BIRTH OF A SALESMAN

Carson V. Heady

Published by World Audience, Inc.

(www.worldaudience.org)

303 Park Avenue South, Suite 1440

New York, NY 10010-3657

Phone (646) 620-7406; Fax (646) 620-7406

info@worldaudience.org

ISBN 978-1-935444-31-2

© 2010, Carson V. Heady

World Audience (www.worldaudience.org) is a global consortium of artists and writers, producing quality books and the journal *audience*, and *The audience Review*. Our periodicals and books are edited by M. Stefan Strozier and assistant editors.

Cover design by Madeline Gorton

"If you have an area of excellence, you're the best at something, anything, then rich can be arranged. Rich can come fairly easily."
—Paul Newman as Fast Eddie Felsen in *The Color of Money*

"Always set your goals higher than you could ever possibly reach. That way, when you barely fall short, you're still better than everyone else."
—Vincent Thomas Scott III, author *The Selling Game*

Acknowledgements

A special thanks to Jake Ruckman for the advice, Nick Watts-Fernandez and Ben Edwards for the years of guidance and brotherhood, all the people I learned from regarding the selling game, Tom Benson and Jason Smith for the multitude of sales memories, Chris Walleman and Jerry Sherwin, Jr. for the laughs and good times, Bart Elfrink for ideas and marketing assistance, my Grandma for being the strongest person I know, my parents Chuck and Janet for being the best any kid could ask for, and most of all to Madison. Without you, I would have a completely different opinion of life and would sometimes doubt my place in it.

INTRODUCTION

Light slowly began to encroach the darkness that enveloped the apartment room. Asleep on the couch, covered in a blanket lay Vincent Thomas Scott III. For that moment, and that moment alone, there was calm.

Vincent is a man whose astounding attributes vastly overshadow his glaring weaknesses. He is a showstopper; a game-changer. His bloodstream flows with the perfectly balanced cocktail of adrenaline, vodka and caffeine, each taking turns running his engine. He is exceedingly intelligent, witty, boyishly handsome, occasionally arrogant, and yet sentimental. Jaded and cynical from his experiences, yet so full of love for his 2-year old princess of a daughter. A bachelor by trade, Vincent is scarred from a few that mattered of the many women that had crossed his path. Numbed by numerous letdowns of life and the antidepressants his chaotic existence had driven him to years ago, he seldom let himself feel much of anything anymore.

Vincent is a man; flawed yet redeemable in many ways. He is not indestructible, not bulletproof, yet puts up a front of both.

His greatest joys: the smell of his daughter's hair, her hand in his, the way she calls his name and runs to him when he arrives to pick her up at the sitter's and the way she would just come up to him for no reason and hug him or declare her love.

There were the cheering crowds and ovations. A basketball player in his youth, Vincent chose work over pursuit of that dream and has had to settle for the adoration of his workforce.

He took pride in the fact he was able to touch so many people in a positive fashion on a daily basis. He truly made a difference and changed lives for the better, even if it was on a small scale – for now.

His greatest weaknesses: vast insecurities that are deeply buried – a fear of not being loved, wanted or of being abandoned or taken advantage of – and he masks them with the guise of an inflated ego. He regularly uses alcohol to supply antiseptic to his incurable pain; it is the ache of a man who had spent the sum of his 31 years attempting to find solace in a world he was coming to realize was cold and brutal. The measure of this man is that the things that have not killed him have made his ambitions stronger.

The meaning of life according to Vincent: working hard so the people you love know you love them and having a positive effect on as many people as possible. Our lives are a mere blip on the radar, so you had better make it memorable.

Emerging from a sea of crayons and a pink hairbrush, the alarm from the phone on the nearby table sounds the James Bond theme, signaling daybreak. Vincent ends the riff with the press of a button, blinks a few times and basks in the silence for a moment. He focuses his eyes, takes Elizabeth's picture from the table and looks at it and smiles before kissing it and tossing aside the blanket.

Aside from several pictures of Elizabeth, movie posters adorn the walls; it is a blatant jab at the existence he was forced to live when Abby called the shots. He was not good at feeling constricted after years of bachelorhood, so after all the fighting, the tens of thousands of dollars he shelled out against his will, the court battle over Elizabeth and the anger, Vincent laid bloody and bruised in the ruins.

Vincent had always been the picture of health, perhaps being hit with debilitating flu every year or two. Outside of physicals for basketball or a sprain after being thrown from a bicycle when he was 8, the man had never seen a doctor. However, life with Abby proved far more than he could take. Anxiety attacks are a powerful thing and Vincent reached a point he could disregard them no more. After not being able to make the 100-mile drive to his hometown of Mankato, Minnesota, because of overwhelming fear and shortness of breath, and experiencing this on a smaller scale on daily drives, he finally confronted them with a doctor visit on his 29th birthday. A few months later, Vincent and Abby were no more.

Vincent flips on the bathroom light and looks at his reflection in the mirror. The short blond hair is just slightly out of place; his face covered in the stubble of a few days' growth. He sees the emotionless stare he has grown accustomed to seeing staring back.

The silenced phone starts vibrating with incoming calls as soon as he nears the shower. It always does. But this is the life he chose and the responsibility that tags along with the power.

Vincent runs a sales department of 220 people. While the frustrations and calamities are never-ending, the adulation of his subordinates keeps him going. While the sales arena is sometimes the bane of his existence and he has contemplated seeking a vocation that does not require this level of overwork and heartache, he would have a hard time turning his back on his calling. He would miss it too much.

These early morning calls are his managers running late, "sick," hung-over, pulled over, "in traffic" (behind a train – that was his favorite). It's all just another metaphor for "I'm not at work when I'm supposed to be."

The water pressure in the shower has never been enough, and the temperature fluctuates every time the faucet or toilet in the apartment above is touched. No matter; Vincent is not a complainer. He will not send back food in a restaurant. He will not ask for help. He will take the beatings, big or small, whether he brought them on himself or not, because he has learned to cope and adapt through years of his independence. That is how he succeeds – by rolling with every punch of every kind and not complaining. Vincent has mastered this trait. Over eight years ago he was an reserved 22-year old college graduate thrust into a sales job with no experience. He got a look because he knew somebody, proving an old adage about "who you know" and made the most of it. When that introvert was interviewed by Shelly Cheekwood for his first management position, she was fair to ask, "You keep to yourself and don't have a lot of interaction with others on the floor. How will you react to having to manage and motivate a team?" His reply: "You have, until this point, seen Vincent the rep. You haven't seen Vincent the manager. I will become whomever I need to be to be successful."

And he did. He was loved by his followers and despised by jealous peers. They tried to figure out the secret to his success but the concept was beyond them. Vincent is not someone you want to compete with because if you try to step on his toes, he does not play nice and he will beat you, no matter what. And, unfortunately for him, no matter the cost to himself.

He is a contradiction in that he can apply so much discipline to aspects of his life but his professional life is a devil-may-care battlezone. He throws himself in front of so many buses to stop injustice facing his people that he is lucky to still be in one piece.

A snippet from his appraisal: "Vincent is difficult to control. His ego occasionally clouds his judgment and causes him to make poor decisions." Of course, this is inches from, "When it comes to driving results, Vincent is without peer. He is one of the best motivators and innovators this company has ever seen."

Vincent's passion and work ethic equate to him making 1,000 decisions or actions – many of them brash or half-cocked in an attempt to fit them all in – in a given day to someone else's 100. Where another person can make 100 decisions and make 1 mistake, he will make 1,000 and make 5 mistakes. One could look at it and say he did 995 things correctly to someone else's 99. Of course, most powers that be will say he made 5 times as many mistakes as the average worker. Sadly, those are the ones with all the real power and who constantly beat him back down. Take heed, reader: Corporate America does not like renegades or crusaders.

Vincent is the champion of the people; they flock to him like the Pied Piper. The same man who flaunts an unabashed ego to motivate the masses is actually humbled by the standing ovations that erupt when he arrives for a morning meeting. His employees trust him, emulate him and they know he would fight until the death for them.

He is the Robin Hood of All Brand Marketing. He robs attention from the rich and showers it to the poor. Unfortunately for Vincent, however, those who dislike him typically know where to hurt him.

He has won more than he has lost, knows he is guaranteed for greatness and will not stop until he gets it.

Now you know Vincent Scott. Now you can witness the birth of a salesman.

*   *   *

The drive to work can be tedious through traffic and annoyingly long, but it is where some of the best ideas are born. Any time Vincent is left alone with his thoughts, his mind is aflutter with activity. The combination of music and ignoring most of the calls that keep his phone buzzing all morning are the only other constants.

Today is a critical day. Christmas comes once a year for the rest of the world, but the last day of any month is Vincent's holiday. Not only that, but his department is caught up in a whirlwind of political chaos that only he can carry them through. It has been 8 years, 2 months and 2 weeks since he started working for ABM. At the tail end of 2000, he graduated from Minnesota State University, Mankato, with his business degree, bummed around for 6 months with his best college friend Ted and newfound love Julie…and suddenly it was time to go. Julie got a volleyball scholarship to play in Minneapolis. Ted was moving his family to Minneapolis. Vincent's antics of showing up at his parents' house at 3 AM after a night of partying were getting old for all. Logic dictated that it was time to move out and forward.

Unfortunately for Vincent, he has a penchant for staying in a situation until it is undeniably clear it is time to move on, if not longer. It explains why he suffered through the effects of Abby for so long. The saddest decision in the world is having to decide not to see your daughter every day because being with her mother is killing you.

He cannot have a platonic relationship with a woman or a friendship with many people because he won't trust his insecurities with anyone. He has made that mistake in the past –getting close to a few people – but it has almost always ended in him being burned.

The euphoria of making-out-at-stoplights puppy love turns into them snooping through your stuff or not understanding when you just want to be alone...it always blows up. That spark may turn into a flame but life extinguishes it every time. And that's what happened with Julie.

Julie was 3 ½ years younger, which at that point was a difference of light-years. She was gorgeous, traded stares with Vincent often and worked in the deli at Cooke's grocery store while he worked several feet away in the meat department.

They spent a lot of time together at her house watching movies, playing video games with her little brother and chasing around their family dog Dax. It was the first semblance of a normal relationship for Vincent and he enjoyed every early minute.

It was off to Minneapolis after the summer of 2001 and Vincent finally put distance between himself and the only home he had ever known: Mankato.

After a seemingly endless month in the deli of Cooke's in Minneapolis, the call came: All Brand Marketing. Vincent's Godmother's sister-in-law was a director of communications with ABM and scored Vincent the interview as she was a longtime contemporary of the hiring manager.

Vincent was expecting some type of customer service role, but what the heck; this would end his life path towards being a permanent meat-cutter.

ABM was typically heralded as a prestigious company to work for and he was open to seeing what it had to offer.

Very shortly into Vincent's ABM career came an unexpected event that rattled his soul: the suicide of his grandfather. Vincent's parents had revealed just a year before it reached fever pitch that his Grandpa Tom, from whom he inherited his middle name, was an alcoholic. The addiction had polarized the family, consumed conversations amongst relatives and prompted multiple interventions.

Vincent found out about this ordeal when it became clear his grandparents were headed to divorce. The day it was finalized, his Grandpa waited for her to leave the house to go to the grocery store before taking his own life with a shotgun to the chest.

After decades of working on a farm and living a life he was happy with, Grandpa could not do the things that made him feel whole. Once gone, only the drink erased the pain. Grandma was the strongest woman Vincent had ever known but, unfortunately for all, Grandpa shut her out as a lifeline and the story ended in tragedy.

Vincent's inability to share his feelings about the tragedy was another dagger to the volatile relationship with Julie. In turn, she did not discuss her issues with her father. The lack of communication spelled disaster for their coupling.

Of twelve to be hired into training, two made it out: Elise Barnett and Vincent. They were not coincidentally the only two from "off the street" who could not retreat to intra-company positions from whence they came. Vincent was also taken aback that 40% of the payroll was on "disability" for varying things like stress leave. In hindsight, that probably should have told him something.

It was near the end of training where the mantra, "This may not be the job for you" was first heard – addressed to the group. Behind closed doors, Vincent was assured he would be a star, by trainers and managers alike. Time would tell, but in his mind, he had no choice but to stick it out.

In the end, of course, Vincent passed training with flying colors. He found himself relating to new teammate Jake Stallings, the best male sales performer on the floor. He found himself chasing Bambi Jennings, the top rep on the floor. Rumors always circulated that she was dirty. Whether she was or not, it was the age old thing: tearing down top reps so you have an excuse for why you cannot beat them. Vincent never bought into excuses. He just beat them.

Darren – the final trainer to teach Vincent's class – was assigned to them once they graduated to the floor. He goaded on the friendly competition between Vincent and Jake.

Vincent Scott, at this point, was just a small town boy living in a newfound world. Yet, unbeknownst to Darren, Jake and the onlookers in this office were about to see the birth of a salesman.

"The Selling Game" by Vincent Scott
Chapter 1
THE ART OF CONFIDENCE

If you are reading this, let me lead off by saying congratulations. Chances are you are serious about selling. You will find, if you haven't already, that many techniques can add up to the same equation of success. One of the challenges of success is determination of your own equation and your own path. My objective is to open your eyes to things you may have never considered to make your path an easier one to tread than mine has been.

But all the books, the scripts, the coaching and counseling in the world mean nothing if you do not begin by believing in yourself.

Everyone, with the right application, has the ability to be a star. It takes brains, guts and tenacity to get there and my goal is for you to attain that glory so you feel like Rocky at the end of *Rocky IV* when they hoist him up and drape the American flag over his shoulders. Trust me, I know that at the conclusion of some days you feel like you just went fifteen rounds with Russian powerhouse Drago; you take such a beating that you'll almost be forced to wait five years for the underwhelming sequel that should never have been made. But seriously, always remember that Rocky won that fight. You can too.

You may be asking yourself if I have ever read a sales manual or book. I have not. My methods are what I have learned over years of doing exceptionally well. I learned by trying a lot of things and applying the principles I will outline on the pages to come.

There are a lot of opinions out there – everyone has one. You will not agree with everything I say, but hey –that's what America is all about.

Sales ability, like oxygen, exists in every living being but like the talent to build bridges, play an instrument, or speak a foreign language, its expression varies across the species. Some people reek of the ability – an illustrious scent of confidence exudes from them – and it dominates everything around them. Others' ability or application in the area reeks – an odor that contaminates their playing field. But, for that, there is a cure.

The day will never arrive where you are no longer called upon to sell something to someone. It can be selling yourself in a job interview, selling your spouse on where to have dinner or selling your child on why to use the potty rather than their diaper to do their business. Sales deals in the tangible and the intangible. The lucky ones get paid for being good at the skill. It's a science and a psychology and, if mastered, it can make all the difference in your world and the worlds of others.

I have crafted this book to cover how to master them all. For I, like you, once sat in a position where I had no idea I could dominate the trade. I once was fresh out of college with no work experience, and when placed in a sales job because I had a high-quality referral, I was at first overwhelmed. No more.

If you are great at something, it is your responsibility as a part of the human race to impart that knowledge to others. We are all here for a short time and should strive above all else to be remembered for excellent and honorable things. I hope above hopes you find what you are looking for in the pages of this book. If not, it would make a great gift. Or, let me know what I omitted and I'll save it for the sequel.

I encourage everyone to keep a journal. Keep a log of what you attempt daily: the challenges, choices, experiences and disappointments. You cannot advance in life if you do not learn from these things. Knowing where you came from is the only way to know where you are going. Mistakes have to occur for any kind of growth. Repeating mistakes will lead to continued failure, but modifying your approach to sales or, anything for that matter, and finding the best method of attack is what will lead to positive consistency. Positive consistency breeds success. And that quest for success is why you're here.

Sales, like poker or paper, rock, scissors, is playing the person across from you. It is not about spouting benefits and crossing your fingers that the listener will cave. It is a psychological tug-of-war where you put yourself in your customer's shoes and realize and utilize what they need to hear before they cave. It is getting in their head by lowering their defenses so you can determine what they need to see before they buy.

Too often I have heard sales reps showcase their knowledge of various products and services their company offers in hopes the customer will eventually hear something they latch onto and just jump up and down and beg to be sold to. This is not going to happen. Rather, your mission is to target a customer's weakness, find if and why they truly need your merchandise and find five unique ways to explain how it is going to cure what ails them. Period. You have to drill that point home until they cave. And if they don't, after you have given them everything you have, know when to pack up and move on.

People are a lot of things, but they are (1) afraid of change and (2) not going to be bullied into it. You have to make the fear of not changing outweigh the fear of changing. You have to hammer home the weaknesses they possess or the undesirable outcome you want them to avoid so they will make the decision to change. You cannot make up their mind for them. You can, however, make them fear that the parade is passing them by and that they are missing out on something groundbreaking. You can show them their competitors that are thriving off what you have to offer. You can cater to their greed (Gordon

Gekko's favorite sin), desire for success, and their will to win. Doing these things is what will lead you to your win.

It all starts with ATTITUDE and confidence. The most important part of becoming someone who can infiltrate the customer's mind, needs and weaknesses is having the mindset that enables you to barrel through any obstacles that present themselves. This does not only take into account the ones your customer throws at you; it can encompass morning traffic, the gas station only having decaf or being saddled with a manager that has no business being in the business. Obstacles will be everywhere, but you cannot be deterred. If you have a set mission, a clear-cut initiative and a drive to achieve that objective by any means necessary, there is nothing that can stop you. You will fall, you will hear "no" frequently, but these temporary setbacks will start to roll off your back. You will welcome them.

I liken this evolution of a salesperson to the movie *The Matrix*. Neo, played by Keanu Reeves, started as an average Joe with no belief in what he was being told by newfound friends: that he was "the one" referenced in a prophecy. However, he latched on with people trying to show him his capabilities and as time went by, he became so ahead of the curve he was able to dodge bullets, outsmart digital agents, and do things mere mortals could only dream about. You can reach that state as well; stick with me and I'll make you a star.

Repetition of a heightened sales strategy, a perfectly laid out call flow (not necessarily a script) and belief in yourself will lead to a high level of achievement.

If you are in sales, someone at some point saw the potential to put you in that post. Personally, sales experience means zilch to me when I interview candidates. I am looking for a personality. People will buy from those they take a liking to or respect. And the fact you sold furniture for thirty years does not mean you can convince someone to change their way of life. Personality, charisma, wit, and charm do.

No two people are going to do something alike, so why would we tackle sales the same?

A lot of sales mastery boils down to the choice and timing of words. Saying, "We have this XYZ program that would be great for you. It does this and this and this," will not work, yet I have heard this approach thousands of times. This methodology is nothing more than throwing yourself out there and hoping the customer says yes to something.

Read this: "Thank you for the information. Based on what you told me, you clearly are very serious about your business and I applaud you for that. That said, I am going to give you something that will actually free up your time to delve more into the business and is going to take care of the fact that with your current strategy you are putting yourself in a position of weakness. I want to put you in a position of strength."

That statement achieves several things. Clearly, information about the business was obtained. The customer's ego was stroked. A benefit was immediately given, but not just any benefit. Most salespeople quote random benefits in hopes the customer will take a liking to one. They sometimes get lucky that a customer asks about one of them, but it's just that: luck of the draw. The skilled salesperson will find distinct, fact-based benefits that are used to purposely entice the customer to think the way that you think. The power of the words used is vital: no customer wants to gamble with their business or personal property. They do not want to be in a position of weakness. As illustrated in the example, you must shift the statement to a positive one as quickly as possible and look into the optimistic future.

To delve into your customer's psyche is about fooling them that you know everything. The fact of the matter is, you *do* know everything about what *you* are talking about, but you want to keep most of that information on reserve. This customer is on a need-to-know basis. They need only know what you have that will cure their weakness and how that treatment will benefit them. Period.

If you want someone to be impressed by everything you know, tell your boss or significant other. Stick to specific basics with the customer. Do not over-complicate sales. You get in, you introduce yourself, state your purpose, and go into fact-finding before you even give them an opportunity to shut you down.

In the early going you are merely on a quest for answers. Do not get over-eager and blow your cover by aborting your mission and trying to "pitch" too soon. Get people talking about themselves, for they have a tendency to open up about their favorite topic. Whether you are trying to sell financial services, advertising, insurance, pharmaceutical services or equipment, health needs or appliances, get your target talking about their situation. It's near and dear to their heart. Find needs and weaknesses and, all the while, drop little bombs of weaknesses in their current approach that plant the seed for what you are going to do later.

Much of the selling game is using strong words, like "we have to take care of this problem immediately." It's about generating emotion in customers, enticing them with your solutions and showing them the power of the future.

Once you have the facts, recommend what is going to fix their problem, show them how it fixes the problem, and close. Salespeople also make the mistake of spending too much time recommending and asking questions *again* after they recommend. You are on a destination from point A to Z and the line is a lot straighter than most people make it.

How you handle the setbacks defines you as a salesperson. It defines you as a person as well. Life is no picnic. But everything, the joys and sorrows alike, is temporary. Maintaining consistency in yourself and staying true to your values and approach is what will lead to what you deem as happiness.

Act like you have the world by the balls. No one will know any better.

Hesitation is an enemy. It's like they say in *Top Gun*: "If you think, you're dead." Sometimes you have to take a flying cannonball into the deep end of the pool. Risk is part of the game. And sometimes you have to be willing to risk everything just to achieve something.

I will let you in on a secret: being confident is often an act. For, even in times of strife, you cannot shed your cape and armor. You cannot let anyone see you bleed. And, let's face it, in a sales game, your enemy is the fear of your customer. The only way to drive through that fear is to break down those walls with your charisma and charm. And, if you don't have much of either, you have to fake it.

Throughout a sales presentation a customer will show their trepidation. They will throw up obstacles here and there (known as objections) and it is up to you to acknowledge them, politely but assertively put them down in their place and move forward to your next agenda item. Every single time.

A lot of putting up a confident front through all of that is bluffing. You will have no idea what a customer's reaction to something will be until you try it. From there, like a pinball wizard, you must be ready at a moment's notice to process new information and answers from them, respond appropriately and move forward.

The reason someone like me is qualified to speak about sales or about life is because I have fallen down – many times. I have made what some would deem as mistakes, but have learned a great deal from every single one of them. And I would imagine that many people reading these lines feel the same about themselves – they work hard but, for whatever reason, are looking for a different approach to selling themselves or their goods.

The greatest sales job in the world is to sell a country on electing them to the highest office in the land. You think those guys don't make mistakes?

Many variables exist in this game of confidence. Namely: what are you selling? Does it have any value? You may be really good and really smooth, but even the best have a hard time dressing up a sheep into wolves' clothing.

Unfortunately, a lot of sales positions tie you to a product or service that has little to no value or flat out does not work. Some managers and companies have no integrity or care if your soul has to be sold to Satan to turn a profit. Others require you to cross the line. Any job that forces you to compromise your beliefs is a waste of your time on this Earth. Find something else. If you can't look yourself in the mirror, that's a sign. If you take too long of a look, that's probably another. But it's also probably a start in the right direction.

You want to be in a position where you can look back on everything you have done and say you would not do it differently. If you can look back and you know you did everything possible to win with the arsenal you brought from within, you have nothing to be ashamed of. Be it a solitary sales call, a presentation, a job interview or even ten years of your life, stand tall with no regret.

Confidence exudes from the way you look, talk and walk. It amazes me; I have hired hundreds of people in my career and they go through various phases of showcasing their degree of confidence. In the interview, they will be at their most brash. Personally, I am looking for someone who knows they cannot be stopped and shows it. Interestingly, once they have gotten their face kicked in by a few belligerent customers, they are at their most timid. They come in, go about their business and leave at the end of the day. But that cocoon is shed upon the completion of the transformation into a closer.

That state, however, is a delicate one. Any wavering of confidence or deviation from the tried and true method that took them to the top can send them into a slump worse than an athlete could experience. It is unwise to drastically alter a batting stance during a hitter's slump yet salespeople who were once great make the mistake of undergoing big changes to their approach in hopes it will take them back to the top. It will not. Stay the course. Do what you know is the right stuff on each call. You have to play the odds in everything. Sales is no different.

Those who take longer to ramp up into that confident closer are more long-lasting than those who emerged from the gates at full speed. The latter horses tire and once they lose that initial momentum, they often find themselves lost and unable to recapture the magic that surrounded their first sprint.

However, do not be so quick to judge that someone's confidence is real. Especially if you are a sales manager, you must learn to discern the disparity between those who talk the talk and those who are able to walk the walk.

It is possible to bottle confidence like a perfume and release it with one quick burst like hot air from the mouth of a buffoon. It is entirely another scenario to produce the scent with one's own adrenaline. If you fall for the futile promises of the buffoon, only you suffer. Some people's motivations are harder to find and those who are not provoked by the usual ingredients like money and family are hard to drive.

Real confidence is like magic; it can be an illusion but if done properly, it can capture the minds and hearts of its witnesses. It is an art form because it is a personal expression and the finished product can be beautiful and life-changing.

16

Confidence will lead troops into a battle they never thought about fighting and inspire people to do things they never previously imagined doing. It changes the cultural landscape, can eliminate fear and it gives people hope.

But beware: it has many synonyms with negative connotations that you want to avoid. Arrogance. Narcissism. Vanity. Self-absorption. Conceit. Those words can turn a warm character profile cold. Or maybe these don't faze you. They never fazed me.

However, if you are going to present yourself as something grandiose and better than the average bear, you have to be able to back it up. A couple of false moves and you are the boy or girl who cried "wolf." Once you outlive your usefulness, many companies and people eliminate you. You are a number. The trick is making your number greater than everything and everyone around you. And if you can't, fake it with confidence.

One of the greatest lines in motion picture history is "If you put your mind to it, you can accomplish anything," from 1985 classic *Back to the Future*. And it's so true. If you want to get to work on time, you will. Sure, if you dilly-dally getting out of bed, traffic might be more of a factor and you may use that as the reason for tardiness when you come face to face with your boss. But you are well aware that laziness was the reason for your delinquency. Now, of course, there is always the unforeseen emergency or family situation, but I have yet to meet someone who has been picked on or terminated solely based on a slew of emergencies. I would venture to guess you haven't either.

In addition, it has never ceased to amaze me the sometimes two drastically different versions of a person that coexist in the same body. One person comes to the job interview. An entirely different one shows up after a string of frustrating days. A big part of confidence maintenance is reminding yourself who you are. Go into your next call, day and week with the determination that you are going to win.

Meeting expectations is a decision. You aren't the first and you won't be the last. If you're smart, you will find out what the best are doing and do it better. Nothing they do or don't do can stop you from fulfilling what you set out to accomplish. Stealing winning concepts from others that are ahead of you in an area is brilliant; finding your personal way of doing it better is more so. The fact you are reading this book and others you are in competition with may not has already given you a leg up, right? Nonetheless, a referral of this book, if nothing else, should be the gift you keep on giving.

You are in control of your destiny. Don't ever forget it. Sure, you will hit some bumps along the way but you determine what you learn from them and how you proceed. The tricks and tips to follow are going to guide you to sales success. Consider this book like the limousine taking you to prom; you could attempt to take a beaten up car and arrive in less style if you arrive at all. However, with these tactics you will head to the top of the charts in style.

Being confident and exhibiting confidence is not easy, especially when factors will throw themselves or be thrown from all corners multiple times a day in an effort to tear you down. That is why only a handful of people claw their way to top spots in any arena: they were the ones still standing. It is survival of the fittest out there and if you do not have what it takes, you will be swept aside by those who do as they scramble past you to the finish line.

One of my best friends, a man I have known for over twenty years, gave me some of the best advice I have ever received about seven years ago after a tough breakup. Getting used to the newfound freedom I had actually prayed for pre-breakup and the negativity over an uncertain future were eating me alive. His advice that I will never forget: when a negative thought enters your consciousness, acknowledge its presence and dismiss it.

You are thinking, "That's it?" I know it sounds easier said than done. However, after seven years of following that advice and perfecting it I now have the ability to pick and choose which emotions I allow myself to feel. Your thoughts will only be inundated with negativity if you let them be. You must acknowledge that a negative thought has entered the picture and eliminate it. Simple dismissal of negativity may not come easy the first time but it is second nature to me now.

Think about it. Like anything else, negative thoughts or beliefs or occurrences will bombard you. That's life. Keep plowing through. Maintain the confidence in yourself. You are great at something – probably several things – so who cares what other people think about you? Nothing is permanent and you will find over time that a lot of the very things you held dear, believed in, or put your faith or stock in were nothing but illusions. It is in those times you find out what is important and what you should be living and dying for.

Everything in life is some form of sales, whether you are closing business or asking someone to prom. Each maneuver starts with confidence burning from within and willingness to be told "no." You can't care about the end result or be afraid of that rejection. We make things out to be greater or scarier in our heads than they are. Fear is in your head. You put yourself out there so you can look back without regret.

If you set your expectations for any given situation high you are only poising yourself for massive disappointment. Go into everything, be it a date, holiday with your family or even a job with nothing but realism. Call it apathy, but whatever is going to happen will happen. Give it your all, enjoy the successes along the way, but realize something is going to chip away at and erode your good fortune. Just be prepared for it and know how to handle it.

That's what life is about, right? Finding some semblance of happiness that carries us through the murkiness of miseries until we find our next semblance of it. Some people subscribe to artificial highs rather than the natural ones, but the natural high of happiness is what we want so desperately. Moping and complaining about what is unfair and that you did not get this or that is not going to accomplish anything. Keep going. Keep moving forward.

Nothing is certain until it is done. Practicality and keeping yourself grounded is important to being able to take the hits success and life will delve you. Your favorite team may have been picked to finish first in the preseason poll but, guess what? They still have to play the regular season.

All of the greats in the sales game have one main thing in common: confidence. Be it in the product they sell, the words that come out of their mouths, their company or especially themselves – it is there. It is in the ability to get someone to pay attention to something they had no inclination to pay attention to. It is not necessarily convincing someone to do something; it is putting something in the language a customer understands and making the decision a no-brainer for them to make on their own.

It is not the ability to explain and analyze everything under the sun; it is not backing down when you are challenged. Customers want to feel like they are getting a deal, which makes it important for you to have enough confidence in putting everything together so you make them feel they are.

Sales is a mind-set; it is not closing with a gimmick or freebie or being able to talk until you are blue in the face. It is picking and choosing the right combination of words that gets the job done. You have to command respect and not whimper away when you are met with opposition. If you anticipate your customers' moves and use the same tactics to overcome their objections and show (not tell) them how they will make back their investment by tangible or intangible means, you cannot help but be successful.

You handle so many visits or calls in a day that you should have a pretty good idea of how they are going to go. Use that to your advantage. Like Mr. Miyagi pointed out to Daniel-san in the dreadful conclusion to the *Karate Kid* series, it is like the banzai tree growing from within; you have to grow and adapt based on what the nature of your sales presentations yield for you, good or bad. Adaptation and rolling with the punches of life are just as important as brimming with self-confidence. It's the confidence that will get you back up every time you get knocked down.

Before you start patting yourself on the back for a habit of closing your first offer, ask yourself why that seems to be happening. Typically, the cheapest and least effective solutions are the ones sold most often. The reason is they require the least skill. They also yield the least results and those who fall victim to them fall victim to last place spots in sales results and standings.

Being a better salesperson is not about making sales. It is the method and quality of those sales. It is about perseverance in the face of uncertainty and defeat. It is about being the best you can be in every area. Walk away from every visit or call knowing there was no money left on the table and why. If you can say – with confidence, of course – that is the case on every call, it was a job well done.

The selling game is like the game of politics. After a long day of calls or scouring the countryside, you are seeing stars – and probably stripes, too – but you have to remain steadfast in holding certain truths to be self-evident. Give the people what they want – results. You have to eliminate the shadow of a doubt that yours is the campaign they should lend their dollars to. Show them how to balance their budget – give them a cost that is justifiable. Prioritize health care – namely, the health of their family or business. Electability is key and no one is going to vote for you if you fold under pressure, can't collect your thoughts and are unable to beckon them into your camp based on a platform of truth, justice and the American way. Take a deep breath before every call, gather your campaign trail persona, make an effective preamble and ask for them to put their John Hancock to contract every time. It takes cooperation and delicate negotiation to form that more perfect union for all.

Ladies and gentlemen, we have laid the groundwork with introduction of the playing field of the selling game. Now it is time to learn the rules and how to be the best.

*   *   *

Vncent Scott can still vividly recall his first sale.

Her name was Mrs. Robinson, from Hereford, Texas. Vincent was fresh out of training and had no expectations of this particular pitch. He used benefits, quoted the price and asked for the sale like they described in training. He even closed his eyes in the seconds that seemed like eternity between the moment the words trickled from his tongue and the unexpected "yes". It clicked then and resonates today: you can't close the pitches you don't make. The road ahead would be strewn with far more "no's" than "yes's" but he had to start somewhere and this was the first of thousands of sales to come.

A month into the gig, Vincent was #1 in the office – ahead of Jake, ahead of Bambi.

People would walk by and marvel while he was on the phone or look up every time he made the stroll to the dry erase board to chalk up another sale. Getting that first taste of success and first commission check changed Vincent; he was no longer satisfied with the small time money he made at Cooke's. That change continued like an avalanche over the years until it became an unstoppable force and an insatiable hunger for more and more.

Also a month in, Vincent's assigned and practically absentee manager Ashley Flowers pulled him into her office, showed him call scores and flunked him on offering "per sales strategy" because he had not offered a $40 per month bill increase to an 80-year old woman and instead had sold a $4 per month wire protection plan to increase her $18-per-month bill.

"You're kidding, right?" he asked in disbelief.

"No, Vincent, I'm not," Ashley said. "This is the job you were hired to do. We have policies and procedures that must be followed."

"You do realize this customer has never had a service on her account in her life and I sold her the Wire Protection Plan, which is a major coup, right?" Vincent asked, pleading his case. "

"Vincent, you're good. But the company wants you to offer the Everywhere and Everything Plan to every customer no matter what. Future instances of failing to do so will result in disciplinary action up to and including dismissal. Do you understand?"

"I comprehend the meaning of the words you are saying," Vincent said slowly, trying to take it all in. Was this really Corporate America? "But this is ludicrous."

"I will continue to coach you on how to improve in this area," Ashley finished before dismissing him.

Those last words were a joke.

Looking back, Vincent would struggle to conjure up a memory of any valuable coaching he had gotten in his 8 ½ years with ABM. He has learned all of his lessons by doing, making mistakes, being reprimanded and being passed over for promotions in favor of someone not qualified.

Vincent only made the mistake of going to Ashley for advice once. With free trial disks for Internet service showing up daily in mailboxes around the country, Vincent had to sell ABM's pricey service and was having difficulty reaching the level of performance he expected from himself. It was when he went to Ashley to seek counsel on how to aggressively position this cost-inefficient service that he learned who he was dealing with.

Standing outside her cubicle, Vincent knocked on the framework to announce his presence. She wheeled away from her online shopping and clicked over to some corporate system before facing him.

"Yes, Vincent?"

"Ashley, these customers are just not biting on our Internet," Vincent said. "I can't get past the fact that everybody gets those free offers from Online Solution. They don't want to pay more for our service."

"Yeah, I know, it's tough out there," Ashley cooed, trying unsuccessfully to sound sympathetic and not continuing with anything constructive.

"Right…" Vincent continued. "Anyhow, what do you recommend?"

"Well, you're not the first person on the team that asked that." Her voice then lowered. "I mean, like I told Deb, if you just can't get past their objections, just send off some disks anyway at the end of the month. That way they won't be able to charge back in time."

"What?" Vincent coiled in surprise.

"Come on, Vincent, everybody does it," Ashley assured him, sounding like your typical high school peer pressure speech. "Just send a few out. It's no big deal. I'll cover for you."

Vincent has also learned over the years that those who tell you they can be trusted are typically the ones who cannot be. In this situation, Vincent knew he could not show drastic shock so he accepted this answer and thanked Ashley for her time. Not then nor ever did he add something to someone's account unauthorized. The thought probably entered his mind at some points, but it never happened.

It was also around that time that Vincent's speculation began that ABM purposely made its bills so difficult to understand in an attempt to force customers to call in. It made perfect sense; they could have *easily* put in an addendum answering all of the frequently asked questions, cutting out one of the ten needless pages of bill inserts so as to not waste paper. But no, they were banking on customers calling in about their confusing bills so the company could add items to their account with some one-size-fits-all $60 package. Vincent had to come to the realization that while what he was doing may or may not have been in the best interests of the customer it was what he was being paid to do. Anything he was being paid to do he was going to do better than everyone else for as long as he was doing it.

Dealing with the public on this scale was extraordinarily rough at times. On the flip side, sitting through ten minutes of computerized prompts while you are on your break at work or you just got home and want to be with your family is enough to turn anyone into a jerk. When that world collides with the world of a lot of corrupt or simply dim-witted salespeople, mass hysteria ensues.

Vincent will discourage anyone from calling ABM and refuses to this day to call most companies for much of anything. He has seen too often how people maneuver rates and quotes and verbiage in an attempt to "sell" (read: screw) someone and something. Sad, but true, that ABM's superiors endorse this behavior by not doing anything about it and, in many cases, praising the "results." A line was drawn in the sand. Vincent eventually learned to straddle that line while he never crossed it. You can't hate that player; you have to hate that game.

Sad to say, when Vincent finally escaped from this over-mechanized, shady part of the business he was at first unsure if he could legitimately sell a product without reliance on manipulation of sales statistics and just swapping around phone packages. However, after further wild success in his next incarnation he could put that fear to rest.

In a call center there are two types of people: those who want to use this experience as a way to better themselves and those who are using it solely as a source of income. It is little more than a human laboratory: putting a diverse group of animals in a building and watching them interact, breed and fight. This is why you see everything and experience everything in a call center. If any of them would open up its security stance, the greatest reality show in television history could be born.

In April 2002 a noteworthy moment transpired, but the significance was unbeknownst to Vincent at the time. A morning meeting in the lunch room was when he first laid eyes on Stacey Worth: a girl so perfectly crafted that when God created her He undoubtedly had to sit for a moment and feel pretty proud of Himself. She wore a purple dress and had a bow in her flowing golden hair. Everything about her was mesmerizing and she lit up the room, looking as out of place amongst this riff-raff as a movie star in a crowd of commoners.

Aside from these occasional breaks in the action, the end of April saw another climactic duel between Ashley's style and Vincent's desire for right and good.

Whether Ashley was really this cruel or the system made her this hell-bent on using process as a weapon remained to be seen.

The conference room where these meetings took place was ominously dubbed "The Aquarium." It was a small room with windows and blinds on multiple sides that was centrally located in the two-story building so it could be seen from many vantage points, hence the name. Its unique positioning made it easy to observe activity there unless the blinds were drawn and this was one of those meetings. Ashley led Vincent into the Aquarium and they took seats on opposite sides of the table.

Ashley set down a folder of papers and pulled out a couple documents that appeared to be call grading forms.

"Vincent, first I have to let you know that this meeting is disciplinary in nature. Would you like to have a union steward present?" Ashley asked.

"I don't need anybody knowing my business," Vincent replied tersely.

"Okay." Ashley shuffled her papers and began to reference them. "This is in regards to a call I listened to from yesterday. Do you remember Adam Meyers?"

"I do," Vincent nodded coolly.

"Is there a reason you didn't offer anything to him?"

"You mean aside from the fact he was screaming at me to disconnect his line?"

"Vincent, you know that our contact strategy says that you go into your fact-finding questions on every call."

"Right, and if you recall correctly, I started asking him about his current Internet service and he started cussing me out saying he hated our company and did not want to buy anything."

"You have five questions that you must ask on every call. They include current Internet service, current television service, their amount of long distance usage monthly, what their favorite calling features are and if they make international calls. You asked one of them," Ashley said, mostly reading off another sheet of paper.

"OK, Ashley, in our last meeting you committed to coaching me," Vincent interjected, seeing this was going nowhere. "Yet this is the first time we have talked since then. How would you suggest I should have handled this customer?"

"I don't like your insubordinate tone," Ashley spat, clearly frustrated with Vincent's point. "Following the call flow is not an option. I have made that clear before, yet you continue to not follow the contact strategy. Effective immediately, you are being placed on performance warning, the first step of our constructive discipline coaching plan, for failure to follow call flow."

"Over one call? I'm serious – how should I have asked him all of those questions? Aren't I doing the company a service by not wasting time on someone who is screaming at me and moving on to another opportunity to actually sell something? I'm the top rep in the office!" Vincent fired back.

"Vincent, I don't care how you ask the questions, you just do it. And if you fail to do this in the future, it could lead to further discipline up to and including dismissal," Ashley continued.

"You would fire your best rep over not asking questions to a confrontational customer?"

"If you're not doing the job properly, you are not the best rep."

"Is this going to impact me becoming a manager in the future?" Vincent inquired.

24

"If you are on a step of discipline, you cannot be promoted," Ashley responded. "This warning will last for six months. Do I have your commitment to follow our mandated call flow going forward?"

"Absolutely, I'll do the best I can," Vincent spat, with sheer and utter disdain.

Vincent returned to his desk and proceeded to cautiously go through mandated call flow for the next 24 hours, resulting in drastically decreased sales. As Vincent was the top player in the office by far, this slide severely impacted Ashley's sales standing in just that 24-hour period.

Ashley pulled Vincent in the following day and removed the performance warning.

Chapter 2:
LAYING THE FOUNDATION

The sales call or visit begins with what you bring to it. What are you carrying in your bag of tricks? Wit? Charm? Swagger? Hopefully a healthy mix of them all.

Think about it this way: no one with any prayer of winning a fight enters without thinking it through. Gordon Gekko was wise to cite Sun Tzu's "The Art of War" in *Wall Street* when he quoted that a battle is won or lost before it is fought. You cannot win with no weapon, be it literal or figurative. You do not win without anticipation of your opponent's strategies and being prepared for every combination of what could be thrown at you. Athletes do not play adversaries without studying tape for countless hours to ascertain their moves and their plays. They practice more than they play, watch game video and memorize playbooks. Knowledge is power so you should have plenty of it going into a call.

The more artillery you bring to the table, the easier it will be to disarm the opponent and whatever barriers standing in your way (such as the dreaded gatekeeper). On the same token, if you are plagued with fatigue and have chosen to succumb to the wear and tear of calls preceding this one, you will quickly be defeated. Not only that, but you will be defeated over and over again. Stamina and a well-conceived plan are necessary for survival once you hit the front lines.

Whether placing, on the receiving end or making a house call, you have to go in full guns-a-blazing. The first two minutes of your call are the most crucial. They are your audition. Whether you will advance to the next leg is determined in those first 120 seconds. When you show up to a job interview, you don't sound like you are going to die or give a half-cocked effort, so why would you at the beginning of a sales call? You have to present the best version of yourself every time if you want to garner the best results.

Breaking down the call and dissecting it into its key parts is central to the process. To master your opening, you have to think about a few different things.

Number one: you are not the only person who has called. Whether you are calling a residence, business, or potential date, you can't sound like every other schmuck who has called and failed before. You must be a cut above the rest. People do not flock to date someone because the person reminds them of everyone else who came before, who hit on them in a bar or a former flame that broke their heart. They gravitate towards something fresh, something new, something clever. Customers are – guess what? – people too, and they are looking for the exact same things.

If you sound like a telemarketer, lo and behold, you will be treated like one. When I think of the term "telemarketer," I think about the episode of *Seinfeld* where Jerry fielded a call from someone trying to peddle long distance and hung up on him after getting a negative response to, "Oh, so you wouldn't like it if I called you at home? Well, how you know how I feel." It's funny because everyone can relate to it. Telemarketers are a punchline; don't let the joke be on you.

What fatal mistakes do telemarketers make? They sound like telemarketers. "Telemarketer" is a curse word in my dictionary and it should be in yours. You are a consultant and a professional. Act like it. If faced with a choice, would you describe yourself to a first date as a telemarketer or as a marketing consultant? You are going to pick the one you presume will wow them more, so remember it is your job to wow every customer. Just like they know their trade, you (should) know yours, and you have to act like you are doing them a favor by contacting them. The whole endeavor of taking time out of your day to make their lives better is a courtesy to ensure they are well taken care of. You have to repeatedly remind them of that when their attention span starts to falter.

That is the whole show: that you are doing them an immense favor with everything you say, everything you recommend and every time you stick to your guns. That's sales. And when a customer inevitably resists, you have to act taken aback, like you cannot understand for the life of you why, with all the antidotes for their weakness(es) you provided, they would stay mired in their level of relative inadequacy you have pointed out.

Take what you do seriously. If you don't, the person you are talking to sure as heck won't either. The beginning sets the foundation for how the call will go. A weak foundation will collapse when rocked. A strong one stays the course.

When customers predictably greet your introduction with, "I hear from salespeople all the time," you meet it with, "Exactly –I understand you are bombarded by my fly-by-night competitors. We are XYZ Company and I am going to tell you why you should listen to me and ignore the rest. How are you currently taking care of this need?" This statement acknowledges dissent in their response, puts it in its place, and does not falter as you forge forward in the call.

Number two: you cannot undervalue how important it is to dictate the flow of the call; transition throughout from step to step and keep on track. Your customer will not do it for you. Quite the contrary, their purpose is to shake your foundation. Unless you train yourself to prevent that, you will fail.

As a sales manager, I had a rep with a fantastic introduction and superb delivery who painted a picture and built rapport like no one I had ever seen. But he could not close often enough because he would get wrapped up in long conversations that went nowhere. Realize that if you can't close on call #1, unless they are part of the 1% of customers who are serious when they say they will think about it, you never will; you might as well put their face on a milk carton. You will never see or hear from them again. That said, you do not have an hour to spend with every customer; you have to get to the point as quickly as possible with a targeted plan for every call. This all starts with a targeted introduction.

I sat behind this guy when I monitored him and just said, "Transition." It was designed to tell him when to move from the intro into fact-finding, then the pitch and eventually the close. A lot of times it just takes small tweaks to put together the masterpiece. I am betting it's that way with you, too.

Your introduction exists to set the stage, state your business and move directly into questioning. If you do anything else – try to get fancy or use big words and talk their ears off – you fall into that aforementioned line of previous schmucks and you run the risk of being run right out of there. You will wind up going to opening day of that movie you want to see all by your lonesome because they are waiting for someone better to ask them out. You are expendable like a mop-up reliever in a blowout; that is no way to give yourself job security in the major leagues.

Number three: realize that the person on the receiving end of does not want to be sold. Your objective is finding a need or a weakness – determining that person's pressure points – and squeezing. That's why your introduction should transition immediately into questions that are geared towards determining cold, hard facts. What is their story?

In the seconds, minutes or hours before any situation you have to consider what you are going into. Once you master this situation it will likely take seconds. Common sense does not prevail enough in the sales arena. Your introduction has to grab their attention with something captivating that will appeal to an emotion. Immediately following you must go into fact-finding questions before allowing them to do so much as draw a breath.

Confidence, as alluded to in the prior chapter, is a big part of this. You have to walk in reeking of self-confidence and kicking the door down rather than politely knocking and waiting to be invited in. That invitation will not come. Make the most of the time you get and go for it. Force your foot in the slightly ajar door and push it open – you're here to stay.

Giving the recipient of your pitch so much as a moment to gather their thoughts will allow them to go into *their* typical mold in such a situation. Trust me, they have a game plan for you as well –getting rid of you. You have to knock them off their game by being better, faster and quicker, doing something out of the ordinary and getting straight into finding out what makes them tick so you know what it will take to sell them.

Yes, a customer has a routine. They may not make or take as many calls as you, but they have a defense mechanism designed to ward you off. To take down their defenses, you have to find a resourceful way of disarming rather than badgering them the same old way someone else tried and failed before. They are immune to that at that point, but you can bet if you do it right they will surrender to your charms. My goal for you is to become immune to their objections.

If you know the first step is introducing yourself and stating your business and the second is finding out about the business, why not conjoin the two?

What happens when you introduce yourself and ask if they have time to talk? What happens when you ask if they want information about something? You give them the opportunity to drop kick you back to where you came from. Do not, under any circumstances, give them that chance. Asking a "yes" or "no" question takes an awful risk; you risk they shut you down with an immediate "no" and make their transition directly into kicking you out the door. You peeked in and they slammed the door in your face. You may think you're being polite but this is just an excuse to shy away from a sale.

Look at the areas where you are stumbling. What is stopping you? Write it down and think through it logically. If you are getting shut down by the same rebuttal or generic line every time, would it not be a prudent investment of your time to come up with a way around that obstacle?

Journaling and chronicling your experiences is very important. If you get tripped up in the same place every time that is what you need to analyze. All the speeches and scripts you will see were designed by someone (most likely and hopefully) that did not have your trepidation about delivering such lines.

For writing down strategies or scripting is not an embarrassing matter; it is an empowering one. When I was a rep I posted verbiage on my computer monitor that I could mention at any time because a puzzle missing one piece is incomplete. Every time I went into my pitch I was referencing the same items at will. A call without those components would not have been as successful. The foundation and every brick in a building are imperative. Without them, the structure will never stand.

This is not to encourage you to follow scripts; it is to encourage you to write down items that will jog your memory during key moments. Scripting yourself can make you sound like a robot but having key words and phrases within arm's reach means you can pull them into battle on command and use them every time to make sure every call is as good as it can be.

I like boxing analogies that mirror sales calls. What you do in the opening of your call, like the boxing match, will set the tone for what is to come. If you get knocked down early, your chances of victory are slim. Circling your opponent is fine, but you have to test the waters with a few early jabs. The customer (your opponent for this exercise) will attempt to strike back. You parry or deflect with acknowledging their statements, putting them in their place and moving seamlessly and immediately on to your next move – punches designed to put them in the corner and on the defensive. A mistake many people make is when they have the customer against the ropes, they inexplicably stop hitting and make no attempt to close or finish them off. An opponent is not going to lay down on the mat for you. We will talk about those critical moments of the close later, but think about it in boxing terms: what boxer in their right mind would stop punching when the end is in sight? None would, so you can't either. All's fair in the ring until you bite someone's ear off.

Do not get me wrong: I am not suggesting you let them know they are being put on the defensive or make them defensive. Rather, you are going to make them defend themselves and their inactivity. That is different; if you put someone on the defensive you will terrify them like a deer, rabbit or squirrel. They will run back into the forest and your hunt is over. However, if you engage them with intelligent banter, you can make them defend their actions and you can counterpoint with the best of them. Once they have run out of counterattacks they are putty in your hands.

One of your goals is to plant the seed of doubt in their mind. Fear of missing out on something, doubt in current methods of conducting themselves and greed over that perceived loss are the things that will prompt them to make the decision to buy. Self-doubt is a paralyzing thing; it may be the very reason you are reading this book. Once you make it your ally, there is no stopping you. Overcoming that feeling in your customer and getting them to step out of their comfort zone is what leads to sales success.

One of the biggest stumbling areas I have witnessed over the years is allowing the customer to take control. Most ineffective managers will just say, "you need to take control of the call" but they will never actually articulate how specifically you are supposed to do that. We will also discuss how to be a successful manager in a later chapter however, for now, let's discuss how to take control of a sales call.

First, you have to psych yourself up going in that you are the chosen one. You are the authority. The person on the other end needs you more than you need them. Why are you afraid of matching wits with them; they should be afraid of going toe to toe with you! And you have to act that way the whole way through. It does not matter what the last customer said. It does not matter what happened on your way to work or that you were running late or that the shower would not run hot water. You are the best, and, like a jungle animal, you are going to circle your prey until just the right moment is spotted before you pounce.

Second, you just have to take that flying leap into the deep end of the pool. People spend too much time over-thinking and over-analyzing every little decision and potential outcome. Will she say yes when I ask her to dinner? Will they like me? Will this customer talk to me? Will blah blah blah. What difference does it make? What is the worst that can happen? Unlike the potential date that can rebuke you and tell your co-workers you could not even say your name without stammering, the customer that hangs up on you or slams the door in your face will disappear from your world afterwards. There is nothing to fear because they will either buy or they will not stick around in your world long enough to matter.

And every statement they make to take you off your game, you have to act like you knew it was coming. In essence, you did, didn't you? I mean, you did not expect them to let you come in and walk all over them, right? So anticipate it, acknowledge it and keep going.

Example: "Hi, this is Vincent. I'm calling today because I noticed you do not have a vacuum cleaner. Obviously it is something you cannot live without and I am going to talk to you about the state-of-the-art XYZ 1000. How are you currently cleaning your floors?"

I identified myself, stated my purpose and went straight into finding out what I need to know. It was a very rudimentary opening and was not very assumptive, but we don't always have every bit of information about a potential client.

Receiving end customer says, "I hate you, I hate your company, go away."

"Exactly, Mr./Mrs. Customer, I hear you and I understand you have a knee-jerk reaction to somebody calling you or showing up at your door. However, as you and I both know, you've got to clean your floor for the sake of yourself and the others living in your home. How many people are in your family?"

Acknowledgment, deflection, moving forward. Ideally, I want to know who he is putting at risk by not cleaning the floor effectively. Children? Pets? Frequent visitors? What's the dynamic I am dealing with?

I am looking for a need. A weakness. A chink in their armor. And once I find it, I am going to hit the customer with it until I force out any and all objections they have to my product or service. Then, they're mine.

And if he or she hangs up? I wear it like a badge of honor. The customer forfeited. He or she did not tell you "no", which is a draw by the judge's scorecards. You're still standing. Stand proud. And get used to it.

If you are in a sales arena, you have to develop a tough skin to the "initial shutdown." The "initial shutdown" is a different animal than the later or ultimate objection. It is the customer's hasty reaction to your opening statement. It is part of their tough facade, their strategy to take you down. And you minimize its effectiveness by anticipating it, receiving it and firing back with something they do not expect.

My two favorite words on any sales call are "perfect" and "exactly." Customers never see it coming. Using these words show you anticipated them saying what they thought they could get rid of you with. It is a stunning move and shocking blow designed to disarm their defenses and take control of the call. This is the quick flurry of punches; it's that moment in *Rocky II* when Rocky switched back to fighting southpaw in the 15th round against Apollo. This is where you turn the tides and take back control on your march to victory.

When you reach that point of sales mastery, the culmination that ensues is again akin to the comparison to the *Matrix* series; you see things before they happen, you can dodge bullets and objections like they are nothing and you are One with the universe. The obstacles of the sales game will no longer register on your radar. You will wave your hands and they will be gone. In the beginning, Keanu had no idea he had this potential. However, as he honed his skills and developed this knowledge through practice and patience, it clicked. That is how you will be. I've been there. That's why I'm here.

If a customer delivers the death blow and you respond with "perfect" or "exactly", do you really think they are going to continue to treat you like an average telemarketer? (I apologize profusely for the curse word. Just trying to make a point.)

You want this customer to start talking about the personal attributes and situations you are trying to sell to. You want a residential customer to start talking about their refrigerator, phone service, computer, their whatever. You want a business owner to start talking about inventory, how they got started, and their clientele. It's near and dear to their heart and you have to earn a spot in that heart to get to their wallets.

I have a 2-year old little girl. She is my soul and inspiration. Get me talking about my princess and I will not stop. Customers are the same way. Find their tender spots. Find their pressure points. Then squeeze.

No one wants to put those things that are so near and dear to their heart in jeopardy. The simple fact is that people get comfortable. Why do you think people stay in horrendous relationships? Because the fear of what else could be out there is overwhelming. That fear outweighs the fear of staying in a relationship that crushes their identity and makes them depressed. That "comfort" factor becomes their crutch. However, your end result is making the customer fear standing pat more than making a change. Sales is not some

32

unbreakable code, it is psychology. Everything is selling; master the processes and you can do anything. Like wearing makeup, the trick is to make it undetectable to the naked eye.

A lot of the introduction is stating the obvious. You quickly say who you are, your purpose, the most insightful thing you can bring to the table in a brief monologue, and a bridge directly into fact-finding so they cannot shut you down.

I say "brief" because I have heard introductions that go on for over a minute. People cannot keep something like that up over a hundred times per day and mean it. Customers will tune out shortly after the start of one of these marathon introductions. This is why you say something zippy like a teaser line for an action movie or book review. A joke cannot be told, a building cannot be constructed and a movie cannot open without that foundation, but it cannot be overstated or it dilutes the purpose to come. The pre-titles sequence to a James Bond movie may suck up the preponderance of the budget but it does nothing to confound the plot. (And yes, James Bond movies *do* have plots!)

Sound like you mean it. Do you want this customer to buy something or fall asleep? You have to not only have the attitude, but you have to find an angle on every call. Is this a limited time offer? Are you able to do something for this customer that puts them in an elite class all their own? Do you have something better than anything else out there? Describe briefly the most attractive thing about what you have to offer. Mention of their competitors, missing out on something or savings that are unique to this customer can always entice them to listen after those first thirty seconds have passed.

If the customer says they have spoken to someone before – so what? Many salespeople feed into this flimsy push-off and say, "oh, so they already told you about this?" or, "why weren't you interested?" No, no, no! Why would you assume your predecessor's introduction, fact-finding, presentation or overcoming of objections were superior to yours? Take charge and ignore the rest; you have set out to be the best.

They will tell you they have no time. Do not let this or anything they say in that opening few minutes deter you. Stay in the ring until that bell sounds. Always remember that. I wish I had a dollar for every time I had been on or monitored a call where a customer indicated a lack of time at the onset only to stay on for ten to twenty minutes or more and even result in a sale. They are simply using defense mechanisms. Weaken their defenses with your wit, charisma and quick reaction and it will make all the difference. Before you are able to sell them on why they need your service, you must first sell them on why they should give you that window of time. Try it, push for it and even if they still refuse to block off ten minutes for you, you are no worse for the wear.

If a customer says they are unable to look at or have not had time to review something, no problem – you will describe it to them. Do not let that live body go. Cling to them for dear life like you did to that first boyfriend or girlfriend you thought you couldn't live without. Keep talking until they force you out the door. That is not to say that you cross the "rude line"; it means that being a pushover will reap no results. It's being strong without being standoffish; bold without being boorish.

Sometimes the most obvious tips are still the best. For instance, RELAX. Michelangelo did not rush the Sistine Chapel, nor should you rush the flow of a sales call masterpiece. A certain amount of apprehension is normal but you cannot let it consume you. Put those thoughts out of your head and trudge forward for strain and fear in your voice will do nothing but undermine your entire call. What are you nervous about? I read once that we spend the majority of our lives worrying about things that never come to fruition. Don't think. Just do.

Be yourself. Talk to your customers like you are talking to a friend or neighbor. If you have the chance to listen to yourself on a recording, take it. A monotone or bored voice will gain no favor with potential customers. Every line that trickles from your tongue must tingle and titillate with excitement. You may be talking about a janitorial service or a kind of paper product but when you describe it the adjectives have to inspire and stimulate the recipient of your pitch to make a change. You can't do that if you sound like Ben Stein in his oft-quoted *Ferris Bueller's Day Off* appearance. Even if you have to act interested, then you give the Oscar-worthy performance of a lifetime.

Make calls, or be available to take them. You accomplish nothing by over-prepping an account, over-thinking or just taking too much time in between calls and losing your momentum. Bulk of calls is important and I am sure you have heard of sales being a numbers' game. Ineffective managers will tell you that you have to make or take more calls to sell. Truth is, it's quality over quantity. It is more solid pitches, more well-conceived presentations and more calls that go the distance that result in sales.

Leave voice mails if no one is available to hear your pitch. You can probably reach up to 100 or so voice mail mechanisms a week and if even 1% of them call back, it is a warmer lead. Find every way you can to put yourself in the best position to win.

Make progress on every call, whether it fact-finding a gatekeeper or turning around the classic "just send me information" deflection. If they simply take down your name and number, that is not progress. If you are forced to settle for a second call, you do not want to start from scratch. The gatekeeper could be a wealth of knowledge and you want to treat them as such.

34

Never rely on someone else to sell your product or service to the real decision-maker unless you have no choice in the matter. Always push to request that meeting with all partners or the person who ultimately makes the decision. Like anything else, you have to sell them on why this is imperative. Tell them it is a courtesy to them to ensure you are there to answer whatever questions the real decision-maker or partner or spouse has, so they aren't put on the spot to try to answer something they do not know.

Imagine what that conversation goes like when Gatekeeper dropkicks you. It is a little something like this:

"Hey, Boss, John Doe called today from XYZ to see if we wanted a radio ad."

"Not in the budget. Maybe next year."

"Yeah, that's what I told him."

End of discussion.

You are the salesperson. They are the Gatekeeper. Do not rely on them to step out of their role to do yours.

Remember that the people you are speaking to are on a need-to-know basis. The Gatekeeper needs to know one thing: the name of the party you are requesting to speak to. Unfortunately, we do not always have that either, but improvisation is critical to sales excellence.

That being said, when you reach a Gatekeeper, do not lose hope. Plow through. They have defense mechanisms just like customers and, like customers, you disarm those defenses. Think rationally: If the Gatekeeper is programmed to keep you out, why would you fall into their trap by telling them every detail of your identity?

Example of what not to do:

"XYZ Company, how can I help you?"

"Hi, this is Vincent Scott of Scott Media Group. I would like to speak to John Doe about your marketing program. Is now a good time?"

Yikes – just writing that made me shiver. Under no circumstances should you ask a customer or gatekeeper or anyone for that matter if it is a "good time." I don't care if you think this is polite or if someone recommended you say it. Don't. Trust me, if it is not a good time, they will let you know. Your job is to bulldoze through to the next step of the call flow and deal with objections as they come, not to give a customer a reason to get rid of you. Asking if it is a good time is like putting your hands down in a boxing match and asking your opponent if they would like to pummel you. Stay away from questions that can and will be answered with a "no."

"Mr. Doe is not available right now, can I take a message?"

If you give your number, they may or may not even write it down and your information is lost in the oblivion of Gatekeeper jail. Every leg of call flow is like a "Choose Your Own Adventure" book I read when I was a lad.

Example of what to do:

"XYZ Company, how can I help you?"

"John, please."

This is a direct, to-the-point request for exactly who you want. It makes it seem as if you know John personally and there is a chance that Gatekeeper will put you through to him sans hassle. Let's say for the sake of this argument that this does not transpire. Read on:

"Who's calling, please?"

"This is Vincent."

Another true statement made without an overload of information divulged. Again, this may or may not work. The Gatekeeper may assume you are a friend of John's and may patch you through. For the sake of your learning, I will pretend it does not go that way and will illustrate a potential response.

"And who are you with?"

Now you have to give them something. If you just state the name of your company, you run the risk of Gatekeeper assuming you are just a pesky telemarketer. Rather than run that risk, try this:

"Sure, absolutely, this is Vincent Scott with Scott Media Group. I am calling to talk to the person that handles your account with us. Is that you?"

This response does a few things. You answered their question, but you also stated a purpose that puts some of their skin in the game and you conceivably overstated the importance of Gatekeeper. Some gatekeepers are more important than they let on; others are simply what their title implies. You will even run into some business owners who pretend to be gatekeepers just to find out what you are after. Either way, take no chances. This response made the call personal by referencing XYZ's "account" with Scott Media Group. Of course, the balance sheet of that "account" could read zero, but that is irrelevant. You have to do whatever you have to do to get John Doe on that line. He may materialize after that statement, or he may not. But you did everything you could and got as far as you could. That's sales.

You will realize after some experience that, in essence, that's what it is all about: getting as far as you can in any given situation. Pressing the gatekeeper, weaving in and out of fact-finding traffic so you can pitch, and getting past their inhibitions about what you have to offer so you can get a yes or a no on Call #1 are your motives. There are no points awarded for a maybe so, and you want to avoid that answer like the plague lest you wind up chasing them around like a lost puppy thinking they may be your meal ticket when, in reality, they are dodging your calls.

Let's get back to the conversation with Gatekeeper. Here is another example of what not to do:

"He is not available right now. Can I take a message?"

"Sure, this is Vincent Scott; my number is 555 555-5555."

This is nothing more than surrender. What should you have said?

"Actually, what number should I call to reach him directly right this second?" And do not be bashful about calling a cell phone once received. They gave it to you!

Or if they give you the old, "he's on the other line," your response should not be that you will call back or that you will go away with your tail between your legs, it should be, "oh, no problem, I'll hold." Catch these people off guard by doing the opposite of what they expect.

In my favorite episode of *Seinfeld,* Jason Alexander's George Costanza found success by doing the opposite of every impulse he had. On the show, it made for a humorous plot where he landed a job with the Yankees and a blonde bombshell but in sales it is essential. Do the opposite of what you are expected to do in situations that could lead to your undesirable exit. Only then can you knock them off their game of keeping you from walking through that door.

This same situation applies to outside or door-to-door sales. Like a newly married spouse, you have to cross the threshold to have any shot at happily ever after. When approaching the secretary looking for the boss, or you are standing on the outside looking in, keep it short, sweet and targeted on breaking through to the other side.

If you walk into an office and are asked what you want, assume this sale: "Yes, I'm Vincent Scott, I need to meet with John (or 'the boss') about your account with Scott Media Group." If they try to rush you out the door, overwhelm them with information or responsibility. "OK, he's not interested? I see – can I get your name and number so if he calls about his account I can let him know you said he was not concerned about the money you are missing out on?" No secretary wants that burden.

If "he is busy," no worries: you'll wait, and you take a seat. Do not play into their whim of your retreat.

Think about it: when are we at our worst? Anytime we are faced with something we did not expect our reactions can be detrimental. When a customer or gatekeeper deals you the "initial shutdown", your unfortunate reaction to it often winds up with you immediately off the phone. The reason is because you did not anticipate their response and meet it with a better one. Because you did not anticipate it and you did not come back with something stronger, you lose.

If you have a new idea or something sounds like a good idea, just because it may not work the first ten, fifty or one hundred times does not mean you stop doing it. You can't win every time, but it could lead you to win more often and there was a reason you came up with the idea to begin with.

The introduction sets the wheels in motion. However, just like the philosophy of making more calls equals sales success, it is about the quality of your introduction. It is about pushing as hard and far as you can go in those opening moments.

Some leads may be better than others, but that is irrelevant; you get paid to treat every lead like a Glengarry lead. Walk into each with a set purpose; you have no idea what response you will get. Leads that "appear" to be more lucrative can turn you down just as often as ones with no perceived value. Head into each lead with intent to sell and determination to not back down or be backed down.

Be up front with your purpose. Far too many "salespeople" lead in with some customer service-sounding prologue designed just to get the customer talking. Guess what; when they learn you are just trying to sell them, they will be miffed and your chances at a sale are now zero percent rather than whatever they were before. Be honest. You don't have to or want to lead in by telling them, "Hey, I am here to sell you something," but if you devise an effective introduction, you do not have to do some weaselly backdoor nonsense and cross your fingers the customer will talk to you. Think about it; if they talk to you because you trick them that you are contacting them to "verify some information," you're history when they discover your real motive.

It is tempting to sneak in with that approach; after all, it gets the customer talking to you after a series of rejections you just encountered. In fact, some salespeople *are* skilled enough to make it work because they can turn on a dime and know how and when to make it a sales call. However, the vast majority of people cannot make that switch. It is not easy to call on someone and act like you are verifying some basic information only to quickly flip the script and start selling. Truth is, this makes it hard to get proper fact-finding achieved and renders a sales presentation difficult to deliver. It is an uphill battle I urge you to avoid.

In all your travels, hold tight to the fact that the center of the sales universe is your customer. Your relationship with them bears many similarities to starting to date someone new; you are calling them on the phone and any mistake decreases the likelihood of Date #2 (I am going to avoid talking about "the close" here for fear of sounding crass). You are constantly on audition and there is not much comfort level until you establish a bond. They have to see that you are out for their needs.

Customers are people, just like you, which is difficult to recall sometimes after a fruitless day of banging doors or talking to answering machines. But when you wade through to find that pearl known as "Decision Maker," do not forget where your priorities lie. Love may make the world go 'round (if you believe that sort of thing), but "Decision Maker" gets bombarded by attention from those lesser than you, so you have to make sure they see you are simply the best and better than all the rest.

Emotional people make buying decisions. You have to strike the right chords with powerful words and phrases that force their hand. They will not judge you by your table manners, but one false step in the opening moments will spell disaster and leave you asking for the check. They will talk about dating other people, like your competitors or some other salesperson, and they may ignore or screen your calls and tell you how you have wronged them in the past. Sometimes they make no sense and they may rebuke you for no reason, but until they walk out of your lives you have no choice but to treat them right or you are high and dry.

They want to be put on a pedestal whether they deserve it or not and be told how great they are. Even people with fragile egos like me need that from time to time. For you, that means complimenting them or something about their current state of affairs that you glean from fact-finding. This is also going to serve to differentiate you from any other "gentleman" or "female" callers that may be in their field of vision.

This is all part of the "why should they choose you" portion of the program; you cannot have a bland attitude or opening – you have to find a good, positive routine and stick to it. You don't sell somebody by talking about ways your company failed. That is the very reason we hide our deep dark secrets from our potential mates for years and years, right? Just kidding.

Gaining respect and trust will wind up being the most important facet of either type of relationship – business or personal. Finding out about them and showing an interest in what they do and hope to achieve is your priority when it comes to finding your way into their heart or their wallet. But you can't get to their wallet without getting to their heads and hearts, so don't try! That is why you don't pitch price before they fall in love with you.

We have broached the fact that customers are programmed to tune you out, just like not every member of the opposite sex is going to swoon to your charms at the bar. You have to break down that wall as soon as you can. There is little time with which to do it, but to borrow from the Al Pacino speech from *Any Given Sunday*, everything we do in life is won or lost by inches. The little things add up, and if you don't do them, you will not succeed.

It's about showing value, not telling. It's making sure they understand how the inner workings of your product or service are going to make their dreams come true. It's taking time to explain how you appreciate or respect them. It's flowers, not just when you screw up. Customers want to know what is in it for them, and if you can't relay that, you'll fall inches short.

Nobody's perfect, but you don't have to be if you show legitimate concern for their well-being. A relationship requires mutual respect and communication. We've got to earn that respect from customers by making sure they know we'll be there for them through thick and thin, even after they sign the bill of sale. When the promises you make during your sales presentation don't pan out in Month 1, that is when you may be called upon to re-declare your love. Take the time to make sure your customer knows what is going on and upsells or residuals could be in your future. If you don't tend to a wounded relationship, whether it is your fault or theirs, it will end.

Don't forget the holy trinity of sales: satisfy the customer, the company and you. Every decision you make needs to cater to those three; failure to do so leads to catastrophe. Failure to satisfy a relationship in life can lead to a separation or a slapped face; in sales it leads to missed opportunity and potential loss. There are lots of customer fish in the sea, but never take for granted the ones you see.

You benefit most by treating your customer, like your significant others and friends, like the center of your world.

"The Selling Game" by Vincent Scott
Chapter 3:
Q & A: ASKING "THE RIGHT STUFF"

There have been several lackluster third chapters in history. *The Karate Kid Part III*, *Matrix Revolutions* and *Die Hard With a Vengeance* come to mind (with no ill will towards their predecessors in the series). However, this one being of dire consequence to your sales flow, you should consider it the *Goldfinger* of "The Selling Game."

Once you force your way in the door the least you can do is get to know the person. Finding a need and exposing a weakness in a current scheme is critical. Asking the right questions is vital to finding those pressure points. Without a master plan and method to the madness you will fail in building a foundation to your desired outcome.

Put it in perspective. For all practical purposes, you are a prosecuting attorney. It is your job to ask expertly crafted questions specifically designed to elicit the responses you need to build and win your case. You cannot convince judge, jury or customer that Colonel Mustard did it in the ballroom with the candlestick unless you paint the perfect picture.

DO NOT ask a yes or no question. We have visited where the customer can take these and, in addition, if you ask a question and the customer says, "Yes," what have you really learned? Find questions you can ask that will broaden the horizon the most. You want to ask the question that causes the customer to spring forth like a fountain.

DO NOT ask too many or ask useless questions that do not further your case. The customer's time is precious (yours should be, too) and you have to envision they are allotting you just enough time to ask the top five questions and move on. People do not block out an hour for you to give them a full report on whatever you are peddling so strap in and get used to the fast pace. Even if you are building relationships, cut to the chase. Spend the majority of your time overcoming objections, not building up to the pitch, because if you do have to settle for call #2, you will not have to start from scratch.

DO NOT ask a question for the sake of asking it. The exception to this rule is if it is to stall as you calculate your next move. Let me explain: the questions you ask are designed to pry a need or weakness from the customer's inner sanctum. Once you obtain that information it is time to fashion your pitch. However, in many sales gigs, it is imperative to do some computer work to brandish your weapon and you may need to throw in blowoff questions to keep the customer talking.

This is important because (1) any question you ask for determination of needs or weaknesses must resurface later. You will use their words against them in a court of law: your law. There is no greater ammunition than the customer's own words, which is why it is vital to pay attention during these proceedings and write down key points. A lot of salespeople think they do not need to log anything but that is foolishness. A waiter or waitress can only go so long before they forget an order or two. That may impact their tip. A gaffe in sales of this magnitude can impact your career.

You want to ask very pointed, focused questions to which you may already know the answers. They are designed with the purpose of determining the information you need in order to pin the "crime" of inadequacy on them so you can show them where your product or service meets their needs. Once you get the answers to these types of questions, you later "trap" your customer with their own words and rationale when guiding them into the end result you desire. Then, it is time to sentence them to life with your superior product.

Also, (2) once you get good at this rapport and fact-finding stuff, customers say a lot of similar things or go off on tangents that are irrelevant to the proceedings. You do not have to listen to or hear everything they say – you only have to hear the things that are going to help you diagnose their dilemma.

When you go to a doctor's office, you tell them everything that ails you, make smalltalk, etc., but their job is to figure out what is wrong with you. At least physically, right? They do a lot of smiling and nodding as you tell them what they do not need to know. The information about your health will help their diagnosis; a story about your cat will go in one ear and out the other. This will buy your time as you prepare the next and delicate leg of your sales flow: the pitch and presentation.

After years in the game, you will learn what works and does not through trial and error. Often salespeople that are still struggling despite the fact I have doled out advice to them is they try to take too many liberties with what we discussed and wind up going too far outside of the box. I have listened to some reps that do a fantastic job of sounding professional, they can talk your ear off and while they sound like someone a romantic partner would want to introduce to their parents, they cannot sell to save their lives. They talk in circles. They ask questions to hear themselves talk. Stick to the flow and you will be a star. Deviate and you will never get off the ground.

In building the sales call you have to use the customer's words to bolster your stance at every turn. They will balk at your pitch. This is a fact of life. However, when you use their own words against them in pointing out their need and weakness, you diminish the credibility of their objections. They cannot ignore their own words; if you make your customer eat them you greatly enhance your chance of success.

If you are at all like me, you think about the job when you are not there and dwell on what you could have or should have said. You think about new ways to approach it. That's a good thing. You want to analyze your trade if you are going to master it.

A lot of times, people ask, "What could I have said to this objection?" Decent question, but often not the one to ask. A common mistake is setting yourself up to fail by getting up to the line of scrimmage without a play in mind. If you do not unearth the right information in fact-finding, it does not matter how good your recommendation, pitch, or potential overcome is. Your offering could be the greatest thing since sliced bread and they will say no and it will boggle your brain. Do you know why? Because you did not use their own information, their own case scenario and their own words against them. You did not ask the right questions, thereby setting yourself up to fail because you could not overcome with powerful, specific logic designed to garner the proper emotions.

Without strategy you lose more often than not. Unfortunately, like the loose pickle jar, people luck into sales sometimes through no skill of their own and defy these rules. If this happens early in a career it can spell disaster because of the false sense of reality it can provide.

I have seen a lot of people have early success in a career and be heralded as great by managers and peers. Personally, I have always respected the salesperson that took longer to get where they wanted to be and showed constant improvement in their trajectory through solid effort. It is one thing to luck into success; it is entirely another to work your tail off to become great at what you do and know what it took to get you there. Those who luck into success fade away quickly. Those who know what it takes to get there stand the test of time. They worked hard to get there and are not willing to let it go.

It is likely some will walk away from this book and try something new for a slew of opportunities and they may not find instant success. After that, they may dismiss this book and go right back to old, comfortable ways of failing. Neither I nor anyone could tell you a fool-proof method of making a sale on every call. It's consistency that wins the race. It's playing the odds. If you do the right things on your call throughout, you enhance your chances. In many sales jobs, if something works 1% of the time it is a huge success. Where people stumble and fall is when they skip steps to the sale.

When you put it all on the line and confront the customer's weakness with your specially crafted resolution, you have to have all your ducks in a row. This is intimidating to some because a lot of people are scared to pitch, hence their litany of questions that last up until the moment the customer has to go back to work. But you cannot be afraid of taking the clutch shot, having the ball in the fourth quarter or taking your opponent down to the wire. And you will not get better without real world experience of doing it.

This is where analysis of your job and determination of what questions you need to ask comes into play.

Think about what you are selling. Are you selling a good or service? Are you selling something intangible like an idea, concept or results? Is it potentially an everyday item or something obscure?

That first question is the segue you are using to get from outsider to inner sanctum. From the information you start to glean one of two things will occur: the customer will go along with your line of questioning or they will try to shoot you down. If they go with the latter you have to treat it like the "initial shutdown" and flip the script to put them on the spot.

As pointed out when discussing the introduction, you have to quickly get the customer engaged by getting them to talk about themselves, their situation or their business. They will occasionally go off track and it's your job to take them back. The boxing analogy of this paragraph: you have them in the corner, they try to get out; you have to get them back there. Keep them in their place. Keep control.

Whatever your first question is should be designed to get a broad answer that is going to open up a tree of future questioning. If you are talking to a customer about their current cleaning needs, vacuuming needs, moving needs, advertising needs, you have to ask first what they use right now. How are the results? How do they track the results? What do they find most frustrating or would they change about the product they use? You are literally scrambling to find something to latch on to at this point. When you do, you want to find out everything about that aspect because it will likely become the weakness you expound upon when you start your pitch.

At the onset of fact-finding, you are fumbling in the dark for light switches. As you find them, the room becomes a little less dim but you certainly are not privy to all the sights in the room yet. Secondary and offshoot questions are just as important if not more than the principal questions you utilize. Do not graze the surface of what you are trying to accomplish; ask questions and find out specifics about the things you uncover.

The mistake many people make here is they think sales is just about having conversations. Sales is about latching on to facts and characteristics of your target audience so you can show them what you have while taking care of their insecurities and fears.

You did not call this customer to write a biography or interview them for the school paper. You need to isolate the five or so questions that you most need the answer to. Based on those, it is likely you will have to branch off and ask other questions on your own to complete your questioning. However, you need a concise game plan to deliver consistent results.

Think back to *A Few Good Men*; Tom Cruise could never have hammered Jack Nicholson on the stand like that if he had not asked all of the supporting questions that proved his side to be true. But any false questions here or there, a second of hesitation, and the General would take the opportunity to attempt escape. Much akin to that, you have to ask questions that stick to the book: what situation are they in? What are they using that is most similar to what you have to offer? Ask about profits and benefits of what they are using. Probe; the more you have the more you can use later when you are dismantling their method and building up your own.

You always have to be ready to pounce. The more you know about what they do, the more likely it is that you will find their need or weakness. Once you have that, you have the tools for victory.

You are basically hacking away at their foundation from the word GO – undermining what they do and performing a great game of "mine is better than yours." If you undermine what they are doing and make them doubt themselves, you have a winner.

Remember that the questions you think of, the questions your company recommends and the ones that seem most practical heading into a sale are just the tip of the iceberg. It is aesthetically satisfying to check off questions on a checklist but that does not help you in the grand scheme if you fail to uncover the real treasure. Often the obvious questions will set the stage; you have to infuse yourself into the rest. Actors in comedy shows are given scripts but the funniest material is often ad-libbed. Where you branch off from the script can be where you make the most impact.

A customer may tell you they advertise in the newspaper. If you leave it at that, however, what have you really learned? Your whole argument come pitch and overcome time will purely be based on speculation unless you glean cold, hard facts. How much are they paying? What do they get for the investment money? How often do they appear? What is the circulation of the paper? What are the results? How are they tracking the results? Every answer to those secondary questions could conceivably be used later when you are "tearing down" what they do in an attempt to show them they need what you have.

No, you do not have to ask them every one of those questions. You will not have time nor will they all help your cause. However, this is another instance of where your abilities, reflexes and intuition will be important to the process. The answers to these questions will aid you in the long run because you will need specifics to more clearly illustrate your points, combat the objections and ice the deal.

Were you one of the people who looked ahead in books to see glimpses at the ending? The call does not bode well for you if your fact-finding is lacking. In addition, you do not want to end up asking more questions after you have half-heartedly attempted a pitch. Once you have made that pitch you have crossed the point of no return. You have committed. Asking questions is ridiculous at this point; you cannot slow down the train once it has pulled out of the station and is full steam ahead to its next destination. Anything you ask should have already been asked, the customer will see you flailing and wonder why you pitched without knowing the answer you now seek.

The best advice I can give on fact-finding is have a plan. Don't ask too many, don't ask too few, don't ask the wrong ones and don't forget to add some more right ones. This aspect of the call flow is the one that will require you to take the most liberties. For some, that is a scary concept but that fear will dissipate after mass repetition.

Everything you do or say from this point forward is based on what you learn during this session. The problem with scripted questions is that often people will ask them only because they have to and not take it upon themselves to make that next step. They fail to realize the impact or importance.

Let's say I am a car salesman and you have wandered onto my lot. I have approached you and engaged you in conversation.

"Good afternoon! I'm Vincent, and welcome to Scott Motors. How are you?"

"Good."

"And with whom do I have the pleasure of speaking?"

"John Doe."

"Fantastic, John. I am here to meet all of your needs today in your quest for a vehicle. What make and model are you looking for?"

There are a million different ways I could choose to begin this line of questioning. The truth is, I do not want to ask about price range or anything that will inhibit me but many users come to your dealership with a specific car in mind. If they state they have one, you will then be looking into the one with the most options. If they do not, sky's the limit.

"I'm just looking for something sporty in my price range."

"Perfect, John, we will definitely be able to find a fit for you today." Stay away from saying there are a lot of options – this is a common sales mistake. In the culmination of this examination, you are going to make a *personalized recommendation* based on what you have learned. You are also not going to take the bait and ask about the customer's perceived "price range." "I know color is important; what color are you looking for?"

46

"Black."

"Excellent choice, John." Constant reinforcement of customer opinions and answers is important. "What options are the most important on this car?" Again, do not limit yourself. Do not ask questions like if they want a sunroof or they want a CD changer or they want additional amenities. Remember you are making a *personalized recommendation* and leaving yourself plenty of room to trade down. Right now you stick to the things you are going to allow the customer to have their say in initially.

"Well, I'm really just looking for durability and style. My last car required a lot of repairs. I want something that will last ten years or so."

This still leaves everything wide open, but the customer is getting more skin in the game with every question. You can still offer this customer anything on your lot, provided it is black, sporty and long-lasting. The questions you choose to use should serve just such a purpose; leave yourself a lot of wiggle room but give the customer what they want.

"I like your thought process, John. Let's face it, these are important factors in making a purchase and at Scott Motors we only carry top-of-the-line merchandise. What will you be trading in today?" This is a subtle reference to a one-call close and a way to give yourself frame of reference on what the customer has been dealing with.

"A 2000 XYZ 123."

"Yes, I have seen several of those in my day. Sounds like she gave you some good mileage." The customer has not committed to buy another XYZ, so again, the sky is the limit. It is likely your dealership wants you marketing a particular car and, in this case, you certainly can.

Let's say the customer comes in and asks for specifics like a sunroof, spoiler, etc. No worries – in your mind, you want to be formulating where you take this customer. We will get to the pitch in a future segment but while you are fact-finding, you simply want to find out what is important to them because you will use it if and when they balk at your initial offering.

"So who will be riding in the vehicle?" This is where you start to circle your prey; you want to know all variables because if there are children you can utilize their safety as cause for your pitch. If the car is simply for them, you will be targeting their vanity and desire for a flashy vehicle.

When you pitch a customer, you have to forge a bond with them through what you learn at this critical piece of the call. Referencing this information repeatedly while you make and draw conclusions about them, the results they are getting in their current means of doing business and as you steer them towards your camp is how you will most effectively wind up closing your sale.

Each customer enters your realm with some built-in fears. You cannot disarm those fears and convince them to make a change they are apprehensive about unless you put them at ease. In their mind, their opinions, thoughts and beliefs are scripture and when you cite and quote it back to them they will be a lot less resistant to your proposal.

All of that said, never gloss over the importance of a thorough but targeted fact-finding game plan. In the selling game, the fact-finding is the physical roll of the dice; it alone determines how far you will advance. It alone puts the wheels in motion. And it alone will take you into the unknown that lies ahead.

*   *   *

Burnout. While a terrible ailment, it is often misdiagnosed. However, at this present day moment November 2009 in Vincent Scott's career as he drove to work, he knew the symptoms were real. He was mired in an impasse and pondered the implications and treatment options available.

Interestingly, there had recently emerged a hint of a line on the horizon.

Everything in his work world was culminating into an inevitable blowup. In recent weeks, Vincent had waged war on the fact his people were not being paid correctly on commissions. In fact, for three years, commissions and clerical goofs in his department had been a punchline. Simply stated, the joke was not remotely funny anymore. When complaints of the workers reached fever pitch and Vincent's boss continued to ignore them, Vincent was the only one who would act. Motivated by his duty to the people he worked so hard to serve and protect, the haze of gunfire caused from Vincent's assault on the clerical process woke the giant and was the spark needed to ignite a mutiny currently in process.

His current burnout or, rather, boredom, would soon be resolved in some fashion – good, bad or ugly – but he could not help but look back 7 years to the first time he experienced the same feelings.

In May 2002, talks with Vincent regarding management began. Once Vincent hit his comfort zone, caused by a few months of leaderboard domination, he let it be known to Ashley that he was interested in that eventuality. While no one can ever be completely ready for what lies ahead in a management role, Vincent would have been better even at that premature stage than some of the managers on hand (such as his own). His goal was to help others and, as no one was having the success he was, his desires were mostly unselfish.

48

Ashley realized that dangling that carrot in front of Vincent could take her places she had previously only dreamed about on the sales report and she had no qualms doing just that.

This put her team on autopilot. Ashley started having Vincent lead team meetings, used him as the thermometer of team chemistry and actually asked his advice when the team voiced dissent. Little did he know, it would be quite some time before potential movement would actually move.

In mid-June, manager Casey Pine announced her departure leaving a vacancy. Two front-runners were rumored for the position: Vincent and Stacey Worth.

Stacey had worked for ABM's wireless division as a manager prior to arrival in their Rockford center. She was shifted to the residential office but deemed not ready to manage yet. She was put in training and had been a rep for 2 months as of Casey's departure, currently mired towards the caboose of the pack in results. However, she was tight with Maggie – Ashley's boss – and came out on the receiving end of the promotion.

Vincent was a little surprised but a month later, Maggie was ushered out amidst the department's struggles and a job was created for her downtown. Ashley again dangled the management carrot to Vincent, presenting a chain reaction scenario that would see attendance manager Sandy Watson taking the vacancy and Vincent taking her place.

However, that scenario also did not pan out and July marked the arrival of Shelly Cheekwood to run their call center.

Shelly brought immediate spunk and fire to a lackluster sales office. She cooked breakfast for the office, implemented games she had concocted while a manager in Rochester and made a habit of running around yelling, "Rockford rocks!"

At that point , Vincent gave people the benefit of the doubt and thought prospects were good with the onset of the Cheekwood administration. That was fueled by a meeting just weeks into the new regime. Vincent was greeted one day by e-mail from Shelly requesting a meeting in her office later in the afternoon. Knocking on the frame of her open door, he was greeted and he entered, closing the door and taking a seat opposite her desk.

"Vincent, thank you for meeting with me," Shelly greeted him sincerely and warmly.

"My pleasure," he responded. "How are you settling in?"

"No complaints yet! Just learning the ropes," she responded, giggling with a bubbly demeanor that would become her trademark. "That's actually why I wanted to meet with you. As you can probably imagine I have been bombarded with people contacting me saying they want to be a manager."

Vincent laughed. "That doesn't surprise me."

"You would be shocked if I told you some of their names!" she continued. "But I wanted to meet with you because I was interested in finding out if that path interests you. You were the only person that did not contact me that I was hoping would."

Vincent, intrigued, responded, "Wow. Thank you. I guess I didn't think contacting you was proper protocol. I have talked to Ashley about my career path and yes, I am very interested in managing."

"I'm glad to hear that. What do you think you bring to the table?"

"Well," Vincent mused, "I have been doing this job for several months with great success and clearly know how to communicate to customers and peers. I know why others fail where I succeed and just want to impact the company in the way I can best."

"I understand. Right now I am looking at the office and intend to make several changes to get us out of the hole we're in. That said, I want to know who my future leaders are."

The 15 minute meeting stretched to 45 and Shelly ascertained Vincent's thoughts on how he would manage people, discipline those who were currently his peers and the like. It mirrored a job interview and Vincent blew her away.

Time in the outside world continued to march on. Vincent's apartment continued to be stocked with prizes he won at work: a microwave, numerous telephones, a DVD player, a television, home appliances and countless gift cards to nearly everywhere in Minneapolis.

The revolving door that is call center hiring, firing, resignations and moves certainly impacted Rockford ABM; in October, some of the changes Shelly had alluded to started to take form. Ashley was swapped out of the Rockford center and banished to Montrose, a suburb which contained little more than a church and a dungeon of an ABM call center. Montrose was also in the Cheekwood jurisdiction and had roughly 40 reps that performed the same job functions to less critical acclaim.

In her place arrived Harriet Raines – an outspoken and strong-willed woman with quite a reputation. She had spunk and seemed to bring the kick in the pants to the team that they needed – at first. A couple other managers swapped out as well and it appeared that Shelly was trying to stir the pot to garner different results. The tactic seemed to work at first; new policies, incentives and a new feel to help the employees feel a little more loved.

Passing by Shelly one day, Vincent mentioned he had more suggestions for office improvement. She obliged, as he shared ideas on peer coaching and ways to get reps to help others. Shelly loved the ideas and reiterated that it was her desire to pursue Vincent for a manager slot as soon as she had the green light to promote.

And why shouldn't she? The managers in place were relatively useless. A frightening truth Vincent would grow to know is that managers are too often not selected for talent. They are selected because they agree to uphold the system, even if the system is flawed, and they will do little to resist. Often they know somebody and it is highly political. It's the same reason that voters make a lot of bad decisions come Election Day.

Coming to a crossroads in life has its advantages and disadvantages. The creative thought it can inspire is a good thing, but dwelling in the past, wondering where it could have gone wrong or thinking about what could have been done to render a different result do nothing to aid the task at hand.

As time continued to pass, Vincent made the same trek to and from work daily with no change and no end in sight. Not only was he starting to feel unfulfilled in his work but those events coincided with the death knell of his relationship with Julie.

Her visits to Mankato were every weekend. A typical argument would be her throwing a fit if Vincent got in bed before her at night. She claimed he had not made her feel special in a long time. He missed being single. The writing was on the wall.

The morning of the end, "When I come home, you need to be out," was uttered, and you do not use lines like that if you are bluffing. He was not. And when Vincent returned, her stuff was gone.

Their pattern had always been (1) there is a miscommunication, (2) Vincent pulls away, (3) Julie chases him down and (4) things turn out fine.

Not this time.

He soon regretted the decision and made futile attempts over the coming weeks to patch things up. That failure – the pure lack of control and inability to win within a perfectionist such as Vincent – began an incredible transformation that was excruciating but necessary to the person he would become.

Had Vincent not felt the pain his mind told him he was feeling after the Julie breakup, he would not have been able to sustain future pains, be they in business or in matters of the heart. Any future "heartaches," paled in comparison. This was the only one he was in a weakened enough state afterwards to allow himself to hurt over.

Vincent made the classic breakup mistakes this go-around: trying to call, writing e-mails professing his love and remembering the good times and forgetting the bad.

Being 100 miles away from Julie aided the quest and, where most people would retreat and let their job performance go to hell, Vincent used the emotions and and the pain to lash out on his customers' objections. It only made him better.

Vincent has two childhood friends with whom he still has frequent contact: Eddie Haskins, whose parents are his Godparents, and Jack Johnson. They had a three musketeer brotherhood growing up and despite life taking them in drastically different directions they still talked several times a year. Jack was living in Colorado, doing the "out on his own" thing and was quite lonely himself around that same time.

They began a series of what they dubbed their "Sunday conversations." The topics ranged from books to booze to poetry and women, and they served as Vincent's therapy. Vincent never forgot the advice Jack gave him a couple of "sessions" in: that in order to expunge negative thoughts and emotional pain from the body, one must discard those thoughts upon arrival. When a negative thought surfaces, acknowledge its existence and dismiss it.

At first utterance, Vincent had the reaction that while this sounds catchy it is also far-fetched. Not so, as he learned through upcoming years of practice, perfection and spreading this gospel according to Jack. He slowly learned how to discard the thoughts of sitting at Julie's house in Mankato and how they would eat pizza and talk and cuddle and play video games and watch movies and watch television and make love together and shower together and play with her dog together and how he would stay until she would fall asleep before returning home and if she was awake when he left how she would cry and how they would kiss forever. As those next few months went by, so did all of those thoughts: out of his stream of consciousness.

Working the next few months, Vincent started to see more and more people terminated for lack of call flow quality. He stayed unscathed, however, and, in return, stayed on top of the sales report for Harriet. No one could touch him. But continuing to bring yourself back again and again at a level higher than anyone else is not an easy thing to motivate yourself to do. This is especially true when you cannot see the light at the end of the tunnel. As time continued and he had to use nearly all his fingers to count the number of months since management had first been dangled to him, he grew fatigued from the wait.

Some people want nothing more than that steady job and paycheck. They will put up with that existence for as long as it is available and are content with status quo. But Vincent had nothing left in Minneapolis right now aside from this job and he was ready for a move. And every day he wondered: "Will today be the day Shelly talks to me about promoting me?"

And every night he departed work and headed to an empty apartment.

There was only so much to keep him sane. For a while it was the utter dominance. Then it was trying to set records in every statistical category. He liked to put on a show for his cubicle neighbors; standing, pointing and trying to entice them through almost a trash-talking type of showing off. His favorite "adversary" was Bryant Edwards, his literal next-door-neighbor, and Vincent's energy lifted Bryant from an uncaring middle performer to the upper echelon.

In early April 2003, Shelly pulled Vincent into her office to again assure him there was an end in sight. And two weeks later: the real interview. Vincent had said all these things before, but he was selling her again —that he would not be daunted by managing friends or defined by the introverted employee he had mostly been to this point.

"Shelly, I have a job to do. If this company is paying me to enforce its rules, that is my job. I will be forthcoming with my ideas and I will be ultimately trying to make twenty Vincent's on my team, but at the end of the day it is my responsibility to uphold the policies of ABM. Would you rather have one Vincent or twenty?"

And days later, what had been dangled for a year finally materialized: Shelly was promoting Vincent to sales manager. Finally, after every monotonous day he had entered that building wondering when his hard work would pay off, he was being rewarded for his efforts. Victory.

However, in an attempt to prevent as much interaction as possible with peers he once worked with, Vincent was being shipped to Montrose. And – the real kicker – he was taking over the team helmed by Ashley Flowers, who was being demoted to a rep position back in Rockford. It was an ironic twist but sweet justice.

Montrose's call center was a dump. It was next to a pizza place where someone had recently been shot to death. Spider webs adorned the windows and the carpets were filthy. Vincent was not thrilled about being banished to the dungeon, but this was his call-up to the majors and he had to take it.

With pressure off, the casting call and audition nailed and the call-up signed, sealed and delivered, Vincent headed into the final week with a new lease on life. And he posted an all-time one-day record that stands to this day that single-handedly dwarfed all other teams in the division by himself. There was nothing like going out on top.

Harriet, who had been a proponent of Vincent's, was also slated to return to Montrose to serve as some semblance of mentor during his training wheel phase. She had grown frustrated with her team as they were a one-trick pony, and allowed her reps to see her bleed far too frequently. With in excess of 25 years with the company, she was ready for a new challenge and the idea of taking Vincent under her wing appealed to her.

And the rumor became fact: Vincent was slated to become a manager effective May 1, 2003 in Montrose, Minnesota for ABM's residential division. Reactions were mixed. Along with Elise, Vincent was the least tenured person on the floor. Bambi was inconsolable. Jake knew from talking with Vincent that this was a guy that could change the place for the better. And that was his mission, one step at a time.

"The Selling Game" by Vincent Scott
Chapter 7:
BATTLING BURNOUT (BE IT REAL OR AN ILLUSION)

Anyone who meanders through days, months and sometimes years of the same general activity with little deviation in their charted course will face something commonly referred to as "burnout." Or, in some cases, they think they do.

This affliction can strike the strong and weak. Like the common cold it has no bias in choosing its victims. However, there is grand news: it is often misdiagnosed and it is treatable.

True burnout is having nothing left to accomplish or contribute at your current post and having no glimpse of an end in sight. This is caused by having no challenge left because you conquered them all. Burnout, even when not actually present, is often utilized as a scapegoat for poor performance by those not really suffering from it. Don't get me wrong: there are several stages and some people can benefit from early detection, but using it as an excuse to not try is more despicable than dignified.

Treatment options are plentiful, no matter the stage or the reality of its onset. First remember that you – no one else – applied for the position you sit in. You hopefully brought your "A" game to the interview and pledged allegiance to that position, saying you were going to come in and give it your all. In essence, you signed a contract to fulfill the obligations to the post you serve. Granted, things, personnel and procedures will change but it is likely the company is not getting burnt out on paying you. Now, if they are, that is a whole different story.

When you did commit to the job, you sold the hiring manager on putting you in the vacancy, promised the earth, moon and stars, and expressed a desire to grow with the company. There is something to be said for paying your dues and fulfilling those commitments. Have you? Have you *truly* done that? Part of this process is being honest with yourself. Yes, you are going to be frustrated with a lot of things along the way but it is how you react and bounce back that define your character and your destiny.

In short, you may think you are hot stuff but until you master the task, shut up.

Don't forget you sold someone on putting you in that spot. You have to constantly re-invent yourself and hark back to that tenacious soul you were on interview day. Often, I have found that floundering in a position (read: the antithesis of burnout) is due to failure to maintain your big picture outlook. Far too many people have difficulty keeping their eyes on the prize. Where do you want to be in five years? It's a cop-out interview question but a legitimate one you need to ask yourself daily – especially when you claim burnout.

Everything you do has to keep you on the path towards that long-term goal. Sure, we get off course from time to time, but only through self analysis and actualization will we follow that general course and make it to that desired outcome. Like in *Rocky III* when Rocky lost that hunger – the eye of the tiger as Apollo called it and Survivor sang about – you occasionally have to have people like Adrian appeal to your best interests to make you wake up and realize you still have what it takes. The Paulie characters that try to drag you to the bar only appeal to your here and now. The rigmarole and monotony and allowing yourself to be mired in the present may turn you into a lightweight when you need to be a heavyweight to survive.

We like to look at athletes and marvel at how much they are paid. On that token, they practice for hours a day every day and have little life outside of their profession. They are benched or have to run laps if they fail to hustle or run out a ground ball. Do you run out every routine grounder? Do you generate millions of dollars in revenue for your company? Do people fork over hundreds of dollars to get off their couches just to come watch you perform? These are questions to ask yourself if you want to draw similarities between yourself and a professional athlete.

A salesperson must constantly set new challenges for her or himself. Michael Jordan was possibly the greatest competitor to roam the earth, but had accomplished what many could consider to be "it all" relatively early in his career. This obviously prompted his premature retirement and foray into professional baseball; unorthodox for most but it was a challenge he set and reached. While subpar by most standards, he batted .202 with 3 home runs in his lone season, but he accomplished a dream that 99.9% of us would be hard-pressed to accomplish ourselves.

All of that said, could he still win championships in the NBA? Once away for a year, this was a challenge again, and not only could he win but he slung together three in a row. He left again at his apex, only to return to try to lift the lowly Washington Wizards into the playoffs. That effort fell barely short but it did not stop him from trying. No other player could have had more impact on that bottom-feeding team than he could have. And that's the point.

Your undertakings will not likely be on as big a stage as those of #23, but that does not mean they are any less significant. In your realm, setting new challenges can be any number of things: selling more of multiple product offerings, making or taking more calls in a day, bettering efficiency, reaching out to peers to help them be better, taking initiative to do more to improve the department, writing scripts for others, being the top rep in the office – the

56

options are endless. A salesperson must set new challenges regularly lest that salesperson will become bored.

The nice thing about sales is that unlike sports, the skill does not diminish over time. After years of wear and tear, athletes cannot do the same feats of fancy they achieved their rookie season and they have to retire. In sales, you should only get better with time. Continue to improve your approach and attitude and you too will be able to hold your hands up above your head and be a champion.

To quote *Cocktail*'s Doug Coughlin (played masterfully by Bryan Brown) to Tom Cruise's Brian Flanagan, "Anything else is always something better." Are you going to love every aspect of your job all of the time? Of course not – that is absurd to expect. However, you need to acknowledge and accept what it takes to get where you are headed and rise to meet those challenges. Productivity and demanding excellence from yourself go a long way in making that leap. Consider that the secret to success.

Another big part of battling perceived burnout is to stop and reflect on what you have and where you have been. Letting yourself slide and looking back with regrets will get you nowhere; be thankful for the talent, the people in your corner that have never wavered and the footholds on your mountain to greatness. These people and things are never more evident than when you lose. Stop griping about what you don't have and realize how blessed you truly are. It will not cure everything that ails you but it can often quell the feelings of negativity welling up inside.

No question: it is easy to get frustrated or feel defeated. Sometimes you will feel like you have been dealt the knockdown punch. The true judge of your growth as a person or a professional is how you come back from such a punch. Are you going to lay on the mat until the ref counts to 10? Or are you going to get back up and be standing when that bell sounds? That is for you to decide.

The challenge you often face in a situation of actual burnout is maintaining a high level of performance during this period. That is where the true leaders emerge. You cannot afford to slip in the rankings because there is no telling when the call-up will come. If you are no longer next in line when it happens, you will be left behind. Hindsight is 20/20; you can use burnout as an excuse to stop trying but you cannot get that time back after you are passed over.

Those who never let up get ahead. There is always a reason to win, even if you have done it many times before. It feels good to be the best. There will always be newcomers for the throne. There will always be new opportunities and new threats. Be the person they can depend on. When the decision comes for promotion or new projects or whatever you desire, be the obvious choice. Several people blip on that radar but when that choice is made it is like musical chairs. If you're out, you're out.

This will be addressed in more depth when we talk about getting the promotion, but realize that when decisions are made you typically have to be the top 1% or better of everyone in the pool of candidates. Being picked over is not a reflection on your shortcomings. It is a reflection of the person chosen. Far too many people claiming burnout have that misconception. It's not all about you.

Now, dealing with being picked over due to nepotism or because you don't pucker up to the right posteriors is also something I can speak to. Those things are *not* fair but they are reality. You will never escape politics. Just know there is a plan for you and you cannot forget that. I have no idea if you believe in God or a higher power but even if you do not I can tell you that like Sleeping Beauty, someday your "prince" will come and you will get yours. We are often all on the same playing fields; your peers are dealing with a lot of the same circumstances and nonsense that you are. Rise above.

That's not to say things will not happen that tick you off enough that your gut instinct is to polish off the résumé or write your letter of resignation. I have done both in my day. But, in the end, the best remedy is often some much-deserved vacation. Spend it with the people and things that matter; the people and things you are working your tail off for. There is no better way to get your head back in the game than to reflect and focus on what matters most.

This is precisely why the person who takes longer to become successful is in an enviable position: they know what it took to get there. Someone who has instant success that starts to fade as they change their approach is the quickest to reach for the burnout crutch. Here is a tip: if you have been doing something for a year or less, you are not burnt out. Unless it is literally doing the exact same activity with literally zero challenge like watching paint dry, it is not burnout. If you are in the high-octane world of sales and you were a top rep once or twice, burnout is not yet possible. Stop making excuses and get back to work. If it was all fun and games, it would not be called work.

Constant reinvention of oneself is paramount to survival. You may be the best at something or drastically underutilized, but don't stop proving it because the second you do, someone will butt in front of you in line. If you don't like your lot in life, change it. If you don't like your job, leave it. If you want to get promoted, get promoted. If you don't get it, keep fighting until you do. The minute you let anything beat you down and keep you there, you are a loser. Excuses are for losers. Only you determine what you do next. Your move.

I was promised promotion early in my career as a sales rep. However, patience has never been much of a virtue I possess and having my appetite whetted for the next step that early was not all that good for my psyche.

It took them another year to bring it to fruition. Many of you have been there: walking into a job every single day wondering how much more you can take. Wondering when you are going to get a new challenge. That was tough: no real end in sight, wondering how much longer I was going to have to keep doing what I was doing.

When you really, truly, madly, deeply feel burnout, you have to face your final challenge head on: maintaining your high level of performance for another 6-to-12 months without missing a beat. If you can do that, either something will pan out for you or you will realize it is time to move on. Trust me. Again, the key is being honest with yourself. Have you really achieved absolutely everything at your current post? Have you done everything you can to fulfill any and all commitments you made to your company when you signed up? Have you kept up your end of any and all bargains? Or are you just looking for something or somebody to blame?

I have reached a point where I feel little sympathy for those claiming burnout as a reason for decreased performance. That's not to say I don't *have* sympathy for real burnout, but the burden of proof is on you. For one reason, that is because I never let it be a reason for decreased performance. If you do not care what a number looks like next to your name, you do not belong in a competitive arena. The people governing you will not be able to stand you. If a number is next to my name, it is going to be great. That is a decision I made long ago. I encourage you to make that decision. If you are reading this book, hopefully you already have.

Second, I have become desensitized to this excuse because I have heard it from people who have accomplished a fraction of what I have seen others or I have accomplished when I wore those shoes. Don't be a one-hit wonder and tell me you're a rock star. Accomplishments, awards and accolades are great but there is no reason why you can't keep winning even if you are mad at the world.

Third and last, succumbing to burnout as a reason for letting yourself slip is like slowing down in a race and letting others pass you.

The burnout card may get sympathy out of the weak sales manager, but they are the ones easily sold on why the rep is not doing what they should be doing and lets it go. The weak manager gets walked on. They are sold, rather than sellers.

Burnout, whether real or imagined, will strike you if you are in the selling game long enough. But it is how you react, how you move forward and how you keep your wits about you that determines your lot in life and your career. Make the right choice and keep on rocking in the free world.

*   *   *

After the announcement of his ascension into management, Vincent took a couple days off before the new position kicked in.

Looking back at those events from 6 ½ years ago, he could only smile. Nothing could have prepared him for what was to come.

Vincent's present day situation had him governing a marketing office for ABM's business and public relations bureau in Greenfield, Minnesota. It is Monday, November 30, 2009, and he is headed to work for what is to be a pivotal day: the last day of the month and culmination of a huge ethics investigation of his current supervisor, Keith Dickhauser.

The drive to the Greenfield office was not all that bad in the wee hours of the day. Vincent made it a habit to get to work around 6:30 or 7 each morning, double-fisting a 24-ounce black coffee and 44-ounce Diet Coke. He was not a morning person but that lethal combination could instill energy into a corpse. And the early hour meant little-to-no traffic as Vincent had little patience for it.

At 8 every morning, Vincent kicked off the day with a manager meeting. He used them to tout the prior day's successes and follies and capitalize on the strategies for the day to come. Any time prior was spent getting work done in peace. When he is on the sales floor he is chased like a member of the Beatles; managers, reps, clerks alike ask him questions, seek his guidance on a number of items or just attempt small talk or flirtation with him. Before 8, none of these rampant distractions exist, hence his early arrival for the proverbial worm.

A common mistake in management is underestimating the power you have in impacting the masses. Vincent has realized his power, uses it and thrives on it. He needs them and they need him; they are certainly affected by his energy and enthusiasm.

Vincent pulls into the dimly lit lot and heads to his parking spot. At this hour, the lot is barren. The next to arrive will be Scott Kinsey, the man responsible for the clerical and commission processes. He is another early riser, often compiling 60 work hours a given week. He has a penchant for guarding his job functions like a fortress and attempting to condescend to others like they are not remotely on his intellectual level. In Vincent's case, that approach has led to some terse conversations between the two.

Vincent swipes his identification badge at the door, opens it and walks into the kingdom. He makes his way down the long corridor to the section of the building where his office resides. Occasionally he will just stand in wide wonder at what this represents: an office under primarily his jurisdiction. No single person has more impact and influence on how the operations run than Vincent, for better or worse. His blood, sweat and tears have helped mold this into a top-flight arena for revenue.

That and the management team he has compiled. It feels like the DC Comics' Justice League of America: the finest team of superheroes ever assembled. With the haphazard rule of the Keith Dickhauser administration, the team has seemingly held the ship together with rubber bands and duct tape. Time will soon tell if that ship will sink or sail in the aftermath of whatever outcome befalls their department.

Vincent sets his beverages on his secretary's desk and retrieves his keys to unlock his door. Once open, he flips the switch and the light reveals an office showcasing little other than clutter and Elizabeth. Between the walls and the desk, the office is adorned with 41 pictures of her in all.

Some say clutter is the sign of an ingenious mind. At least he knows where everything is. For everything he adds to the energy and sales arena, he lacks in patience or the ability to sit still. He has the hardest time forcing himself to sit down to put documents in a binder or organize a cabinet or do just about anything that takes time away from his passion of driving results. Keith, quite the opposite, obsessed with tidiness, had finally given up on trying to get Vincent to conform to that organizational standard.

Keith had abandoned getting Vincent to conform to a lot of things by this point. The confrontations those two had gone through over the 2 ½ years Vincent had worked directly for him had made one thing clear: Vincent had put himself in a position where he was so necessary to the operation that he could get away with things most people never could under Dickhauser's rule. While that was good for Vincent and allowed him wiggle room in fighting his many battles, it is not to say he can get away with anything.

His first duties in the morning: creating the schedule their dialer will perform that day, compiling updated manager and rep sales reports and logging into the dialer to prepare the campaigns. If either Vincent or Eric Aames, the IT guru who served as Vincent's right hand man were to depart, Greenfield's advertising bureau would be finished. Vincent loved this part of his job. He had created his own position through ingenuity and the fact Keith had no idea what it took to run a center. He had no idea of everything Vincent did in a given day.

This division of ABM was different than any other. It had been formed 4 years prior when ABM decided to add an online marketing engine to rival the big dogs. They threw more and more money into the engine and began this division to hock their wares. ABM was notorious for spending lots of money to invest in capital ventures and partnerships but sadly did not invest in its talent and keeping the wheels properly greased.

Dickhauser has always been notorious for his infamous gang called, "The Boys," and he surrounded himself in each entity he worked in with people he felt he could trust. He originally appointed his best friend Derek Walters as the head of his operation. Shortly thereafter, he brought in Scott Kinsey to run the clerical functions. Keith promoted Mark Rogers, whose father was a close friend, and who was struggling as a rep. Not long after, he added Danny Boyd as another sales manager – his third stint working with Dickhauser – and lastly there were Mike Enderle, Mick Farmer, Haley Jones (the lone female, whose father was another of Keith's best friends) and Adam Sandberg, all former reps in Dickhauser's previous venture running the advertising endeavor in Minneapolis years before.

However, there was only so much of the gang to go around and Keith and Derek had to look elsewhere for talent to in lifting this group off the ground. His résumé shining above all they sifted through, Vincent Scott became their next pursuit.

Now, nearly 4 years later, Vincent was at the helm and had seemingly created his own empire.

Vincent, mid dialer recycle, clicked the button on his phone to begin play of his voice mails. The voice of Agnes Landry, the employee ethics investigator assigned the Dickhauser case, came on the speaker phone.

"Vincent, this is Agnes again. Lydia and I received the files you sent. We are getting ready to close out the case and have just a couple people left to call. You mentioned appraisals you were forced to change and documentation that Keith falsified in order to terminate an employee. Please send any supporting documents on that and anything else you may have pertinent to the case. Thank you again for your help."

Vincent sat in silence for a moment, thinking again about what he was caught up in. He opened his e-mail and located his personal folders. Scrolling down, he found his folder labeled, "Keep." He clicked on it and was flooded with the past in all the e-mails he had saved dating back to his promotion. In fact, the first on the page was the announcement that had gone out to the division about that very promotion, all the way back in 2003. Following that announcement was a flood of messages from Stacey.

Stacey Worth, a management peer in the wake of Vincent's promotion, started calling him regularly starting on that first day: May 1, 2003. Vincent embarked on the long drive to Montrose and began his career in management.

Vincent and Harriet were two of the three managers in Montrose. The third was Lucy Hansen who, like Harriet, was another longtime employee. She was more concerned with grading calls to a tee than coaching, developing or generating morale. Her prickly demeanor resulted in not a lot of people getting along with her and her selfish attitude alienated her from her contemporaries.

Vincent has monitored thousands of calls in his 6 ½ years of management but that day provided the first. It was also the first time he realized just how horrendous many people who claim to be salespeople really are. ABM could throw the majority of its employees in prison for the literal slaughter they perform on their call flow, bludgeoning it daily until not remotely recognizable. Now that was Vincent's job: to police these misguided masses and bring order to the chaos that was their sales approach.

As the day wrapped, Vincent's office phone rang. Stacey greeted him on the other line.

"How was your day?" came her sweet voice.

"It was definitely interesting," Vincent replied.

"I'm sure it was," she said, giggling adorably. "Tell me about it."

"Just met the team, set up my office, the usual I suppose. Listened to calls. I can't believe how horrible they are. I had no idea what I was getting myself into."

"I hear you," she said, laughing again. "It gets better."

And he truly had no idea what lie ahead. His rebirth as a sales manager was upon him.

"The Selling Game" by Vincent Scott
Chapter 8:
HOW TO EARN THE PROMOTION

So you have risen to meet and topple all challenges, battled burnout and are the best of the best. Now you say you want to be a manager.

To earn the call up to the major leagues, you can't just be another pretty face or random positive sales statistic. It's like they say in *Top Gun*, there are no points for second place. Management is not easy and getting there shouldn't be. If it is, your skin may not be as thick as it needs to be. Granted, there are a lot of terrible managers in the world but you do not want to be one of them. That said, there are many ways you can enhance your chances and be that lady or gentleman who gets the nod come decision day.

I wish I had a dollar for every time someone said they wanted to be a manager or asked about promotion. It is very easy to ask this question; as easy as asking what time dinner is or if we're "there yet." It is easy for someone to say they are ready to be or want to be a manager. Truth be told, this is a prime example of when you as a potential candidate, viable or not, have to walk the talk. There are several attributes vital to this process and you have to be aware of where you stand relative to those attributes and relative to your competition for the post you seek.

Talk is cheap. If there is no hustle behind the muscle, you are irrelevant and those in the position of authority to promote you will write you off as such. To put it in perspective for you, probably twenty-to-thirty percent of a workforce will tell you they are or delude themselves into thinking they are ready for promotion. Five percent or less will be ready. Often one percent or less will be selected. Being realistic about the scope of the landscape is your first step.

Paul Newman said in *The Color of Money*, one of my all-time favorite movies, "Pool excellence is not about excellent pool. It's about becoming something. A student. You have to be a student of human moves." In that vein, sales excellence is not about excellent sales. You must master several facets of the business before you are ready to influence others to do as well as you can or have done. Doing something is one thing but getting others to follow your lead is entirely another. There are numerous things taken into consideration when looking at the candidate pool for management prospects. How do you fare? Where do you rank?

Number one on your report card is attendance. If you cannot show up to work it is not fair to your peers who have the capability of showing up or to your manager who has to answer for you. Your company was not made profitable by people who could not show up to work. On the same token, if and when you become a manager it is the people who do not show up that are the bane of your existence. People who are not at work have no chance at generating revenue, miss out on any message the manager delivers and equate to more work on the manager's part to catch them up. Besides, if and when you become a manager, your employees will know your attendance reputation and will not take it seriously if they know you didn't either.

Second is a successful track record relative to the expectations and peers on any measurements of work that exist in the job. If you are one in a pool of 200 and you want to be promoted, you have to be better than the top 1% across the board to be "the one." If you have spotty performance or were a one-hit wonder, regardless of how smart you think you are, you have not set yourself apart; at least not in a positive way. Numbers do not tell the whole story but you have to prove your worthiness to be taken seriously and instill belief into anyone's mind that you would be capable of driving results in others. When it comes to achievements you want the person deciding your future to believe that you can clone yourself as a coach. That makes you more valuable in a higher position than just having the productivity of you and you alone.

Finally, and most importantly, comes having a positive attitude in the face of adversity. This is a broad concept with broad terms. This attribute will be the biggest challenge of all. Remember the company is paying you to implement and enforce their policies and procedures, uphold rulings and to deliver its messages regardless of your personal feelings. That does not mean your input is not welcome (well, let's hope that's the case) but when a decision is rendered it is incumbent upon the manager to carry out orders.

Adversity is a beast of many faces. That adversity could be wading through hang-ups and not wearing them on your sleeve, standing the test of time with little to show for it, disagreeing with policies and procedures but grinning and bearing them, losing a sales dispute, or finding yourself in the midst of a rumor mill or political crossfire. It can be a change in hierarchy or seeing someone promoted that you are more qualified than. It could be coming back from lunch realizing someone is in your parking spot or getting a lousy fortune cookie while you were there. It's everything thrown at you. How you deal with it is the thermometer for how you will deal with management because, trust me, you may think you are ready but you likely have no idea what you are getting yourself into.

It's easy to "be a manager" but demanding to be a good one. You can't fake it, fudge it or forego it; you have to take on every challenge and master every aspect to truly be ready.

Luke Skywalker may have been able to do some fancy tricks with his lightsaber but he failed miserably by going up against Darth Vader too soon in

The Empire Strikes Back. In the years between that ill-fated duel and his follow-up in *Return of the Jedi,* he transformed.

There is no shame in not being ready. Frankly, that is what the build-up is all about. The best coaches played the game and played it well and you gain the most respect if you mastered it before you took over the team. Be honest with yourself: if you are not showing up to work on time or at all, is it really a priority? I have gotten up at 4 AM to work out and shower, get my daughter ready for the sitter, brush her teeth and dress her, drive in the opposite direction of my job to drop her off and then turn back around for a 45-minute drive all to get there an hour before my subordinates. It was a priority to me. If you are sauntering in a minute or two early you are tempting fate. If you are sauntering in late you are not first rate. Make a conscious decision to make these things matter and prove it to all the eyes that are on you. Managers that are worth their weight will notice, and being noticed for positive things is huge in making the step to the next level.

Working, like life, will see you dealt some hard-hitting hands. It is all about how you react to those hands and how you choose to go from there.

Take on new challenges. If you are tops in one area, can you top others? Always silence the naysayers. What would someone say is your weakness? Improve that area. Are your statistics indicative of your skills? Get them there. It's about what you do when life hands you lemons. Don't just make lemonade. Make the best darn lemonade this world has ever seen. That is what sets the best apart from the rest. You want to think about what your detractors would say about you and right whatever wrongs may exist, whether perceived or real.

If you squawk about every injustice you see, you will drive yourself and others crazy. Never present a problem without a solution. Those who complain get a bad reputation and will never make it in a leadership role. Remember you will manage people who are privy to your reputation. You will never gain their respect if you are notorious for negativity.

If you deserve something, go get it. Prove it belongs to you – through actions, not words. Talk is cheap. Sometimes we may not make the right decisions, be it as a leader or just a human being, but we are all in this together. No one in a sales environment is preventing someone else from success and you are all on the same team at the end of the day.

That is why true leadership is reaching the point where you are more concerned with the performance of a team or unit than simply your own. Acknowledging the existence and importance of those around you is key to being regarded as a viable management candidate. Spock himself told us in the *Star Trek* saga that, "The needs of the many outweigh the needs of the few." That is at the heart of management.

Management is acceptance of responsibility guiding and molding other parts of the whole. Management is about taking it upon yourself to innovate and better those around you. Management is about caring enough to figure out what is important to others and what makes them tick. Respectfully, a lot of people can put up good sales numbers but that does not mean they have what it takes to be a good manager. A lot of people can get a college degree but that does not mean they have it in them to lead twenty or more people across a finish line in harmony.

That said, there is an open casting call every day on the sales floor for the next leaders in the business. Leadership should be looking for the person that can take the hits, handle making unpopular decisions, do their job without being deterred, rise above whatever is keeping others down, succeeds where others fail and can motivate others to do the same. Just because someone can sell does not mean they possess these traits or can conjure up the best in others. This by no means diminishes your value; it merely means if you are serious about moving into management you want to figure out where you can improve your aptitudes in these areas.

Consider famous leaders – what do they have in common? There are a wide array, from decorated war generals to Presidents to coaches and movie directors. The best possess confidence, clear purpose and the ability to motivate others to achieve. They are straightforward and honest in their approach and their message. I have interviewed countless management candidates over the years and they brought varying levels of each to the table, but what interests me most is willingness to listen and adapt. You can be brash and have vision but the promotion-worthy candidate is one who stays true to their roots, fights for the cause and is good in every area, not just great in one.

Professionalism is important to command respect from the broadest number of subordinates. A challenge I faced when promoted at age 23 was getting all walks of life to respect and accept me as their leader. Sure, I had tossed up more sales records than I knew what to do with, but why should someone working to pay a mortgage and support two kids listen to a kid that was two years out of college? Because I was generally concerned for their well-being and would stop at nothing to help them be as successful as they wanted to be.

Sadly, ineffective managers far outnumber effective ones, yet they were all selected based on perception of merits and analysis of the playing field. But like any selection process, you are going to come across your share of bad apples in the lot.

To score the promotion, you must embrace the selection process and what it represents. Hopefully your own manager will be forthcoming about what you need to do to achieve that next step and get their stamp of approval. Even if that is not the case, do not let this impede you from constant self-analysis and improvement.

What are you looking for or expecting in the person managing you? Emulate those attributes you want to find in an effective leader – and if you cannot find a real life individual to pattern yourself after, fit the mold of what you would want. You will never please everyone and you have to have a very thick skin to shoulder the burden of managing several personalities. Nonetheless, you will want strong approval ratings to attract the following you need.

I will say this; the perception of the workforce, whether fair or not, will often be taken into consideration when your promotion is considered. Will the masses listen if you are in a position of authority? Can you succinctly and effectively deliver a message and sell people on why they should do this job day in, day out? Can you take the responsibility of going to the people who need to be aware of the problems being faced if you cannot fix them yourself? There are so many variables in the management game and picking the person to take that mantle should involve weighing every one of them.

Those looking for someone to fill management shoes are looking for the best. Plain and simple, you have to maintain your standing as the obvious choice in order to be that pick. Being the best is difficult because people will constantly attack you, question you, put you under a microscope and try to tear you down to their level. Just try your best to never give anyone a real reason to attack you. As for the fake ones, the people that matter know the truth and you cannot let these things break you down.

You will tick people off. It happens. You have to be okay with that, no matter what position or walk of life you hold. If you do not have that ability, you cannot be the best and you cannot lead without second-guessing yourself. Inability to stick to your resolve and obsession with pleasing everyone will only render you ineffective. Not everyone is cut out for leadership, which is why you should ask yourself why you want to lead. Is it because you just want to get off the phones or the streets? Is it just about the money? Are you bored? These motivators do not a successful manager make.

Do you want to better your fellow man and woman? Do you want to help people find success? Do you want to spread your wings and realize your potential? Do you want to do more for the company, your family and yourself? These are the things that drive successful managers. These are the things you talk about in a management interview. These are the things you make your manager aware of so they can lobby on your behalf.

Having someone in your corner is pivotal. When candidates are considered, people in on the decision sit around and ask for suggestions. If someone is adamantly opposed to your ascension in the hierarchy, that is going

68

to be a tough mountain to climb. You will want and need the support of everyone in the capacity to make the decision. You will also want and need someone lobbying on your behalf that knows what you bring to the table and that you would be more valuable in a supervisory role than your current station.

Patience is another must when it comes to earning the promotion. We have talked about burnout, alleged and authentic, but either one can lead you to irrevocable actions that force your downfall. When that decision is made, you want your name to be synonymous with what leadership is looking for in joining their ranks.

Take every opportunity you can to shine. Share with others, volunteer to do more and seize any and all chances that present themselves to make a bigger and positive impact on the team as a whole. Stand out from the rest – it's the only way to be the best.

In the end, earning a promotion is like earning anything else. Deserving it is merely a fraction of it; showing you deserve it, proving you deserve it, maintaining greatness in all areas and striving for more for all and not just yourself will lead to the prize you seek. It may not happen when you want it to, but if this is something you are capable of achieving, make it happen. The single most important person in determining your promotion to management is you.

*   *   *

Those first weeks and months of Vincent's management career, while the training wheels were on, he took the natural approach of getting people to like him, giving people the benefit of the doubt and attempting to care about everything. He started out believing people when they said they would try their best or attempt something new he pointed out and that the "rah-rah" approach would go a long way.

He got to know his people. There was Dick Knoll, a portly fellow and family man rumored for promotion. There was Terry, the caring father who acted like a womanizer to impress the population. There was Marcy, a beautiful expectant mother. There was Susie, who was living paycheck to paycheck after she and her husband had split. There was Nancy, a disability queen with a short temper. There was Lacy, who had the potential to be a star but was a rollercoaster between her troubled relationship with her daughter's father and battles with Ashley Flowers. There was Anne, a newlywed with a heart of gold. There was Katrina, the matriarch of the bunch with the most seniority.

Vincent plopped himself at the desk of one of the reps on disability right in the middle of the team and turned on music, made himself accessible to anyone in the heat of a fight that could be won and made the group noisy and notorious. He very much utilized the systems he was provided, listening to calls, playing them for the team and showing them where they could have risen rather than fallen. He learned to study reports and draw conclusions. He spoke with authority. He hopped on the phones. He wisely invested his time.

It was a slow ascent because the team had been so misguided before him. But Vincent was determined and wanted to learn. The hard work kept Julie off his mind. The calls and e-mails from Stacey aided that endeavor as well.

What started innocently with calls and e-mails just checking in quickly took a flirtatious tone. Vincent unabashedly flirted back – he had nothing to lose. Naive Vincent knew this flawless beauty who was married with two children could not possibly be coming on to him.

The frequency climbed with each passing day. A week in, they were swapping e-mails 20-to-30 times daily.

E-mails graduated into phone calls which graduated into phone calls off the clock. Stacey claimed each step of this burgeoning "relationship" would not turn into the next, yet they always did. Vincent was not sure exactly what to do – she was a great sounding board about the job and attention from her made his thoughts of Julie dissipate. So it persisted and he did nothing to stop it.

As for work, Vincent continued to learn the system.

Dick Knoll was promoted two weeks into Vincent's management career and moved to Rockford to take over Harriet's old crew, making him Ashley's boss. Truth being stranger than fiction, he was ultimately forced to terminate her for basically having phone sex with a customer months later.

Vincent quickly picked up on Shelly's inadequacies; she was seldom at work and when she was, she was in no way punctual or useful. It made sense why she had tapped Vincent and Dick to management roles – they were workhorses that would get things done. She needed their efforts to mask her shortcomings in the way of work ethic.

Shelly let people see her bleed a lot, often overheard in her office shouting at her husband turned ex-husband turned roommate, or whatever he was, disappearing for hours at a time, and never meeting any kind of commitment she made. In her stead, Vincent took the opportunity to rise to more prominence. He was able to sit in for her on some of their district manager's daily conference calls as either the top daily manager or because Shelly's appearance at work in the mornings was sporadic.

Their district manager, Max McKay, was a super-cool, old school cat who was all about sales and making money. He had swooped into town to take Vincent and Dick to lunch as Minneapolis's Top Guns for the prior month and he laid out his philosophies: "The perfect balance of sales and service to our customers is where we win." "What a customer experiences before they experience you is irrelevant. While you have them, you are the center of their universe. Act like it." It was this type of mentality that Vincent fully subscribed to. Sadly, there were not a lot of leaders in the business like Max.

Rockford operated an after hours center: they worked their reps until 7 PM on weekdays (as opposed to Montrose's 5 PM close) and the reps had an off day during the week if they had to work Saturday. The managers, irreverently of assigned location, rotated Saturdays. Four Saturdays in, Vincent was assigned to work with Stacey in Rockford. This would equate to his homecoming and first face-to-face encounter with Stacey since his departure.

He picked up sandwiches for several of the reps and grabbed one for her as well. He did not ask if she wanted to eat with him – that would have been too much too soon. He was just testing the waters. Of course, she came to his makeshift office for the day to ask him if he wanted to eat with her in the Aquarium and "listen to calls." Of course he did, and it was then Vincent started piecing together the puzzle that was Stacey Worth.

She was born in Chicago and her parents moved to Minneapolis when she was in grade school. Towards the end of high school, an interlude with longtime friend Oscar Worth led to her becoming pregnant. Despite lots of drama in their relationship that persisted to this day, she married Oscar and the rest was history. Or was it?

She had wanted to go to school out of state, but Oscar's domineering ways kept her in Minneapolis. She gave up practically everything she had aspired to someday do for his demands. She gave birth to their son Jason and for quite a time things were manageable. Stacey became pregnant again a couple years later; however Oscar cheated on her while she was in the hospital after delivering their second child Sarah.

Despite the falling out, Stacey had not been willing to tear apart the family and after counseling, they decided to stick it out. The two had gone through quite a rollercoaster through 7 years of marriage and two children. However, it begged the question: what was Vincent in this equation? A distraction? Or was this something meaningful?

Vincent saw another wounded bird; someone who could have done bigger and better things but had been held back by another. Was she unhappy? Probably not overall, and she did not claim to be. She had seemingly grown to accept her lot in life. There was the hint of regret in her voice and tone, but the way she talked about her children redeemed it tenfold. Clearly Stacey was a complicated character but none of it altered Vincent's opinion of her. If anything, it made him more interested.

It was certainly not the typical fairytale but they undeniably had chemistry. She was witty, intelligent, fun to talk to and beautiful, all while keeping him on his toes and completely intrigued.

71

Vincent asked her to coffee the following week. Stacey was hesitant at first, but gave in to her temptation.

Working in this fashion began to get more difficult for Vincent. Stacey started calling 5-to-10 times daily, so much so that he had to stop answering the phone. It was not easy for him to be crazy about someone knowing she was going home to someone else every night, especially when she called constantly and would not let him forget about her. He knew he should not feel the things he was starting to feel but he was quickly becoming more and more enamored with this woman.

This amazing lady, who embodied everything Vincent wanted in a partner (save the lack of availability) had to know the thoughts and feelings that were creeping up on him. Whatever response it elicited was of no consequence, he could not go on wondering the outcome, motive or what the end result would be.

In late June, 6 weeks after the ordeal had begun with his promotion and culminated with the "coffee date," Vincent got irritated enough over the curiosity that he sat in his apartment with his Jack Daniel's and Coke in one hand and telephone in the other, dialing a florist. He sent a lengthy note telling her exactly how he felt, plus sunflowers, a favorite flower they happened to share.

Vincent laid it all out there; he was exceedingly interested in getting to know her better, thought she was unbelievable in every way, beyond beautiful, caring, kind and compassionate. He told her there was something about the way she carried herself, it was so unassuming and humble. He dared not speculate why she was deviating in any way from her husband to direct her charms at him at such a high frequency and but win, lose or draw he wanted to know where he stood. A little after 1 PM the following day his office phone rang.

"You are unbelievable," she said, her voice full of emotion. "I love the flowers. Were you going to call me today?"

"You're the unbelievable one."

"I am not sure what to say to everything, I am so overwhelmed," Stacey said.

"Just say what you feel."

"Of course I am attracted to you, too. I do have feelings for you. But I love my children and my husband," she managed, then paused. "I know this isn't fair to you," she began.

"I'm not worried about fair. What I want to know is if you are in love with him."

There was silence for a moment before she responded.

72

"I love him. I don't know that I have ever been in love with him. But I guess it has just always been enough…I guess until now."

"Is this common for you? I mean, what we are doing?"

"No, absolutely not," she replied. "It's not like I have any intention of cheating on him. I don't know what this is. I look forward to talking to you. I like spending time with you. You are one of the first things I think about in the morning and one of the last things I think about at night." She paused momentarily, summarizing everything in her mind before asking, "Does that make sense?"

"I suppose," Vincent responded. "I'm glad to hear the feelings aren't one-sided. I wanted you to know how I feel."

"I'm sorry I don't have all the answers right now," Stacey said. "I have to go back up to the office now, but I wanted to call you and hear your voice and say thank you. Call me later?"

"I will."

Vincent was actually surprised at the turn of events. Could this be the start of something? That coming Saturday, Vincent awoke with his next move in mind. He rolled out of bed, got candles from the closet, and picked up juice and two bacon, egg and cheese biscuits from McDonald's. Just days prior, Stacey lamented that she missed them and had not had one in some time. Vincent eyed this as the perfect opportunity to impress her with some romantic flair.

Stacey was assigned Saturday patrol in Rockford, and Vincent stealthily made his way into the Aquarium and set up shop. Putting out paper plates and napkins, he unwrapped the sandwiches, put straws in the juice containers and looked over the feast with satisfaction before making the call.

"Hello?"

"Good morning, beautiful."

"Hey, what are you doing up this early?" Stacey smiled in realization it was Vincent.

"Just thinking about you."

"Is that right?" she gushed.

"It is. How was your night?"

"It was OK. Got griped at for the fact I hadn't paid the bills yet. What else is new?"

"I wouldn't know."

"What are you doing? Did you just get up?"

"Something like that. I'm in the Aquarium."

"Shut up!" she loudly whispered.

"Come meet me," Vincent said, hanging up the phone.

Minutes later, Stacey snuck into the dark, candlelit room.

"Oh my goodness," Stacey uttered in disbelief upon surveying the scene.

He rose and moved to hug her. She looked great, Vincent marveled; her hair was down, she wore a black shirt with a tan skirt and was every bit as ravishing as the first time he had seen her. The face was out of a painting and the way the candlelight danced across it made her all the more breathtaking.

"This is crazy," she said, half-elatedly and half-worriedly. She double checked that the door was locked and after their embrace she flipped on the light and proceeded to blow out the candles.

"A little much for you?" Vincent asked.

"It's super-sweet. I just... Wow..."

"I know. I just wanted to surprise you."

"You did."

Stacey took a second to take it in and smiled at Vincent – the most beautiful smile he had seen. They sat and ate. Once the pleasantries and small talk was over, the conversation made its way back to the task at hand.

"So, I have to ask; are we actually headed somewhere meaningful or am I just a temporary distraction for you?" Vincent asked point blank.

Stacey paused awkwardly and smiled, revealing that she was struggling with the situation.

"I don't know." She continued, "I do care about him. The life I have. But I admit, I don't know what I'm doing."

"Well, when you figure it out, can you let me know sooner rather than later?" Vincent asked, half-seriously and tempered with a wry grin.

Stacey did not respond verbally, only gave a pensive look crossed with a smile.

The meal came to a close and Stacey needed to return to her duties. Vincent discarded the evidence and they stood together at the door. Stacey hugged him.

"We all need to get together for some kind of happy hour or something soon." As the embrace ended, she continued, "That way we could be together when it's not...wrong."

"Name the time and place; I'll be there."

With that, Vincent snuck back out. With the newfound energy of the management team between Rockford and Montrose, the month saw a huge resurgence of the Cheekwood sales unit and they won an award for most improved for June 2003. The reward? Max McKay was coming to town from

Rochester to take them out for a night on the town. It was the "happy hour or something" Stacey had alluded to, literally weeks later.

Vincent can still easily recall that night; they had continued their e-mail and phone conversations, which even bled over into weekends when Oscar was working. She wore a gorgeous black dress – Vincent's favorite color. They sat opposite each other at the table.

After dinner, the group went dancing. Vincent was dragged to the dance floor after refusing to participate in a few numbers. As typically goes, the other folks departed and Stacey and Vincent were the last ones standing.

They stood across from each other at a small table off the dance floor. He circled it and moved closer to her, trying to hold her hand. She seemed timid despite her obvious affections for him.

"I am dying to hold you," Vincent whispered in her ear.

"Anyone could be around," she said nervously, scanning the area.

He maneuvered her hand under the table with his, out of the sight of a naked eye.

"So what's your curfew tonight?" Vincent asked as they finished their last drinks.

"I have to leave here by 10 at the latest."

Vincent checked his watch: 9:15.

"Do you want to go someplace and talk?"

"Absolutely," she replied.

They walked through the parking lot to her car and got inside. She opened the sunroof, they reclined their seats and she turned on the radio. The two looked up into the sky staring at the stars.

"I had a really good time tonight," Stacey said.

"Yeah," Vincent acknowledged. "I did too."

"What are you thinking about?"

"Are you going to be with this guy for the rest of your life?"

Stacey laughed slightly. "Why do you have to ask me that?"

"I'm just curious."

They continued to talk, they held hands, and she rubbed his hand warmly. Vincent kept glancing at the clock in the car. At 9:54, he decided it was now or never.

He leaned in. She leaned in. They kissed.

They kissed for quite some time. Kissed and talked and kissed and talked and she smiled a lot and the moon was full and it was bliss. She departed a lot closer to 10:30 than 10 and called him just prior to her arrival home. Vincent blared Marvin Gaye's "Let's Get it On" in his car, sang along, and was on cloud nine all the way home.

It wasn't even a week later that Vincent picked Stacey up on lunch and took her back to his place where they made out profusely and had each other's shirts off before they realized what they were doing and stopped. And it wasn't two days later before they were right back there and didn't stop.

Stacey said from the beginning that she would never dream of cheating on her husband. She "did not know" what she was doing but now she and Vincent were lovers.

The experience was magical, like something from a movie. The ensuing moments where they first told each other they loved each other added icing to Vincent's already appetizing cake. It was all happening so fast and Vincent, who had just recently sworn to not fall in love again was now not only in love but was in love with a married woman.

It was clear that cheating on her husband was new and difficult for Stacey; however she expressed no regrets afterward as he held her in his arms.

Vincent truly believed they would find happiness together. And he rebuked negative feedback he got from friends and family – he felt it was none of their business to weigh in and tell him he was ludicrous for falling for someone still bound by the sacrament of matrimony. He was completely blinded to reality by the perception he was being overcome with.

She was never anything but honest with him. She did tell him she would not be in this situation forever, she was conflicted, that she did care about Oscar and that she never wanted to lead Vincent on. Vincent saw a hopeful end to the 7 months of drunken depression since Julie. No one else had intervened to pull him out of that fire, so he thought he was climbing out of it on his own.

In reality, he had only shifted the dependence of his temperament, his mood and his emotions. These were telltale signs of a weakened and vulnerable soul.

She dressed in his bathroom afterwards and he came up behind her, embraced her and kissed her neck. They looked at each other in the mirror and in that moment they both wondered if the other was their destiny.

Then it was back to reality.

Work saw Vincent's first real taste of management, having to discipline Katrina to corral her offbeat call flow. Monitoring revealed it was atrocious and he made the irrevocable decision to write her up. She retaliated by going days without speaking to Vincent and posted vile results during that time, but came around a week later. They always did. Vincent continued to climb, reaching the top quartile of the teams in ABM's residential division. Harriet held the #1 spot,

Dick was a few spots behind Vincent and Lucy and Stacey were towards the back of the pack.

Stacey, a tender, loving soul, was a softy when it came to managing salespeople and was not destined to be a leader in the revenue rankings.

Needless to say, Stacey consumed the vast majority of Vincent's thoughts. He would stop by Rockford 2-to-3 times per week on his way home to kiss her in her office until half an hour after she should have left. He could catch her scent on himself for the rest of the evening after those visits; the best and worst things in the world wrapped into one. She would leave the neighbor's backyard to "get a sweater" so she could call him. It was like they were teenagers.

She told him no other guy had been so sweet and taken the time to write poems and make CD's for her. She believed he would do anything for her. They continued sneaking around, spending time in Vincent's apartment, parking lots and the monitoring room in the Montrose office. Vincent asked her to get a divorce, but she said the kids were happy being a family. This was something that, at that point, he did not understand. She would say she would probably not be with Oscar forever, that something would happen, but it became clear she would not initiate it.

It caused Vincent to pull away, which caused Stacey to become upset, which caused her to cry and Vincent to come running back. This happened a few times until the dreaded vacation week.

Stacey and Oscar had planned a vacation for quite some time to take the kids to Florida. Vincent obviously was not thrilled with going a week without seeing her but of course was less thrilled with the prospect of her potential rekindling with Oscar.

Upon her return, Vincent played coy and made her make the advances. She revealed that while they were gone, Oscar re-committed himself to her. He had told her how lucky he was to have her, that he never wanted to lose her and all the stuff she had obviously been longing to hear. She kissed Vincent at the door but it was time for the good thing to come to an end. She loved him but the guilt was too much and she could not tear apart her family.

Vincent's ego may be bloated to cover up his insecurities but underneath it all, it was fragile. The thoughts jumped around at light speed; the positive was that it flushed Julie from his system. The negative was that he once again was left without a clue of what he was doing and how this "soul mate" character could be so elusive.

What had started out with such promise was nothing more than a seven-year itch.

She made the right choice: she chose her family over Vincent. He could not fault her for that, especially now as he saw e-mails from her while surrounded by pictures of Elizabeth: the most important piece of his own life.

He had only corresponded with Stacey via e-mail a couple of times since his departure from the residential sect of the company and last report, she was happy. And that was good. He had no ill will towards her. True love is wanting someone to be happy even if it makes you miserable. Vincent never forgot that.

Vincent scrolled down, past the e-mails from Stacey and back to the present. He located the requested files on Dickhauser and forwarded them to Agnes.

His cell phone rang, breaking the flashback. It was the practically everyday 7:15 AM call from Keith Dickhauser himself.

"Hello?"

"What's up?" Keith boomed on the other end, his voice naturally gruff and emotionless until the bear was poked.

"Prepping the dialer and running the reports," Vincent answered. "Today's going to be big."

"Good. I got fucked up last night. Too much vodka. Did you go out?"

"No," Vincent replied.

"Have you heard any more about the investigation?"

"No, nothing," Vincent responded. "They probably don't want to talk to me."

Vincent deflected the question for multiple reasons. One, no one being investigated is allowed to talk about it. Second, no one involved in the investigation is supposed to talk. Third, he had no idea what to say; anything he uttered could lead Dickhauser to suspect him in the fracas.

"Well let me know if you hear anything," Keith grunted. "I can't figure out which one of these fucking managers is trying to tear me down. There are enemies among us. We can't trust anyone."

"I understand. I'll keep you posted."

"I was in the training class yesterday. Why do you hire so many black people? There were only a couple young white guys."

Vincent's eyes widened; it was like he had no control over the verbal vomit. "I hire the best of who I see."

"OK. I will be there a little before 8. Are you having a stand-up?"

"Yes."

"Are you meeting with these fuckheads at 8?"

"Yeah, I am going over the conversion rates and efficiency for November and goals for December. Since it is a short month, I'm opening the floodgates on the best leads tomorrow instead of waiting two weeks."

"OK, sounds good. Our only problems are management problems. Don't be too easy on them."

Nearly four years of talking to this man had taught Vincent that Keith never says "goodbye", he just hangs up.

Vincent did not view Keith Dickhauser as an irredeemable individual. He had the propensity to be a decent human being but the value he could add to this evolved division had diminished to the point of nothing. Dickhauser's days were the days of the face-to-face lunch and drinks meeting, the golf meeting and the work until noon and take off the rest of the day routine. He was a relic of an era long gone in ABM. ABM's price gouging of its customers and disregard for growing competition led them to losses in many of its ventures. This burgeoning department's success was its only chance to get out of the red.

Dickhauser would curse you up and down for a minuscule detail but send flowers when a relative passed; he would take the entire team of managers to Christmas dinner every year and was legitimately concerned when the topic was family. He had lost his father at an early age and cared for his mother for years until her death. When Dickhauser was assigned this division, it was his last shot. He had already been demoted for verbal bashings he administered employees as head of the Minneapolis advertising office. He had been shipped to Dallas for a year and monitored closely before being given this last opportunity at redemption. The company had no idea if it would pan out or not, so putting Keith in the role was no risk.

The ABM Online team started with 10 sales representatives, trainer Nancy Wilkes, Derek Walters and Dickhauser in November 2005. Nancy trained the basics of the product for one week. They were unleashed on the phones, dialing manually at that, calling accounts listed on spreadsheets. It was hardly the technology age. The company had little-to-no expectations of them and thus set minimal objectives for them. They made an early splash in some significant markets and the company told them to grow to 100 reps. That is where Vincent came in.

Embattled from his experience working thanklessly for Shelly Cheekwood, tired of seeing lost love Stacey Worth regularly and stifled time after time by the administration of the residential division, Vincent made no qualms about the fact he wanted out. His unparalleled success and sales management expertise was exactly what Keith and Derek were looking for in a manager for their budding team. That prompted Keith, on a cold October afternoon, to call Vincent, ask him to lunch and start proceedings wooing his talents to the advertising bureau.

The road to Vincent's hatred of the residential division, however, was a long one. Once the Stacey diversion ended, Vincent's new focus was winning the sales management game, whatever the cost.

His team began a slow descent after its initial spike. The initial impact that coming in, changing things, shifting the energy, bringing positivity and giving people the benefit of the doubt brought ran out. When your team is up, ride the wave. When they are down, make them behave. Harriet taught him that.

Next came the announcement the Rockford and Montrose offices were being consolidated in Rockford. The dungeon was closing. Vincent was going home.

This meant he would be face to face with Stacey daily, something that took a toll on him in rollercoasterish form over the years to come.

That move occurred at the beginning of December 2003, just months after their relationship came to a halt. Vincent was ready for it. The reps in Montrose worshiped him for his spirit, confidence and positive attitude. He brought something new. His product knowledge and knowledge of the sale were without rival and everyone knew it.

And the merge of offices commenced.

The other major change of note: Max McKay was being put to pasture. As corporations often do, they isolate those who are not aligned with desired principles and, if they have racked up lots of years, they take the path of least resistance and move them to some kind of staff job. In this case, Max was being moved to a "special project" over clerical functions for the department. His "sales first, discipline later" mentality, one that Vincent clung to for the duration of his career, was not aligned with the business.

December 1, 2003: Vincent made the shorter trek to Rockford's office, a trip he had made hundreds of times in the past.

At first, everything appeared to go Vincent's way. Dick and Harriet pointed out to that they could tell his presence was getting to Stacey; it did not help her that the vocal Montrose employees were making loud and clear their love for Vincent. Be it immature or a justifiable defense mechanism, Vincent made the decision to ignore Stacey when at all possible. Basically, she did not like the cold shoulder treatment, which was exactly Vincent's motive. He felt that either sharing or showing his hurt at the fact she had spurned him would only serve to be to his detriment. Truth was, the daily sight of her was eating him alive.

Sans Stacey and her attention, Vincent turned in his moments of solitude to the bottle and back to Becky, his ex-fiancé. She was still in love with him and the emotionless but intense interludes were exactly what he felt he required to tune out what had happened in his personal life.

The truth was Vincent was terrified of being sober and alone with his thoughts. If he was alone, no one was making him feel desirable or validating his rising status or preventing him from being riddled with self-doubt. While he had no intention of trying again to forge a relationship with her, Becky filled the gaps in Vincent's wounded psyche so he could keep crawling forward.

Vincent met Becky in early 1998. She worked in the miscellaneous sector of Cooke's Grocery Store, alongside Ted's future wife Robin, and caught Vincent's eye.

Becky was a hopeless romantic and, for whatever reason, Vincent felt he needed to jettison his college partying ways and he proposed to her in October 1999. While his heart is often in the right place and he can eventually address changes he wants or needs to make within himself, the way he addresses them at first is often misguided.

Their engagement lasted 3 months. They fought constantly and had nothing in common save the desire not to be alone.

With Julie and Stacey out of the picture, Vincent wounded emotionally and feeling alone in the world, he turned back to Becky for meaningless anesthesia.

Their involvement led him into the new year: 2004. Interestingly, he found out early on that their fearful leader Shelly Cheekwood was pregnant by her estranged husband against whom she had a restraining order. It was also announced who Shelly's new boss would be: Dirk Slabor – a short, cocky 32-year old known primarily for his marriage to the woman running the company's incentives program and for his lack of compassion. What an interesting year it would be.

In February, Vincent admitted to Stacey his envy over her taking on confidantes in Dick and Shelly over him. His resentment would fester and it caused Vincent to act infantile in their working relationship and tension between the two in general.

She agreed to the difficulty in the situation and they agreed to work on things. And this happened off and on until the day they parted ways. They would commit to being close friends, Vincent would get agitated at her for something, strain would ensue, things would get unbearable, someone would snap and they would start the process all over again.

Vincent had also, to this point, taken the approach of giving his employees the benefit of the doubt; working with them and avoiding disciplinary tactics at most all costs. He was, however, miffed that he had been saddled with disastrous Barbara Allison in the stacked-against-him draft prior to the convergence of Shelly's two offices and was unsure how to proceed with this notorious problem child. He was pleasantly surprised when she promised to turn over a new leaf for him but he promptly discovered her not answering a call and hanging up on a customer the first week on his team. Thus began his string of Perry Mason-esque moments. Vincent prided himself in the art of playing prosecuting attorney as he already knew the crime and how to prove it and, while others would not have the confidence in themselves to hammer final nails into these reps' coffins, Vincent took pleasure in on the knowledge he would not allow himself to be played. It was the ability to know the answer to questions before he asked them. Typically he would use catching them in the act as leverage to force them to try hard the rest of the day, week or month. However, in Barbara's case, he saw his opportunity at a first kill that would be worth its weight in gold.

The initial kill can be difficult – almost intimidating – to a brand new manager. You can be overcome with nervousness, shaky as you lead them to the conference room that becomes their final resting place. After six years of management, Vincent has come a long way. In his current post, they have a joke about it. As he has weaned several into management, they liken the experience to becoming licensed to kill in the James Bond universe: it takes two. Vincent's first– Barbara Allison for call avoidance and misconduct – was a far cry from terminations later that had him licking his chops at the chance to eliminate losers who refused to try or defied him at every opportunity.

Vincent swore as a rep that he would be a crusader for the people that worked hard for him and he has been just that. They get that initial benefit of the doubt. At the same time, he feels confident that if he is unable to coach someone to victory no one can. And if they give up trying, he gives up on them. Hence the delight that started to ensue when he was able to eliminate those limbs from the tree through the years to come. Barbara had sworn up and down she was going to go all out for Vincent when she landed on his team. She promised to get herself off the bottom of the sales report. This incident was a slap in Vincent's face and he did not have any sympathy. It was time for her to go.

The difference between that and the direction Shelly was unsuccessfully trying to guide Vincent into and was successfully guiding Dick into was this: she wanted everyone straight out of the gates, regardless of effort level, to be held to impossible standards. The problem with big companies is that most, if not all, rules are made by people that have no clue how the world works for the people they are governing. They often do not care. It is also the very reason Vincent wants to rise to power: so he can lead and make policy in the best interests of all.

Vincent does not hesitate to voice his dissent towards that system. It started with simply ignoring perceived marching orders. It continued with questioning authority in private and then in front of others. As most things have a habit of doing, it came to a boil and resulted in tempers flaring. Of course,

Vincent being outranked, he lost every time. Questioning authority is not always wrong. It is just like the old adage that the customer is always right. But Vincent would misstep when he failed to respect the position of a supervisor even when he did not respect the person.

Sadly, many people are in positions of authority that have no business being there. Shelly started out as a rep in Rochester where she was above average due to her spunk and giddy charm. She was an adequate manager in that she was not deathly boring as many are and she sought out softy Max McKay in sharing her marriage woes. Max felt for her and pulled for her promotion and shipment to Minneapolis to get her a little distance from the loon she married.

Shelly knew Vincent was a legitimate threat to her; she was seldom around, late daily however Dirk Slabor did not have the morning calls that would expose this inadequacy. Rather than helping Vincent, she made it harder for him because she knew he would kill himself to win. Her mentality was that of her superiors: discipline first, coach second. Vincent ignored these directions and did things how he saw fit because they were working beyond belief. He climbed to the top manager spot in all of Minnesota's precincts in March. Next up for him was the top spot in the company.

Once you do things your way with great success and see that those who are supposed to be mentoring you doing nothing of the kind, you lose respect for them. In late March, Vincent went too far when he questioned her in front of others. The night prior, she had asked for volunteers to get gift cards and he offered to do so after work. She never responded to the e-mail because she left an hour and a half early. The next day, with Vincent already mired in his work, she asked him to leave to get the gift cards. When he stated he was busy and suggested in front of Stacey and Dick that Shelly ask Lucy, who was perched at her typical last-place position, Shelly was outraged.

Shelly had already grown irritated with Vincent's cockiness and the way he was regarded by the majority of the floor as its leader. Vincent's scripts were all over the office, the reps sang his praises at every opportunity and he was the in-house authority on everything. He had a hard time with humility because of his quick shot to stardom and an ever harder time becoming acclimated to management because he never got any guidance. Rather than coach him, Shelly took this opportunity to do what she thought she could do to corral Vincent and put him back in his place: threaten demotion for insubordination.

This was the first of many shouting matches between the pair, which always resulted in the same thing. Vincent wryly played the, "this whole thing is new to me, I'm just finding my bearings" card and would get Shelly to commit to coaching him. He documented the conversation. No coaching followed. In essence, there would be little she could do and if she tried, he had the upper hand and knew this. So she threatened him occasionally to bring his ego back to earth but rode the wave that was the result of his budding greatness. All the while, she was clearly grooming Dick for the next level undeservingly because he did whatever she asked. Such is the fate of the renegade in a sizable company.

After March concluded and Vincent got his commission for the top performance in Minnesota, he took his team to dinner, which became a regular occurrence with the accomplishments to come. The newfound success and money was euphoric to him but as he was a frugal individual, he invested the rest.

Frustrating was the fact Shelly divvied up training classes and awarded the best potential to the lowest performing teams, dooming them to cellar dwelling Lucy and ensuring that Dick got better picks than Vincent. In fact, now that Vincent's performance was tops in the office he typically got the untalented ladies and gentlemen that had no business being there. Over the first half of 2004, however, he did manage to get two acquisitions with some potential: Peter Swansea and Jeff Mason.

Peter was a former bartender at the establishment Dirk Slabor's boss Ed Green frequented. Jeff had worked at a separate entity within ABM scheduling flights for executives and once his time was up he joined because it was the only office hiring in Minneapolis. Because Shelly had high hopes for neither, she gave them to Vincent but they, being around Vincent's age, latched on to his attitude and aspirations and listened to him, at least at first.

Vincent was starting to learn that sales is manipulation of the playing field. You can't change the field, but if you know something will be rewarded and you can find a way to boost that statistic with little effort, take advantage of it.

Green and Slabor held conference calls monthly that praised reps and managers in other offices who were blowing out revenues on international calling plans to boost their rankings. Of course, only a small percentage of prudent customers calling in to gripe about their account would actually make a conscious decision to purchase one. These swindlers' mastery of "including it in the bundle" and just quoting a price rather than the increase to the bill was a misleading masterpiece. Vincent decided to study the revenue streams, the ease and frequency by which he could manipulate the rankings and he started writing verbiage for each product. He would not cross any ethical parameters, but would straddle them better than anyone else was crossing them. If these other clowns could get praise for this stuff, Vincent was determined to do it better.

Upon getting the verbiage approved by the legal team, he unleashed it on his team. Their productivity on the Internet dial-up service, which had a free month attached, exploded immediately. It rapidly boosted their percentage to objective totals and, in turn, Vincent's. They also got verbiage on everything else from the top of the line comprehensive package all the way down to basic phone

84

protection plans. He mandated that his team read these on every call, offering incentives like thirty extra minutes off the phone for excellence in these areas and they started an unparalleled ascent up the charts.

Vincent did not learn until later in his career that sharing the secrets to his success was a better leadership trait than hoarding the knowledge and annihilating everyone in his path with it. Oh well. A star was being born. This Vincent was more selfish than his future self, probably because there was no Elizabeth. And he had many lessons yet to learn so why not pound his competitors while he could? And pound he did.

After leading Minnesota in March it took only two more months to climb ahead of all 117 managers in the residential division. And he did not stop there: he stayed #1 for three straight months. Commission checks were big, the team dinners got bigger. Drinking was prevalent. He was becoming a creature of the environment and was caught up in the money. The sting of Stacey weakened with every fifth of Jack Daniel's he drained and every female sales rep that threw herself at him.

The problem with being a workaholic has meant that most of Vincent's trysts have been in the workplace. Having attained the unattainable Stacey Worth made Vincent legendary and his status as ABM's most eligible bachelor attracted quite the female following. Many of them threw themselves at him and his willpower was at about zero.

Vincent parlayed his burgeoning power into bringing his friend Ted Benton on board as well. Ted had dabbled in teaching since the two set out to Minneapolis from Mankato, but had recently jettisoned the career due to clashes with the clueless school principal. Once he caught a whiff of how much money Vincent teased him with, he signed on and Vincent recruited him to his growing team.

As the young lion surpassed the old lion, Vincent rose as Harriet decided it was time for her to go. She started interviewing for other positions and Vincent continued his dominance. This turned Vincent and Dick into bitter rivals who talked negatively about each other behind the other's back. Dick could never pinpoint how Vincent was so popular and successful and why his own mentality of firing his "weak links" did not bolster his results to Vincent's stratosphere. Vincent could not understand why no matter what he did, no matter what records he set, no matter what he accomplished, Dick was what the corporation seemed to want.

Shelly praised Dick's "coaching" methods. She would gloss over practically everything Vincent achieved. When she talked to Dirk Slabor about her team, she described Vincent as a vagabond and decadent agent. She praised Dick as ready for the next level. To the sales floor, however, Dick became known as "The Terminator" while Vincent was the most popular person in the building. However, big companies and those in decision-making authority do not care about nor do they like people that go against their grain and have uncontrollable popularity and personalities. These diamonds in the rough scare the heck out of them. Especially ones that often prove their own individual grain might be better than the company's. How dare they?

Dirk decided that Rockford would need an acting area manager upon Shelly's pregnancy leave and it was a fight to the death between Vincent and Dick. Dick started rumors that Vincent was a cheat and his sales tactics were dirty. He tried to convince some of Vincent's top talent, now including Peter Swansea, Jeff Mason and newcomer Danny Nance, that following Vincent's lead would get them into trouble. These three characters of extreme prowess and potential all sat in what was dubbed "murderer's row" along with already upstart Ted, and were the foundation of Vincent's team.

Vincent's only way of combat was winning whatever the cost. He obliterated Dick's numbers monthly but the backstabbing and hint that what Vincent was telling his team to say was unethical was poison in the water; Peter called Ed Green directly scared for his life, Jeff contemplated shutting down as well and Danny tried to distance himself from the assertive tactics also. Ted continued doing what his friend told him to do and was the top rep in the company his first and second months on the floor. Imagine that.

Vincent has always cared a great deal about what others think about him. The hint of impropriety planted in Peter, who continued translating the message to Ed Green, caused a very negative light to shine on Vincent. He fought on, however, publicly blasting the few people listening to this garbage. That also got back to Green, making clear Peter was the leak, but neither Ed nor Shelly seemed pleased that Vincent handled it in this rogue fashion.

Vincent dropped Peter from his inner circle, got Danny and Jeff back on board and let Peter be swallowed whole by cancellations. Others stepped up to cover the deficits while Peter was buried and suffered. Vincent did not. He had no time for this nonsense and was not about to bleed any further over this traitor he had once taken under his wing.

Amidst heating up of this Vincent and Dick dual, Harriet departed. Realizing she would not make it any farther up the division, she left for downtown Minneapolis as a product manager developing systems for the call centers. She would have been the easy alternative to keep the peace between Dick and Vincent in the pending interim area manager situation. However, there was to be no such luck.

And the inspiration for Vincent faded quickly. He had risen to unbelievable prominence in just over one year of helming this team. What he struggled with was why Shelly continued to reward bad managers with good reps which did nothing but ruin their potential. Why did she not give reps with some potential to Vincent so he could take the office even higher?

Instead, her philosophy of what she claimed was fair and balanced did nothing but neutralize the office. Vincent was at the top of his heap every month but Shelly was near the bottom of hers. She incorrectly assumed she could force Vincent to get her worst reps to succeed and that people with potential would sell anyway despite the lack of motivation or guidance from poor managers like Lucy. She was very wrong.

Shelly saw what happened when she continued to give top reps to Lucy yet she persisted. Vincent continued to get the worst trainees sent his way, such as Jessie Stone, who was so bad that not even his friend Dick that referred him to the company wanted him. Jessie was the worst rep Vincent had ever heard on the phones. However, after Vincent put him on mandatory scripts including products that were easily manipulated and required no skill he actually won Top Gun for his first quarter on the floor. Dick, along with everyone else, was flabbergasted. Nothing they tried to keep Vincent down with worked.

The gaps got wider. Vincent crushed Dick one month by 23% to objective. The next it was 46%. But his bad boy reputation was his undoing. Being promoted to management at 23 meant Vincent still had a lot of growing up to do, and he showed his immaturity in how he arrogantly wore his crown. Had he had some guidance or coaching, perhaps the evolution would have been more comprehensive and fluid.

Shelly still touted Dick as most ready for the next level in discussions with those who mattered – when she actually showed up to work or was not sneaking downstairs to smoke cigarettes with Stacey every hour on the hour. Yes, while pregnant.

The summer months started winding down and Shelly was slated to depart in August. At the tail end of July, Vincent entered the Aquarium, as it was his opportunity to meet with Dirk for quarterly feedback. Dirk came across as the classic inferiority complex type guy but used his position to lash out at those who probably would have bullied him or stolen his lunch money. Dirk stood and shook Vincent's hand. Shelly sat at the end of the table.

"Vincent, how are you?" Dirk asked, greeting him robotically.

"I'm well. How was your flight in?"

"No complaints. Vincent, first I want to say that revenue-wise you are throwing up some impressive numbers. I do, however, have some concerns."

"Do tell."

"First, Shelly has described to me some run-ins you have had which were borderline insubordination."

Vincent coiled in surprise and looked at Shelly. "Um, actually I have no idea what you are talking about. We have had some situations we agreed were misunderstandings because of our dominant personalities. I assume that is what you are referring to?"

Shelly passively gazed back, saying nothing.

"Vincent, I know your ambitions. Shelly and I agree you have a lot of positive attributes. Clearly you can motivate a workforce to do things that others cannot. However you cannot become victim to your own blind ambition."

"I see," Vincent muttered, realizing to what degree the fix was in.

"Last month, your team averaged 50 of the Internet dial-up programs per rep. The next team down was 21. Do you think that is something to be proud of?"

"Well, let me ask you something," Vincent said coolly. "Citing your conference call messages, your mechanized sales tool provides the products and services that our customers have the highest propensity to buy based on the mandatory fact-finding. That in mind, should I not be proud for doing it better than everyone else?"

"I'm not looking for a smart-aleck response, Vincent. While you clearly have some strong leadership qualities I have serious doubts in your maturity."

"I'm a kid," Vincent said simply. "I'll be the first to admit it. I'm 25 years old and the top manager in this company; I must be doing something right. Why is it that managers elsewhere started this with international calling plans and they are talked about like they live in Camelot and I come along, do it better and I am the devil?"

"You have a lot to learn about Corporate America," Dirk responded. He never missed a beat. He was so mechanical, so programmed by the system that Vincent saw he did not stand a chance in this room.

Vincent had to learn that, despite the unfairness of lots of things around and especially above him, he had to become skilled at when to speak and when to bite his tongue. Vincent did not know how to conform to that; it was too easy to fight back and, to this point, he had not lost anything in doing so.

Vincent wished Shelly was not in the room, but it occurred to him that was probably the very reason she was. Shelly knew Vincent would take any opportunity he got to hang her out to dry with news concerning her late arrivals, early departures, hourly smoke breaks and the fact she rarely emerged from her office long enough to do anything other than yell the occasional, "Rockford rocks!" en route to doing incentive shopping on company time with Stacey. The fact no one could see this, the fact no one knew what Vincent had to deal with on a daily basis and was still rising to reach result levels above everyone else, was a death blow to his spirit.

The conversation did not go uphill from there and it was clear Dick was going to be the choice come temporary-promotion time. Vincent walked out of the Aquarium, cleaned out his office, put in for 25 job transfer requests to other departments and went home for the day.

How you bounce back from adversity is what defines you. Dick was announced as the temporary area manager one week later. Vincent was about to define himself. And it would not be the last time he would be forced to do so.

"The Selling Game" by Vincent Scott
Chapter 9:
HOW TO BE A SUCCESSFUL SALES MANAGER
(AND OTHER STORIES)

While not everyone is interested in management as their eventual destiny in the sales world, it can even be valuable to an employee who strives to do well to understand what their boss grapples with and what they look for out of you. Knowing those attributes and the weight on your supervisor's shoulders can go a long way in molding your approach to making them satisfied with your performance and effort.

We have visited the fact that just because you may have gotten the title of manager, it is far from easy to be great. It is simple to say you play baseball, but can you play in the major leagues? It is effortless to hit a golf ball but can you join the Tour? The same analogies can be applied in management. In any position, there are people who are successful and there are others who are not. The ones who are not make you appreciate those who are.

Good salespeople do not always make good managers. They often possess more potential because they have already most likely mastered the game they were playing. However, that is only part of the battle. We visited what it takes to get the promotion. Now we are going to talk about how you master the art of management.

Like sports, those who understand the game and played it well can often find success coaching because (1) they know what they are talking about and (2) they can relate to the players and build trust with them. That is the key component: gaining respect. However, on the same token outlined above, there are a lot of great athletes who find no success on the coaching end. It is a crapshoot because being great requires being a leader and team player.

Do not forget this: respect is not friendship. Gordon Gekko was not far off when he said, "If you want a friend, buy a dog." Getting subordinates to like you and thinking that is the key is a one-dimensional blunder that befalls many managers in the early-going. Yes, I did it at first. I'm glad I did, because I learned through that experience that it is not about making friends or gaining popularity. Managers afraid of losing their perceived popularity make a lot of foolish choices and errors in judgment. Sometimes, inaction when action is necessary can be one of the worst such mistakes. Thus, they are not effective because their people take advantage of them when they catch a whiff of their weakness.

So you have earned your promotion and now have people working for you. Congratulations. Managing people is about looking out for their best interests and always staying faithful to one fundamental principle: without their presence, there is no reason for yours. Never overlook that essential part of the dynamic. If you remember that and revere them the way you want them to for you, it is the cornerstone of a successful career in managing. I have seen far too many people forget that concept to their detriment. I never forgot it, and I have found success in management beyond my wildest dreams.

That is not to say I have not tried many ways at achieving the respect required for success. You will not see eye to eye with the people you oversee, and vice versa, but this is where effective communication comes into play. Just because two people have a difference of opinion does not mean they will always fail to see each other's side. It does not mean they will fail in communicating to one another what is important to them or be unable to compromise. Meeting each other halfway and identifying common ground and purpose are important parts of the manager-subordinate relationship.

Care about the right things. Care about what your people need in order to achieve your collective goals. Care about earning their respect. Care about working hard to make their jobs meaningful and your team goals accessible. Managers who fail are often unable to cope through the difficult times or they choose to ignore the problems of their group. They occasionally choose to discount the "little issues", thinking they will go away. They don't; they only fester into bigger ones. When it comes to supervising others, just like being a salesperson promoting a good or service, elimination of obstacles and objections still comes into play regularly.

Morale in a sales environment is a huge driving force to the ultimate line between success and failure. The manager will always be looked to, right or wrong, for the answers and solutions to problems that spring up. The troubles of a nation cannot be pinned on one individual, yet they always seem to fall on the shoulders of the leader.

Even if you do not know the answer, know where to go for resolution. It may be your boss, peer or a network you liaise with, but your job is to tackle and respond to the questions and concerns you are presented with. If you drop the ball a couple of times, you will be written off and as far as respect goes, good luck getting any semblance of it from your subordinates.

So much of being a successful manager correlates to all other relationships on the sales hierarchy food chain. That chain starts with the customer-rep dynamic. The rep reports to the manager, who reports to a senior manager, and so on up the chain. This is important because you must identify within that relationship the same steps in satisfying your subordinates as those subordinates have in satisfying the customer.

Identification of strengths, needs and weaknesses (or areas of opportunity, as you will call them) is what being a supervisor is all about; you will spend your time perfecting processes based on these things. Instead of fact-finding and overcoming objections, you are asking your team members what they require from you, finding out what they need or want help in, determining their areas for necessary improvement based on conversations, observations and documentation and putting it all together to recommend a course of action. Just like selling a customer something, you have to "sell" your subordinate on why they should do things your way. You have to sell them on why they must change their way of doing things. You must convince them that their success hinges on an imperative tweak to the way they do business. See the connection?

Morale plays into this because you must constantly have your fingers on the pulse of your team. What do they need to be motivated? What fears and issues exist that stymie results? Your ability in determining these issues and eliminating them will determine your success. However, I am sure you can very quickly see how much easier that is when your frame of influence is one person: the customer on the other end of the phone line. When it is a team of 10, 20, 40 people, the game changes and your approach has to change with it.

Morale on a sales floor will always have peaks and valleys and that will directly impact the approval rating of a management team. Eliminate excuses, maintain a steady hand in managing the processes and wade through them. That is what effective managers do. A manager does not win with threats or by goading someone into a task; a manager wins by lighting the way through the woods to the clearing of success.

One of the biggest disconnects between managers and their employees is the lack of realism; if a manager fails to show his or her team that a goal is realistic and how it can be achieved, chaos ensues. The team members will take their own sporadic approaches to tasks and become nothing more than a bunch of individuals. The effective manager can corral all of these personalities and pack a powerful punch with their combined talents. An ineffective manager will have a zoo on their hands.

For, management, like everything else, is sales. Based on what you have learned about your team member through conversation and what you know of their hopes and dreams, you have to chart a course and every step towards it. Not only that, but when the going gets tough, you have to sell that person on staying on that course.

Many of us are parents and if you are, you understand a level of caring you never understood before. A good manager has to have a legitimate concern for the well being of their team members. They have to know their people – what motivates them, what they need and how best to address their concerns. The successful manager may have 20 different personalities that all need love and attention and sometimes morning coffee and bagels, too. Some days your crew will post numbers that break through the stratosphere and the whole world will smile with you. Others you put up a stinker of a day and the entire attitude shifts; you can feel the defeat in the air. It is the way the cookie crumbles. But consistency wins the race and keeping your head up will prevent the negativity from overtaking you or your team. They look to you to be a leader. So lead. It's called self-fulfilling prophecy; believe you are a winner and you'll come out ahead in the end.

Get over the niceness as quickly as you can. That is not to say you want to be a jerk, but if you have "friends" on your team that know they can prod you into letting them off the hook for missing work or bending rules, you are headed down a dangerous path. It is nothing but trouble if your employees think or know they can get you to look the other way on rule infractions. Not only does this mean they will further push the envelope and try to get away with bigger things, but other team members will cry foul when they see a peer get away with something they cannot.

This is a tough one, because I have also been fooled in my day into thinking some of my employees were my friends. I learned the hard way that they were not, but consistency in the way you manage will go a long way in getting consistent results. There can be no doubt in your employee's mind what the cause and effect of every scenario will be. A clear cut policy needs to be in place and enforced the same way every time to ensure there are no signs of favoritism and no one trying to get away with something. Even if you are concerned with what a subordinate thinks about you, if you live by the stance that you are paid to enforce the rules and it is not personal, you can gain their respect even if they don't like it or you.

Many in management positions allow themselves to be walked on because they are afraid of people not liking them and think that if their team likes them they will work hard for them. Others let the power go to their head, forget their roots and rule with an iron fist. Neither approach works.

The things that matter in sales management in the order they matter are (1) constant attention to and supervision of the right stuff – the processes, conversion rates, hustle stats, efficiency metrics, etc., (2) momentum, (3) morale and (4) the skill of your team. An ineffective leader puts priorities in the wrong place or simply cannot focus on the big picture well enough to put all of this into perspective. I have seen countless managers who get so caught up in things or desperate that they panic and do little things they think make a difference when in reality they fail to make a dent. They lose sight of the big picture that will help them on a high level and these misconceptions cost them dearly.

First, constant attention does not mean berating your team, lending too much credence to these items or failure to consider the sum of a team member's parts. Everything has to be taken into consideration when you are diagnosing a subordinate and your most important job is to find a way to get the most out of your day. I found that I had to be content with getting about 75% of what I wanted to accomplish completed in a given day of sales management. The effective managers streamline their processes and get everything completed that *must* be done and should be done. The ineffective allow themselves to be overwhelmed and swallowed like they are in quicksand as they are ill-prepared to handle all of the fires that constantly come up. Far too many managers poorly budget their time and stop what they are doing for every little thing that comes up which, in the end, equates to nothing of substance getting accomplished.

When you arrive at the onset of a day, week, month or year you have to map out your intentions. Like a call flow, your adversary (in this case, your chaotic day) will derail you at every turn. You want to stick as close to the game plan as possible to make sure you can be as effective as possible.

Take heed: the biggest goal you should have as a manager is to have a positive effect on as many people and things and sales opportunities as possible without spreading yourself too thin.

Many managers in a sales arena think it prudent to constantly teach by doing, whether on the phone or in the field. Don't get me wrong; this is a great tactic when breaking in a new hire. However, once someone has the training wheels off and is fully versed in everything they need to know, spending such time with them is a waste of yours. After someone knows the ropes, they need only have checks and balances to keep them on track. This is where studying of their statistics comes into play. This is where diagnosing their strengths and areas of opportunity comes into play.

A lot of managers are apprehensive about pulling reps off the phones or out of the field for any amount of time because they fear loss of revenue. Get over that very, very quickly. I once had this same trepidation but you have to look at it this way: if the time spent away from the trenches is quality time, it is a quality investment into their future calls, visits and sales attempts. If you have a positive impact on futuristic calls that you will not be privy to or riding shotgun for, how is that a bad thing? Isn't the very reason you sit with or accompany a rep so that you can impact that one call? Is impacting one call out of thousands they make in a month while others on your team flounder a worthwhile use of your time? Especially when it is a more seasoned rep, believe me – you are not making a difference by sitting there for one or two calls, even if they ask for it or say they need it. Your best bet is studying their statistics, making recommendations based on their efficiency and metrics across the board and monitoring to ensure they are following your example.

This is where the concept of managing processes over people comes into play. Your initial instinct is to keep someone on the phone as long as possible without breaks in the action so they are always there to make money. You may sit with them from time to time and help them and try to minimize any deviation from that schedule. You may give them performance reviews by just putting them on the desk while they are on a call and coming back later to get their signature. Wrong answer! They will continue to do wrong things on every single call you fail to impact. Having a drive-by conversation on one call or giving them some notes on a performance review that you fail to enunciate will not lead that rep to the path of success. Investing time in them off the job function that will positively impact every opportunity they make in the future while you aren't looking and while you are free to help and impact others is how you effectively perform the juggling act known as management.

After laying the groundwork, chart a course to greatness with each subordinate you have. You always analyze where they are now versus where you need them or where they want to be. If a rep has mediocre efficiency, mediocre results and is gravitating towards just one of your product offerings when you have multiple, there is a lot of room for improvement.

First, there is no need for them to have mediocre efficiency if productivity is low. What are they doing to fill their time? You have to determine that and sell them on why and how they can spend more time selling. If they are only promoting one of multiple product offerings, they are a one-trick pony because they lack confidence in the others. Why? Your exact question needs to be, "What is holding you back from discussing Product X with your customers?" "Where does Product X fall out of the bundle you are discussing?" Just like the call flow, fact-finding is integral to determining corrective steps of action with employees.

If you have a good coaching session with a rep for 30 minutes to an hour, it is true they missed out on placing some calls or scheduling visits. However, they are far more prepared for the ones to come. You have managed to positively impact the largest number of future actions and calls as possible. You also did it in an effective means; you spent a fraction of your day with that team member and can move on to someone else. That's management.

Another key principle that people in leadership roles must understand is that follow-up is vital to the process. If I coached the aforementioned rep on expanding their horizons when it comes to pitching the product line or on shortening the gap between calls because they were doing unnecessary research, no one is helped if I fail to follow up and ensure they are doing it. Even if your company does not mandate it, keep a file of what you are working on with every single team member. No doctor or dentist can remember the afflictions or last check-up of all their patients; that is why they have charts! You too must keep a chart on all team members and reference them every time they are in your office.

The key in setting these benchmarks is figuring out what milestone you and the subordinate need to reach by the next time you talk, be it a week, month, or however long out. You should become intimate with the term "improvement plan" as you will want to use it in every meeting. Document an improvement plan with the rep of where you are, where you are going and what you are going to do to get there. Keep it in their binder and reference it every time you meet with them. Furthermore, especially if you have several people on your team, you will want to have little "touches" on a daily or semi-daily basis with everyone. This could be in the form of just walking by casually to see how the rep is doing that day. In these little fly-by meetings, reference what you are working on and what you have discussed. This counts as a touch and, not only is it easy to squeeze dozens of these into a day, but they make a difference because they keep you in your team's heads. That's a good thing.

Maybe the rep is struggling with pitching Product Y; have them keep a tally sheet of how many times they recommended it that day and the reasons customers declined it. That journal activity will give the two of you tremendous talking points when next you meet up. Do not just blindly and stringently follow the guidelines of your department; many of them will only require you meet with someone once per month. Work smarter and not necessarily harder so you can optimize your results efficiently and effectively.

Many managers take the path of least resistance and have a drive-by conversation with everyone and call it a day. I have seen managers who think they accomplished something because they talked to everyone that day and know what personal problems they are facing. Using a personal problem to explain to me why some rep is flailing around is a poor excuse indicative of an ineffective manager. Those who want to be successful will do what I have outlined here.

I encourage you to think creatively about how you want to implement this style. By no means did I invent the wheel; I simply perfected it. It took me quite some time to get there; you will witness or hear many different approaches at management. You will hopefully get training on how your company or boss wants or expects it to be done. I am simply telling you the most effective way to be successful. My best advice: always complete what is expected of you. Offer up your thoughts and suggestions on how the process can be streamlined. Find a way within the confines of your job to satisfy the needs of the company and of your team. This is where the holy trinity of sales fits into management and that is how you will find success.

A lot of impediments will be removed from your path once you realize you cannot and should not take for granted someone knows how to do something or will do something correctly left to their own devices. Just because you mastered being a rep all by yourself and worked well independently does not mean you should take for granted that your subordinates know how to or will conduct a proper call flow. In fact, the very reason you were plucked to lead them is because you mastered it and the company wants you to train that mastery to others. That said, you should always assume your team is a blank canvas; teach them everything the way you want it done and follow up to ensure it is being done the way you expect it to be done. Inspect what you expect. I heard that a long time ago and it is very true.

The reason I make it a priority to point this out is because I have seen many managers pay lip service to a lot of things to their detriment. Yes, you can "come down" on bad behavior and talk big but after your team sees a couple instances of you not following through on holding them accountable, they realize they can get away with murder. When they realize you are blowing hot air, they will not respect you, your "rules" hold no water and your results suffer. You will look back one day and realize your collapse is an avalanche you cannot stop. These are the managers who get trapped under the weight of failure. These are the managers who allow themselves to become overwhelmed. Do not give them an inch, despite your fears to the contrary about compromising morale; they really will take a mile and you will be much worse off in the end.

Remember when these people came into the business they wanted a career and to make money. You have to remind them of this regularly. You will also want to use that when charting their course to greatness. Something makes everyone tick. It is your job to figure that out and utilize it as motivation as you guide them to that goal.

It's funny; I have heard contemporaries complain that they had employees who were content just making a paycheck and collecting benefits and that there was no way to motivate them. Of course there is. For them, what makes them tick is a place of employment and the benefit package it provides. If they are not carrying their weight, you have to make them fear losing the only thing keeping them going: that job, those benefits. Once you determine someone is not going to push themselves out of self-respect to shoot for the stratosphere and you have given them all the advice you can to no avail, there is no shame in holding them to the letter of the law with the threat of losing their job.

Unfortunately, while tragic, many managers threaten first, coach never. The refreshing thing is that these managers never defeat the managers who coach and develop. Threats and intimidation can "work" in some areas but people never go above and beyond for a boss that rules with fear. They will do just enough to get by and hold on to their seat.

Never forget your roots. Do not let go of the person you were and from where you came. To get buy-in, gain respect and get people to go above and beyond the call of duty for you, it is vital you show them you can relate. My employees knew I was the best salesperson around, that I would walk through fire for them and take bullets for them. They knew if they brought me a concern, if I could not fix it myself I would take it where it needed to go. They knew even if I could not win a dispute on their behalf I would die trying. I fought all the battles. It was important to me because I knew it was important to them. I never once had to threaten first; I gained respect from my team members and they did a lot of hard work for me. I did not reach everyone, but I reached enough to reach success levels I would never have thought possible. That's management.

Mistakes are par for the course. Get used to them. Your mistakes will be your merit badges; they are what qualify you to be able to teach and guide others not to make the same mistakes. It is akin to parenting; how many times have you thought as a parent or heard a parent say they want to help their kids not make the same mistakes they made? You stumbled and fell in your past life as a sales rep and your subordinates can be privy to those obstacles at much earlier stages in their careers thanks to you. And, by reading this book, you can learn from mine and find success without the tumbling.

Great success can be found through elimination of every single excuse your workforce has. Hear them out but do not buy into them. Managers who lend too much credence to their team's excuses try to use these excuses to cover up their own inadequacies. Do not fall victim to that. However, find a way to eliminate what they are complaining about. If that is not possible, sell them on why these perceived obstacles exist and what the alternative, which is often worse, would be. Once objections and excuses are eliminated and overcome, what other excuse do they have not to sell? None; and that's the point. Show them you are willing to go that extra mile and they will do anything for you. And, if they don't, they have no excuse left and will certainly see it coming when a disciplinary plan is right around the corner. You have them right where you want them. That's management.

One of the few bits of advice I got from a manager back in the day was, "When you're up, ride the wave. When you're down, make everyone behave." I have utilized and taught this principle for years; believe me, these are words to live by. When you are exceeding expectations there are not a lot of boats you want to rock. By all means, you want to continue tracking the progress everyone is making towards a goal, you want to ensure policies and procedures are being met and you want to make sure you complete all of your assigned tasks; however you do not want to mess with your momentum. Like sports, sales is a game of streaks and runs; when you are riding a hot streak you do not want to question it or do anything to cause its demise. While you will still probably have a few people in your group that are always at the bottom who need to be kept in line, for the most part you want to leave the upper crust of your core alone so as to not disturb the balance.

On the flip side, you will inevitably encounter lulls in the action no matter how effective you are as a manager. What goes up must come down.

98

Get used to it; you will see a lot of peaks and valleys, more so the higher you climb the corporate ladder and the less control you have over the people on the front lines. I cannot say this enough: that is where management of process over people is so vital in determining if you are going to be a phenom or a flop. When you experience these breaks in the action, it is important to ensure everyone is playing by the rules and living up to their potential. By no means do you want to let your team see your frustration nor do you just want to start having knee-jerk reactions that are inconsistent with your overall style. However, it is important to be willing to pull in the reins lest this race will get out of your control.

When it comes to efficiency management, it is about ensuring your team members see the statistics daily and that you are calling out any and all discrepancies. If someone was short two hours on their time they should have been on the phones, they need to account for their day. If they repeatedly fail to provide a satisfactory answer, your improvement plan for them should entail some kind of documentation of every activity they partake in that takes them away from their job. If you still fail to see improvement, sadly, it is time for disciplinary action. The trick, however, is charting a course and showing them how feasible it is to make the tweak all while selling them on why it is important to their performance and their quest to obtain whatever big picture grail they seek.

In order to achieve your desired metrics in efficiency, you must sell your team on realistic expectations. It is important to get their buy-in that the goal is attainable, worthy of their attention (as in there is something in it for them, like increased productivity or keeping their job) and the commitment it will be done. From there, it is all about holding them accountable to that commitment. If you are smart about how you manage, you will never have to surprise anyone with a conversation or discipline or termination; they will always know it is coming.

As for call flow and sales management, most jobs also have steps in place for these types of measurement of work. You are likely bound to many of these internal rules yet do not let that inhibit you from putting your own stamp on the processes where your team is concerned. Many a time I have heard managers that worked for me complain about the fact their lesser-skilled sales reps did a good call flow and they had a hard time flunking them. Believe me, if a rep cannot sell, they are not doing the call flow justice.

The way to fix this is by giving your own personal definition to each bullet point of the call flow. Be succinct and targeted in explaining to your team exactly what you expect to hear on every bullet point of that flow. Document that you had the conversation and hold them accountable on every call to do it the way you outlined. Something as general on a call flow grading format as "Offered Product X with benefits" could be marked affirmatively by the ineffective manager just because the product was mentioned. However, this same point would be marked with a negative response by the effective manager who outlined with his or her team the expectation that at least three benefits were utilized and a close was attempted. You are well within your rights to manage your team as you see fit until or unless you are not cutting the mustard. That was always my philosophy and it should be the same in your situation.

In my time as a manager and as a manager of managers, I mastered those positions by perfecting the art of diagnosing my employees based on the sum of their statistics. I can tell so much by looking at each quantitative and qualitative measurement of work; I can tell if you talk too long, prepare too much, send too many proposals, take advantage of the full suite of services in your arsenal or are a one-trick pony. Basically, I can tell if you've been bad or good so be good for goodness' sake.

It is not like you are requesting your employees submit a different cover sheet for meaningless TPS reports à la *Office Space*; expecting them to uphold basic measurements of their work is far from outside your realm as their supervisor. You have every right to set expectations and hold your team accountable to strive for and exceed them. In fact, your ability or failure in doing so will make or break you. Someone will always be holding you accountable so you should by all means do the same to those who are a reflection of you every day.

It is not about whether they love you or not. It is irrelevant if you are on their Christmas card list. The only gift you care about is their effort, attitude and application. When an employee listens to you and does what you tell them out of respect, that is a huge step in the direction of success. We have probably all had times in our lives where our parents or guardians or someone in a position of authority was not our favorite person. However, if they were consistent in their approach, clear in their intentions and expectations and their methods resulted in personal growth, we can look back on the experience and respect them now.

It doesn't take great results and accomplishments in your previous existence. It takes patience, understanding, team orientation, striving towards a common goal, the ability to put yourselves in their shoes, being able to relate to them and doing absolutely everything in your power to help them achieve their goals no matter what those goals are. Sometimes you cannot do any more for them and you cannot fix a perceived problem but as long as you can show them you did all you could, stood up for them or took a hit on their behalf, they will follow you anywhere.

Coaching your team to success is the most integral part of management. It always pained me when I heard reps complain of any manager that failed them in this area. Some managers try to hide behind their responsibilities and say they do not have time to coach as much as they want. Do not make this mistake.

100

Make the time for developing your team. Period. Failure to do so results in failure. I don't care what personal tweaks you need to make to your time management; they need to be done to ensure you leave no stone unturned in the evolution of your team's approach to the mastery of the job.

There were many days in my management career where I would look up late in the day and not necessarily be where I wanted to finish the day. My busy work would be piled up and I had committed to myself I was going to finish some things in that vein that were not yet completed. Despite that, I put it aside; sometimes you have to make the decision to put aside other things for the sake of your real goal: money. Your results are ultimately what you will be judged off of; find the time to do the busy work but make the time to impact results.

The best thing about being a manager is that you dictate when you get in the trenches and when you do not. While I could never stand those who just wanted promotions to get off the phone or out of the field, I looked forward to a career step that would unchain me from my permanent home at the telephone. On the same token, it is nice to be able to get out there and get some positive chatter and enthusiasm going because the boss is alongside the team members making stuff happen.

Again, your time is best spent impacting as many futuristic sales attempts as possible. Always keep that in the forefront of your mind. However, especially with newer team members, there will always be good opportunities to get out there and show by doing. One of the toughest decisions I would have to make in these situations was if and when to take over the call for fear the rep would lose the sale; I would scribble notes on a pad of paper to feed them lines and would whisper instructions but would often not take over unless I saw that sale slip-sliding away. The reason this decision is tough is because doing something for someone else is not teaching. They need to learn. Be sure you know when and how to draw that line so you are not making them dependent upon you; they have to learn, grow and prosper independently of you.

As for coaching sessions with reps off the phone in my office, these were my bread and butter. I love these sessions more than nearly anything in sales management because this is what I found had the most impact.

Unless you have nothing useful to say, you should pull them off their usual duties in an instant in the attempt to make them better. You invest in the stock market, you invest in mutual funds and you invest in your people. It pays dividends and that is how you make gains.

The art of coaching an employee is delicate because you are dealing with feelings and emotional topics like performance. This is where many managers fail; they are unable to deliver the tough messages necessary to get the point across in the most effective manner. Giving bad news or telling someone they need serious work is not easy, but, like selling products and services, the words you choose to use and how you deliver them are keys to getting through to them proficiently.

You do not want there to be a negative connotation of coming into your office. Often, reps will hum some kind of horror theme when one of their own is summoned to the office, but you want to dispel that feel quickly. Regardless of my forthcoming message, unless of course I was terminating someone, I would always let the rep know it was a privilege for me to meet with them and that they should consider themselves fortunate that I felt they warranted additional time to form a plan of attack. Especially when I was managing managers, if I included a rep in a session, it was their lucky day to get my advice in addition to their superior's, even if not everything they were going to hear was the easiest thing for them to find out.

Whether covering a call or visit or some aspect of their performance, you always want to open by asking them how they are, how they feel about that particular call or aspect and you want to ascertain where their head is. This will give you a window into how you want to approach this session. If they are defensive, you need to be relatively delicate in your approach but will have to sell them on your legitimate concerns. If they are arms wide open and a willing sponge to soak up your pearls of wisdom, first consider yourself lucky but second be sure you understand your obligation. The manager-employee dynamic involves egos and you have to be mindful of that as you proceed.

No matter what message you are about to deliver or how poor the employee is at the item at hand, always acknowledge whatever good exists first. Even if the employee only managed good tone or saying their name properly, you want to lead off with a positive to set the tempo for what is to come. No one wants to simply hear a laundry list of their downfalls. That is especially true of someone in an employee's shoes. You must also realize that they may often have a differing opinion from yours so be prepared to back up every aspect of your diatribe. That said, you should also be prepared to stick to your guns.

Speaking of laundry lists, do not administer one. People's attention spans are not equipped to handle every single thing they could have improved on. If you consider what you are trying to communicate, it is likely some of the items are higher priorities than others. That said, you want to lead off with the important, high end stuff. I have heard many managers just read off everything the rep did wrong; if you fail to discern that you care more about the passion and enthusiasm they displayed during offering than the fact they read the scripted introduction, they will likely not know which to apply more emphasis in improving.

Never leave them guessing; your coaching session should by all means outline what needs improvement yet it should center around a select few high end priorities that will be their marching orders going forward. Like a sales presentation, you want to lay out what you expect to be done to fix these items, the benefit to them of fixing them and how they can feasibly do it. Plausibility of a goal is one of the most important things on the minds of your team members. One of the most frustrating things for an employee is a goal they feel they cannot reach; if you can show them how they can take and make steps towards the goals you have discussed, you have done them a great service.

Highlight the main bullet points you want them to have in the front of their minds, recap them and have them repeat them. Writing them down and giving them a report later of what you discussed is always a good idea; this works wonders for the file you are keeping on your team members as well. It also serves as quick reference for the employee; every time they glance at the paper it shows what they need to be working on. Implementation of improvement plans like having them keep track of the things you want them improving on is very helpful as – at any time of day – you can get an up-to-the-minute update on how they are progressing and they know you care. Stopping by someone's desk to check their stick tally of an improvement area takes seconds but it is working smarter and not harder towards effectively managing the processes that make you successful. That's management.

While you may make several valid points during your coaching session with a rep, they will not remember everything. Map a game plan and be creative with the steps you want them to take to get to the "X" that marks the spot. This can also be a great time to revisit what you expect on their evaluations; that while they may have mentioned Product Y or asked a customer if they were interested in discussing Product Y, they did not recommend it with benefits and therefore they missed the point. Not only that, but as assumption never works in management, you must outline the wording you expect to be used and show them how you expect that recommendation to take place.

Heck, it may have even been a progression for the rep to actually start *mentioning* Product Y, but it is still not being done with benefits. So, in keeping with the theme we just discussed, you would first commend the rep for getting over their fear of discussing the product. Then you would chart the next step of recommending it with benefits, all while showing them how you expect it to be woven into their call.

Much of the conversation with an employee should be dictated from the fact-finding you undertake with them. It is one thing to ask them what benefits are of Product Y and to have them quote your training manual in giving you ample belief they know their facts. However, just because someone knows benefits of something does not mean they can or will sell it. In fact, quite often, that is the very case: you could have a very intelligent employee on your hands that knows the products inside and out but they have no idea how to position it or win the psychological tug-of-war with their customer. That is where you have to show – not tell – them how to integrate it into their call flow.

I have found a lot of success in management by instructing employees to write their own scripts in their own words that they feel would address shortcomings in the call flow. After they have completed writing the script in their words and voice, I will tweak and bless it. It is always important to let your employee have a strong hand in the progression of their career; it is hard for someone to just follow orders, they want to have some skin in the game. Besides, writing sales scripts is second nature to me but I am the only one who will deliver it exactly the way I intended. Having them craft it in their mold and having me oversee and tweak it to my satisfaction is teamwork. That winning combination will lead to success.

Once a script is born from a collaboration and coaching session, make following it mandatory if necessary. Make sure the employee understands you will be listening for that script every time you monitor them. Document that discussion. Follow-up to ensure it is being used. Inspect what you expect. See, a lot of management is going above and beyond just paying lip service to the clichés you will hear every day from your supervisors. You have to take the initiative to put your own mark on things, be creative and look for the best ways possible to improve the processes in your group. A common fear of a manager is that once you turn your back on one rep to turn your attention to another, Rep #1 will misbehave or relapse into old behaviors that will not work. Your attention to their progression, your dedication to following up on them and your consistent approach to managing policies, procedures and processes will be the deciding factor on whether you win or lose. That's management.

Always keep your eye on the big picture and ensure your employees do the same. All of them have some kind of motivation, but you have to get to know them to uncover it. I know, the correlations between the sales flow to a customer and the coaching flow to an employee are very similar; the same relationships often exist in slightly different forms as you climb the sales food chain.

Just like you can never assume your subordinates know something or know to do something, you can also never assume they will keep their own eyes on the big picture. In fact, for many, this is a very difficult undertaking and it is another place where you come in. You have to keep their eyes on the prize; that is how you motivate your team members from the bottom-feeders all the way up to the climbers. Some of them need more attention than others. Some of them deserve attention more than others. Based on the quality of the investment of your time, you have to and get to determine how to divvy it up. You call the shots on what you do and when you do it. Sure, you have a guideline, but you need to keep all of these factors in mind when deciding how you are going to play your hand.

With all the joys and successes also comes unrest. Being a master negotiator, mediator and being adept at conflict resolution will all be skills you must learn and call upon in your quest for management greatness. Like anything else, it is not all fun and games and you will regularly be tested in your position. Nothing worth anything is easy, and if you take on the role of manager be prepared for plenty of challenges. You may be the best time manager in the world and may plot out every second of your day, but those are the ones that will most quickly be derailed by the problems that undoubtedly arise.

As frustrating as things can get, never respond with a knee-jerk reaction. Your gut instinct to catastrophe – which is nothing more than a decision without the facts – will only further the spread of potential disease. Always remember your top priority and responsibility is not letting your team see you bleed, not allowing them to witness your frustration and ensuring they view you as nothing more or less than the authority on all topics. You may have chinks in your armor but you do not want to expose them to your team.

Whether the situation is a subordinate taking a spill requiring medical attention, a fight or argument between employees, a disagreement with a peer, false accusations attacking your character, or a sales dispute that has people up in arms, let cooler heads prevail and do not be afraid to sit back and gather all the facts. People will want or expect an immediate decision from you when often that is not possible or not wise. Granted, if someone falls in the parking lot, you follow protocol and may call an ambulance. But if two people are fighting over a lead, get the facts, make sure everyone gets the impression you are out to play wise King Solomon even if you have already made up your mind, and always let everyone get everything off their chest they desire to. If they are convinced you have their best interests at heart, it will be easy to sell them on giving you enough time to make a thoroughly investigated and informed decision.

Keeping your cool when you are under fire can be even more difficult but I can tell you that anything you do to respond out of anger at a false statement or accusation will only serve to undermine you. The people that matter – even if it is just you sometimes – know the truth. You have to let things roll off your back. Great leaders attract jealousy. Remember that you have to hold yourself to the same high regard you asked for and earned. With management comes a responsibility to yourself, others and the company. Take it seriously.

Put all of these things together and the better you oversee these processes, the more effective you will be as a leader. Anyone can carry the moniker but what does it take to be the best?

The best managers are the go-to-authorities for the team; they are a wealth of knowledge and have a plethora of tips and trade tactics. If you are going to coach you should know the game; the ins and outs, the idiosyncrasies and what makes the machine run. Anyone can schedule a meeting with employees, but the best managers have an outline, a game plan and talking points plus the allowance for the team members to have their turn to talk. Where the ineffective manager allows this open forum to get out of control and fails to address concerns, the effective manager has the answers, dictates the flow of the constructive "bitch session" and follows up on anything he or she cannot answer that second.

The effective manager upholds all developmental plans, knows where everything is for the purpose of personnel binders and keeps everyone in line with office standards and expectations. The best manager volunteers for additional responsibilities while peers sit back and do status quo. The best manager leads in overall performance – sales, efficiency, paperwork and hustle stats like conversion rates and whatever else your department comes up with. The best manager is always looking for a new area to reign.

Can you get people to work for you? Do they want to work for you? Can you bring them together as a team? Can you get their performance to its peak? Are you worth more to the company as a solitary rep or can you replicate your success in others?

The best managers can voice their opinions and the opinions of their subordinates behind closed doors in making policy; then turn around and embrace whatever the outcome, even if they are not in 100% support of it. They are ambassadors of the company and have to sell their teams on how to tackle the mission statement of the company, no matter what. The best manager can answer the 20 questions per day they field from each of their employees. The best managers are subject matter experts (or can effectively fake it) on every topic.

The best managers do not and cannot care what others think about them and must develop a thick skin. While they are concerned with what their detractors and naysayers would spout about them strictly for self-development purposes, they will never let anyone see them bleed. The best managers have a clear cut understanding of all reports and why they are important, plus the ability to sell their importance to those working for them. They can break down the reports, make them make sense to others and get the buy-in and commitment to excel in every facet of the job. They keep the information in their faces whether it makes them comfortable or not, are not afraid of having tough conversations and are not unsettled at the thought of disciplining an employee when necessary.

The best managers lead by example and leadership rather than threats, fear and intimidation. The best managers know how to plot out their day to give the most of themselves in the least amount of time. The best managers care about their team and the success of the whole. They care about recognizing successes of all shapes and sizes, improvements and milestones. They are competitive but not at the cost or to the detriment of themselves or others.

106

The best managers commend rather than tear down. They do not show their frustration or take it out on others. They have to be patient and understanding but temper it with their duty to the business and the team as a whole. They reach out to others to share and learn; they are interested in best practices, no matter where they originated from. They are not afraid to delegate work to others and put faith in employees who are ready for additional responsibility. They understand that promotion from within reflects positively on them and are not intimidated by those who work for them. They are secure enough in their position and approach that they can mentor others and have a succession plan.

The best managers have a strong enough support system that they can take a day off without the kingdom crumbling. They have gained enough respect of the employees that they work when the leader is out of pocket and know there will be repercussions if they fail to do so. They empower their teams to have a say on as many issues as possible such as work flow, approaches, incentives, team bonding exercises and the like. They care about momentum and morale and know how to keep it strong. They show strong respect for those with the will to succeed while they assist in improving the skill to get there.

The best managers never judge themselves versus peers that are not meeting expectations or goals; they always judge themselves against the expectations and goals of the company and of themselves.

Like anything worth anything in this world, being a manager will never be easy. However, when you see that light bulb go off in an employee and they "get it" – when it all clicks and comes together for someone you have been working with – and everything pays off, being a manager can be one of the most rewarding things in the world.

That's management.

*   *   *

While Vincent has experienced several disappointments at the hands of his occasionally reckless actions over the years, he would not change a single one of them if given the opportunity. All of them, even if they were knee-jerk reactions to injustice or persecution, led to lessons, learning and to the man he was to become.

For better or usually worse, every single thing any oppressed employee had wished they could do, he did. He does so because he feels he earns that right through everything he has given and endured, and here to now he has not been punished so severely he can't eventually pick himself back up.

Vincent was unquestionably hurt after being snubbed for this temporary promotion. Sure, he had done a few things that had gotten him in hot water with Shelly. Sure, he had gotten himself in a mess with Stacey. But now these things were costing him an opportunity to further prove himself. He just wanted that chance.

Shelly sent an e-mail to him that coincided with the announcement of Dick's rise to power. Its contents told him that if he wanted to talk she was available. It also ensured that he knew how important he was to the office success. It was a real fluff piece. An e-mail *after* the announcement? It was a typical classless display.

Perhaps Vincent was not yet ready to run a department, but that was not the point. Neither was Dick. There had to have been another solution, even if it would have required some creativity on Shelly's or Dirk's part. This just felt like a slap in the face.

Vincent's reaction the following day after polishing off a healthy helping of Jack Daniel's and Diet Coke was to schedule three weeks' vacation. Needless to say, upon receipt of his request, Shelly summoned him into her office.

"Is this how you want to handle this?" she asked.

"I have given this office my blood, sweat and tears for 3 years and I'm denied what should be my birthright with no explanation," Vincent responded calmly, as he had sorted through all possible thoughts in his head by now. "How would you expect me to react?"

"How could I put you in that position? You do a good job managing your team but you have not effectively worked with your peers. How do I have them reporting to you? How do I have Stacey reporting to you?"

"How do you have us reporting to Dick? The guy has stabbed me in the back multiple times and now you have your star player answering to him?" Vincent fired back.

"Vincent, I had to make the decision that left everything in the best hands in my absence. Dick is going to be dealing with basic behind the scenes stuff. Did you ever think that maybe I can't afford to have my floor general be off the floor during this critical time?"

This was a great line Vincent temporarily bought.

"I get that, but the entire floor is going to know that he is in charge when his skills are no match for mine."

"I'm not leaving, Vincent. I'll be back. And I will still be doing everything from afar. This is a glorified, temporary assignment. It means nothing in the grand scheme of things. Now, if you want some time off I understand. You deserve it. But I don't know that 3 weeks right now is in the best interests of the department."

"Fine, I'll take a day and I'll be back Wednesday," Vincent answered.

"Vincent, you can take more than that. That wasn't what I meant."

"I only need a day. I'm not going to a Top Gun luncheon that Dick hosts. I don't care if it's free or if I was the top manager in the company. I'm not getting an award handed to me from that man who doesn't deserve to even hold it. Beyond that, I'll be back. And I'll be better than ever until the day I walk out of here. Is there anything else?"

Shelly had no idea what to say. She dismissed Vincent. Vincent took the following day off, which was Dick's first at the helm and he intentionally missed a free Top Gun recognition luncheon. Instead, he spent the day drinking and thinking and plotting his next move. A new day was dawning for Vincent. Every time he had been dealt less than desirable cards from a seemingly stacked deck he has taken a breather and come back better than ever.

However, every time he had to dig even deeper to conjure up strength, he had a little less in the tank.

Harriet's team was divided and Dick's was given to Patrice Carnes, a newly promoted acting manager. Vincent dealt Peter to her and the day before he relinquished him he slapped a disciplinary warning on him for his abysmal call flow. Many managers would look the other way when their star performers missed points on a grading sheet. However, after Peter betrayed and sold him out to Ed Green, Vincent had to teach him a lesson. It served the traitor right, and this was proof of the three emotions that Vincent could never squash: anger, impatience and revenge.

Vincent quickly took notice of the massive deception from Shelly as he witnessed Dick doing far more than "basic, behind the scenes stuff." That did not stop him, however, from heeding the words she used in calling him a floor general and he took the mantle in cavalier fashion. He compiled reports for the floor that painted the office's strengths and weaknesses in light the reps and managers could see. He went above and beyond to share verbiage and make the office better. And with those steps, he became better.

The reps questioned him daily as to who was really in charge – him, or Dick – noting that Vincent was the one sending out the actual important information, verbiage and scripts, strategies and the stuff they needed and Dick was just following up his e-mails with some lame attempt to get in the last word. Vincent could only smile. Dick may have gotten a temporary lead in the polls but Vincent was not about to "lose." Perception is reality, and the perception was that Vincent was the leader. He probably took it a little too far during this experiment but no one could or would do anything to stop him.

He was going to make himself the only viable candidate for any future real promotion. Period.

Either that, or get out of Shelly's clutches. It very quickly became clear she had lied about Dick's new powers; he promoted a new manager – Phil Colin from a competing office – sat in on all the departmental conference calls, conducted meetings and sat in on terminations. He was doing everything Shelly would have done, minus the smoke breaks and he only left one hour early every day instead of two. The office numbers actually went further down, unbelievably. Vincent's numbers, however, continued to soar.

One of the most difficult things for Vincent over the years has been time like this in limbo with no end in sight to the frustration and little to nothing keeping him sane. The remainder of 2004 saw few changes to that dynamic.

The endless summer of Dick Knoll at the helm seemed to drag on forever. Dick returned to his regular duties in September. However, he conned Shelly into giving him half of the administrative duties that Stacey was unable to handle (though her predecessor Sandy had encountered no difficulties completing them) and a dream team of 15 hand-picked reps from his former team. He had grown tight with Shelly, talking to her daily during his time at the top and Shelly confided in him. She was not one who stayed tight-lipped about things, as she once shared her marital woes with a training class on their first day, but Dick was her opportunity to play mentor. Even a fractured mentor is better than nothing and Dick was eager to lap up the spilt, albeit sour, milk.

Shelly made clear to Dick that she was in his camp; that she tired of Vincent and the fact he always said and did whatever he wanted. Dick secretly monitored Vincent's team and, upon Shelly's return, would slip her calls he disagreed with or would attempt to find any type of disciplinary items on people Vincent called friends. The unfortunate souls on that list were people like Ted or now Jeff, who was quickly becoming fast friends with longtime buds Ted and Vincent.

And when Dick returned, as the management team had added Patrice and Phil and was now "welcoming" back Dick to the fold, it facilitated an office-wide team shakeup. Vincent had seen enough of this to make his head spin: fielding and building a top team from little talent and taking them to the top of the (un)civilized world all while being handed the runts of every training class litter. That prompted him to have a clever idea.

Dick was not well-liked among the personnel of Rockford – his underhanded shenanigans, the way he salivated over terminations of anyone who had a bad call and his discipline before coaching mentality all marred him as an undesirable leader. In addition, he had also promised Ty Monk, a trainer in the office who was formerly one of Dick's top reps, the management spot that ended up going to Phil Colin. It was a purely political move putting Colin in there because he was endorsed by a friend of Shelly's, but it was deceitful nonetheless. The stage had even been set for Ty's transition; he was going to take his current training group into on-job training and make them his team. Ty was one of the many people who sought Vincent and his counsel over the dirty politics of the Knoll regime. And all of that sparked Vincent's idea.

He went to the Cheekwood bargaining table with a detailed proposal. Vincent offered to take the brand new class of 12, pick up two new trainees from a separate class, hand pick 7 people that used to work for him on his award-winning team and would take the office's Union steward, who was last in the department in revenue in an attempt to appease the other managers. It seemed like a no-brainer to the others, as no manager likes breaking in people out of training, much less 14 newbies, and it was a big enough risk that the doubters saw this as something that could deflate Vincent's ego.

Dick was ticked, however, as he wished he had thought of it, and even went around saying that maybe *he* was going to take over that group! In the end, however, Vincent closed the sale by guilting Shelly for all he had been through and proffered that this was a much-needed challenge to keep his head in the game. Two could play at the political spin game. He did not have much, but he was the top manager in the company. Occasionally, that fact alone prompted Shelly to yield on what she felt were minor battles. In this one, Vincent got his way.

He retained Ted and Jeff so he could protect them from Dick and Shelly as much as possible. He held on to some other faithfuls and welcomed the 14 newbies who were ecstatic to be under his tutelage. The first week on the floor, Vincent even jumped on the phone for a couple of them and in five calls sold more than three-quarters of the reps in the office for the day by himself. It was all coming together. Again. And when that happens, something always comes along to spoil the party.

In November, the first full month for the new incarnation of Vincent's team, they were #1 in the company. Another challenge accepted, met and exceeded by Vincent Scott. That said, Vincent realized it was certainly time to go. He had once again set a challenge and obliterated it and there was nothing in his mind left to do here.

He had again come to that same realization, here and now present day 2009, sitting on the verge of the nearing eruption in the ABM Online advertising bureau. He felt the same emotions and had the same thoughts that raced through his mind in all of 2005: being master of his domain growing impatient awaiting the next move.

Other people come and go and are forgotten. He wanted to be remembered for greatness long after he departed; both the sales world and the Earth. People in Rockford to this day remembered him fondly for the energy and support he brought to the table. Some remembered him not so fondly, but the preponderance was a positive reflection on his time there and what he left them. His verbiage was still utilized there years later. His e-mails were still saved by some and read during times of low morale. He had left his mark and that, after all, is all we can do in this life: positively impact others and hope it impacts generations to come.

Another similarity between present day and 2005 was the presence of a woman he ignored at every opportunity to mask his emotions. Then it was Stacey Worth. Now it was Phoebe Wells. Her story is to come, but the utterance of her name was enough to make Vincent coil in disgust at himself for again allowing himself to be hoodwinked.

He had come to put Stacey in perspective during 2005. He realized he could love someone but not need them for his survival. If there was such a thing, which Vincent felt the jury was still out on, whatever he and Stacey had could not have been "true" love, right?

Katie Barnes, a former co-worker and friend of Vincent's, made one prolific statement that stuck with him to this day: that if he was ever going to settle down it would have to be someone who floored him in every way, someone he felt was on his level and challenged him. It was true. He was type-A and much more concerned with the welfare of Elizabeth and of taking over the world so he could fix its problems, so the concept of a doting wife would have to take a backseat. Or maybe not come to fruition. It was not that he had never wanted this companionship. He had convinced himself to forget about it because his search to this point had rendered nothing but pain.

He had put Stacey on some kind of pedestal. It was one that no one, even she, could live up to. But that was also the measure to which he would hold accountable anyone to come. It was one of many reasons Abby failed in his eyes. It is why Phoebe's lies stung him so badly, because he wanted to believe her when she promised to be something she would never be. Vincent had to realize that these people did not put him in their priorities. Therefore, they were not worthy to be his.

2005 tied up loose ends. It provided a few final challenges that completed Vincent's duties for the residential department. It allowed him to put a lot of things in their proper compartments in his mind and his heart.

He watched as Dick Knoll terminated a man the week of his wedding as the rep reached out to a hard-up customer by crediting something that maybe he shouldn't have. Coaching would have been understandable, but termination before his wedding? Vincent watched as Stacey moved into a new house with her husband and showcased pictures of their trip to Hawaii. He watched as Shelly was around less and less and pulled on Vincent's reins when he got out of line with her questionable strategy.

He was still rough in many areas of both life and management style and during that year to come he fine tuned it all by – you guessed it – making more

112

mistakes. A lot of the year was also finding new ways to stay entertained. Ted, Jeff and Vincent made light of as many things as they could, often dragging in a few of the new members to the team who came from Ty's class: Cliff Marlin, Jay Zander and Jane Daughtry. Vincent put them all in close proximity to one another and found that to be the life of the party.

One day doing side-by-side monitoring with Jeff, they came up with creative lines to use based on the coherence of the customers calling in. As soon as they identified the customer as pretty aloof, they dove in, quoting Rolling Stones songs, Stallone movies, or even making as many references to medical terminology or mechanic lingo as possible. A typical line Jeff dropped, "Ma'am, I have no sympathy for the devil that added this to your bill; however I assure you wild horses could not stop me from ensuring you get satisfaction. Start me up, I'm on this and time is on your side. I'll be back in a jumpin' jack flash."

With Phil Colin's name an easy target, the trio blared Genesis and Phil Collins music, serenading one another to strains of "Groovy Kind of Love." They would post pictures of the singer with word bubbles touting items like "Our TWO HEARTS have a GROOVY KIND OF LOVE for ABM speedy Internet service. Cut through the LAND OF CONFUSION and TAKE ME HOME where I can enjoy it with my family. I WISH IT WOULD RAIN DOWN enough money that I could buy everyone this product. I CAN'T DANCE but anybody can surf with ease with ABM! Even SUSSUDIO agrees that TONIGHT, TONIGHT, TONIGHT we are going to surf online with ABM and doing business with a competitor is taking your money and THROWING IT ALL AWAY! The power of ABM is IN THE AIR TONIGHT. Let it reach out to you with its INVISIBLE TOUCH. THAT'S ALL!"

Cheesiness like that abounded. It was the only way Vincent could maintain sanity in this otherwise mundane, monotonous existence.

Vincent continued his obliteration of Dick on the sales report, month after month. Shelly was back to telling Vincent that there was some kind of end in sight, that a peer of hers would surely retire or depart in a competing office and she would throw his hat in the ring. He had his hopes up that the inevitable would soon come.

And it did.

In early March 2005, it was announced in a management meeting that Dick Knoll was chosen over Vincent and would be promoted to take over the last place Oklahoma City office. It was yet another dagger to the heart. It was a heart that could take little more.

As shocked, betrayed and shaken as Vincent was his initial move was to be first in line to congratulate Dick, shake his hand and walk away. He ignored the familiar e-mail from Shelly to talk to her if he needed "someone to talk to." She had done enough.

Vincent was flabbergasted, much like every other person who had any idea of Dick's work ethic and inability to effectively manage employees. The attempts to console Vincent came from all sides but it was not until drowning the event with Jack Daniel's that any solace was realized.

Initially, Vincent fell into a lapse of two weeks' apathy: he lost the ability to push himself harder and farther at work. He had created everything in the office that had given them any success, ran the top team and was insanely popular with the reps. He deflected questions about how he was doing with pure lethargy, just explaining he had nothing more to give and clearly his dominance and superior work ethic were not what the company was looking for.

However after that initial sting, he finally came to realize that no matter what falsehoods were emitted from the mouth of Shelly Cheekwood that she was his worst enemy and Dick's jealousy was the biggest thing that brought out the bad in him. Vincent emerged with the realization that being the best and doing the most work was irrelevant. He stopped taking his work home. He tried to be less obsessive with his dominance at all costs mentality. The decision to jettison that mentality actually brought him some semblance of peace.

Shortly thereafter, Dirk Slabor resigned from ABM amidst a fallout with Ed Green due to his own arrogance backfiring. He left to help run some fly-by-night competitor and was never heard from again. Dick Knoll quickly started terminating Oklahoma City employees in hopes he could lift their results. Of course, it did not work.

Slabor was replaced by Dana Warsaw, becoming the next in a line of leaders Vincent would see in his career. Every time a new boss enters the picture there is always a sense of hope; could this be the person who needs to be impressed and will actually reward for hard work and stellar performance? Vincent has seen so many of these people come and go and has come to realize that if there is a Shelly or a Keith Dickhauser wedged between him and that person, he is not going to get noticed.

With Dick gone, with talk of demoting Patrice and promoting pal Jeff Mason, with no one left in Rockford for Shelly to turn to so she had to tread lightly with Vincent, things got a little better. Phil Colin had relied too much on Dick while he was there and was headed towards the dark side. With him gone, Phil started looking at the coach-first methods of Vincent, saw them working and it led him back on a path towards the forces of good.

Lucy was stripped from sales duties and given a meaningless special project as her approach led to last-place performance no matter who was under her guidance. Once that change was made, the teams were split between Vincent, Phil and Patrice. Vincent, ever the negotiator, convinced Shelly to let

114

him hand pick a cross section of 34 people while Phil and Patrice both got 20, giving him a bigger span of control. With it being in the best interests of the office, she allowed him to do it.

The new incarnation of his team found its way to #1 pretty much immediately per usual and he lifted Shelly to the top spot. Vincent did the math: without his team's numbers, Shelly's office would have been 7th out of 14 teams in their district. And the first time Vincent met Dana Warsaw, he was the #1 manager in the company. No better place to be.

Dana visited monthly and would take the management team to dinner and drinks. Initially it seemed Dana would be a breath of fresh air. She seemed receptive to Vincent's ideas and genuinely interested in what he had to say. She actually called him when he was the top manager in her district her first month at the helm.

Stacey would purposely sit next to Vincent during these visits. She would try to find angles to talk to him, like asking him about rumors regarding him being romantically linked to staffing manager Jackie Parsons. She would find random reasons to touch him like asking if a watch he had owned for a year was new and making contact with it. Stacey looked flustered any time one of the ladies made mention of Vincent's eternal bachelor status and he blew off questions about whether he would ever settle down.

The existence of these lingering flirtations was the biggest reason it took Vincent so long to get over her; she wanted attention while once again not getting it at home. The prospect of rekindling may or may not have been there but Vincent knew he was not going to allow himself to go down that path another time. He would ignore the advances and regret it later but all the while knew that until or unless she laid out all the cards he was doing the right thing despite his emotional consequences.

He typically left once Stacey had a couple of drinks and her advances became obvious to the table. He tried to ignore being crazy about this woman, but was faced with her daily. The allure of a challenging, intriguing female in his workplace always outweighed the knowledge the fallout would be ten times worse.

He would make his escape from such events and use bourbon to try to make his memories and pain go away.

Dana Warsaw revealed her true colors not long after by saying she expected everyone to have a termination for call quality under their belts. She came to be known as "The Saw," as every time she came to town she made an example of someone in the office and "sawed" them off at the knees for a singular bad call of the hundreds they would field that day.

Vincent continued applying for every job he could because Shelly told him he would be releasable. When he was called by an area manager in another office whose wife worked for Vincent he was stoked; it was a proposal management gig where he would spend his day writing. Shelly quickly changed her tune, refused to let him interview and blocked him from making any attempts at a lateral move. He was stuck unless he found a promotion. And in this hostile climate, that was unlikely. And every day he stayed here, he ran the risk of taking his challenges of Shelly's inadequacy one step too far.

In an August conference call, Dana opened the floor to suggestions on departmental improvements. Vincent took it very seriously and saw this as an opportunity to be noticed for something positive on a grand stage.

He wrote a 9-page synopsis of the ailments of the department, how to fix them and how to make the entire experience better for all, using feedback from managers and reps alike. He spent hours concocting it and was extremely candid; so much so that Shelly seemed hesitant to let Vincent actually expose these truths to her boss. However, the fact Dana never read it made clear how his future fit in with this cesspool.

In September Jeff Mason, after his dangled promotion never occurred, finally got out, heading to the advertising bureau where his new girlfriend had a job in proofreading. It was with that move Vincent took a serious look at his options; could this be a potential venue he should pursue or should he resign? Nothing was worth what he was going through.

He actually typed his resignation letter and kept it in his binder. Still to this day, it was there ready to come out at a moment's notice. From time to time he would re-read or tweak it and had actually done so not long ago as the torture from Keith Dickhauser had reached fever pitch.

Vincent stopped reminiscing and continued his morning rituals of compiling sales reports and shooting them out to the teams. It was time again to re-focus on this final sales day of November 2009.

He sorted, cut and pasted and color-coded everything as he saw fit and issued praises and biting commentary where he deemed prudent. This was the biggest reason he could never walk away. Finally, after all those years he toiled as a manager under incompetent regimes he was leading his own salesforce. He was still under a bungling administration that treated him and his team like garbage, but he enjoyed aspects of the job he had created for himself and most days he came out 51%-to-49% in favor of staying.

Vincent was a statistical junkie; he always had to be the best at everything. Those were the challenges he would present himself and that is what kept his head in the game. Now he was the conductor, the Gepetto manipulating the sales statistics and it was a rewarding place to be. He knew his thoroughbreds cared about where they placed in these areas. This is why he went to painstaking detail to make sure every statistic and every top earner was accounted for.

116

Making the people see where they appeared, where they were strong, where they were deficient and where their peers appeared versus them in every category: these were his motives. While he could not control it he hoped everyone would latch on to at least one of the statistics and benefit from his pearls of wisdom. Showering his team with statistics was a quick, easy way of impacting everyone with relatively little time spent before they even arrived to work.

For that was the fun to the statistics: breathing life into them. If someone can produce ten times that of another, clearly the "another" should and could step up their game.

After sending his reports and witticisms it was time to prepare the leads for the day's dialing. It is a science he thoroughly enjoys. The department was not as ramped up as the residential team but it was good enough for Vincent. Vincent felt like a founding father here. The scripts, the reports and his own job were his brainchild. Only he knew how these things worked. Vincent was happy with what he had accomplished here. Granted, he could do so much more on such a larger scale but he had single-handedly added millions of dollars to the company's bottom line. Sadly, no one was trumpeting that to the right people.

He had used what he felt were good ideas from the residential division. He jettisoned a large amount of things he felt did not work. One thing he certainly learned was why they tried to make their employees robots: because more often than not, employees left to their own devices are hapless and hopeless. The problem, however? Making those rules also govern the people who deserved to be allowed to run wild. Like Vincent.

When Vincent moved from Rockford to Greenfield, he obviously also saw the opportunity to get a clean slate with a new boss. He was able to stay in line with his perception of the goals in this new department for quite some time. It was not until he worked directly for Dickhauser that he saw how corrupt the man was.

The last day of any month to him was a magical day, one where anything could and often did happen. All could be forgiven and be right with the world at just the right sales call. In a call center, this was the type of stuff you live for.

As time ticked towards 8 AM, Vincent started printing out 17 copies of the reports he wanted at the meeting. He grabbed his weathered binder he had gotten on his first day in the advertising bureau 3 ½ years ago, tucked the reports into it and made his way to the conference room. It was game time.

As he turned the corner heading towards the meeting room he walked right past Phoebe Wells and her current boyfriend, overweight and goofy-looking sales rep Denny Price. He acknowledged neither.

Vincent met Phoebe on his first day in ABM advertising. She certainly stood out as she wore outfits that flaunted her fantastic figure; she had bleached blond hair and a significant amount of makeup. The voice and laugh Vincent once found charming now screeched in his brain like nails on a chalkboard.

Phoebe was a thrill-seeker always attracted to the wrong guy. She would set her sights on the guy in a committed relationship or the one who was forbidden fruit. In Vincent's case he was even more appealing because he was in a position of authority and any personal interaction between them would be taboo.

Phoebe would coax her prey into the web, promising the earth, moon and stars, showing initial affection and acting like she cared. Her true colors came out when she would start making time for everyone but the guy she was "committed" to and failing to follow through on any and all commitments. She had done it to the father of her daughter. She did it to the guy she married and the guys in between. She did it to Vincent. And, after Vincent finally cast her off, she did the coup d'état; she spit in his face by contradicting everything she told Vincent by bunking down with a rep in their building.

His transformation into cold-hearted bastard had taken another major leap and he had Phoebe to thank.

Now, Vincent's life was all about Elizabeth and the job. She was his salvation; he had endured a lot of pain over the last couple years fighting to be with her but it was all worth it. The pains he had felt were dwarfed anyway when compared to that of relinquishing the person he loved most to the person who had hurt him most every two weeks due to a custody arrangement.

That was where Vincent Scott was now. He had fought a lot for a lot of things. First, it was his career, then his subordinates and now his daughter. He was always on the side of right, but his rage, intolerance and occasional quests for vengeance would do nothing but hold him back or hinder his fight. He was not perfect, but he was trying to be.

He did not need or want for anything else. Sure, he enjoyed writing his book and hoped he could touch lives with it and his teachings. But as he climbed the corporate ladder he realized that more and more loonies came out of the woodwork to take potshots rather than to take notice of what they should be doing that would make them successful.

He walked into the conference room and, like King Arthur, took a seat at the head of the large round table. He set down his binder and coffee and took one last deep breath before the mayhem would begin.

* * *

"The Selling Game" by Vincent Scott
Chapter 10:
TIME ON YOUR SIDE –
THE IMPORTANCE OF EFFICIENCY AND TIME MANAGEMENT

The Rolling Stones claimed it was on their side. Marty McFly had to get back in it. Jean Claude Van Damme, if you recall (which most of you likely will not) was a cop of it. It is one of life's most precious gifts yet many of us take it for granted. It is time. Time is money; whoever uttered those words knew what they were talking about.

Early in our world's history, mankind created a means to track time in seconds, minutes, hours, days, and eventually months and years. Surely, while they were etching prehistoric cave drawings, they knew that one day efficiency statistics and metric reports would be a prominent fixture in the sales world and would add immense value to the human race. Boy – they were certainly ahead of *their* time.

With everything life has a way of throwing at you, when that alarm clock sounds it is easy to lose focus on our mission of juggling everything we must accomplish in a given day. After all, we have to make ourselves beautiful, possibly get kids or significant others ready, be productive citizens and follow the Golden Rule, all in the same day! Often, we do not prioritize effectively and allow lesser priorities to the forefront only to allow our time allotted to those projects to expand and cut off the things we may not put in their proper place. This is what can get us into trouble.

Wasting time is like wasting food, clothes, water or money. It doesn't help anyone – least of all the person doing the wasting – and other people suffer as a result. Realize this: just an extra 30 minutes per day of talking to customers equates to an extra 2 ½ hours of talking per week and 10 extra hours per 20-sales-day month. That could be injecting 3 or more additional days' worth of work into your month. Who couldn't use that kind of time? Believe me, at the end of a disappointing month, if someone said out of the clear blue, "Hey, I'm the great and powerful Oz and I am going to give you another three days to accomplish your September goal," you would jump all over it, right? Well, basically that is the power YOU have when you decide to make your day a more productive one.

In a sales environment, whichever side of the fence you are on – management or non-management – you have heard the term "efficiency." Likely you have looked upon this nugget as your enemy: something you have been

119

chastised for, something you have tried to no avail to figure out or something you have flat out given up on (or, unfortunately in some cases, never paid attention to to begin with). Now we are going to talk about something that would make Mick and Keith proud: getting time on your side.

After all, it is easy for a manager to play Monday morning quarterback and look back on your prior day's statistics and judge you, right? Sure it is, but when you crunch the numbers and realize you could have taken five less walks to the printer while putting together a novel-sized proposal your customer will put in the trash can or made three fewer circles driving around the gas station to check out the cutie pumping gas, you can learn from your mistakes. This type of analysis and corrective action can make all the difference in the world next time you leave the huddle and head to the snap.

Constantly looking back at past behavior (not dwelling on mistakes, mind you) and bettering yourself because of it is how we grow as salespeople and human beings. If we do not learn from our mistakes we inevitably repeat them and garner the same poor results. The reason time management and utilization of efficiency as measuring sticks are discussed here is because you can never undervalue how much they impact your bottom line. Poor management of your time can greatly inhibit you from reaching your potential.

Time management in a sales occupation is one of the most critical elements. Everything you are judged upon is based on qualitative and quantitative measurements contrived from actual numbers and productivity results. How many visits you schedule, calls you make and how much time you devote to the cause are all part of that quantitative dimension. You can be the greatest objection-handler in the world, the most career-focused person on the planet but if you fail to manage your day wisely, you will never reach your potential. I have seen it happen plenty of times: someone has a solid conversion rate, but if they are not engaging enough customers they never become first rate. Even if you are oozing with talent, failure to put it into play leads nowhere fast.

It all begins the moment you wake up and constitutes everything you squeeze into your day, whether at work or play. Whether your manager brings you doughnuts or you are in a coffee club, something needs to get you going. No matter how well you map your day, things will pop up from out of nowhere that will try and sometimes succeed in throwing you off course. The trick here is that these unannounced and sometimes unwelcome visitors to your schedule do not care about whether or not you meet your commitments. However, your supervisors do, and you should, too.

Be smart about it. Never schedule your *entire* day in advance leaving no margin for error; have some method to the madness and prioritize the items that must be tackled but leave plenty of wiggle room to allow for the unexpected. A pipeline customer you have been waiting to close for weeks may give you a ring and unexpectedly take up a chunk of your day. Leave some cushion for the unexpected but be sure to finish everything that is expected of you. The most important thing to keep in mind when it comes to management of your time is being able to justify your actions and account for any time you could have been pounding the pavement or hammering the phones with justifiable facts that will eventually or already did equate to revenue.

Allow plenty of time to arrive to work. The last thing you need is to get your day started rushing to arrive on time. The moments before your sales day begin are when you mentally prepare for what is to come. It is also often when you put together your game plan, get coffee or just sit in meditative silence before the melee of the day begins. When that starting gun sounds the start of the race, there is no turning back. You also do not want to get into a habit of walking in late, especially if you want to be promoted someday. Superiors do not get into the habit of promoting those notorious for strolling in past the school bell.

Wholly embrace the numbers' game; this means it can be manipulated in your favor if you tackle it the right way. Statistically speaking, every job has a close ratio. If you are making enough calls and your flow is sound, you should have no problem eking out a spot for yourself at the top of the charts. However, even if your call flow is on point, if not enough decision-makers are hearing your value story, you will never reach your apex. Alas, there is nothing more tragic in the game of sales.

Never judge yourself against others in any peer group who are not meeting minimum expectation in that area no matter what rung of the corporate ladder you find yourself on. Regardless of other people's performances, you always want to look at your results versus the goal in place, whatever the area. Any job with any purpose has goals, measurements of work and expectations that show you what level you should achieve. Targeting status quo will equate to just such a result, if that. Targeting whoever is at the top of the heap will, in turn, result in the best case scenario. Aim as high as you can – even higher than you may think you can reach – for that will keep you shooting for an outcome that will accomplish your aptitude.

Using the poor performance of a peer as an excuse for settling for less leads to nothing but mediocrity. Do not fall into this trap; it is for the underachievers of the world. If there is a goal, it can be hit. Hit it.

Efficiency reports take the guesswork out. They are not absolute but they do not lie; they chart the amount of time you were at work, available to make or take calls and how effectively you executed your day. Use these items to your advantage.

The healthy balance of all statistics makes the star. The reports exist for a reason. Make your reason striving to be the best with a healthy balance in every area.

Whether your manager requires it or not, it is important to be able to account for your day and how you spend it. Hammering the pavement or the phone early and often is essential to building the momentum that will carry you throughout your day. How you approach your day, just like how you approach your call flow, sets the tone for the end result. Once you connect the dots through the day's events you can start to see what was worth the investment of your time and what was not.

For instance, I have seen salespeople take a huge chunk of their day prepping or preparing individual accounts. In some cases, such as account management scenarios when you are assigned those accounts until the end of time, this is understandable if not done in excess. However, I have also seen reps prep accounts when all they are doing is cold-calling or going door-to-door in a hunter role where the odds of them even speaking to someone are slim-to-none. This type of prep is grossly overrated; it does not help to become over-prepared for a situation if it is at the expense of making other calls and drumming up additional business. This is where analysis of efficiency is extremely valuable.

No manager *should* want an employee that shows up to work just to throw 150-200 calls on a report and call it a day with nothing to show for it. On the same token, you can schedule ten visits with business owners or homeowners to hock your wares to the average seller's three or four appointments per day but if you are not closing, you are just posing. While you need to be provided a snapshot daily of your efficiency performance from the day prior, if you are not taking advantage of it as a learning tool, you are doing yourself and your managers a disservice. These reports expose missed opportunities and if you have any desire to better yourself, which I believe you do, this is where you should start.

If you spent more time preparing for calls than being on them, what does that tell you? If your average talk time per call is short, are you doing an effective job of transitioning through the flow and taking and maintaining control of the call? Say you are having long conversations – sure, that looks good on paper but if they are not resulting in sales, what should you do to modify your flow to address this deficiency? The more you talk, especially unnecessarily, the more you run the risk of that customer getting out of the conversation without closing. You run out of time and have to start all over if you ever speak to them again. Talking to hear yourself talk or thinking the customer wants you to do that have no place here. Your prime directive is finding the appropriate mix between talk time and sales results so you know you are at your optimum levels.

122

Take advantage of everyone whose attention you are lucky enough to capture as soon as you get in front of them. When you have gleaned the answers you need from fact-finding, it is time to visit the magical realm of Pitch-Land. After that pitch, it is time to overcome objections and keep going in for the close until it sticks. You have no time for anything else. Analyze where you stand in that equation and trim the fat. Keep an eye on the clock, be it internally if face-to-face or your computer if over the phone, and realize you have to make every minute count.

If you feel the need for a long-winded conversation, be sure you have a pitch on the table first and that the lengthy part of the conversation is overcoming objections and attempting to close. That way, even if the customer makes an early exit, you have your cards on the table and there is nothing left that needs to be done but the close. I know some of you fancy yourself this "relationship-building" salesperson. That is fine and good. But if you spend too much time spinning your wheels in build-up, you will never get to the close. Obviously, you can't sell if you don't pitch. You also can't close if you never hear the customer's objections. Leave plenty of time for these essential segments of the sale and you are giving yourself a better shot at a successful conclusion.

I want to make sure you understand that attention to efficiency and adherence to your schedule is NOT micromanagement. That word is one of the most often misused words in the sales language. Checking with vocabulary guru Noah Webster, one would find the definition is "to manage or control with excessive attention to small details." The amount of time you are available to talk and are talking to potential customers is far from a small detail. Furthermore, a report or two is not excessive and the details of the reports sure aren't minor. And good managers are not afraid to use them.

Afraid to look at them sometimes, but never afraid to use them.

Athletes who are injured or fatigued after sporadic stretches of playing time are less valuable than those who can go the distance or outlast them, regardless of the statistics they put up in those short bursts. Don't get me wrong; there is a happy medium between efficiency and results – if you push yourself too hard or too far trying to make or take too many calls or be on the phone too long, you will burn yourself out (the real kind). However, far too often there are people with a natural gift that cut themselves short because they do not wisely budget their time.

From a rep standpoint, efficiency should be a tool to expose additional opportunity. From a management standpoint, it is a whole another ballgame; this is where holding people accountable and enforcing subordinates' justification of their time come into play. An effective manager will furnish and produce these reports daily to guide and help, not to criticize and tear down. They will keep the information readily available and point it out to their teams consistently all while ensuring the offenders have to answer for their inadequacies. Ineffective managers have no idea how to police it, are inconsistent in doing so and let bad time management run rampant because they either have no clue what they are doing, are too lazy to care, or have no one to show them how it's done.

Remember: there is only one number in sales that is absolute – revenue. Whatever tracking method that is used to track dollars and cents tells the tale of the tape. While everything else pales in comparison, if you are not taking advantage of your time you should and typically will be counseled by management on how you can better optimize your day. An athlete with drastically reduced minutes will not score as many points.

Your efficiency time is the one statistic that you can personally manipulate. There is no chance involved, unlike your results. You do not have control over how many people will answer the door, listen to your story or what objections you will hear. However, you do have control over how early and often you are doing your job.

You have personal control over your adherence and efficiency and you need to flex that muscle. That phone is your friend, or at least, it wants to be; it does not discriminate, does not hold grudges and will always give you what you seek even if you try to forsake it. You have to take advantage of the numbers' game and the fact this is a contact sport. It's not all quantity and it's not all quality. It is cross-section at the nexus of both.

Pay attention to how long you have been in the conversation at hand. Remember, these customers do not allot the time necessary for you to explain and illustrate every idiosyncrasy of every product. They are there long enough for you to do some quick fact-finding and make a pitch, but they will not always stick around for the entire main course or dessert. Not every call or visit will be a one-call close but if there is to be a second conversation you had better get as far in the first as possible. That takes time management on your part and you have to get it right.

Rapport is great but dancing around topics or asking a lot of needless questions that serve no purpose while your call ticker or watch counts off thirty minutes and you still have not reached the presentation is an immense waste of time. You do not want to undercook or overcook your meal – it has to be just right. After many successful calls you will master this craft but you need to constantly work on tightening up the process until it is as lean and mean as possible.

When in doubt, here is the rule of thumb: everything that comes out of the customer's mouth should be addressed and acknowledged, then overcome and deflected if it detracts from your flow all while you make a seamless transition into your next topic on the agenda. Do not stick around in any particular leg of the call flow for too long and do not let your own hesitation of what to pitch prevent your progress. Let common sense prevail; if you effectively ask the questions you need answers to, your customer will guide you to the pitch best for them. You dictate where the call goes but leave nothing untouched because if you fail to address any concern or objection anywhere along the way it will only fester and take you down later.

Top sellers master optimization of their time. That is not to say they are on the phone or on sales calls all day every day. It is to say they have found the healthiest balance.

It really all boils down to accountability of your day. One of my mottos has been that if I can justify something I will do it. If you are at work for 8 hours in a day, you need to be able to account for all 8 hours. Simple, right? Granted, there are breaks, lunches, bathroom breaks, etc. Those are typical factors that impact everyone. But as we broke down before, adding 30 additional minutes per day of dialing, meetings or being available to take calls is 10 additional hours in a typical 20 sales day month. Forget how happy your manager could be; this could make or break you.

Also, always remember that a lead's warmth diminishes the moment after you touch it. It is like the depreciation of a car once you drive it off the lot. What this means is that if a lead is warm, strike while that iron is hot and get the customer to close the deal. The more time that passes between you engaging that customer and you trying to get them to sign on the dotted line, the greater the chance they will escape. On the same token, far too often people spend their time trying to continually chase down someone. By calling the same customer over and over again just because a long time ago in a galaxy far, far away you had one out of 1,000 attempted proposals pan out does not make it right. You are always better off drumming up a new potential customer than beating the hell out of the dead horse that is a touched lead. Flash it or flush it; tout the sale or get it out of your system. Play the odds. New and fresh beats recycled every time.

Some sales jobs and some customers dictate that you must occasionally bow to the request for a proposal or to "send some information." The problem is that far too many salespeople cling to this excuse of "being polite" to the extreme by backing out of the sale the moment a gatekeeper or decision-maker tries to get rid of them with this line. Let's face it: that is all they are doing. Now, if you have gone around and around with a customer, answered every objection they have and still deem the lead valuable even after they refuse to close, settling for this may be your only option. If the customer called you and is asking for a service and you did your due diligence in making a personalized recommendation and meeting their needs and answering all questions, it is still likely you can close them later. However, in the vast majority of all cases, a proposal is a complete waste of time.

The reason is because your time is better spent drumming up new business than chasing one person that will never close. Call #1 is when you got to know them, hit them with all your best shots and overcame their objections; you will never reach that plateau of greatness again. Unless you have loosened the pickle jar and are practically guaranteed they will answer the next time you call to close the sale, cut bait. Do not let them leave you twisting in the wind; you want them to dump you or marry you. Call them out, all while respecting their time but requesting respect for your own.

Of course, there are exceptions to every rule. Someone will read this and question my sanity because, of course, you did once upon a time call someone fifty times and finally closed them. My challenge to you is this: could that time have been better spent and yielded fifty brand new calls that could have led to multiple sales where the fifty you made yielded just one? Think about it.

Sales is a quick hit, run-and-gun playground where numbers reign king. Efficiency is important because you have to make enough calls and enough witty statements to people that need what you have.

Maximize every day, both in sales and in life. Squeeze the most juice out of everything that comes your way, be it a lead or your day. When you signed on to whatever position you are in, you pledged allegiance and that you wanted a career, to make money and to be successful. Prove it. Hopefully those are still needs and wants and, if they are, remember that time is money. Use it well.

Productivity is important in everything we do. Before a work day, I wake up at 5:30 AM, hit the snooze a few times and around 6 something goes off in my brain like the voice of Michael Douglas in *Wall Street*: "This is your wake-up call, pal. Go to work." Minutes later, I am in the shower and half an hour later I am out the door (unless, of course, I am getting my daughter ready which takes another 15-30 minutes depending on her level of cooperation). I don't like to contend with traffic and my best ideas come on that drive to work.

I want to be there long before the school bell sounds because yes – the early bird really does get the worm. I get more accomplished before the troops arrive than at any other part of the day and I take full advantage of it. I recommend you try the same. The beginning of your day sets the tone for the rest, which is why you do not want to be running late in a panic and waltzing in without a second to spare.

Methods to track productivity are in place to impact the variables that lead to your end result. If the sum of your parts does not equal or exceed the expectation, no one is wrong to expect you to change the variables in the equation. That is what tracking your productivity accomplishes. If you are blowing out your revenue expectations, great. However, if you are not, and your efficiency numbers are not flawless, what on earth are you doing?

A lot of people are good salespeople because they tested things and failed before finding their niche. I, too, have fallen for the "just send me something" line of bull once or twice. It is human nature for us to want to believe that putting together a good-looking proposal that took us an hour to type will catch someone's eye and they may actually make a purchase because of it. It's that same naive part of us that deep down wants to believe that the entire human race will do the right thing for their fellow man and woman if given the chance, or be honest, loyal or faithful. I hate to break it to you: all of these things are illusions. Trust in anything too much, you're gonna get burned.

The reason it is so hard for us to let go of these "customers" is because we are afraid to lose them; like a dying relationship we think that means it's time to ignore requests of leaving alone an uninterested partner and turning on our charms full blast. We truly think there is a chance they will receive the proposal and it will not end up in the trash can. We truly think they will read that 20-paragraph e-mail diatribe we put together. We believe in Santa Claus. Actually, I'd bank on Santa getting stuck in my chimney before I would bank on any of the aforementioned myths. These customers are like that weary soon-to-be former lover; your overtures are ignored and the flowers wind up in the waste basket.

Think about it; if the customer was too busy to take just a smidgen of their time to listen to someone who was passionate about the product and could answer their questions on demand, do you really think they will peruse the novella you faxed them? Sorry, but get real. Okay, if you want to get technical, yes, there is a chance. Feel lucky? Buy a lottery ticket instead.

Again, we cannot be afraid of losing what we do not have. Fear costs us more than anything in life and in sales because it keeps us from going for what we deserve. It may be fear of rocking the boat by offering what the customer really needs over what you think they will say yes to. It may be fear of giving the customer a little bit of pushback because you think they might buy something even though they won't even listen to reason. It could even be fear of defending yourself on the phone and standing your ground because you don't want to piss them off. Activities such as these do only one thing: they shift the balance of power on the call in favor of the customer.

If you do not truly believe the customer needs what you are peddling more than you need them, you are at their mercy and you might as well stand in their driveway with a cardboard sign and beg for money. Simply accepting your customer's control over the call is as submissive as Jim Carrey's character in *Dumb and Dumber* celebrating one in a million odds by saying, "So you're telling me there's a chance?!" Grasping at straws is more like it. Reek of desperation and it will show in your results.

Since you are not asking the person you have been batting your eyes at for weeks out to the movies, it is A-OK (and actually preferable) to hear "no" right out of the gates. You should expect it and meet it with tenacity.

Anything but a "yes" is a "no." You do not want a "maybe so." I know that sounds bizarre but I took my sales management career to unparalleled heights when I convinced my team of that. The "maybe so" lingers on like that relationship where you twist in the wind in limbo while they will not tell you it's over but they treat you like you do not exist. Tell the customer, "Look, your time is valuable to me and my time is valuable, too. I spend all day every day signing customers up for programs that generate revenue. You wouldn't still be on the phone if you weren't remotely interested, but honestly, why would you wait to pull the trigger?"

Why would anyone wait another day if they believed in the results you promise?

People succumb to the "send me something" rebuttal for the same reasons previously noted: they do not want to rock the boat for fear of scaring off a potential customer. I say risk it. You have nothing to lose and you are no worse for wear. Rather than trying to call that customer 20 times over the next month and getting their gatekeeper as your new best friend, they saved you that trouble and you called 20 diverse customers, some of whom will buy. They did you a favor by cutting you loose. You should thank them. Literally the only thing that will change in between now and two weeks from now when sitting around thinking will magically make up their mind for them is that they will miss out on several opportunities to use what you have to offer. They are not going to think about it and buy later. Don't fall for it. When someone in a relationship "needs space," it's over! The same applies here.

Getting over that obstacle in your own regimen will drastically improve your time management, your efficiency and your success. No amount of *War and Peace*-length e-mails or proposals is going to force their hand better than your time with them in person or over the phone. Believe me, when it comes to "pipeline" just don't let it linger too long. It's like fresh meat; it should not stay in your refrigerator for more than three days. Grill it or put it on ice before it sucks your productivity down the garbage disposal.

I can tackle every time-related topic as it relates to sales except for laziness. Unfortunately, that coupled with a bad attitude and a defeatist outlook can spell the biggest disaster for foreboding results in this area. Think about all the reasons you should care about the time you allot to tasks and how you budget it. The pros outweigh the cons and when it comes to friends in the sales game, Father Time should be the one you want in your camp most.

Time is on our side until we fail to make it our ally. Every tick of the clock is time you can be investing in your well of leads, your team, yourself and your company. In the end, those are the relationships you need to satisfy during your stint wherever you are. It is what you make of it and the time you spend doing any of those things is in investment in your future.

Undoubtedly win, lose or draw time will still march on. Just ask the Byrds: there unquestionably is a time to be born, a time to die; a time to cold call, a time to close business in style. We have all the time in the world, but it's what we do with it that defines us.

If you're not the best salesperson, be the best time manager and no one will know the difference.

*   *   *

8 AM marks the beginning of the sales day for the management team. Of course, many waft in anywhere from 8 to 8:05 on a good day, sometimes later. Vincent has tried to clamp down on it a few times in the past but, like anything else, it works for a while and then they relapse. This is one of few areas Vincent picks and chooses his battles. If the department is having a rare lull, he may take exception but otherwise he tries to be lenient about it.

After a few minutes they are assembled. To Vincent's left at the table sits Mark Rogers, his lone counterpart in the division. To call him an equal would not be comparing apples to apples as Vincent's few weaknesses are Mark's strong points and Mark's shortcomings mostly through lack of experience are Vincent's bread and butter.

Vincent had no ill will towards him. In fact, as time went by Vincent actually started to respect him. Mark had been a rep under Dickhauser's tutelage years ago and when Keith started rounding up people to become managers in his new center he tapped "The Boys" whether qualified or not. When Dickhauser saw the opportunity to move him to commandeer a new inbound venture under their umbrella with ridiculously low objectives, he did so and those numbers masked Mark's inability to achieve results.

Mark meant well and played the political game well, which is why Vincent suspected he would be the type of guy the company wanted. It was nothing like Dick Knoll, who he had to actually try to whip on the sales report. Mark did not try to sabotage Vincent behind his back and his results were no danger to those of Vincent's.

Continuing around the horn to his left, sat Scott Kinsey, overseer of all clerical and commission functions. A very pious and condescending fellow he was. Kinsey was a sanctimonious bastard who was nothing more than an overpaid accountant, making a salary more than twice that of pretty much all of the sales managers. The man was a computer wizard but his people skills and ability to work as part of a team were pathetic.

Vincent sardonically regarded Kinsey the greatest salesman in the business, however, as he somehow sold Dickhauser that there were no problems with clerical and commission items while reps and managers screamed bloody murder about them. Kinsey had recently gone through a divorce and it made him all the more biting with his commentary. Kinsey and the managers battle regularly but Dickhauser refuses to keep him in check due to the tight-knit boys' club that exists to protect one another.

Next to Scott was Danny Boyd. Another of "The Boys" from way back, he had been exiled from Dickhauser's old team after having an affair with a married direct subordinate. He came on board the fledgling division and took over a stacked team that regularly ranked second after Vincent's. When Vincent got the job running the salesforce that Danny had also interviewed for, his spite for Vincent grew and the two of them clashed frequently.

Betty Cross was next at the table. She had spent years developing ad campaigns and joined the team when her job was downsized. She served as liaison with the Labor department, handled special projects and was one of the few people Vincent enjoyed talking to on a regular basis. She actually seemed to understand him. Her only drawback was that it took her half an hour to explain something that should take five minutes. Vincent's impatient nature caused some rifts over his impulse to walk away mid-thought but overall they got along fluidly.

The motherly Helen Johnson was next to Betty. Nary could a disparaging word be said about the woman, she was nice as could be. In her early 50's, she had been with the business for quite a time, mostly in service capacities. She was good at saying uplifting or inspirational things, but did not have the apathy and killer instinct to perform adequately here. She could not have the tough conversations and keep her troops in line. Be that as it may, she was the den mother and everyone loved her.

Maria Fernandez was next – a case of a book you do not judge by its cover. She had a small build, a short woman of Spanish descent who was strikingly beautiful and deliberate in her mannerisms. If you saw her on the street you would think her timid; the irony being she was anything but. Maria was the top rep in the history of the team and a bulldog on the phones. Vincent previously had the pleasure of working with her on his own team and once he took over the floor she was one of the first he promoted. Her results had not taken off in management as quickly as she would have liked but Vincent helped her stay the course and she learned quite a bit from the woman sitting to her left, Gina Baker.

130

Gina was something else. She had been with the company 9 years, mostly in service functions and had come on board to Dickhauser's team the same day Vincent did. The two of them clashed at times as managers as Gina was another strong-willed individual who would do whatever it took to win. She did not have the kind of success she was looking for early on and often relied on intimidation with her reps to get the job done. When Vincent took the helm he saw in Gina a very moldable employee who had a lot of the tools in place. Gina had no qualms about speaking her mind and telling her subordinates what she thought of them, yet at that point her criticisms were mostly bad. Vincent tried to help Gina harness that and find a balance. And now she was the top manager in the department for the second straight year.

Haley Jones sat next to Gina. Vincent remembered when he first met her, as she came on board in early 2007, another of those Dickhauser recruited from his outside sales days. Her father was Dickhauser's first boss, mentor and friend. Vincent had thought her strikingly attractive and could see why she had been an outside sales rep. Over time, they had an interesting dynamic as they often had different views on but their combined efforts made for a healthy sales endeavor. She helmed an offshoot team that contacted recently acquired customers and helped them tour their new programs. Vincent had annexed that team for himself in early 2009 after they went several months without scratching the surface of their expectations. They had not missed expectation a single month since Vincent took over.

He knew she was another that talked poorly about him behind his back. But again, he was not above using the fact that these people needed him to his advantage.

Haley's best friends in the business were to her left, Adam Sandberg and George Flaker. Sandberg had been an outside rep with her and they came on board the online division the same day. Sandberg had been a force to be reckoned with as a manager, competing with Vincent at times, and he made the move to the lucrative inbound team. He was sidelined by stress issues, mostly caused by working with Dickhauser, and was now returned to the fold. After a month to get his bearings, he was back near the top.

Flaker was a former member of the military and had come from a family with money and respectability. He was the first person Vincent promoted, as he had shown significant promise as a rep and his cockiness and way he carried himself were very much in line with what Vincent was looking for. His downfall was his occasional laziness and use of excuses but when the pressure was on he was someone you wanted on your team. Bar none he was probably one of the top five salespeople in the building. He just had yet to reach his potential.

Continuing we come to Randall Darwin. Randall was entering his 29th year in the company and had been an outside rep and manager. When his job was downsized, Dickhauser brought him on board as a favor to Darwin's former boss, Derek Walters. Keith was frustrated when he was not able to quickly adapt to the call center atmosphere, despite the fact no one had trained him how. He had reported to Mark for months with no traction. He was moved to Vincent and started showing promise.

Randall could get a good cheer going but at first had no idea of how to fine tune his skills for the call center setting. At the onset, he did not like Vincent's arrogance and was put off by his speeches. After working together for months, seeing his results spike and seeing Vincent serve as the buffer between Dickhauser and the management team, he respected him.

While Vincent put on that front of over-inflated ego, often just to elicit a laugh from his followers, he would do whatever it took to guide his people. Randall was a prime example. His job had been on the line and now, after Vincent rolled up his sleeves and did everything he could to help, he was fighting back and felt he had an ally. He was a guy with a long career that he did not want to see end. Vincent knew that and respected it.

Next up around the table was Jimmy Sander. Jimmy had been with ABM for 10 years, formerly working in an IT capacity and, when his job was eliminated he interviewed with Vincent for a rep position. Jimmy was one of the nice guys, often to his detriment. But when Vincent met him he saw the attitude and determination of somebody that wanted to win and would put forth effort to do it.

Jimmy, along with Abby Winters, was in the training class Vincent sat in on for a week shortly after he joined the division. They chatted over burgers at lunch and beers after hours and Jimmy was one of the few people Vincent trusted. He had been the only person Abby trusted with the relationship she was having with Vincent after hours and the two had swapped female woe stories for years now.

While Vincent had gone through the ringer with Abby and Phoebe, Jimmy had ended years of relationship rollercoaster by tying the knot with on-again, off-again girlfriend Carrie Harper. Carrie had a son from one of the guys squeezed in between interludes with Jimmy, but Jimmy took the boy in as his own. She lost her job because she could never show up to work and she financially raped Jimmy for years, ruining his credit and his life before leaving him for someone else. What a gem.

Through their woes, Vincent and Jimmy stayed tight and had family Halloween's together and their kids were at each other's birthday parties. Some days they just sat in Jimmy's basement playing video games and drinking beers to wash away those dark times. Jimmy was a true friend.

Clyde Barton sat next to Jimmy – yet another who had faced job elimination and Vincent recruited him from the telecommunications side. Clyde brought that assertive, open-minded and revenue-oriented coaching style, which Vincent liked. Clyde was a bit of a scoundrel, however, in probably every sense of the word. Fidelity was a punchline to the man and Vincent was not sure if he could trust him but, Clyde ran a top flight sales team and seemed to say the right things.

Clyde had been the spearhead of the operation to unseat Dickhauser. It was during that uprising that Clyde gained favor in Vincent's Cabinet. He was now a regular in the Breakfast Club meetings every morning down the street at McDonald's. He seemed to be a good person to have as an ally, despite his shady demeanor. He and Vincent often had different opinions but they learned from each other. They worked well enough together to warrant keeping the relationship alive. Despite their differences, one would identify the other as a friend.

The spark that began the uprising targeted on ousting Dickhauser was an attempt Keith made to suspend Clyde for speaking out against him and Scott Kinsey. The issue originated when one of Clyde's reps lost a huge sale due to it never being keyed by the clerical team, which was commonplace around the office. Vincent went to bat for the sale and lost. Clyde continued to push the envelope and Dickhauser did not take kindly to it.

Keith, flexing his political muscle, tried to twist Clyde's words and hammered him with the accusation that Clyde was trying to get Keith to violate the company's ethics code by paying a rep for unrealized revenue. All Vincent and Clyde wanted Keith to do was lobby to get some kind of incentive payment for the rep, which was well within his ability, however Keith adamantly refused. Keith went so far as to usurp Vincent from the process by conducting the threatening meeting with Clyde using Kinsey as a witness and Betty Cross as a note-taker.

This was one of the many mysteries surrounding Keith, Kinsey and Danny Boyd; it was unclear why they refused to fix the problems that were so clearly damaging the department. It was unclear why they would not lobby to pay someone for work they did. It was ambiguous why they were nothing but a barrier for Vincent and the managers, who just wanted to get things done correctly. It was almost as if they profited from the improper payment of sales personnel.

Clyde had friends in Human Resources, and hated the way Dickhauser made it sound like he "saved" Clyde when his previous project management job was surplused. Clyde actually interviewed for a few jobs and his first choice was this one, but Dickhauser held it over his head that he had saved him by bringing him on board. That was typical Keith; because he had scratched the backs of "The Boys" over the years, they were indebted to him and he never let them forget it. They would do anything for him, mostly because he pressured them to feel like they had to.

From that event, Clyde organized what he referred to as "The Brotherhood," which was several managers banding together against the Dickhauser regime of oppression. His intent was to drum up enough support to initiate an investigation that would result in Dickhauser's downfall. It was quite a plan; one that nearly everyone wanted to see come to fruition but most were terrified to kickstart.

One of the reps who previously worked for Clyde, Frankie Rivera, sat to his left. He had gone through two stints as a rep for the department and a few months into his second he was tapped to be a manager. Dickhauser had always liked Frankie and he was one of the few people Keith would actually listen to. Frankie had made his rounds, having slept with several reps in the department, including Abby at one point while she was sleeping with Vincent, and was trying to get solid footing on his inconsistent sales team. Vincent was none too pleased when he learned that little tidbit.

If there was a member of the team who was most embattled and beaten it was Steve Zimmerman, the next around the circle. He was a hard worker but could not motivate a roomful of kindergartners to go to recess. Steve was hired because of his prominent last name; his father sat on the board of directors. He was still with the business because he had the good fortune of some high-quality reps over the years. But his luck was about to run out.

Cathy Schumer was next; she was formerly a bartender and was very much into the music scene as she headlined a band of her own; someone who was good at putting up with the public and did a grand job as a rep getting customers on board with ABM advertising. She was the most recently promoted and had taken over the former last place team when Vincent had to cut its manager loose. And she had lifted them well over expectation in a short period of time, proving her mettle.

Next up around the circle was the life of the party: Johnny Slade and Cal Riley.

Johnny had been another of the most impressive reps the team had ever seen, to the benefit of Zimmerman, who often tried to claim he had created him. Johnny was one of the hardest closers in the game. He was smart, diligent and ruthless. Vincent had taken a liking to the guy upon first sight in the interview. A product of some boiler rooms scattered across the country and several sales jobs, this guy was in line with what Vincent wanted in the business – a guy who would not back down. He set all kinds of records in the division but was very outspoken about his problems with the department's inadequacies in the commission and clerical realms which caused him to butt heads with lots of people. Again, this made him right up Vincent's alley.

Though he disagreed with a lot that Vincent had to say his first year as a manager, Johnny rode the wave of some strong reps and did things his way. His first year he was one of the top managers on the team and was lucky not to have to manage a lot of processes because his reps wanted to win badly enough that they took care of him. Unfortunately, in year two he had a much different clan and they required a lot of babysitting. As Johnny had not heeded Vincent's advice in year one, he collapsed early in year two but was becoming better learning what it took to build himself back up. Vincent had more respect for him now that he was learning through experience how to manage the processes that led to success.

Cal was Mr. Charismatic. He brought the party. He managed to accomplish more with a lesser skilled team than anyone in the business because he was crazy with energy, full of life and as flamboyant as it gets. Cal had grown up in a small town in a broken family and had done most of the work in caring for his mother and sisters. He was the first person in his family to make it. Cal came into the company at 21 and was rough around the edges – not the most scholarly but he was more than willing to compensate with hard work. He was introverted at first until he learned the ropes but once he started closing business and closing the ladies of the office he turned into a maniac on and off the phones. Cal was the guy other guys envied and the ladies wanted. He would walk into a bar or party and the females would flock to him. He did not pay a lot of attention to reports and details but when it came to rallying the troops with sheer unbridled enthusiasm, he fit the bill better than most.

Finally, rounding out the round table was Dean Yamnitz, likely the most intelligent and well-spoken member of the team. He had an MBA, was well traveled and Vincent wondered what on earth prompted him to apply for the rep job to begin with. In fact, even at this point as a manager he was overqualified, but if climbing this corporate ladder made him happy, so be it. Yamnitz was the polar opposite of Cal yet their teams were stationed next to one another's (on purpose) to play off each other. He was the straight-laced disciplinarian and student of statistics, well organized and analytical. He had what Cal did not in the way of discipline and analytics while Cal had what he did not: the animation and the goofiness. Dean had worked to become more of a driver in that capacity and it aided him on his climb to the upper echelon of the sales pack.

The top manager in the unit was Gina, but also near the top were Yamnitz and Clyde. Cal was in the fourth slot followed by Sandberg and Haley. Maria was coming on strong this year as well and she, along with Cathy were the brightest spots of the relative newcomers.

Vincent put the multiple reports at the end of the order and they began being passed around to all.

"Good morning, team." Vincent led off.

"Good morning," came the collective reply. Some days he had to elicit another because the first was weak but lately, with the commotion in the air and this being the final sales day of a month, the response was upbeat.

"Scott, do you want to lead us off?" Vincent often deflected to Kinsey early so he could deliver whatever message he had and he or Mark could bring the meeting home with a sales message at the conclusion.

"Sure. Managers, as you saw on Friday we released the latest outstanding contracts report. I know today is the last day of the month but we really need to get this cleaned up by Wednesday when the preliminary look at the next list is released. I have the report split into two tabs. One shows stuff from last week and the other shows stuff from before last week. I will have bins set up outside my office for each set. Danny, do you have anything?"

Boyd nodded. "Yes, we have noticed that many of you are turning in multiple copies of contracts. This is not going to help anything get keyed into the system more quickly. Please refrain from this activity."

A few managers looked away to control snickering or showing a reaction. First, the "outstanding contracts" report was a catastrophe. The managers received twice weekly looks at lists of contracts that were alleged to be missing. Many of them had already been turned into the clerks at least once but still appeared on the report for reasons that no one had been able to pinpoint. A lot of them had not been checked off, been misplaced and twice a missing contract was found in the bathroom after being turned in to the receiving clerk. In short, the process and this report were disasters.

The state of the clerical team was varying. There were some who cared and were diligent. There were others who shopped online during work hours, had the work ethic of a stuffed animal and were more interested in spreading the latest gossip than doing their jobs. Others had vendettas against managers who had tried to turn them into Kinsey for their crimes. Scott did nothing to manage them nor did he want to implement any kind of measurement of work for them that would hold them accountable to do their jobs properly. Why create more work for himself, right?

Unfortunately, Kinsey was where the buck stopped because he would not allow any management input on ways to fix the process, would not hold his employees accountable to do the work properly, and anything that was reported to him fell on deaf ears. With Dickhauser wrapped around his finger, getting anything accomplished in the clerical world was a crapshoot; therefore, getting reps and managers paid properly was not something that happened often enough. The troubling thing was that no one could quite figure out why this cluster at the top did not want to pay people properly and promptly.

No matter what offers Vincent, Mark or the managers made to chip in, help out and help improve the process, they were rebuked like they had no idea

136

what they were talking about. All the while, Kinsey sold Dickhauser on the fact that all was right with the clerical world and that commission issues were a figment of everyone's imagination. He would give Keith some lengthy explanation using big words that went over his head and somehow convince him the managers or reps were mostly to blame for any gaffes in this area.

To Kinsey's point, a chunk of commissions *were* paid properly and a *majority* of clerical functions were done properly. The problem is, in a large sales environment, "a majority" does not cut it. Large discrepancies make for unhappy people and when neither Scott nor Keith cared enough to fix the problems, the fallout fell on Vincent and the managers. Not only that, but since no clerks suffered but the reps always did, it did not make for a healthy work environment. Keith and Scott may have been able to slink into their closed offices or out the door early every day, but some unhappy managers had to deal with the regular fallout and it was not an enjoyable experience.

Scott's disdain for salespeople and his apathy towards people getting paid properly while he pocketed his $130,000+ per year were not well hidden. His unwillingness to listen or care about what they had to say was the main thing people in the division took exception to. That and the fact he was quick to put down and talk to people like they had no business even sharing the same Earth as he did. Most people would not challenge him, but a few of the stronger managers and Vincent surely did.

The reason contracts were turned in multiple times was, as Cal told Vincent just days before, "Dude, I'm going to keep turning that shit in until it comes off the report. I've turned some of them in four times." It made Vincent chuckle but he certainly could not argue with the logic. The process itself was anything *but* logical so Cal's attempt to be a smartass may just be exactly what was needed. Keith was going to scream at all of them and curse them out for the reports regardless, so they might as well attempt to finally get some of the contracts removed from this fictional report.

The thought on everyone's mind was that with a company this size, why does it have such a hard time processing paperwork and why was it so difficult to pay people their hard-earned commissions? In addition, when a rep made a mistake that cost them a sale, they suffered. When a clerk made a mistake that cost the rep a sale, the rep suffered. They were given no compensation for the sale in either their results or their wallets. And that caused a big rift between management and commission folks. In fact, Danny Boyd's mere presence out there at this point was a testament to recent progress made from a war on clerical waged by Vincent just months before. Danny was typically stationed downtown but after the war began, Dickhauser had to move Danny to Greenfield to try to fix the broken process. Vincent's antics had a way of getting things done for the multitudes he represented but this also attracted the resentment of those he waged war against.

Desperate for another challenge and hovering above the ABM earth like Superman waiting for a crisis, Vincent had heard the pleas of the people for so long. It had been the punchline to a long-stale joke: "Why should I sell anything when I'm not going to get paid for it anyway?"

Vincent's stance on management, just like being a rep, is to eliminate the excuses, eradicate objections and get rid of all obstacles. When no excuse remains, there is no justification by the other party to not submit to your wishes. Of course, that is unless they were just lying to cover up their laziness, but this was a way to purge that behavior as well. And if salespeople and managers claim they will not sell or cannot get motivated because they are not getting paid properly, Vincent can only hem and haw for so long about how if they sell above chargebacks they will never notice them. When every single manager, even those at the top and those who never make excuses, comes to him with an issue, he must lend credence to it. And he did. And he made a huge dent in the problem because no one who should have would.

After listening to one of his top reps go on a tirade in his office and confirming these issues with a couple of his trusted managers, Vincent decided to do the one thing no one had ever had the audacity to do – throw himself into the melee and show up Scott Kinsey's refusal to fix their problems. Like *Superman IV* when Superman made the decision to rid the world of all nuclear weapons, Vincent Scott decided to rid the division of all clerical and commission problems. (Certainly not a fine piece of cinematic art but it paints the appropriate metaphor.)

Vincent sent an e-mail to the division soliciting perceived issues regarding clerical or commission questions. He did not design it as an attack. And it was not – it was coming to the aid of the reps and managers. That, after all, was his job. They were the ones making his money and he owed it to them to rid their world of this problem if he had the power to do so. And he knew he was the only one who could or would.

The problem with a lot of people in Corporate America is they are so consumed with fear of a poor reputation or not being liked by superiors that they just sit back and let themselves be flattened. Vincent sees injustice and fights back, despite the damage it does to his reputation and career. That is why some people greatly admire him even though they have too much trepidation to follow suit. It is also why those on the receiving ends of his attacks are not fans of his work.

In this case, Vincent was flooded with problems from the team. All they wanted was someone to care. It would have been different if Kinsey would have shown some sympathy or willingness to help. He did understand a lot of flaws in the process, but when someone was not getting paid properly a typical

138

response was, "I understand your rep isn't getting their full $11,000 commission check, but they are at least getting $6,000 so what is the problem?"

He consciously processed incorrect commission reports on a weekly basis and most of them did not have the time to do the research to prove him wrong. Had he merely stood in front of the salesforce to say, "This is the problem and the people that need to know about it do know about it and I am going to stay on them until they fix it," that sentence would have worked wonders. But since he was not willing to say it, Vincent did. Doing so earned him even more admiration. It also earned him more haters.

Danny Boyd had never enjoyed being a sales manager because of the hard work involved but he was relatively effective when it came to supervising organizational functions and putting processes in place that could theoretically work better than what was there. After the shot across the bow from Vincent, Dickhauser started to take notice and brought Boyd in to help clean up some of the problem.

There were cartloads of hundreds of contracts sitting around that no one knew anything about until they slowly tried to make dents in them. Clerks were losing contracts, making keying errors and no one was doing anything about it. The process was deeply fractured. Even if Vincent could not single-handedly fix the process, he was the catalyst who could at least get the attention drawn to it necessary to get the ball rolling in the right direction.

"Betty?" Mark prodded.

"Yes," Betty began, sifting through papers. "The call grades that were due last Thursday are still missing from a couple of you. Also, if you could have your observations finished and in the system for November by end of business tomorrow, you will be in compliance for the month. That's all I've got."

"Thanks, Betty," Vincent stated. He looked around the room and thought, *Here goes.*

"Team, here we are. I don't want you to look at it like the last sales day of a month. I want you to realize there are 19 sales days left in this year. Overall, it has been a solid year. I want to thank Gina and Dean for leading us so far— both have already exceeded their annual objective. Let's hear it for them."

There was applause.

"This month has been a shortened one and I hope you all had a great Thanksgiving holiday. I hope it reminded you why you are here. It did for me. I bust my tail here to support my daughter and for the amazing payday we are going to get come March. We go through a lot of nonsense and put up with a lot of craziness to make this place tick. I appreciate wholeheartedly what you guys do. I understand how difficult your job can be but it is about focus on a high level about what is important."

Vincent scanned the crowd. All eyes were attentive.

"We have focused this year on working smarter and not necessarily harder to accomplish our goals. Managing processes instead of people. Holding people accountable and making them justify what they do. Holding them accountable to do basic call flow items. And we have gotten better at it. Believe me when I say, ladies and gentlemen, this is the most talented team I have ever worked with. I know I sit up here and beat the hell out of you some days but it is only because I love you and I want you to be the best you can be. That is what you should want yourself. Someday, if not today, you'll look back and realize I had your best interests at heart."

Vincent grabbed one of the pieces of paper in front of him.

"Here is this month's sales report. As you can plainly see, we have some huge disparities between top and bottom. Those of you at the top of the heap – Clyde, Dean, Cathy, Cal, Maria and Gina – are doing it in every category. I've heard that these meetings seem redundant at times and you know what? You are completely right. I am pointing out a lot of the same things over and over again. I am at a loss as to why we are not doing a more consistent job *across the board* of managing this process of conversion rates of our products. I cannot understand why some of you have an uncanny ability to keep your people on the phones for the vast majority of the day and others of you have literally no control over your reps. I myself cannot figure out why I have to repeat myself on a seemingly daily basis. But rather than harp at you today, I'm going to open up the floor to the best in each category and let them talk about why they are where they are. You hear enough from me."

Vincent was elated to see some people looking up from their note-scribbling or text messaging and paying more attention than usual. He was right. Sales management is often about saying the same thing over and over until it finally sticks. As long as you can look in the mirror knowing you did all you could for the person and they made the decision not to meet you halfway, you will be able to sleep that night.

"Maria, your team leads the pack on our search programs. How do you drive that behavior better than anyone else?" Vincent inquired.

"It's about accountability," she responded without hesitation. "When they sell something without it, I make them call the customer back. I inspect their pitch-screen in the middle of a presentation to make sure their bundle includes it. They know if they don't sell it they have me to answer to."

Vincent smiled. "Great, thank you, Maria. Clyde, your search results are booming all of a sudden. Care to tell us why?" Vincent asked with a wry smile.

140

"Well," Clyde began, returning the sardonic smile with one of his own, "after being passed over for monthly MVP honors multiple times, I realized I was going to have to if I ever wanted to win." The group laughed. "Seriously, it was just another step in the process. I have the reps report to me every pitch they make. When search wasn't included, I stayed on them about it. They knew I was going to hammer them if they didn't include it and it finally started to stick. I guess they just got tired of hearing me talk about it."

"Good answer," Vincent chimed in. "See, team, Clyde and Maria have been very clear with what they expect and have followed up to ensure their coaching is working. Holding the team accountable for this basic component is all it takes. They are working smarter and not harder by doing something minor that impacts every call their reps make. When you sit with a rep, you impact one rep one call at a time. When you do exercises like this, you impact every single call everyone makes going forward."

Vincent glanced again at the reports in his hands.

"Cal, your team is consistently at the top of our bundle conversion. Why are they pushing this better than the rest?" Vincent asked.

"Well, you know we're always going to do what we do," Cal answered with authority in his voice. "It gives us the capability to sell double the amount, these guys know it, and they get paid quicker. So it's good for them and they know I'm going to hound them when they don't do it, so it's just fun for the whole family."

"Eloquently put, as always, Cal," Vincent smiled. "Bottom line, team, it just makes sense. And when you see sales announcements that say the customer refused one or the other as part of the bundle – wrong answer! We've got to get used to saying, 'Mr./Mrs. Customer I hear what you're saying, but all of the components I described are automatically included in our bundles for new customers. Typically the price would be $X per month but because you are a brand new business I can discount it to $Y per month which, we've already established, is just 5 customers before the pure profit kicks in. Now, let's sign the papers.' And yes, it's that easy."

Vincent looked again at the reports in his hands.

"Dean, your conversion of upgrading to websites and selling into larger geography is off the charts. What gives?" Vincent asked.

"For starters, Vincent, my authorization is required for any small geography sales. That shows I mean business on this category. Even though 60% still get sold in the small areas, it makes it a little painful and it makes them sell me on why they are advertising the less effective programs that are not truly indicative of where they do business. The fact they are always thinking about it and pitching the bigger programs is in their heads has gone a big way in changing the behavior," Yamnitz responded. "As for websites, we all know it is paramount for any business to have one so we talk about this in each of our three daily stand-ups. I think it is the repetition that drives the point home."

"I love it, Dean. Team, you have carte blanche to run your team as you see fit. Unless, of course, you aren't hitting expectations and then you'd better believe Mark and I are going to put in two cents. Or more, in my case. Dean has three daily stand-ups to keep a firm grasp on what's going on, and he has taken it upon himself to mandate approval forms for something he wants to drive a behavior in. Fantastic," Vincent marveled.

Vincent turned to another page and held it up.

"Okay, team, lastly it's on to efficiency or, in some cases, lack thereof. Gina, you are always best in show here," Vincent observed. "What words of wisdom can you impart on your peers to guide them in this area?"

"I've been doing this for 3 years now and I know the game. These people may not like me but they know what happens if they can't answer for their time. I'm not in this business to make friends but I will help those who help me," Gina said assertively. "Let's face it - some of you have to get past the popularity contest. Some of you have to remember that this is *your money* and you are letting these reps ruin it for you. Where are they going to be when you can't make a house payment or buy your kid a Christmas present? They don't care. So you have to keep them honest, keep them following the rules but at the end of the day squeeze every penny out of them you can."

Vincent could not help but grin. "I couldn't have said it better myself," he said.

"Seriously," Gina said. "Let's all keep it real here. Some of you are letting your people get away with murder. Idle threats don't get you anywhere."

"You've got that right," Vincent echoed. "Gina, thank you for your candor."

They both laughed. Gina had become the person Vincent used as an example on a lot of categories. Her methods were rough sometimes, but she drove results. During the year they were managers together they frequented each other's cubicles to vent. Even now as the area manager, Vincent made daily stops by Gina's cube to vent and just discuss matters at hand.

"Before I turn it over to Mark I have one last thing to say. As we close out a month and soon a year, let's realize what our real challenge is. We have to constantly reinvent ourselves in this game, constantly look for new challenges. Some of you have mastered the job or gotten close. Others of you have mastered one or two aspects and have several more to go. Whatever the case may be, whatever you want your future to be, keep your eye on the prize and remind yourself every day that we are lucky to have what we have. We are lucky

142

to have this job, to have each other and to have at least a handful of people who want to make us some money. Let's get out there and get ours!"

The table cheered and Vincent signaled for Mark to take over. "Good morning, team!" Mark boomed. "Good morning!" came back the reply.

"As usual, Vincent covered pretty much everything. I'm just going to add a few points," Mark stated. "I want to thank a couple teams that posted over $1,500 in monthly revenue last Wednesday."

Vincent grimaced when Mark did this: thanking teams, reps or managers that did not hit what he had put out there as a much higher daily target. These were rookie mistakes and he sometimes wished he was the only one running these meetings. However, Mark often did point out relevant information or something Vincent wished he had thought of. But it was not often enough.

The table finished clapping for the top daily managers, the feelgood moment over.

"We have a lot to accomplish today and I wanted to talk about the different lead sources we have going," Mark continued.

Vincent blinked, cringing again. They knew how to call the leads. They knew what to say. He had covered it a billion times before. No matter what was said in these meetings, nothing struck home except the tough concepts. Lead them off and leave them with bright spots but other than that you had to hit them with cold hard facts between the eyes. Talking yet again about how to dial lead sources was not the way to go.

Mark was articulate and knowledgeable; he just was not adept at managing managers. The managers liked him personally, they just looked to Vincent for most everything. Vincent was able and willing to go to bat for the team against Dickhauser. Mark would not. Vincent jumped into action any time their sales or methods came under fire from other offices whose accounts they were borrowing and selling. Mark would not.

The two of them were complete opposites and that was just the way it was. Mark ended with a, "Let's get out there and do it, team!"

"See you guys in Block 1 for an 8:30 stand-up," Vincent announced. "Make it a great day, team!"

"Yeah!" Cal boisterously proclaimed, clapping his hands as everyone got up from the table and filed out.

Vincent had been here hundreds of time before, about to start a sales day by leading his troops into battle. Being able to do this had been what he had wanted for so long. He knew he probably had fewer days ahead in this office than behind but he knew when he left, just as when he left the residential division that things would never be the same and he would be remembered fondly for the contributions he made.

"The Selling Game" by Vincent Scott
Chapter 11:
THE VITALITY OF SALES STATISTICS AND FINDING CONSISTENCY

In order to achieve consistency in results you have to maintain consistency in the things you do to drive those results. In the sales arena, this means finding a flow that works and sticking to it. After all, you don't tinker with the ingredients of a recipe and expect the taste and texture to remain the same, do you? In the same vein, you have to find what works for you and repeat it however many thousand times it takes before you get to whatever next step you are looking for.

Sports figures in slumps should not make drastic changes to their approach. You should follow their lead (in this example, of course, not in taking steroids or extramarital affairs). The thought process is that you want to repeat what brought you success rather than trying to recreate it by doing something different. If it worked at one point, you were on to something and just because you have had a run of bad luck does not mean something drastically different is going to get you results you once enjoyed. Recapturing the old magic is what you need. It is likely, similar to the slugger stepping wide or dipping their elbow, you have accidentally lost a few important steps from your call flow that you need to get back.

The strategy you follow is an energy that surrounds us, penetrates us and binds the sales galaxy together – like "the Force" in *Star Wars*. You cannot see or touch it, but when you get good enough you can see things before they happen, manipulate the minds of weak Storm Troopers and maybe surpass Billy Dee Williams in level of cool. Okay, that last one is tough to do. Unfortunately, when customers try to shake you off your flow, you cannot lop their heads off with a lightsaber.

There are a million, if not more, ways to conduct your call and a great deal may be effective. However, if you attempt to stray from the structure outlined in this book, you could quickly find yourself floating around lost in space. The points I illustrate are to be confident, block out negative energy and throw yourself into the fray, ready for everything that will be thrown your way. Once adept at following the schematics outlined here, navigating through sales calls should be second nature to you.

We have outlined what happens when you fail to administer the call flow properly; the same thing occurs when you deviate from it in an attempt to escape a slump. No hitting coach or golf instructor is going to advise to make drastic changes to the swing to make it back to the top of their game. In *Tin Cup*, Cheech Marin recommended everything *but* changes to Kevin Costner's character's swing, including changing the location of his keys in his pants pocket and turning his cap around. The meaning of this is that it's mostly psychological. Take your mind off the numbers and put them back on doing the right stuff. Dwelling too much on anything will just bog down your brain and render you less effective.

Never get fixated on a number you are supposed to achieve for a revenue target. People call this the "goal," the "quota" or the "objective" but frankly it's just status quo. Your intention should be to reach a mark much higher. If you do the right stuff on every call, you will look back on the week, month or year and the numbers will be there; you do not even have to think about it. Focusing just on the numbers is misdirected focus. Focus on the process is where you should allocate your attention.

Deviation from the call flow results in you pitching based on your own pocketbook and knowing nothing about the customer's expectations, needs or wants. This leads to under-pitching and selling your customer and yourself short. Because the best fit for the customer was not determined and their situation was not taken into account, the desired results will not be there for any of the involved parties and that does not bode well when trying to form lasting business relationships.

An individual in sales must possess the skill to evolve and grow based on the changing factors that surround them. The landscape will not be consistent so to resist the upheaval that life tries to deal you, you have to roll with the punches. The product may change, needs of the customers change, but one constant will be the importance of staying at the top of your game. Finding consistency means adapting to the playing field.

Sales conversion rates are often not as high as we desire them to be or the number of opportunities we receive are not conducive to breakthrough. You may be a solid hitter but if you are only getting one pinch hit per week, it is doubtful you are going to do enough to crack the lineup. In hockey, there are not a plethora of 100-goals per season superstars. Teams make 1 or 2 shots out of 40 attempts in contests so you have to relish every opportunity on the net.

It is imperative you always bring your best. You cannot afford to get a decision-maker on the line only to perform like a faulty relief pitching staff. Studying sales statistics can guide you in seeing where you are strong and where you are not so much. Far too many people look at the primary, highly regarded statistics like number of closes or raw revenue and gloss over other items that lead to victory such as performance in specific areas, efficiency or conversion rates. Those who rack up assists or sacrifices or defend their scorers are just as important to the cause of the victory but their statistics do not get all the praise.

Either way, do not forget their importance when selling because you will not succeed if you look past key variables.

Chances are, in whatever sales arena you are in, there are several buckets that are measured to determine how successful you are. Your percentage to goal can often be derivative of several metrics whose summation equate to true mastery of your post. You may be selling a specific product but surely there are idiosyncrasies, add-ons, additional products and services that can be taken advantage of to make more value for your customer and money for yourself. Studying these and knowing how to make them part of your repertoire is to the benefit of everyone in the equation.

Why would you ever want your name next to a statistic that is not indicative of your ability or less than spectacular? If you do, stop right there; sales is not for you. However, becoming a student of the game will better your chances at survival. You need to know all the nooks and crannies of the stadium, where to put the ball so it will not be caught or retrieved quickly and how you can manipulate statistics to get where you want to be.

Many leaderboards are not solely based on revenue. Nowadays companies are getting into the scorecard approach; they weight the importance of several statistical drivers that equate to what they deem success.

You may see several different components of your performance weighted to determine your worth. Be smart about your approach; figure out what can be most easily manipulated and make a huge dent in that area. Have a gameplan for each component, especially heavily weighted ones, so you can stack the deck in your favor and get that extra mile or twenty ahead of your competitors.

Mastering all components of your trade is what will get you the positive press you likely seek. These are the things your supervisors want – not to have to worry about you. To mark you down as one of the good ones that needs little attention and will always deliver. To have you assist in mentoring peers to be as effective as you. To deem you a more valuable asset than the vast majority of those in attendance.

Autonomy is a typical attribute of the successful salesperson and is something supervisors want to see in your bag of tricks. With solid performance will come little flak and probably not a lot of additional pressures from the powers that be. A support network of people in the job who are making the magic happen always helps. These are the people from whom you are going to get ideas and bounce ideas off of. I have seen independent groups gather at lunch of their own accord to share ideas that have brought them success. I personally formed committees whose purposes were to ascertain the needs and wants of the populace to keep morale high and share strategies. Committees bring all kinds of ideas to the table and serve as acknowledgment that no one person has all the answers. It is important to recognize that teamwork makes everyone more effective. Surrounding yourself with success is also a way to improve you.

The art of finding consistency is paying attention to everything at your disposal, be it statistical readouts, your peers or anyone that can help your approach get better. These things are everywhere so your best bet is to be open to solutions, wherever you may find them.

If you go out there determined to master every facet of your job, you are already better than practically everyone else. Odds are your results will reflect this as well.

Do not lose heart when things fail to go your way. I have seen too many people succumb to the loss of a sale, a tough day, week or month, or a chewing from their supervisor and use these as excuses for their subsequent lack of effort. Believe me, I have had plenty of losses, but after licking my wounds and regrouping, I am back better than ever. You started the fight for a reason; don't lose sight of that.

Consistency wins the race. The horse that comes out of the gates first is not automatically declared the winner. The ones leading throughout the race are also not prematurely given a coronation ceremony. The best sprinters cannot necessarily condition and preserve themselves for marathons.

My philosophy is to complete a job well done, not just a job done. I encourage you to study the game and realize where you can make your easiest advances.

Like "the Force," the ability to sell is in every living creature. Some of us have learned to control it, some have taken the time to master it and others have the brass to strike down Jabba the Hutt's henchman in the Mos Eisley cantina. A lot of people can call themselves salespeople but what you have probably already determined and started to understand is that to be the best – to be the Jedi Master – it takes discipline, willingness to learn and lots of practice.

You do not want to be a one-hit wonder, a flash in the pan or "Where Are They Now?" subject matter. To evade that predicament, learn what it takes to put forth solid results in every area. Study the spreadsheets. Listen to others. Have the courage to try new things from time to time but stay faithful to the flow that made you successful to begin with.

In the recipe of a successful sales career, the ingredients start and end with your effort, determination and desire. With those ingredients and your application, the sky is the limit.

*   *   *

When you find yourself in a situation you know you have to get out of, sometimes impatience can envelop you and make you go crazy. Vincent felt that way with the unfair promotion of Dick Knoll, the regime of Shelly Cheekwood, the ridiculous leadership of "The Saw" and seeing Stacey Worth every day as she played hot and cold with his emotions. The alcohol, partying and pool-playing that took up his time outside the office and witty banter and camaraderie with Jeff, Cliff and Ted could only do so much to keep Vincent sane.

However, on Wednesday, October 12, 2005, his office phone rang. The caller ID shot across a local number. He figured it was someone he knew.

"ABM, this is Vincent."

"Yes, is this Vincent Scott?" came the gruff voice on the other end.

"Yes it is. How can I help you?" Vincent asked.

"This is Keith Dickhauser; Director of Sales for ABM's Online Advertising unit. I posted a requisition online that you recently posted for."

"Ah, yes, Mr. Dickhauser, how are you?" Vincent asked. His mind raced as he wondered which of the 35 jobs he had applied for this could be. As he asked the question he was already accessing the job database so he could track it down.

"I'm fine, thanks. How did you hear about the job initially?" Dickhauser inquired.

"Well..." Vincent began as he had yet to determine what job he was discussing, "I read the description online and it sounded very similar to the items I do every day here. The position was also an opportunity to move up and around in the business to take on a new challenge," he said vaguely but cleverly.

"Sounds great," Dickhauser said. "I reviewed your résumé with great interest and would like the chance to meet with you to discuss the opportunity. How is tomorrow for lunch?"

Vincent found the job posting and skimmed it: the senior sales manager position with ABM's advertising bureau.

"Tomorrow is great. What did you have in mind?"

"Do you like Italian?"

"Absolutely," Vincent answered agreeably. He would have said yes to whatever they were eating in *Indiana Jones and the Temple of Doom* at this point; this could be his big break!

"There is a new restaurant in Greenfield called Francesco's. Have you heard of it?"

"Uh, sounds familiar," Vincent's classic answer when he had no idea what someone was talking about but did not want to convey his aloofness. "I'm sure I can find it online."

"How is 11:30 for you?"

"That would be great," Vincent replied. "I will run it by my boss but I am sure she will have no problem with it. I look forward to it."

"So do I. Thanks, Vincent."

"Thank you, Mr. Dickhauser."

"Call me Keith. I'll see you tomorrow."

"Sounds great, thank you."

Dickhauser hung up on the other end. Could this be victory?

A few minutes before 11:30 the following morning, Vincent entered Francesco's and looked around. To his left, a gentleman in his late 40's with short, dark hair and glasses, also wearing a suit, approached.

"Vincent?" the man inquired.

"Keith," Vincent stated, holding out his hand.

"How are you?" Keith asked, taking and shaking Vincent's hand.

"Very well," Vincent responded. "And you?"

"Good, good. Does this table work for you?" Dickhauser asked, motioning to a corner table.

"Sure, fine by me."

They took a seat at a small table by the door, ordered and talked shop. Dickhauser asked Vincent about his duties in Rockford, described the job at hand and gave him back story on the advertising bureau; where it had been, where it was and where it was headed. Vincent talked about his life, where he had come from, his career thus far and his aspirations. Dickhauser asked him taboo questions like his age and religion but Vincent did not really care, he answered them and it impressed Dickhauser all the more.

As the meal began to wrap and Dickhauser had put his credit card in the payment book, he looked back at Vincent.

"Thank you for lunch," Vincent said.

"No problem. So, Vincent, do you have any other questions?"

"Yes, when should I tell my current boss that I'm reporting to you?"

Dickhauser bellowed; a deep, hearty laugh that Vincent would hear hundreds of times in the years to come. "Well, I am bringing on board another guy who I have worked with in the past. The only issue there is I may not be able to hire you both simultaneously due to, er, hiring restrictions. He is also a white male."

"I see," Vincent replied, deflecting the odd response.

"Your résumé was by far the most impressive I've seen. I will see how this pans out. If by some chance I can't pluck you now, there is a possibility of expansion in first quarter 2006."

"I understand," Vincent acknowledged. "Just know that I am very interested in this opportunity and I look forward to your call. Thanks again."

Vincent and Keith rose from their respective chairs.

"Great meeting you," Keith said. "We'll be in touch."

They shook hands and departed.

A week went by and Dickhauser called again. The promotion was not happening at this point. He assured Vincent that if and when expansion took place that he was "earmarked" for their next available opening. So, for Vincent, it was still nose to the same grindstone.

On the work front, Vincent's team was blowing out expectations while Lucy's and Phil's were barely, if at all, reaching 80% on the sales report. The polarizing disparities were resulting in Shelly's unit sinking in the division and she found herself at the center of a lot of unwanted attention. "The Saw" was on her regularly about what she was doing to resuscitate the office. As Shelly was obviously aware of the casualties Warsaw had left in her wake, that pressure was quite uncomfortable. She had left behind a higher body count than Schwarzenegger in *Commando*. Dana forced Shelly to change up the teams again, and, to Vincent's chagrin he could say nothing to dissuade her.

Vincent found little remaining to celebrate in the department or his situation but the way the new teams was announced was something he could never forget. Each rep was given cake, ice cream and a certain color of napkin (the brainchild of Shelly and Stacey over smoke break). Those with a red, green or blue combination were designated to a certain manager. Lucy, Phil and Vincent were all in the Aquarium and were announced by Shelly to the unit so the reps knew who their "new" managers were. Red was revealed first and those reps were reporting to Phil. He emerged and there was a smattering of applause. Green was next and those reps who would report to Lucy gave a polite golf clap.

Uproar began and, the cat out of the bag, Shelly revealed that blue was reserved for those reporting to Vincent. He emerged to a boisterous ovation. It was awe-inspiring to him; these people were so excited about the prospect of working for him. Vincent hoped he had few days left in this place but the applause meant the world to him.

Flash forward to present day: he felt the exact same way. Applause from those who appreciated his work meant the world to him and is what kept him going. The reps and most managers legitimately looked forward to every golden nugget from Vincent's arsenal. He entertained and titillated and they often hung on his every word.

Vincent watched Mark lead off the morning stand-up. Every day one of them would invite top reps and managers from the day prior to speak about their successes. This day was no different; Mark called up four performers from the day before Thanksgiving and they came to the middle of the circle to talk.

Block 1 was one segment of the online sales division. The team had gotten so big since its planting in Block 3 they had to expand into another section; this one being the one Vincent moved his office to upon expansion. He made the move to put as much distance between his office and Dickhauser's as possible. With his former office right outside his boss's it was always the first target during one of his rampages.

For the morning stand-ups, everyone stood gathered around as Mark, Vincent and occasionally Keith himself would stand in the middle of the room and speak to the crowd.

Standing back in the crowd to observe reactions and issue some last minute direction to Jimmy Sander that would involve his portion of the stand-up, Vincent could witness the lack of enthusiasm when Mark spoke. He knew Mark had to get frustrated over this but that was not Vincent's problem. Mark would try to end his segment of the meeting by following Vincent's typical ending: getting some kind of cheer out of the troops.

"So, do I have everyone's commitment to do their part today?" Mark shouted, almost mechanically.

"Yes," came a monotone and unenthusiastic reply.

"I'm going to turn it over to Vincent from here. Vincent, do you have a few words?"

Vincent paused briefly. "No, I'm good."

There was some chatter and Mark looked at Vincent, perplexed.

"Okay…" Mark muttered, not sure what to do next.

"I'm joking, everybody," Vincent announced, as they started to laugh. "I'll never pass up the chance to hear myself talk."

He started to prance towards the middle of the circle as the reps and managers began to laugh and to cheer for him. This was what he lived for. This was his livelihood: the morning speech. He just did not know how many more he had in him.

Some days, this walk was the hardest thing in the world to do. Through everything the last couple of years had done to Vincent, he still had to stand up here every day and sell 200+ people on coming to work, trying their best and exceeding expectations at a job where they were not even paid properly and the people that were supposed to care didn't. Whether he was fully engaged or holding himself together with alcohol and apathy, he did the best he could.

"Good morning, everybody!" Vincent shouted.

"Good morning!" came the rousing welcome.

"I woke up this morning and couldn't sleep. I ran through my house to get to the shower because I felt like a kid on Christmas morning. You see, in a sales environment like ours, Christmas doesn't come once per year, it comes 12 times. The last day of the month is our Christmas. Are you ready?"

The crowd laughed and answered back, "Yes!"

"Good to hear. I hope everyone got their rest and had a fulfilling Thanksgiving weekend. Today is our final sales day of November and we have to post another $16,000 in monthly billing to hit our objective. I'm not sure why we always have to cut things so darn close, but we have so we might as well finish what we started."

A few in the audience shouted their approval with a, "That's right!" or a, "Yeah!" Vincent held up the color-coded sales report that was recognizable to all.

"But wherever you are right now on the report, don't be defined by these numbers. They don't say who you are. They don't talk about any level of effort you have put into this job any day, month or year of your life. You are the one who breathes life into these numbers so don't even look at them as you start your quest today."

With that, he flicked the report from his hand and its three pages flew and descended to various places on the floor around him. The audience loved it.

"Don't look backwards!" Vincent continued. "I need you right here, right now. Looking back in time does no one any good. You can make objective or define yourself in one moment, one call. And one person hitting objective does not make or break anyone else's chances of doing it, so we should be sharing our knowledge daily and I thank everyone who does just that."

Some more applause and positive chatter ensued. Vincent only spoke louder.

"I want to ask you, by a show of hands. Who here is satisfied with where they are on the sales report this month?"

Some hands considered going up but stayed down. A hand or two went up here or there.

"It's okay, don't be shy," Vincent said.

The hand of Andy Gamble was up and Vincent laughed.

152

"Andy, it is okay for you to be happy with where you are this month; so am I," Vincent said. Several people laughed. "Bottom line, many of you are not satisfied with where you are on the report. Yet you continue to do things the way you see fit regardless of what your managers or I say. Right?" Vincent continued. "It's OK, be honest with yourselves!"

People looked at each other, muttered things to each other and mostly nodded.

"Looking at those numbers I just threw on the ground, clearly your way isn't working! The way you do things is leading you to numbers you are not satisfied with. Right? So why do we continue to do things we know are not going to lead to the results we want?"

Vincent paused only briefly, allowing his points to strike and sink in.

"Normally, I would open it up to you to answer, but I've been doing this long enough I already know the answer. You are doing it out of desperation. Trust me, I was a rep, and nothing sucks more than going any stretch of time without selling or seeing other people beating you at anything, any time. And if you bring yourself in here and go a day without selling and it festers into another and another, this place sucks and you wake up in the morning and you think to yourself, 'my God, do I really have to go into that hellhole today'?"

More laughter and chatter of agreement resonated throughout the floor.

"A lot of you jump to the conclusion you should bail yourself out of a slump by throwing out some low-priced program that doesn't work just so a customer will buy. Does a slugger drastically change his stance to get out of a slump? No! So why should you? And why do you think that pitching a program with no value out of desperation is your key to success? Even if a customer says yes, did you really win something? Absolutely not! You failed the customer, the company and you: the holy trinity of sales."

Vincent paused again momentarily as there was a solid mixture of laughter, agreement and chatter throughout his salesforce.

"Team, I'm not just eye candy, I know what I'm talking about," Vincent announced to more laughter. "And when I listen to our calls I love the product knowledge I hear. You guys know your stuff. But I gotta tell you, you absolutely must ignore your instinct to throw out everything you know to these poor customers. It's great that you know these things and I admire you for it, but we're not giving book reports here. We are finding out their weakness, finding their pressure point and squeezing. They aren't going to make a move unless you convince them the parade is passing them by. And you have to find five different ways of telling them how you are going to cure their weakness and say them over and over and over again until they cave or hang up on you."

"Yeah, that's right!" someone in the front row shouted. Many others echoed their sentiments. Vincent continued.

"And a lot of you just throw out everything you know and you spend your time basically just trying to sell the person on why they should stay on the phone with you. What does this accomplish? If you get stuck in one segment of the call flow and you never move on, what's going to happen? That customer is going to have to go and if you actually ever speak to them again, you start from square one! We're not building relationships here. If you want that, you should move across the hall."

Laughter ensued again, as this was a clear reference to the other advertising team housed in the building that handled existing accounts and had their own assignments. They were certainly not known for success.

"This is in your face, get in, find out what you need, shoot a pitch from the hip and close it down. That is what we do."

The audience greeted this with cheering as well, clearly liking his assessment of their job function. All but those like Haley, Mark and Keith Dickhauser; they viewed Vincent's gunslinging mentality as bulldozing good customers and leaving their dead bodies in his wake. They would silently cringe and look at one another. Of course, the fact that Vincent had led them to this unbelievable level of success was hard to argue with. And Vincent would purposely make these comments because he knew it got under their skin.

"Team, if you do nothing else, write this down and tack it to your monitor. I don't care who you talk to, if you don't hit them between the eyes with this one statement on every single call, you have not done your job. Are you listening?"

The signaled they were.

"'Mr./Mrs. Customer, I understand you say you need to think about this but you and I both know if you believed it would work and you'd make a return on investment, we would be signing you up right now. So, with the hundreds of thousands of directories and the thousands of online searches to your category monthly, how will you not get the, for example, five customers you need for a return on investment?' Then – *stop talking!*"

Vincent stopped for a moment. His mind was racing – what was next?

"You've got to find out the *specific* reason this customer does not want our customers. Period! They may tell you to call them back in a month or so, but you and I both know that if you say you will you might as well file a missing persons report; you will never talk to them again!"

The collective group laughed. Vincent smiled.

"Challenge it, team. They have their own gameplan against people like us. They have a gameplan against – and I am going to curse, I apologize," and he got quiet as he whispered the word, "telemarketers" to the extreme amusement from the entire team. "If you act like one you'll be treated like one. What's the worst they are going to do? Say no? Hang up? How are you any worse for wear? You're not! And if they hang up on you, it isn't a loss – it means you knocked them out of the ring. You should wear a hang-up like a badge of honor."

The agreement amongst the team continued with enhanced cheers and shouts.

"There is only one real objection and it took me 8 years to figure that out. I'm imparting that wisdom on you now so you can progress more quickly than I ever did. The only real objection is lack of belief. They are going to tell you anything and everything else but that's what it boils down to. Hit them with that lack of belief question and you did your job. Make sense?"

The team, loving every minute, yelled back, "Yes!"

"Okay, team. I'm not going to take up any more of your time. We've got a goal to hit. Are you going to do your part?"

The team erupted with a resounding, "Yes!" and they started cheering wildly. This was always Vincent's favorite part of the program. These ovations sent energy through him like very little could.

"Let's get out there and do this! We are the champions!"

Amidst the cheers, Vincent pointed to Jimmy, standing in the corner at his cubicle. Jimmy hit the switch and Queen's classic, "We are the Champions" erupted from the speakers, filling the quad and fueling the fire of motivation, adrenaline and morale.

Vincent raised his hand to wave to the crowd as he walked away amidst the cheers. He high-fived, shook hands and patted some backs as he waded through the crowd back to his office.

Fortunately, the department's revenue objectives were actually amplified for the reports the floor saw so Vincent and the managers only needed to achieve 80% of what the targets depicted. That said, his part of the department consistently hit 120-130% of their "objective" under his direction each month.

Playing music during stand-ups had become commonplace as he liked to play songs from the *Rocky* series and other motivational things to get the crowd going. He was not above anything that would push their buttons and get them going. It was taken as immature and tomfoolery by some, but Vincent would do whatever it took to get the desired results regardless the response.

As he headed to his office to turn on the dialer for the day's work, he passed Clyde, who muttered, "I'm McHungry."

"You and me both, brother," Vincent replied. "Give me fifteen minutes."

"I'll be waiting," came the reply.

Once the stand-up dispersed, the reps and managers broke up into their crew level powwows. Vincent activated the dialer and began his schedule, which required him to be there every time a campaign ran out, and the managers regurgitated the morning message with varying levels of skill and accuracy.

No one but Eric Aames knew the dedication it took for Vincent to be there every moment a campaign ended in the dialer and a new one needed to be activated. He could have pawned off this responsibility but he wanted complete control over the schedule. Often he would make decisions on a whim or play with the leads and he alone knew how to get the best results out of any lead set at any given moment. It was a cocktail only he knew the ingredients to.

However, every day around 10 AM, Vincent made sure the dialer was set on a campaign that would last until 10:30 or 11. Reason being? "The Breakfast Club."

It started with Cal, Slade, Jimmy and Vincent, over a year and a half ago. They started to go to McDonald's and discuss the state of the union. As time went by, Frankie and Clyde would tag in and they would all end up there. Eating, drinking coffee and sodas and eating greasy breakfast to soak up the hangovers from the night before were the orders of the day. They discussed happenings in the department and the treatment they got from Dickhauser. Lately, they discussed what should and would be his fate.

With tensions high amongst the team in anticipation of the eventual conclusion to the Dickhauser investigation, they were not going to miss an opportunity to discuss the latest.

"I hear the calls have stopped," Clyde offered. "A little birdie told me that they anticipate he will be put to pasture in a staff job downtown and away from us." A "little birdie" was code between Clyde and those he kept close to the vest for Agnes Landry's best friend Helen Johnson.

"What is the timeframe?" Frankie inquired.

The group also had a pool, drafting the days they anticipated the demise of their falling leader. Each had a vested interest as the pot was over $250.

"No telling," Clyde responded. "But they won't waste time. Every day they take he is a liability to the company. If he makes further movement against someone they can sue ABM for inactivity."

"He knows, boys," Vincent dropped. Everyone looked at him with concern and disbelief.

"Shut up," Slade muttered.

156

"Mark told him," Vincent offered up.

"How do you know?" Cal inquired.

"Keith told me," Vincent revealed. "Don't worry, I played cool. Hell, I had to, I wasn't about to let on that I knew something. I just played it off like – 'why would they want to talk to me? I'm the bad boy of ABM'."

"Well played," Clyde said.

"I anticipated this and intended to reveal knowledge of the whole thing at the end," Vincent continued. "It sounds like we're there so I will go to him today saying I got the call. I can't have them say they talked to everyone and him not hear from me that I got a call," Vincent concluded.

"Are you sure that's the right move?" Jimmy asked.

"It is," Clyde said. "Vincent can't do anything to expose him or us as traitors."

"Precisely," Vincent said.

"And then the Vincent Scott regime begins," Cal boomed.

"From your mouth to God's ears," Vincent said.

This was not *really* mutiny. This was years of oppression and it had finally culminated into enough people wanting to do something about it. Vincent was just along for the ride. He had not initiated this fire. He had received a call and, as he knew more than anyone and could provide a unique insight to the tactics and demeaning activities, he did just that. He told the truth.

But would this company actually promote Vincent Scott to Dickhauser's vacant position? He had a track record of battling superiors, bedding females in the company, a child out of wedlock with a former rep in the department and a known affinity for alcohol – he was the last thing this company wanted.

The conflict for Vincent was that no one took the time to look at the reasons for any of those things. It is easy to cast stones at people like him. He was like a D-list celebrity; Vincent could feel the pain real celebrities must face while insolent slobs sat at home in front of their televisions attacking them. They knew nothing about what the real world forces on people who have power, responsibility and visibility, no matter what the size or the scale. Vincent may not have always reacted to things the right way, but he was never prepared by anything or anyone for some of the attacks thrown his way.

Vincent battled superiors for the greater good of the people who worked for him. Yes, he was sometimes borderline insubordinate but he thought he was doing it with just cause. He became romantically involved with females in the company because he was a workaholic and never had the opportunity to meet anyone else. He may never admit it, but he got lonely like everyone else. When they threw themselves at him it was tough to resist because it was not like he was going to get much play or attention elsewhere.

He drank like a fish because it was the only way he was willing to pursue to wash away his considerable pains. He had to escape from his own mind, his debilitating fears and insecurities.

The company needed Vincent Scott but would much rather someone else – anyone else – who would march to their drum without controversy, would come about.

"But you know that will never happen," Vincent lamented, continuing his thought after the brief mental escape to a world where he would actually get the reward he deserved.

"Vincent, you know that's the whole goal of this," Clyde said. When Clyde said it, he wanted to believe it.

"They aren't going to put a wild card like me in that post. They will bring in someone who knows nothing about our business, which could be more dangerous than our current situation," Vincent stated.

"Vincent's right," Johnny Slade agreed.

"The 'evil we know is better than the evil we don't' philosophy," Frankie offered.

"Exactly," Vincent said. "That's why phase two is my letter to the executives in the aftermath of Keith's removal."

"What do you mean?" Johnny asked.

"I'm going to tell them what their play is. Very respectfully, of course," Vincent tempered. "If they don't want to promote me, that's fine. They would be better off having no one take Keith's job. Let Mark and I run this as we are now. Keith is nothing but a political figurehead who has worn out his usefulness and beats the hell out of the people making this place successful. I will offer to be their single point of contact, maybe a temp promote on a trial basis until they feel comfortable making the change permanent. Meet them halfway, as it were."

"That's smart," Cal said. "Because you're right, you look too risky on paper."

"It's the only move I've got," Vincent said.

"Then it's settled. The Brotherhood's mission is near completion," Clyde said, beaming from ear to ear.

The group toasted with their McDonald's cups, then dispersed. It was back to the ranch. Of course, any time a clearly laid out plan is in motion, a wrench will introduce itself to throw the entire plan off course.

Upon returning, Vincent walked across Block 1 to his office. He noticed people looking at him, whispering, but he did not think anything of it. He semi-waved and continued his gait. Once he got in his office, he unlocked his computer interface and logged in to see how many leads were left in the campaign bucket and check his e-mail. The company's instant messenger system had several incoming messages. The first he opened was from former subordinate and friend Danny Nance.

"Yo, Vincent," the communication read. "Don't know if you saw this yet but you're not going to like it."

A link was attached. Vincent clicked the link and it led to a blog about ABM's advertising salesforce being a scam. That did not faze Vincent; in fact he chuckled slightly. However, as his eyes continued to scan the message board he felt his whole demeanor shift. A post with the handle name, "VincentScottNailsSubordinates" read: "Thank goodness for ABM! Without them I wouldn't have a daughter!"

Vincent stared at the post, making sure he got his interpretation of what was said right the first time. He felt the blood boiling inside of him, the rage welling up in his veins. Who could have perpetrated this assault on his lone sensitive spot?

His 95-words-per-minute-fingers leapt into action. He penned a quick e-mail to the webmaster of the blog to have this libel removed. He followed it with a response to which he signed his own name, "Those who hide behind anonymity are cowards."

He was so tired from these constant anonymous attacks. But he had to put this out of his mind; he had a job to do and he could not lose his cool.

And now Vincent knew what he needed to do. With the Dickhauser investigation seemingly over, he had to go to Keith and tell him something that would keep his suspicious eyes off his back. Vincent did not feel guilt for applying nails to the coffin for Keith. The relationship had been tumultuous since the starting gun of his ascension to running the department. He had been cursed at, yelled at, hung up on and threatened so many times he knew how his subordinates felt and then some. He had been their only buffer and lately even that dam was weakening. There was only so much he could now prevent and with the floodgates opening against them, they took the opportunity to return fire on Keith. He had to go and Vincent felt no compassion; he had brought it upon himself.

Vincent walked across the building, passing the crew areas for Clyde, Cathy and Steve. He could never make a journey from any particular points A to B without being stopped by people with questions about accounts, sales strategies or soliciting advice on some idiosyncratic situation and this trip was no exception. About five minutes later, Vincent walked past secretary Marla Mooney's workstation and rapped on Keith's door.

"Is he available?" Vincent asked.

Marla scoped the phone line situation and nodded, "Yeah, he just got off the phone."

"Come in!" came the response from behind the door.

Vincent opened the door for what seemed like the millionth time and walked in, closed the door and parked himself in the chair facing Keith Dickhauser. When summoned into this office, Vincent never closed the door. He could always tell if there was a hint of danger to the meeting when Dickhauser asked him to close that door. This time, the door needed to be kept secure.

"I got the call," Vincent said.

"Really? When?" Dickhauser asked, focused on Vincent. For Keith Dickhauser to give anything the preponderance of his attention was a rarity in and of itself. He was a classic case of a disturbingly short attention span, even notoriously walking away from people mid-sentence on occasion, but this was one conversation he did not want to miss.

"This morning, first thing. She called during our stand-up and I called her back."

"Who was it, Agnes or Lydia?"

"Agnes. And don't worry," Vincent answered coolly. He paused momentarily before adding, "I took care of you."

Vincent had wanted to deliver that line so badly for so long. Obviously Dickhauser would interpret it to mean he smoothed things over. Vincent meant it in quite the opposite fashion. And he did not tell a lie.

"What did she say?"

"It was pretty much like Mark described. She asked if I had seen you tell someone in an open forum that if they couldn't do their fucking job you would find someone who could. I said I had never heard you curse in an open forum," came the selectively worded reply.

"Right," Dickhauser said, clearly on edge. "What else?"

"Just the same stuff, apparently. I told them we have to have tough conversations sometimes to get our point across."

"I just want to know who ratted me out," Dickhauser grumbled with anguish. "Did she give any hint as to who it is?"

"She said there was an anonymous call and then two who revealed their identities to her."

160

"Goddammit, I am too old for this shit. I just want to ride out my three years and get the fuck out of this place."

"And I just wanted you to know that I got the call."

"Thanks for letting me know. Obviously we have to have each other's backs."

Vincent nodded as he rose and left the room.

Those final words did not resonate guilt within Vincent, primarily for one reason. Four months prior, Vincent had been under a firing squad all his own, spurred by an "anonymous call." The call was made by Scott Kinsey, and reported Vincent for a meeting where he said "if you choose to ignore this report, you're a damn fool." Kinsey had waited until just after some internal movement that made his action less conspicuous and practically untraceable.

Vincent's tight-knit team would not bury him, of course. In fact, of 20 people in that room only 6 admitted to even *hearing* that uttered and only 4 said anything that would amount to constructive criticism of Vincent's occasionally overenthusiastic style. When Vincent faced Agnes Landry and Lydia Rawlings, who were clearly out for blood with the way they posed their questions and the hateful way they read off his purported crimes, Dickhauser had every opportunity to defend him. Quite the contrary; Keith allowed Vincent to be under fire and lied to cover up his own faults.

Vincent's disgust lingered and now he had silently enacted his revenge. He had given proof of Dickhauser's wanton ways by sending a voice mail where he had referred to the managers as idiots and said, "Fuck them." He had provided e-mail proof of abuse, evidence of Dickhauser ordering falsification of documentation and plenty of first-hand account of his horrendous dictatorship. Vincent had merely told them the truth. And may the truth set them free.

The last day of a month for Vincent was actually the easiest – like Election Day. He had done everything possible, busted his tail during the campaign, drummed up as much support as he could and now it was time to sit back and watch the results roll in.

He loved numbers. He analyzed every lead source, every dialing statistic anything he could try to tweak or manipulate to squeeze more money out of this engine. He found himself now pretty much finished tweaking. This was the optimized beast. He was scrambling to find another challenge to keep him interested.

The last time he had felt that way was Rockford, four years prior at that tail end of 2005. While still topping the charts monthly he had little left in the tank and was running on fumes. Oklahoma City offices under the guidance of Dick Knoll changed the dynamic of their teams and made "Dream Teams," putting all the best reps getting the best calls on one team and splitting the commission earned amongst all managers in an attempt to gain office momentum in the sales pack. Vincent was the only manager in the company able to compete with these Dream Teams without having one.

In fact, in December 2005 and January 2006 he was in the top 4 both months out of all 115 teams and the only teams that beat him were these contrived Dream Teams. As they were only comprised of top talent with literally no weaknesses, this spoke volumes towards what Vincent what able to accomplish with his super-sized group. Rather than reward him, however, they investigated his sales and monitored the calls where he was racking up extreme sales. He was clean. How dare they question him *and* refuse to give him any accolades?

With every rung of the corporate ladder he climbed, the attacks became fiercer. Was it really all worth it?

Vincent, pompously undeterred, put another proposal on the table to take 52 of the 78 reps in Rockford. He wanted to hand pick them and Lucy and Phil could split what was left however they saw fit. The reason for 52? Because Dick Knoll's entire unit was 51. He wanted to, for the sake of his "final" challenge, out manage Dick by taking more reps single-handedly than Dick had with a little help from his friends.

That was another thing with Vincent; the concept of potential failure never entered his mind. If he set out for a cause, there was no stopping him. When Dana Warsaw used Shelly as her instrument to announce to Vincent she would entertain this idea only once he terminated someone through the call flow process, it became clear what they were doing: compromising to get him to use their inherently flawed system. It was against every fiber in his being. His team was always at the top so why fall back on this weak way of managing? It rubbed him the wrong way because he had already proven himself by taking 37 misfits that comprised the worst team in the office to the top of the department's sales charts – why do they still not trust him and give him this challenge he needed?

That pipe dream put to pasture put Vincent's final charge to pasture. He had nothing left but clinging to a hope and a prayer that this advertising venture was going to rescue him from Shelly and Dana. And the thing that proved it was all meant to unfold in this fashion occurred: a trip to Dallas for the entire residential division was announced. This trip would not only put faces to names of many of his adversaries on the sales report. It would also bring him face to face potentially one last time with Dick Knoll.

Vincent was already on everyone's radar because of his extreme sales and they were certainly expecting him to be a pretentious ass worthy of their disdain. So he decided to go out of his way to be the complete opposite. Buying drinks for all of Dick's managers who had been trained to hate him. Going out of his way to make first contact with Dick himself; shaking his hand in front of a large gathering of onlookers. Making conversation with Dana like he gave a damn what she had to say. Going out on top, in style, undefeated and untied. This trip enabled him to seemingly mend any fences that needed work.

And upon his return, he got the call from Keith Dickhauser: effective March 1, 2006, his promotion would take effect and he would be leaving Rockford's residential division to helm a crew of advertising consultants in the brand new online division. Victory.

Over the final two weeks, things went quickly. Shelly lobbied to get Peter Swansea promoted, passing over Vincent's protégé Jeff Mason, who, despite now in the advertising sect, had put his hat in the ring. It was an obvious attempt to get in Ed Green's good graces by promoting his bartender buddy and prevent Vincent's influence from spreading.

On the final day, there was not much to do but say goodbyes – mainly to the people he actually cared to say goodbye to, a list whose roster had depleted many times over the years.

And there was Stacey.

She asked him repeatedly that last day when he was leaving, hovering around him more than usual. When he finally decided to depart he went to her office. Tears welled in her eyes and she hugged him.

"So…you're going?" she asked.

"I am."

She pulled back and looked at him hesitantly.

"You'll have to come visit sometime."

"I would have to have a reason to do that," Vincent said back coolly. "Why don't you come visit me sometime?"

"That would…take me out of my routine," she said nervously.

"I figured," Vincent said, knowing this was never going anywhere.

"Good luck. I'll…miss you," Stacey managed. She hugged him again.

As Stacey pulled back, she kissed Vincent's cheek. He looked into her eyes, wanting more but not pursuing it even though it was his last chance.

"I have to ask; do you still have any of the things I gave you?"

Stacey blushed and, per usual, dodged the question.

"Stay in touch, Vincent."

"I could live for a thousand years and never understand you," Vincent said.

Vincent stood there and they looked at each other, wanting to say or do a million things in that moment that they knew neither one of them would act on for a million reasons. Stacey hugged him once more. And Vincent walked away.

With that, Vincent Scott left the building that had been a springboard to his career, where he had learned to close, deal with heartbreak and how to manage. It was where he had experienced birth as a salesman. He was now about to take those skills to a bigger stage.

*   *   *

When the online sales office began four years prior, it had been housed in downtown Minneapolis in the form of strictly outbound dialing reps and managers. As time went on, an inbound offshoot sprung up which Mark and Danny were assigned to and the originating outbound bunch was moved to Greenfield due to capacity.

After several months Dickhauser decided to use some of the remaining downtown space to form three outbound crews that would report to Mark. It fit in their budget so it made fiscal sense if they could make some additional revenue off new blood. Unfortunately for Keith and Mark, the downtown outbound project was a flop compared to the pioneer circuit. The outbound team Vincent helmed in Greenfield defeated Mark's sect by 25-35% to objective every single month without fail. Desperate for excuses, they blamed the lack of synergy in a small office and taller cubicle sizes for the gap in revenue. Anyone who manages knows it is easier to get a small group to do what you want than it is a larger one.

Now, in present day 2009, all outbound teams were immersed in Greenfield and they were on point. Vincent's influence on those teams, however, was never lauded as one of the reasons for their surge. The truth was well-known but was not one of those things acceptable to talk about as Dickhauser and Mark had regularly reported to superiors that "tall cubes" were the reason for the 30% gap in percent to objective totals. For Vincent and his posse this was a punchline, but it was par for the course in Vincent's unsung managerial career. It was tough for anyone with sense to tag tall cubes as the culprit, but it was better than actually thanking and appreciating Vincent Scott.

On the final day of a month, Vincent's dialer regimen could be hectic to maintain due to his devotion to cycling through the best leads available at any given moment.

Vincent would cycle through all of their highest propensity-to-buy leads in the order of their profitability.

164

The leads with the highest chance of success were the enhanced complimentary listing leads; situations where someone had taken time out of their day to visit ABM's website, create a username and password and add information to their complimentary listing. They were referred to as ECL listings and were the most popular in the department as a solid 12% resulted in sales conversions.

On the flip side, the leads that kicked off the month were customers who had a phone number with ABM's telecom side of the house yet no presence in any of their advertising mediums. Those leads yielded 0.01%-0.6% success ratios; they were not highly regarded but Vincent's program was set up to force them to be as good as possible at the lesser desirable leads. The low conversion rates were due as much to lackadaisical presentations as to the value of the leads.

When Vincent had begun his career with the advertising bureau, admittedly he had been very intimidated: surrounded by people who had spent their careers in the marketing part of the business, knew the product and were used to selling it. Vincent, while he knew he could straddle the line in the residential division better than his adversaries crossed it, had no idea if he could legitimately sell. He was good at manipulating statistics and convincing people to take things, but felt unproven in real sales.

The first time Vincent walked into the downtown Minneapolis building it was a daunting fortress. Standing 45 stories it was ABM's Mecca in Minnesota and one of the city's tallest buildings. This citadel housed several factions of ABM subsidiaries including publishing, marketing, advertising, customer service, human resources and the like. Jeff Mason was now located on the building's eighth floor and Harriet Raines on its 30th. The top couple of stories housed some of the local officers of the company, managers 3-4 levels above Vincent in the hierarchy. Full-fledged training facility, full service cafeteria, immense parking garage: this place was real Corporate America to Vincent and his Rockford duds paled in comparison.

This was the stuff out of movies: the women and men in the hustle and bustle of the morning, newspapers and *Wall Street Journal*'s tucked under their arms holding their lattes and heading to a busy day at the office. He had arrived.

The assignment was located on the eleventh floor. Upon arrival, March 1, 2006, he met Derek Walters, who was to be his supervisor, and was introduced to Mark Rogers and Mike Enderle. The "Boys Club" empire that Keith Dickhauser formed did little to shake Vincent's initial intimidation.

Derek was a respectable enough fellow: a married father of two in his second tour with ABM. He had left a few years back to work with a competitor but Dickhauser wooed him back with a hefty price tag for this project. There was really nothing unlikable on the surface about Derek, Vincent would soon realize, and even his regular 2:30-3:00 afternoon departures did nothing to faze him. Derek stayed out of Vincent's way. He did not praise him, but he did not praise anyone. He was strict, upheld the rules of the land and did not put up with nonsense. While he may not have done much in the way of guiding managers, he knew about business and set parameters for the fledgling department to follow. Derek and Keith set the wheels in motion for this little bicycle to roll. Vincent took off the training wheels.

After the first manager meeting, Derek and Keith pulled Vincent into Derek's corner office.

"So, what do you think?" Derek asked, slightly beaming. He did not smile often but when he did, there was slight upturn of one side of his mouth.

"I'm excited," Vincent said. "I'm looking forward to being an asset for a new part of the business."

"Let me tell you," Keith started in. "We have very high hopes for you. You were our top draw."

"I can't wait to sink my teeth in. When will I join a training class?"

"Here is the game plan," Derek began. It was always clear when Derek and Keith were in the room together that Derek was the one with the vision and he took charge of the conversation. It was clear in present day that the reason Walters was a more effective buffer between Dickhauser and the managers was because Keith considered him his best friend. Vincent did not have that relationship with the man and no matter how much Keith claimed to respect Vincent's intelligence and his growing business sense the kid was too brash and his management style too kamikaze for his liking. "We have just been given the order to grow from 10 reps to 100," Derek said, never changing emotions. His constant poker face was another trait Vincent admired.

"That's fantastic. I saw your prospectus; your first two months were off the charts versus objectives," Vincent offered.

"Yeah, and now they want more people. Like yesterday," Keith guffawed, always there for a cameo comment designed to elicit a laugh that mostly amused only him. Vincent offered a polite chuckle.

"You've done hiring before, right?" Derek inquired.

"I have been involved in some candidate job visits before. I know what to look for," Vincent answered, trying to say something as close to what they were looking for as he could.

"We are going to insert you into the hiring process," Dickhauser said. "You will be the first face the candidates see. If you like them, Derek or I will meet them and make the final determination."

"So...I will do a preliminary interview before you guys do the real one?" he asked, not quite certain of the importance of this function.

166

"We want you to weed out those who have no hopes of success. You have managed successfully so you will know what to look for," Derek explained. "That way Keith and I don't have to look at all three hundred candidates just to get our one hundred. Make sense?"

"Perfect sense," Vincent said, digesting everything. "Sounds good. And will I sit in on one of the classes?"

"At some point," Derek answered. "Right now, this is the most important thing on our plates. It's a big responsibility."

"I'm up to the challenge," Vincent answered.

"Great," Derek said. "I'm going to introduce you to the ladies in HR that will be coordinating interviews with you. In fact, let's head down now. We have some interviews scheduled later today."

"Baptism by fire, eh, gentlemen?" Vincent laughed. Keith responded with his signature bellow.

"Oh, and one other thing," Dickhauser said, stopping Vincent. "Don't fuck the help."

Vincent did a double take. "Come again?"

"Don't fuck any of these girls here. I don't need the distraction."

"Oh…okay…" Vincent muttered.

Derek led Vincent to the elevator and they descended to the mezzanine overlooking the lobby. They walked through the glass doors and were greeted by Melissa Worthington and Phoebe Wells.

Near retirement and the former life of the party, Melissa was as feisty as ever and proudly Phoebe's mentor in the ways of getting what she wanted in the company. She had dirt on the higher-ups through years of parties, gatherings and indiscretions and did what she wanted when she wanted.

Phoebe was initially a sight to behold. Shoulder-length blond hair, exceptional physical figure and the clothes to complement it well. She wore a significant amount of makeup but her face was appealing. She was flamboyantly attractive, one who attracts a crowd wherever she goes and whom every guy with confidence sets his sights on.

"Good morning," Derek announced. As he did, eyes turned to him and Vincent.

"I want you to meet our newest sales manager, Vincent Scott,"

"Good morning, ladies," Vincent stated with a slight hand wave.

"Hello, Vincent," Melissa said, quickly sidling up to him and shaking his hand firmly. "We are looking forward to working with you."

"Likewise," Vincent said.

"We have some interviews scheduled for this afternoon. I will send up the schedule and one of us will bring you the interview packets. I'll go over the process with you this afternoon. How does one o'clock sound?" Melissa asked.

"Works for me," he answered.

"So this is the new talent?" Phoebe inquired, looking at Vincent coyly.

"At your service." He took her outstretched hand by the fingers gently and shook.

"So you're not from these parts – how do you plan to manage a product you don't know?" she asked brazenly.

"I catch on quick. I'm like a Boy Scout," he said back, not missing a beat and without looking away from her eyes. "So what is it you do here, answer the phones?"

She laughed slightly, continuing the game.

"It's a little more complicated than that."

"I'm sure it is. Excuse me," Vincent said, backing up to leave but maintaining eye contact. "It was a pleasure."

He and Derek headed for the doors.

"Ladies, I look forward to our future interactions," Vincent proclaimed. "Melissa, I will see you at one."

"We'll see you soon," Phoebe offered.

"Good meeting you, Vincent," Melissa said. No sooner than Derek and Vincent vacated the room, the two began conversing about the newest advertising employee, Vincent Scott. The seed had been planted. He had no idea it would grow into a weed.

His first day was positive save the start of a trend for a few months to come: reps from the initial project asking him questions about product information. His standard line had to become, "I promise I'm actually here for a reason other than my good looks. Wait until I learn this product and I'll run circles around everyone here." It was heavy billing, but what was he supposed to say? As long as he was a hiring mastiff he had to keep the troops from thinking one of their lieutenants was just a prettyboy placeholder.

Vincent fielded a couple calls that day from former Rockford reps. Shelly, Phil and Peter wasted no time in gunning for his former team. They slapped two of them on call flow warnings on Day One of his absence. It was nauseating. Their real plummet was beginning right on cue.

In the days and weeks to come, Vincent scored lots of points with Keith and Derek, helped hire dozens of new employees and despite the fact in early April she became engaged to her boyfriend Nathan, he was both receiver and giver of useless flirtations with Phoebe Wells. He pitied the guy she went home to that trusted her to be tame. In hindsight, he should have figured it out then.

The Rockford office held its annual awards banquet in early March and, as Vincent had been their lone management Top Gun he was one of the award recipients. Dana Warsaw came to town for the banquet and she and Shelly were hosting the event. They were not thrilled their least favorite former employee was on the itinerary but there was nothing they could do about it.

To their credit, they did use the company's stipend to rent out the banquet hall of one of the most lavish restaurants in town after the company decided not to send them on a trip. Peter Swansea was honored as a rep as his pre-"strike" efforts on Vincent's team had been strong enough to get him in the top 100 reps in the division for the year. Ted Benton was an honoree and so was Jane Daughtry. In fact, only one of the handful of honorees had not worked for Vincent during the prior year, a fact not lost on anyone in attendance.

The only rep there who had not worked for Vincent was very self-motivated Laura Meadows, who had actually started as a rep working for Shelly when she was a manager in Rochester. She, like Shelly, had been part of an abusive relationship and fled to Minneapolis and as, for lack of a better word, luck had it, they found one another again. She was one of the people who worked for Dick Knoll who helped pad his stats.

It was clear Shelly had been drinking for quite some time and on his way to the bathroom Vincent had seen her looking a little shaken while smoking in the lobby. She confided in him that Dana had informed her to start looking for another job. The kingdom was crumbling and Vincent knew he had been the only thing that could have kept it together.

Shelly was sobbing uncontrollably in the bathroom when it came time to give praise to Jane. The fact she had been there to go on and on to praise Laura when her time had come added salt in an already growing wound, as many had seen what Vincent had seen in recent months: Shelly was a lame duck.

The top reps in Rockford saw their ship sinking and saw escaping lifeboat Vincent Scott. With Vincent's best friend Ted and now Rockford's top rep Jane on board, the exodus was underway. In just the first month, 11 reps from Rockford called Vincent in regards to coming downtown to the new online team under his tutelage. What started out as a joke turned into a disaster.

While Vincent did nothing to recruit these individuals and Dana had even half-jokingly told Vincent not to recruit on the evening of the banquet, he certainly did nothing to dissuade these people from pursuing a better job in a superior environment. And he quickly became the scapegoat Shelly so desperately needed to lash out at.

Keith and Derek already had their close-knit circle of influence. Vincent saw the opportunity to start building his. But Shelly was none too pleased that her people wanted to flee to a brand new department just to escape her collapsing organization. And while Vincent again did nothing to coax people to his more attractive pastures he relished the sweet revenge this provided.

Ted departed first, which was no shock to anyone considering his status as Vincent's best friend, but when Jane's defection became known, the friction was too much to bear and the war began. When Vincent sent a strictly business e-mail requesting Jane's appraisal, Shelly called him and went on the offensive.

"ABM Advertising, this is Vincent," he answered the phone, knowing full well from the Caller ID pronouncement who was on the other end.

"Vincent, this is Shelly," came the chilly response.

"Hello, Shelly, what can I do for you?" Vincent sat back in his chair, grinning.

"Vincent, I have been made aware of some actions on your part recently that are cause for my concern."

"I'm not sure I know what you mean," Vincent answered.

"Vincent, some of my top reps are in contact with you to transfer to your department. I don't appreciate the lack of head's up which would have been a professional courtesy."

"Professional courtesy, Shelly?" Vincent laughed as he sat forward in his chair. "Quite the contrary – the reps of whom you speak have asked me questions regarding the pursuit of another job in the company. I have done nothing more than answer questions."

"Vincent, what do you want here? I was your biggest fan and biggest supporter. Why are you trying to make waves?" The desperation was evident in her strained voice.

"My biggest fan? Let's not get out of control here," Vincent fired back, glad he was finally Shelly's peer so he could speak candidly. "You did nothing over the last two years but stifle my every attempt at advancement. You threw your support to Dick, who can't hold a candle to me and now because you think your reps would rather work for me than you, you want to act like I'm committing treason? Please. I have done nothing to recruit anyone and am simply following protocol by obtaining the personnel files of those who have successfully qualified to work here. I should not be crucified for that."

"Vincent, be careful about the bridges you burn," Shelly said, trembling on the other end of the line.

"I'm not burning any, Shelly. And if I did, it was a weak one to begin with."

"Okay, Vincent. Best of luck to you," Shelly spat.

"Yeah, you too."

170

Vincent put the phone back in its cradle and smiled.

While he had not gone out of his way to steal these people from his inept former supervisor, he also did not have to have his fingerprints on the paper trail luring them to his department. He chose to because it was his simple way to let them know he was getting redemption for the way he had been treated, passed over, ignored and dismantled during his time there. If he burned whatever bridge had existed between him and Shelly Cheekwood, may its flame light the way.

Shelly had very intentionally hurt him and now was his primitive chance to hurt her back.

In the days to come, Shelly caused such a stir that Dana Warsaw and Ed Green both got involved. Ted and Jane had already eked through to safety but they clamped down an injunction preventing the other nine from the greener pasture. They threw accusations at Vincent of breaching their code of ethics, illegal recruitment efforts, etc., and it was enough to get the injunction in place initially. Of course, as the dust settled in April 2006, the sum of the crimes she tried to tally against Vincent totaled zero, the Union stepped in and eliminated the injunctions and the floodgates reopened. And Shelly learned not to stand in the way of Vincent Scott again. It was the last time she ever tried.

Rockford finished April dead last in the district and near-last in the company, the first time this had occurred since Vincent had taken a management position in their now disgraced halls. Rumors ran rampant that Shelly would soon be ushered out and that the fallen office would be swallowed by some other department and absorbed. Everyone knew Shelly was not only responsible for blocking reps from pursuit of another job opportunity but that she had made up lies in the smear campaign against Vincent that was her sole means of stopping the bleeding. Both backfired and she had lost any support she once had.

The hiring in the online division continued and Vincent picked and chose who he actually wanted from Rockford's ranks, turning away those he did not – all through the guise of Derek, of course. He told Derek who to choose and who not to, and the progression towards 100 reps moved forward. Vincent certainly met some characters through hiring and as they neared the century mark in number of personnel, Derek informed Vincent he would be sitting in on week one of the class slated to begin April 24.

That class, hilariously enough, seemed to contain some of the most interesting personalities of all. There was Chad Willman, a former car warranty salesman and 22-year old trapped in a 16-year old face, body and voice. There was Jimmy Sander, who conveyed his passion about staying with the company and convinced Vincent he could sell even though he never had. There was Kevin Verne, a hyper, high-energy goof Vincent took a chance on despite not knowing if he could live up to the hype (he went AWOL on Day 2 and was never heard from again). There was Sahim Saundura, a quiet but intellectual character who shared some of Vincent's same passions in writing, literature and screen. And there was Abby Winters.

She was 22, a strikingly attractive brunette with brown eyes and an appealing smile. Vincent was attracted to her right away. She came across deceivingly as the nice girl-next-door, Southern-values type. That happened to be what fascinated him most.

Vincent was the first to finish every morning quiz and work exercise. He quickly put his fears to rest and was ready to conquer what was to come.

Keith and Derek only allowed Vincent to sit in on one week of training so he had basic knowledge of the online portion of the curriculum. Unfortunately, in the years since and with all of the new products they have started promoting, he still has just that one week under his belt. But you would never know it to hear him speak. And that was the real trick.

"The Selling Game" by Vincent Scott
Chapter 4:
THE WIND-UP, THE DELIVERY, THE PITCH

As you continue building the foundation of your perfect sales call, crafting of the pitch will dictate just how devoted you are to a healthy balance for the holy sales trinity: the company, the customer and you.

Relationships fail because they are one-sided. Satisfying all three components of this relationship is tricky but you must take everyone into consideration when formulating your presentation. In the short term, failure to do so can cost you your customer. In the little-bit-longer term it will impact your wallet. In the long term it can impact your job.

The best decisions when pitching a customer are made when the salesperson is irreverent to cost and sells based on value to the customer. I know that is another sales cliché so I am going to deeply elaborate my point by telling you exactly how to do it. Furthermore, this is where it is vital to remember that you are not calling this person to give them some kind of speech or dissertation on the history of your company. Keep the pitch lean, mean and clean for best results.

The relatively short attention span of the worn-out customer must be kept in mind at all times. Remember, they have heard it all before and you are far from the first to try to sell them something. The more unique you can be every step of the way the better. The majority of salespeople make the mistake of saying too much and telling the customer everything they know about a product just hoping the customer will latch on to something and purchase. Tell the customer what will benefit them about your product all while weaving in what you learned during fact-finding, and make sure the customer understands how your strength is going to cure their weakness. Previously, we looked at asking the correct questions. The importance of that step is no more evident than when we branch out into our pitch. We impose limitations on ourselves more than any situation, customer or other outside force ever could. Those limitations enter the picture if we do not ask enough questions or choose to pitch out of our own pocketbooks thinking the customer will not spend much money. On the flip side, we also limit ourselves by asking too many questions to stall making a pitch because we are terrified of this part of the sales process.

There are two parts in the call where you have to just close your eyes and take a leap of faith: the presentation and the close. This chapter will show you how to begin one and transition into the other. Sure, the task of making a "perfect" pitch can be daunting at the time but once you have the basic information you need from the customer, it is time to begin. Each customer has a relatively short window of time with you and if you are cut off while playing 20 questions you will never sell the customer.

I always tried to operate with and train the stance of pitching inside of or as close to the 10-minute mark as possible. If you are on the phone, that is pretty easy to track. If not, try to utilize your instincts to gauge your progress, but inside of 10 minutes you should be able to determine everything you need to know about someone to pitch them. In fact, your pitch itself is really only going to utilize a few of the things you just learned so stalling this part of the process only hurts yourself.

Part of conforming to these proven sales methods is having the capacity to corral yourself in any situation at a moment's notice. Are you reading this book because you are already a sales master and want to see if there is anything I know that you don't? Or are you reading it because you want to become one? There are exceptions to every rule; I have met one person in nine years of sales who was able to exceed expectations while asking little fact-finding. However, the dollar amounts of his sales were small and he had to sell a lot to get there.

I have also listened to a lot of salespeople I swear talk so much to hear themselves talk or because they think the customer will respect them since they sound intelligent and buy from them. Those people sold little to none because they never got around to the close! The customer did not stick around for the meat and potatoes of their seven course meal. It was too much; they may have been able to speak articulately and spark a conversation but they had no instinct when it came to making the pitch. Too much talk can kill you. Knowing when and what to pitch and not being afraid to do it makes all the difference.

The session of fact-finding is placing the ball on the proverbial golf tee. The pitch is squaring to fire it down the fairway. Far too often, narrowing questions are asked rather than broad questions that will allow for more wiggle room. If you ask questions that start with, "Do you only," or "Do you just," you are almost forcing your pitch to start out smaller. You may or may not consciously be doing it but that is where self-analysis comes into play. Take the opportunity to listen to a recording of your presentation. Find out every possible angle you can use on a customer.

A lot of the fear of making a pitch is the fear of the word "no." I have to tell you, if that word scares you, you're in the wrong business. We're not asking people to prom here, this is sales and "no" is part of the game. You *want* your first pitch to result in a "no." Otherwise, you did not do them justice.

One, if a customer jumps at your first pitch you could have sold them more. Maybe you pride yourself as someone who is "only going to give them what they really need," and you say you are not going to gouge them. Fair enough, but far too many bad salespeople hide behind that mantra to cover up

174

their inadequacies. If you do a good job of presenting something to a customer and they accept your terms, how did you gouge them? Whose responsibility is it to investigate those terms and sign off on them if they agree? The onus is on them at that point, folks, and you did nothing wrong.

Second, you have to leave yourself a lot of room to play. If you ask limiting questions and start with a lowball pitch just because you think they will agree to that price, where do you go when they say no? Sales is not only psychology, it is negotiation. Potential car-buyers do not waltz into the dealership with the mentality of paying the sticker price. Again, this is a case where understanding your customer, their motives and their vantage point does you a lot of good. Hiding behind your own prejudices and fears serve only to hinder your effectiveness and results. Do you think a dealership only posts the lowest price they are willing to accept on a vehicle? Heck no, they post a high-end starting point and have a price in their head they are willing to be negotiated down to. Your mission is, in essence, the same thing.

If you are talking to a customer trying to sell them a kitchen appliance, you are not doing yourself a favor if you ask them if they are the only person who would use the device, if they ever make a specific type of recipe or if they only would use the device for cooking for certain occasions. This is narrowing your results. You want to open up the playing field so you can pitch your product to the maximum number of users, situations and occasions. Ask how many people use the kitchen. Ask how many would use it or would cook were it made extremely easy-to-use. Dad may not cook but if Mom is away and it falls upon him to make dinner, your product can be used by more people if it makes it easier to cook. That is yet another benefit. Ask what types of things they cook; this raises the probability they will walk themselves into extra benefits you can bring up during the pitch. Ask the questions that will cause customers to open the doors. The rest will fall into place.

Once you ascertain these items, you want to pitch the earth, moon and stars. A critical means by which to catapult yourself to super-stardom is pitching without fear of the response. Fear prevents us from pitching seemingly big programs or dangling the meaty price tag because we think a customer will say "no" solely based on price. Never forget: price is a fake objection.

It is a reaction, an illusion and this bogus excuse masks their lack of belief. We will discuss how to truly overcome it when we discuss overcoming objections but you should not let the fear of it deter you from pitching a quality program.

Knowing when to talk and when to temporarily cease fire to bear the fruits of your labor are necessary ingredients to the sale. It is important to hit the customer between the eyes by calling them out and forcing them to give you a specific objection of why they do not believe. *That* you can overcome. Some bogus, generic excuse like price you cannot. That is why they hide behind it so frequently. Don't let them.

If I tell you to donate $1 to the Vincent Scott Aston Martin foundation, the likelihood of that donation is slim to none. I gave you no benefit to yourself and, therefore, you see no value. On the other hand, if I tell you to get me $100 and I guarantee I can invest it and turn it into $1,000 overnight, you would scramble to the ATM to fill my request. Why? It is simply because you see the return on investment. You see the value and the benefit to yourself. And that perfectly illustrates why a customer would say no to a $1 investment but yes to a $100 investment.

Understanding that price means nothing is one of the most important steps to sales success. Customers will do everything they can to hide behind it but you have to force them out every time.

Sure, occasionally customers may be under the constraints of some kind of budget. The "I can't afford it" rationale is occasionally true if only because they already made a poor investment in something else. That, however, is not to say you should not attack their attempt at justification by attacking what is more likely a lack of belief. Leave price out of it. That will be something broached in the chapter about closing – my personal "three strike rule" – if and when the decision comes to concede to this excuse. Bottom line, however, is you should not allow your customer to hide behind price. You should not hide there, either.

Many salespeople also justify lowball pitches because they may have identified the customer as ripe for a specific small component of the potential offerings. Absolutely, most every customer will be ripe for a certain offering that you want to lean into and lead with to pique and keep their interest. You should not hesitate to gravitate towards that and lead with this particular element to start reeling them in. However, do not inhibit yourself, your results or your company's profitability by being one-dimensional and only focusing on what you have isolated their need is.

If you work for a radio station and think playing a nightly spot for the customer is a great fit, by all means tell them that is part of the bundle you are going to set up to increase their exposure and get their name out there. However, in addition, to ensure the customer has the maximum exposure you can provide and the best probability at return on investment, you are also going to throw in the mid-day spot, the online ad on the station's website and you are going to feature their business on the mailers you send out for the station. As long as at the end of your spiel you show the customer where they will be and how they will make a return on investment you have iced the deal. They set out with one particular part of this bundle in mind yet, because you did not limit yourself or the customer, you sold four.

That is what sets the great salespeople apart from the rest of the pack: the ability to branch out and package something together leading to maximum exposure and prosperity for the customer, maximum commissions for yourself and maximum profitability for your company.

It is irrelevant that the customer's first choice would not include that online ad or that they would not have asked for the mailer ad by name. Do these extra features and these extra potential customers hurt their business? Of course not. Hence if you show them that the total cost for this package is easily made up with however many customers it takes based on what an average job will yield them, congratulations – you have yourself a sale. This is not cracking the meaning of life. It is about offering additional products and services in a way they appear most attractive.

Another snafu in pitching is a dangerous inclination many people have that makes them think they should provide a complete book report on everything they know about a product or service they introduce to the table. Knowledge is power, however over-utilization of it is what is commonly referred to as "talking yourself out of the sale." If you lead brilliantly with what the customer is gravitating towards most and what will help them most yet insist on telling them every single bell and whistle of a service that comes along with the bundle you are recommending, it will serve only to elicit an, "I don't need that." Needless to say, when a customer says that, it is detrimental to the cause. Lead with your strongest foot, how it addresses the customer's need and weakness and quickly outline the other components of this puzzle all while weaving into your close and just how easy it will be to make a return on investment.

You do not want to verbally vomit on a customer about everything you know. It is great you know these things and I am sure your manager is very impressed that you got perfect scores on quizzes in training class. Pat yourself on the back frequently for your knowledge of the product. However you must remember the customer is on a need-to-know basis and all they need to know is how they are going to make or save money.

That is what it is all about. Kitchen devices, vacuum cleaners, advertising products, services, vehicles – they are all pitched after figuring out the customer's need and the reason for them to buy is based in what is in it for them.

So – what *is* in it for them? Will this device mean Dad can make dinner instead of ordering pizza every night? The family is healthier and has more money to spend on a night out together. Will this vacuum only need to be replaced every ten years instead of every two like the ones you have been buying? The house will be cleaner and you can save hundreds of dollars over the years that you would have spent replacing the darn thing. Will the advertising you are offering put the customer in more places and give them a strong chance at getting the five-to-ten customers they need to turn a profit? Other advertising already in place is irrelevant; if you show them this one would work, that is what prompts people to take that gamble. Will the construction work service you offer keep the customer's costs and frustration of doing it themselves down? Will the vehicle you recommend keep down expenditures on gas and repairs? It all comes down to benefits. Show them what they need to see to be closed and you give yourself the best chance at success.

So, let's say a customer tells you they do not need the extra vacuum appendages you throw in there. They tell you they do not want five of the items you are throwing into the kitchen set or that the sunroof and power windows are unnecessary. They ask you the cost without these items. What do you say?

"Mr./Mrs. Customer, I totally understand you are looking at cost and that is an important factor in your decision. While I built your program around the item we discussed first, the other parts are all components of the bundle I created for you. Why, with everything that comes with this bundle, would you not believe this is worth the investment? For what specific reason do you not believe in the value?" You should, given opportunity, go so far as to ask them if pertinent, "Why would you turn away the additional opportunity to save or make money?"

You have deflected their request. A lot of getting around the price objection is deflecting it; making it about lack of belief.

"I have already shown you how this will benefit you and save you money. We both know you would jump all over it if you believed in the concept. For what specific reason do you not believe this is going to work for you?"

We often have a mental roadblock that leads us to believe throwing in more stuff a customer did not specifically ask for is going to prompt them to say "no." I will not deviate from my theme: you must overcome and get past all of your own roadblocks before you can get over theirs. They put you on the defensive all the time. Return the favor. Just because you throw out a comprehensive bundle including stuff they did not ask for by name does not mean you will rock the boat. Do it delicately, as previously described, and you give yourself the best chance at success.

Seriously, how can you make up a customer's mind for them? How can you pre-determine that a cost is out of their price range or a certain type of results is all wrong for them? Recommend something, back up why you recommended it using the customer's own words and philosophies and needs and wants and make the customer defend their lack of belief if they say they do not want it.

Once you have gotten over your own inhibitions about the pitch, that is half the battle of moving forward at this stage in the call. We looked at when you time your pitch— by or roughly 10 minutes in, after you ascertain the information you need to move forward – and we talked about the fact price is irrelevant, pitching as much as possible is key and that you want to keep it to the point. Now it is time to make the pitch.

First, acknowledge with gratitude that the customer answered your questions. It marks a line in the sand that the question-asking phase has passed. Please be sure you asked all pertinent questions – from this point forward you should not ask any questions unless you have to clarify items while overcoming objections. Your pitch is a locomotive; it is now leaving the station and you cannot stop its momentum or the journey is over. If you are still asking questions in the midst of your pitch, it becomes herky-jerky, no momentum is built and the effectiveness is completely shot.

For example, I have heard a lot of people start and stop during the presentation, almost waiting for some kind of indication from the customer if they are interested or not. Doing so not only gives them the chance to shut you down and escape, but it also shoots yourself in the foot; you get absolutely no synergy going. I have heard the customer stop the salesperson, the salesperson scramble, panic and start asking more questions and the opportunity is headed towards a fatal destination.

At this transitional stage in the call, you also want to briefly recap the items you have learned which are pertinent to what is to come. You are going to use the customer's own words in crafting the pitch and overcoming objections so revisiting what they said as often as possible is a very bright thing to do. Doing so keeps it fresh not only in their mind but also in yours.

Immediately following the recap, state your personalized recommendation by name. As I stated before, each customer has probably one or two needs that you can address with a specific part of your product offering; always lead with what they gravitate towards most. It will serve to entice them and get them hungry; you will skim the details of the other components pertinent to or included in your pitch and then you will end with a question that serves as your close.

BUNDLE when you can. Even creating your own bundle when your company did not is more than acceptable.

Never give the customer too much information up front. If you have them hooked because of the benefits of one part of your service but want to sell them others, great! Entice them based on those main attributes and let them know the other portion is along for the ride as a courtesy; it is all part of the bundle. You can explain the benefits of the main angle you are taking but leave the rest of it as a simple mention as part of the bundle.

Always keep it simple until/unless the call necessitates complexity. Do not over-use statistics. They can be your friend but can also be your undoing. Statistics are like alcohol: in moderation they can improve your health but too much of them will lead to mass destruction and chaos.

Always end your pitch with a question. It forces a response. If you just dangle a statement out there, awkward silence will often ensue.

If there are freebies and gimmicks associated with your product, DO NOT talk about them until after the customer indicates hesitation. Don't fire every bullet from that gun because if the prey keeps coming at you, there is nothing left to battle with. If they attempt to run away, there is nothing left to keep them in the game.

"Fantastic, thank you for the information about your family's vacuuming needs. Based on what you told me, your husband, you, and the kids use the vacuum cleaner from time to time. You are replacing it every three years and using it twice per week, meaning you get a little over three hundred uses out of it. There are some hard-to-reach places in the house where you have to clean by other means. All of that said, I recommend our Scott Super-Suction 1000. It is simple to use, making it easy for everyone to share in the work whatever their age or cleaning skill level. Whereas your current vacuum lasts 300 uses, this sucker goes for 1,000 uses, meaning it will last you ten years to your current one's three. As a courtesy, I will also include in the bundle the five additional appendages that make it easy as pie to reach all types of surfaces, crevices, nooks and crannies. Typically, each of these components purchased separately would cost $1,000 but because you are a brand new customer I can give it to you today for just $750. I can have it out to you within 5 business days. To what address should I ship the Scott Super-Suction 1000 today?"

Let me dissect; first, there was gratitude. Second, there was the recap of all pertinent information I intended to use in making this presentation. There was the name of the recommendation followed by benefits that addressed each aforementioned need or weakness. I skimmed over the "additional appendages" rather than detailing every single thing they could possibly do or clean and I stuck to how they benefited the original weaknesses and made sense for the customer. In fact, I threw in "as a courtesy" making it sound like I was doing them a favor by bundling them into the package. I quoted a perceived discount, dropped the price despite it being relatively high for a vacuum cleaner, and ended with a question as my close so the customer will be forced to answer.

Failure to utilize the information learned in the fact-finding is a major mistake that – believe it or not – I have seen many a time. Why would you ask questions if you have no intention of addressing the needs and weaknesses you overcome? On the same token, how can you effectively interest the customer and make them believe they need what you are peddling if you find out nothing about them? What you learned in fact-finding must be used at this stage and the vacuum presentation illustrates how you can effectively weave everything you learned into that brief but effective pitch.

Next, skimming over additional parts to make sure the customer understands what comes with the pitch but so as to not divert much attention from the main component of the bundle is important for momentum. People like to watch magic shows yet a magician does nothing to divert your attention from the tricks themselves. They do not show you the levers, pulleys and hidden compartments that make up the show. You see the end result; you see the part that is for the purpose of your entertainment. In that vein, the customer needs only see the part that is there for the purpose of profitability.

"As a courtesy" makes it sound like I am doing you a favor and treating you special just because. People like to feel special. Lots of people stay in terrible relationships because once upon a time the person made them feel special and they are holding out hope it may happen again. The desire to feel special is powerful and you want to shower your customer with statements that make them feel as such as often as possible.

Then we come to pitching price. This is obviously the most delicate part as evidenced by the fact it is what often instills the most fear in the hearts of the seller and the sold alike. No customer wants to hear it and no salesperson wants to drop it. The trick is prefacing the price and softening the blow by any means possible.

If I called you and said I could offer you a vacuum cleaner for $750, you would hang up on me. The price is seemingly ridiculous unless the vacuum cleaner will also wash your car, do your laundry and take care of your kids' homework. So, clearly, that approach is out.

Many salespeople attempt to get around the hefty price tag by going straight for the cheapest program available. Let's pretend for the sake of this exercise the cleaner itself is $300 and the appendages that were bundled in bring the price to $750. Some people would actually call a customer and lead with the angle that they have a durable vacuum cleaner for $300. They seek the path of least resistance but what they do not realize is they gave no benefits, found out nothing about the customer and they short-changed themselves, the customer and the company. If the proper questions are asked, proper benefits cited and price is effectively packaged, you can sell anything to anyone.

In the vacuum pitch, I quoted that market value of each of these items combined was $1,000 when everything is purchased separately. Showing that there is a built-in discount for this customer because they are a "brand new" or "preferred" customer is yet another way to make them feel special and to draw attention away from the price tag.

These principles apply to every walk of the sales life. The trick is not to make a pitch the customer will say "yes" to; it is the ability to anticipate and address their reaction, whatever it is, and continue undeterred on your road to the sale.

This customer will almost undoubtedly laugh at paying $750 for a vacuum cleaner and appendages. However, if you have done an effective job to this point, you have a lot of wiggle room.

For starters, you have several overcomes to their objections; this customer gets 300 cleanings from their current brand and would get 1,000 out of yours. This sucker lasts three-and-a-half times longer than their current cleaner and let's say they are paying $250 or so each time they purchase the kind they use now. Obviously that would be something you would have determined during fact-finding. That said, you can show the customer potential savings in the long run. In addition, this cleaner is easy to use, making it potential fun for the whole family. Anyone who is the prominent doer of the chores would probably love to have assistance from other potential contributors. Finally, this cleaner can reach anywhere and saves time, effort and additional cleaning methods to get those hard-to-reach places.

In addition, if and when worst comes to worst, you have a lot of room to trade down. Starting out by pitching the unit itself for $300 and later finding out the customer would need an appendage leaves you fighting an uphill battle. Starting out by pitching the unit itself for $300 and having the customer say "no" leaves you with nowhere to trade down. Starting out with something huge and leaving yourself a lot of room to play as the call continues is the best way to give you the best chance at success. That is what sales is about: finding the best methods that give you the best chance at success. That, and having and finding the ability to repeat them thousands of times until you get promoted.

That price is cost justifiable and there is and should be no shame in putting it out there regardless of what the customer says back to you. You pitched this program for several reasons and will have plenty of time and opportunity to defend your choice.

Where a lot of slumps begin and continue is when dominant pitches fail to work for a string of calls, desperation sets in and we try to take the shortcut or pitch the valueless pitch or stop going with the flow we know we should use. Never succumb to desperation in any walk of life. It will lead to settling for less than what you or anyone else deserves.

Finally, each close needs to end with a question. When a question is asked, an answer follows, and in the event you have not already noticed, the point of the call flow we have discussed is to give the customer the chance to talk only when you dictate it. When you delivered your introduction, you went straight into fact-finding so they could not get rid of you. Even when they try to take you off your game during fact-finding, you acknowledged their statements, put them in their place and moved on. And now, you are pitching them what they need, not stopping during that pitch to even draw a breath, and you end with a question that will force an answer.

Many salespeople make their statement, say the price and stop. What function does this serve? It will lead to an awkward silence. You should not expect your customer to jump up and down and beg you to close them. If you delivered an articulate, to-the-point and masterful pitch, you have to put the finishing touch on it and that finishing touch is your close.

If I am a waiter and I tell you, "I'll be back with your drinks and to get your order in a few minutes," that is a statement that does not require an answer. Well, hopefully you will say, "Thank you." But if I say, "OK, I will get right on those drinks. Do you know what you would like to order?" society dictates that you have to and will answer.

Therefore, if you ask a customer specifically, "How did you want to pay for this today?" or "we just have to do a voice recording of your authorization; I'll be back on the line in thirty seconds, okay?" or "we can have that out to you within 5 business days, okay?" they will answer you. They have to.

Sales is guiding the customer to make the decisions and have the reactions you already anticipated they would have. Too many people take it too seriously, over-think it or over-complicate it. They think they have to talk for hours to illustrate everything they learned once upon a time when they read a training book. It is quite the contrary; a customer will purchase when they are able to identify their needs and weaknesses and the fear of changing is outweighed by the fear of not changing. If I see that your vacuum cleaner is going to save me money, be better for the kids to use and will clean places I currently have to get down on my hands and knees to clean, I'm in. That is not to say you have to show me all of those things; I may purchase based on any of the benefits at hand. That is sales.

The most important thing to realize when pitching is that you are building something. The pitch is neither the beginning nor the end but it is the engine of the sales car; without it, your call cannot move. What you learned in the beginning must be sprinkled throughout. You have to pitch without fear of rejection or price. You preface your price by softening the blow. And you end with a question to force a response. You are almost to the satisfying conclusion. Make it count.

*   *   *

Vincent was asked to aid or take over several projects through the years and he never came in to boss anyone around or start throwing around his weight. He approached the situation, studied it and learned it before offering his advice or making changes. He solicited opinions and feedback from those in the trenches and formulated his hypothesis.

In the original downtown 11th floor setup, Vincent could be heard throughout his section of the floor getting animated with customers. Reps in adjoining areas would wander over or not dial their next customer, listening for a nugget of his proficiency. In present day Greenfield, Vincent's rants to customers attracted a wider audience and garnered a different response.

As Vincent made his morning march through the kingdom, he would be stopped by several reps and managers alike, faced with questions about how to approach a potential sale, handle a local rep somewhere encroaching on their sales process, how to appropriately apply the credit policy or a discount, how to handle a sales dispute and so on and so forth. On this morning, November 30, 2009, he was flagged down by newcomer Ernie Carville.

The life expectancy of a rep in this center was not long. For someone to reach and maintain peak performance it was very challenging as the smarter, more industrious reps could see that the department was meagerly held together with duct tape. The commission and clerical problems that plagued the division could eat away at the soul of even the strongest rep, manager or Vincent himself. And the ineptitude of the people that should fix it and their unwillingness to do so was tearing the place apart.

The place thrived off of "at the moment" superstars. A scant few were constant performers who won the annual Top Gun trips. But one misstep, bad string of events or faulty voice authorization and they fell from grace and Dickhauser pushed to have them terminated for a first offense of any kind.

Ernie was one of those at the moment stars. He was perceptive and eager to learn; a breath of fresh air to Vincent who was trying like hell to keep his wits about him. As Vincent approached he saw Ernie doing battle. He glanced at the screen: a $500 monthly program with practically everything ABM had to offer. Ernie muted his phone.

"Can you talk to this guy?"

"What's his occupation, average buy, location?" Vincent said coolly.

"He's a doctor – physical therapist. Average client is $1,000. He is in Tulsa."

"What's the hold-up?"

"He doesn't want to start this big."

Vincent smiled. Most reps would start peeling away components and start throwing desperate, paltry programs at their customers just to get a sale. "What's his name?"

"Dr. Sumesh."

"Let me at him," Vincent said, taking a seat on the edge of Ernie's desk.

"Dr. Sumesh?" Ernie said into his headset. Vincent picked up the handset and unmuted it. "My supervisor is standing by and was going to go over some of the specifics of this program for you."

"Dr. Sumesh?" Vincent asked, announcing his presence.

"Yes," came the reply.

"Hi, this is Vincent Scott with ABM Advertising. I'm Ernie's supervisor and just happened to be passing by. How are you today?"

"Doing well, thank you."

"Fantastic, Dr. Sumesh." Name repetition: check. "The reason for our call today was because you actually came to us recently and opted to add some additional information about your practice to our online directory. First, I want to thank you for that. Honestly, I wish more of our valued customers took the time and cared as much as you clearly do." Ego stroke: check. "Let me ask you – what are you doing right now to market your practice?"

"Ah, well, uh, I am in some medical magazines, the local paper and have done some radio spots. Stuff like that."

"Tremendous, Dr. Sumesh. Obviously you're a man who is serious about his business. What types of results are you getting from those mediums?"

"Eh, well, I'm not 100% sure."

"What do you have in place to track it?"

"Uh, nothing right now."

"OK, fair enough. I am sure you are a busy guy so your goal is to put yourself out there wherever you can – I get that. When you enhanced your listing with us were you just hoping someone would see it or do you actually want new customers?"

"Oh, well, yeah, I would certainly like new customers."

"Perfect. This is cosmic, then, us talking like this. Reason being, right now, and pardon me for saying this, I am concerned you might be putting yourself in a position of weakness with these other mediums, especially if you are unsure of the results. Sure, they occasionally work, but it's a crapshoot. It's a gamble. See, with us, we saturate the web with your business, so it's like playing with loaded dice; we put you in a position of power." Powerful words: check. "I'm looking at the program you and Ernie were discussing. I applaud you for being interested in advancing your practice and taking it to the major leagues. How far out do you attract customers from geographically?"

"Oh, just in Tulsa."

"Fantastic. See, that's exactly what we do; we put you everywhere you need to be to be seen so those customers know about you. Right now, you are merely listed with a basic listing on our site. Our featured listings are plastered all over the web, you get guaranteed searches – 100 per month in your case from the program you guys were discussing – and you also appear in our physical publication. Obviously one customer pays for two months of this program. What we do here is get the ball rolling through voice authorization. I'm going to bring on a recording device where Ernie will basically read through the items and you can walk through them together." Softening the blow: check. A perfectly executed sneak attack. "We will be back on the line in about forty-five seconds, okay?"

There was hesitation. He was closing in.

"Oh, no no no…I just can't do it," Dr. Sumesh lamented. "That's just too much."

"Too much? Okay, well, certainly, Dr. Sumesh, I understand it's probably more than you spend on your current advertising. That's why I don't want you to look at this like additional advertising. It's an investment in your business. See, here we give you the highest probability at a return on investment. You do understand the concept that one customer would pay off two months of this program, correct?" Cost justification: check.

"Uh, yes, of course, but—"

"Of course you do, you're a smart guy. So here's the thing: with the 500,000 books I am putting you in, the 100 searches per month we target for you on the major search engines meaning 1,200 over the course of the contract and with the business listings we post for you on some of the most highly trafficked sites in the world—" he paused for effect, "how do you not get the minimum of seven customers you need in a year to make this a goldmine?"

He stopped talking. There was a pause of decent length that Vincent had absolutely no intention of breaking.

"OK, but I don't see why it's so much money. I mean, I talked to Online Plus the other day and they have a similar program that is only $200 a month."

"Yes sir, exactly, Dr. Sumesh, and again – I applaud you for doing your homework. You clearly care about your business. That in mind, I care, too. Personally, it does me no good to set you up with something that does not work. I am not comfortable moving forward unless you're comfortable. My reputation is at stake, quite frankly. And consider what you're getting here. How many guaranteed searches do you get from Online Plus?"

"Uh, I'm not sure. They said something about bidding on keywords."

"Certainly. Any respectable business would do that for you. How many keyword combinations are they bidding on for you?"

"Uh, well, they were going to put me under physical therapist in Tulsa so I come up on the first page on the major search engines."

"Okay, that's a start. What else are they giving you for that $200 monthly fee?"

"Uh...I would show up on their site, too."

"Sure, sure, Dr. Sumesh. What else?"

"Uh, that's all they told me."

"Certainly, Dr. Sumesh. And it is my obligation to tell you, especially since you took time out of your busy day that I want to make busier to fill out a listing on my site, that you've got to compare apples to apples here. Look away from the dollar signs you see. I want to show you ones you can't currently see. It's like you are investing stock here. You are thinking about dropping $200 into a program with a competitor that I will not disparage on this recorded call for fear of FCC retribution and showing up on *one* site. That's how thin that program stretches your $200. Now, with ABM, a company who has been in business since our great-great grandparents roamed the earth, I am putting you in 500,000 books. *500,000.* In addition, you not only are featured prominently on our site, but there are several additional sites with the same listings and similar placement. Lastly, while Online Plus is going to bid on, what it sounds like, one keyword combination for you, we bid on hundreds. Hundreds, Dr. Sumesh. Do you know why that is important, Dr. Sumesh? It's important for multiple reasons. One, let's say you have an area of specialty, like – let's say sports injuries. We would bid on 'sports injuries'. We would bid on 'sports injuries Tulsa'. We would also bid on the misspellings because, let's face it, not everyone is as articulate and gifted as you and me. We bid on misspellings so that if someone misspells physical therapy or sports injuries or, God forbid, their home city of Tulsa, they still will find Dr. Sumesh. That's where your $500 goes. And that's why this is a no-brainer."

Vincent paused again briefly for effect and for the sponge to soak in as much as it could.

"Clearly, you owe this to yourself. You work hard. Let us start working for you." Time to close again. "So basically what happens here is I am going to go ahead and bring on that voice recording system. Ernie will come on and just basically read off a script that protects you and will tell you the details here. You have the chance to walk through this together."

It was a poetic, beautiful close that was anything but beating the customer over the head with a blunt object.

"We'll be back on the line in about forty-five seconds, okay?" Always ask a question. It forces them to answer. Even if it is not the answer you want, it's the answer you need to hear to know how to proceed.

Pause.

"Okay."

"All right, Dr. Sumesh, congratulations on this step towards major success with your business. Ernie will be back on the line with you in just a moment."

Vincent put the handset back in its cradle as he hit the conference button on the phone. He looked up and practically the entire floor, mostly staring in wide wonder, erupted in applause. Vincent did a double-fist pump and high-fived Ernie. What a rush. The close. It was the best physical high that could be had within ABM's policies on its premises.

When Vincent was on the phone, people listened, jotted down notes and knew he was for real. Vincent waved to the crowd as he walked away, smiled and winked at Yamnitz and made his way to his regular home base at Cal's desk where Johnny Slade would always saunter up shortly thereafter.

"Guess that went well, huh?" Cal asked, smiling.

"Yeah, you know. Gotta bring the jersey down from the rafters every once in awhile so you pups know who is still king," Vincent cheesed. Cal laughed.

"Yeah, I just got off the phone with a customer, too," Slade said, looking disheveled as usual.

"Did you close it?" Vincent asked.

"He told me he was going to call the police if we called him one more time," Slade said seriously. Vincent and Cal laughed hysterically.

"Dude, seriously, how can you keep calling these leads?" Johnny asked.

"Dude, seriously, have faith in me. When have I steered you wrong?" Vincent asked. "Calling these ECL leads twenty times is better than calling non-customers once. Would you rather call those?" Slade shook his head. He was susceptible to pessimism and allowed the job to eat him alive more than most. Dickhauser's assessment of Slade was that he was the one who constantly cried "the sky is falling".

Sammy Kaplan and Helen Johnson had been the next two managers hired into the division in April 2006 following Vincent as the team was assembled. Sam now helmed one of the inbound teams downtown and was known as the conspiracy theorist of the bunch. While relatively astute and knowledgeable, he had little spine to stand up to the Dickhauser administration and was always making excuses for poor performance. While the exodus from Rockford was in swing, Vincent tried making a play to get Jeff Mason installed as a manager. Though Dickhauser promised Jeff a job telling him he was "earmarked" for the position at the interview, he was inevitably passed over for nepotism.

Steve Zimmerman was the third in a line of Zimmermans who had worked for ABM. His father was a ruthless businessman who ruled with an iron fist for years in another sector of the business. To Steve's credit, he never rode his father's coattails nor did he so much as mention him. To his discredit, he could not motivate a cheerleading squad at the pep rally the day before the big game.

Clyde sauntered over to the trio as the 11 o'clock hour approached.

"What's for lunch?" he inquired.

"I brought mine," Slade said.

"Who cares, let's get Chinese," Vincent responded.

"I'm game," Cal said.

"You know Sander won't go for it," Clyde said.

"He'll go. We have to discuss the next leg of the plan," Vincent said.

"Good point. I will gather the Brotherhood," Clyde whispered as he backed away.

Vincent looked at a nearby computer monitor and saw a blank dialer screen.

"Damn," he muttered. "We're in 'stop' mode."

This meant the dialer was out of leads in the current campaign and Vincent had to sprint to his office in the other quad to move to another one. Nothing made Vincent's skin crawl like idle employees, hence the sprint. He darted down the hall and back into his quad. Of course, employees were just standing around shooting the breeze. A couple threw a small Nerf football around.

"Nobody throws a ball until they hit objective," Vincent pointed, laughing.

He ran into his office, unlocked his computer desktop, ignored the blinking instant messages from managers telling him they were out of leads in this campaign and moved the reps to their next revenue-generating venture.

He looked and had received 27 new e-mails since his last stroll on the floor. He sat in his chair, sipped his Diet Coke and smiled. This life may give him a heart attack but he didn't know any other way. A job with less responsibility that was not as fast paced would bore him to tears.

"The Selling Game" by Vincent Scott
Chapter 5:
OVERCOMING ALL OBJECTIONS, FOREIGN AND DOMESTIC

Overcoming objections is like a Presidential debate; all eyes are on you and if you fail to address every issue on the table, you lose. This, I'm sure, is the chapter everyone has been waiting for, right? This is where I dispel the myths surrounding objections and tell you how to plow your way through them.

It's funny; when I started in sales I actually believed in all these different types, shapes and sizes of them. You know all of them – you're heard them, right? There is "lack of money," "it's not in the budget," "I have to talk to my wife," "I have to talk to my partner," "I'm going out of business," yada yada yada. What would you say if I told you that through my Indiana Jones-esque adventures of cracking open the lost ark of the sales world I finally figured out there is really only one objection? Yes – *one*.

It's true. Want to know what it is? It's *lack of belief*. Period. I don't care how you slice it; it all boils down to that. Your mission, should you choose to accept it, is to twist and turn to bring all objections back to that home base. Yes, I am going to show you how.

Sales is about getting into the shoes of the person across from you, whether in person or on the line. Like playing cards, you have to make your moves based on speculation of what the other person is holding, which is knowledge gleaned from your brief interview.

Don't get me wrong: the objection of lack of belief will appear in many different forms like the devil in the Bible. He can pop up from the get-go if you ask a closed-ended "yes or no" question. He can show up if you try to give a less than compelling sales pitch. Even the best will face the dark lord. In fact, a call without an objection is one of the biggest rarities in the world. Those are pure gift where no sales prowess is involved. Those are the ones that even the weak links can pick off. If you want to be the best, you have to learn to annihilate the rest.

A lot of salespeople and a lot of customers are afraid of "the close" because it is too often used as a blunt instrument. Do not bludgeon your customer over the head. We discussed how to introduce the close with a gentle subtlety and finesse and, in that vein, overcoming objections and "re-closing" are similar feats. At this point, you are basically playing that old board game Operation; the slightest false move one direction or the other will spell disaster. Be gentle; even soften your voice a little. They do not want to feel like they are being sold and you have to make it a completely painless, logical next step in the procedure.

One common mistake of overcoming is the same of calls in general: belief that throwing every piece of information you know and hoping, wishing, praying they will latch on and say "yes" is the way to go. It is far from. Find the objection, hone in on it and literally, you will need to find, in some cases, five different ways to illustrate the exact same point until it sinks in. Not every customer will buy. But if you hammer home that point – the magical one that illustrates how you cure their weakness – you give yourself the best shot possible. And that is the only chance you've got.

No customer – or person, for that matter – tunes in or listens to things that do not interest or concern them. You tune out or skip past commercials. Customers will try to circumvent your flow by saying, "Fine, let's cut to the chase; how much is it?" They often have a one track mind and short attention span on issues that involve opening their wallets. Because of this, the most important function of your interview is to ascertain the customer's sensitive spot. Once you have uncovered something you can do better or something that puts them in a position of weakness you have your bargaining chip. From there, the call requires having the patience to wait on mounting your attack until just the right moment.

The whole call is laying groundwork; we have talked about that. Once you deliver your closing question, the customer will dictate where you have to go from there. At this point, it is all about prudent and timely reaction on your part. In addition, you cannot falter. Another great line in *Cocktail*: "Never show surprise; never lose your cool." You have to make it appear you have anticipated their every answer and every move.

This is where my two favorite words on a sales call come into play. As I mentioned in Chapter 2, the words "perfect" and "exactly" can go a long way in disarming any objection your customer unfurls on you. Think about it this way; in the back-and-forth game of sales, your customer has probably delivered a lot of knockdown punches like, "I can't afford it" that caused the salesperson to back off. They expect that to work on you as well. Truth be told, if they could not afford what you were peddling they would not last a day of electricity costs. They do not believe what you are selling will work for them, which is why they are trying to get rid of you. You have not inspired them or conjured up any dreamy potential outcomes for them. Better luck next time.

Here is an example of how to head off a standard objection:

"Yeah, no thanks, I can't afford it. It's not in the budget."

"Exactly, Mr./Mrs. Customer, I can appreciate that your initial reaction is saying you cannot afford this. Let's face facts; you already told me that you are doing something that we discovered does not work as effectively as the option I presented. That said, how can you afford not to do this? If you believed this was going to work for you, you would jump all over it. For what specific reason do you believe this will not work?"

First, you disarm their objection by showing that you anticipated it. Let's face it; after a day, week or years of selling, you certainly should and do anticipate a little pushback, right? You hear most of the same objections so none should throw you that far off your game. You also have to sidestep the objection by turning it into something else and using the customer's own words to do it. Using their words to show weakness in their current platform and strength in yours makes it law. They do not believe anything or anyone above their own ideals, principles and words, and utilization of those things to cement your case makes it even easier to get the job done.

Furthermore, you have to turn the tides and make the objection about lack of belief. For, that is what the objection really is. If you believed you would get a desired outcome, you would spend the money, whatever the cost. That very principle is why insider trading is illegal!

"Mr./Mrs. Customer, I hear what you're saying, but earlier you told me," is how you begin pretty much any attempt at overcoming an objection. Let's say you are selling furniture and they balk at cost. You determined earlier their kids are going to use it so you once again hammer home your point about the stain-resistant upholstery. Let's say you are selling advertising and they balk at cost, saying their current advertising is cheaper. "Certainly, and of course it is, because look at what you are getting," and then you outline what they are paying for now, how it puts them in a position of weakness, and the way your method trumps it.

Once you have acknowledged their objection, put it in its place, dismissed it and moved forward with your lack of belief question, you have accomplished the sequence necessary to overcome objections. Then it is time to "re-close" with another attempt at asking for the sale and ending with a question.

This psychological tug-of-war we call sales is a wobbly balance; it can be won or lost with the slightest tweak here or there. When you fail to acknowledge that, you lose. If you fail to view objections as anything more or less than lack of belief, you lose. When you realize that your customers have all heard it all before, that is the big lesson to learn in not sounding like everybody else.

No business would turn down customers. No person would turn down an opportunity to save money in their homes. So why are they turning you down? It is because they do not believe. Economy schmonomy; now is the perfect time for a business to establish that they are in this for the long haul. Being dominant during the hard times is what causes a business to stay the course. So why is someone tightening their purse strings rather than opening them for you? It's called fear.

Overcoming objections is better described as dismantling customer fears. A lot of people are scared of objections and this is where their call flow falls apart. A weak salesperson will start throwing gimmicks, freebies and discounts out there too soon, will respond to a cost objection by trading down to the cheapest program possible without defending their stance or will just bail out. The effective salesperson will stand their ground and react based on what they have learned and what they know. Sales is a formula, a road map and a recipe. Objections are illusions. Sell past them.

I want to spend more time on the "cost objection" because it seems to be the one that knocks people out most often. You have to understand that an objection to cost is rarely an objection to cost. I acknowledge there are some people who cannot afford a complete overhaul to the way they live or do business. However, you have to acknowledge that if you are selling something of value, you have figured out how it can effectively fit in this customer's life and you have done a bang-up job of presenting that, it should be difficult to sell you on why they are sending you packing.

Our gut reaction is often to trade down to something else, but there is a reason you offered your first pitch first, right? Hopefully you put together that recommendation because something the customer said triggered that response. Stick to your guns. Tell them, "Mr./Mrs. Customer, I understand your gut reaction is to question this price. However, the reason I made this recommendation is this gives you the best chance at winning. This is the best value for you and gives you the best probability at success. Sure, I could have given you a less effective program or bundle, but I don't want you calling me in two months asking why somebody else is getting better results than you or why your program doesn't work. Besides, let's face it, if you believed this was going to work out favorably, you'd jump all over it. Why specifically do you not believe that?"

Any trade down you provide the customer will give them lesser results. A $1,000 per month advertising program certainly gives the customer a better probability at return on investment than a $50 per month program. They simply do not believe they will make their money back, which is why they are reluctant to make the seemingly larger or riskier purchase. You may or may not have illustrated how easy it is for them to do so. Either way, you have to do it again. You have to challenge that lack of belief. You have to ask them for specific reasons they do not believe they will get that return. Only by doing that will you oust the "underlying objection."

The underlying objection is the one the customer is guarding. In *Superman II*, a staff member was hiding the President from menacing General Zod for his own protection. Some probing on Zod's part revealed the real President. You have to do the same. Lack of belief is often hiding behind other disguises like "cost" and "my partner." Some objections are lurking in the dark and you must bait and lure them into the light. If you fail to find the "real objection" you will succumb to their excuses and never close them.

Put the customer more at ease, "Mr./Mrs. Customer – clearly you see how this program would benefit you and we have gone through how you will make a return on investment; what could possibly still be holding you back? Why do you not think this will work for you? I do not feel comfortable moving forward unless you are completely comfortable. Let's get all the cards out on the table. Shoot straight with me – is it price?" Your customer will respect you more and you will have forced any remaining objections to the surface so you can overcome them. People buy from people they respect and they respect people that respect them.

If you immediately back down or trade down, you show you have no belief in your product or pitch. Why would you offer something only to jettison it at the first sign of trouble? Be faithful to your pitch and it will be faithful to you. Just find a million different ways of diverting your customer from their scheme of getting rid of you.

"Expensive? Actually, if you consider what you are getting for the cost, it is a phenomenal rate. Let's look at what you said you are doing right now. You get X for $X. Now, what I'm talking about gives you X, X and X for $X. Fact of the matter is, if you truly believed this would work for you, you would do it. Why don't you believe this gives you the better outcome?"

"I understand you have a set budget and I do not want you to look at this as some additional expenditure. This is an investment; like putting a billboard in front of everyone that is driving down your street and ten others, just to make sure they know to go to you. I have the people that will make this worth your while, but how will they find you if they don't know about you?"

Putting your customer on the defensive is one of the most important parts of overcoming their objections.

"These customers are ready to buy right now and every month you wait is a missed opportunity. They will just go to your competitors. What is going to change between now and a few months from now with your financial situation? What does waiting another day do to the playing field despite more missed opportunities flocking to your competition because they can't find you?"

Customers will tell you to call back later, check back with them in a few months or follow up after some time has passed. Hogwash, I say. You, as a sales wizard in the making, must realize this customer is only attempting to getting rid of you. Do not allow the customer to leave you twisting in the wind. Get an answer, even if it is not the one you prefer.

Remember in *Back to the Future Part II* where Marty located a sports almanac detailing the outcome of every sporting event from 1950 until 2000? Going back to his time would have resulted in him being able to bet on those

194

contests and be guaranteed a win every time. That is what the customer wants —
a guaranteed win. We have to get the customer to realize that, while neither we
nor anyone else can provide that guarantee, we provide the next best thing. If
you convince them they will have that probability, they will sign up, however if
you do a poor job, good luck finding a flying DeLorean to help you erase that
missed opportunity of a sales call.

When your customer says they are not a believer, you have to act
dumbfounded. It all continues the game and the show. Truth be told, this act
looks a lot better if you set yourself up for victory with a solid foundation to
your call. Failure to do so will just make you look dumb. Not dumbfounded.
There is a big difference.

Some customers try to keep it general to guard their misgivings from
you. You must bring them around using specifics. Just telling you they are "not
interested" without the courtesy of elaboration is like the great and powerful Oz
hiding in the smoke and mirrors; you must direct all your attention to the
objection hiding behind the curtain.

For example:

"Yeah, I'm just not interested."

"Wow, really? Honestly, Mr./Mrs. Customer, I have appointments lined
up all day every day to set up programs for customers that work. I am not
comfortable moving forward unless you are; my reputation is done no favors if
this pans out badly for you. That said, what specifically about what we have
discussed are you not interested in?"

Notice how I keep talking about specifics; it is key to obtain specific
reasons from customers why they are not interested so that you can attack each
one individually. Leave no stone unturned and no objection unaddressed.
Failure to tackle an objection will lead to just that: failure. You don't leave
athletes unguarded in any sport lest you get burned when that pass falls into their
open arms. The customer who just says they are not interested is holding
something back. Call them out.

Let them hang up on you. You knocked them out of the ring and they
did not come back. Something you have to let go of is the fear of losing
something you do not even have. So many salespeople are terrified that a live
customer will walk away from them, so much so they start doing all kinds of acts
of desperation to keep them engaged. When a relationship is over, it's over. No
amounts of flowers, cards, apologies or sweet gestures can resuscitate a
relationship on its deathbed. This is because one or both of the parties have
thrown in the towel and there is no comeback from that. Showering the
customer with desperate actions to keep him or her on the phone will lead only
to a more embarrassing breakup and loss of dignity. Stay strong, stay defiant and
keep them engaged with legitimate belief in yourself and your product.

Keeping an unhealthy relationship alive while deluding yourself into thinking it will pan out in a positive fashion is something we as human beings are far too prone to do. Cut the cord, folks. He or she is not going to marry you. This customer is not going to buy from you. Most purchasing decisions are pretty simple; are they in or out? What do they need to see in order to make up their minds? Every second, minute and day that passes will make them forget your allegedly award-winning sales presentation, so why run that risk? Get an answer from the customer by asking the right questions when they object. If you did an effective presentation and it still does not instill the desire to come over to your camp, cut bait and let it go.

Acknowledge their need and be sure they understand you can provide for it, all while making sure they know you are not comfortable moving forward if they are not comfortable. You have shown you care, you respect their needs and you will stick with them until the end. Chicken soup when they are sick doesn't hurt, either. This is also the trick to a long and healthy, loving marriage (so I hear; I have never been accused of having a good relationship). Thank me later.

Always acknowledge their objection, put it in its place, deflect it and ask another question.

"I don't need it; I have too much business already."

"Oh, perfect, and I applaud you for the incredible business decisions you must have made to put yourself in that desirable situation. However, what I am offering is the opportunity to pick and choose from a more lucrative client base. What are some high-end jobs you do that we can send you to pick and choose from? Is there an additional product line of services you market that we can attract customers to?"

"If I called you right now as a customer, would you actually turn me away?"

Yes, some customers may have an established client base or product line so get creative; find something you can do for them they have not already thought of or are not already putting out there to the public eye. Applaud your customer for the good fortune they are currently in, but how long can that pipeline of business last? Statistics say it will turn over within 10 years. What potential audience or benefit can we put them in front of they are not currently thinking about? What work can we provide that would not take up any manpower? Do they have an additional offshoot product line that is not being marketed? What are some high-end jobs you can give them so they can pick and choose their work from expensive gigs rather than handling low-end as well? Find some way for your product or service to fit and suit them. Chances are there is something you can do for the customer. If not, move on to someone else and relish the numbers' game.

196

The customer may tell you that they do not use what you offer as their preferred means of satisfying that need. "Exactly, Mr./Mrs. Customer, it sounds like you have a fantastic plan right now for getting the results you want. However, why would you discriminate against the type of results I have just because they came from a different source?" Trust me, no one wants to discriminate. Using words with emotional connotation can get people into the game.

"Your current plan of attack has gaps and it is imperative that we address them immediately so it stops costing you money and customers. Why do you feel it would harm your business to put yourself where people are looking for you?"

If a customer says they do not get customers from the radio, the newspaper, the Internet, or wherever you are trying to put them – of course they're not! They do not appear there! Those customers are going to their competition! You have to point that out. Then hark back to what they said they were doing and show them they are being one-dimensional relying on one or two means to lure new clients while you can open up a whole new world of business for them. If you entice them through any combination of playing to their fear of loss, greed or ego, you are well on your way to a successful close.

In case you have not noticed, a lot of overcoming objections is hitting the customer with a question they will have difficulty answering without falling into your trap. The analogy has been made that you are a prosecuting attorney and, that said, you are asking questions that are designed to elicit the responses you desire. You are painting a picture, building a case and putting the finishing touches on a masterpiece; you are leading the customer to water. You cannot make them drink but if you get them close enough a lot of them will fall right in. All through your fact-finding you were asking questions looking for facts and for the customer to say just enough that you can utilize against them later. Referencing the customer's own words, facts and figures make it an open-and-shut-case.

Some people just say, "No, I'm not interested." Your questions in that scenario will be designed to force out the reason they are not interested so you can fit them into some other objection category. Others give you a reason and your questions are designed to keep the conversation flowing and find your angle.

Some have tried your product before and did not like it. You are not going to win a former lover back without repenting and promising that this time will be different. You are also not ever going to win them back if you do not address the specific concerns that led to the downfall in the first place.

"Yeah, I tried it before and it didn't work."

"Certainly, Mr./Mrs. Customer, I understand completely how you feel. Obviously you saw the value in this to begin with so where did the situation go wrong? What specifically did not work about the program?" What did the customer have? Can you figure out why it did not work the first time? Once you figure that out, you can show the customer why it did not work at first and why this time it will not fail. Remember, they saw a benefit to doing this at one point. You have to reignite that flame to rekindle the romance.

An objection that can rear its head for those selling over the phone is that the customer does not make transactions over the phone. Again, do not feed into these things! If somebody called you and said they were going to mail you a check for a million dollars and just needed your address, would you do that transaction over the phone? Your pitch may not be as compelling, but if you instill belief, they will buy.

"I understand your skepticism, Mr./Mrs. Customer and, quite frankly, neither do I unless I'm doing business with someone reputable. In this case, you are doing business with a company that has been doing this for quite some time and has produced thousands of very satisfied customers. I can and will send you copies of everything along the way and will be your personal contact if you have any questions on the program. We make many transactions in life like paying bills, paying taxes and making appointments without ever seeing a face. Fortunately, this transaction is one that will actually benefit you. Truth be told, if you believed this was going to work for you in a positive fashion, you would jump all over it. That said, why don't you believe in that positive outcome?"

Every objection can be woven back into the only objection: lack of belief. You have to figure out how to do that with each and every scenario presented to you. Once you accomplish that, you will be a star.

You will also encounter those who tell you they have to talk to a partner or spouse. These *can* ultimately turn out to be dealbreakers, but that does not mean you abruptly lay down or even accept these at face value. The follow-up approaches and questions from this point are all designed to push the envelope as far as you can without upsetting your prey but you cannot and should not rely on this customer to sell that partner or spouse. Selling is your job, not theirs.

"Sure, sounds good. I need to talk to my partner about it and we'll get back to you."

"Hey, that's perfect. What is your partner's name?"

Believe it or not, some partners are a figment of the imagination. Asking this and seeing how they respond will gauge how real this person is.

"John Doe."

"Fantastic. However, I don't want to put you in the awkward position of having to sell John on all of these benefits. I want to be able to help answer his questions. How about we get him on the phone with us right now?"

Remember, if you let Decision-Maker #1 "talk" to Decision-Maker #2 about your solution for their business or lifestyle, that conversation is going to go a little like this: "Hey, Vincent Scott called me today about Scott Marketing." "Yeah, we can't afford it." "Yeah, that's what I told him." Then, you are history. Do not allow that to happen.

"Well, he's not available right now. I'll talk to him tonight and we'll get back to you."

"Perfect. Let's set up a time tomorrow we can all three sit down to talk. How is 9 AM?" By asking that question, you keep the timeframe close and you also try to force all decision makers to be in the same place at the same time. Again, the partner or spouse objection can lead to a dealbreaker but that does not mean you sit back and let it steamroll you.

I have never had a rep or manager give me an objection I could not overcome. Unfortunately, I cannot speak specifically to you or set up a 1-800 objection hotline to address specific ones you may have encountered. (Well, maybe that will be my next business venture…) However, the best advice I can give when it comes to overcoming objections is journal your experiences. The next customer you talk to has no clue about the miscues you made on the call before. There is no better momentum-building activity than learning from your past.

Write down what a customer said and did to get you off the phone or out of their office. Analyze it later and come up with the "what you should have said" response so you can use it later.

Everyone has been in a squabble with a significant other over something. Of course, you come up with the best zingers hours later – the things you wished you had said to have really socked it to them. In the dating world, it can be a while until you get the next chance to use a zippy comeback line like that. In the sales world, the next opportunity to dazzle is right around the corner. Journal what they said and keep reminders of what you want to say back under these circumstances when history repeats itself.

Keeping these reminders around as triggers to your conversation is a great idea. When I was a rep I had note cards decorating the framework of my computer monitor for just such occasions. When I was going into my pitch or faced with a common objection, I needed only glance at these notes to make my brain take me where I needed to take the customer. Do it several hundred times and it becomes second nature. Your current customer has not heard anything your last customer heard and you cannot build the foundation for a sale without every vital brick.

There are lots of situations when you see what works and what does not. The beauty is that you can find many different ways to accomplish the desired result. You will find your way of doing it. Granted, you may fall flat on your face with something you thought was a good idea. Even still, that may not mean it was not a good idea. But if you follow the map, no matter what side roads you take, you can still reach the intended destination of closing the sale.

You cannot under any circumstances leave the office or get off the phone with the customer until you know the specific reason why they did not purchase. In looking back on any individual attempt, can you identify that? Them just saying, "I'm not interested" or "I hate your company" is not a specific reason. However, if you go toe to toe with them, address all of their concerns but figure out that they are flat out afraid it will not pan out and cannot afford to take the risk, there is your answer. You can show them every which way but loose how this will work and can minimize the perception of risk, but you are not going to close them all. However, if you can answer the question of why specifically they did not purchase, congratulations – you did your job.

This also applies to those sly customers who try to get rid of you with the "just send me something" or "leave me your information and I'll call you when I want to do business" lines. Do not fall for them.

"Absolutely, Mr./Mrs. Customer, I can send you whatever you want to see. What specifically do you need to see that will help you make your decision?"

You want to make it sound like you are going to comply with their wishes only to continue your sales flow when they answer your question. They likely have no idea what they would need to see to guide their decision, meaning once they stutter and give you some other blowoff nonsense, you accomplished your goal. You hit them with a response and a question they did not see coming. In turn, you furthered your cause because they walked directly into your next question and attempt to close them.

"Well, I just like to see the facts so I can make a decision."

"Perfect, Mr./Mrs. Customer, take out a pen and paper so I can tell you what you need and it will be right there in front of you. Let me know when you are ready." This disarms the objection; if they need to see facts, perfect – let them write them down. No better collateral piece than their own scribble in the comfort of their own hands. "The only thing you need to see is dollar signs and I am showing them to you. Let's face it, if you believed this was going to work you would be all over it. What specifically is holding you back?" Make it about something else because it always is.

Some customers give you the "send me something" objection right up front. In fact, there is a whole another objection called the "initial objection" and it is just what its name implies: the objection a customer gives you in the beginning to get you off the phone and out of their lives. You want to get the

200

customer asking you, "OK, let's cut to the chase. How much does it cost?" When they ask that, they are interested. No ifs, ands or buts. How you handle that question is delicate and will determine your success, but if they say this line, they are interested in what you have to offer.

The customer's prime directive is to shake you off your game and yours is to shake them from theirs. Both of you are selling. You are selling yourself and a good or service. They are selling you as to why they do not need it. The initial objection is dropped from the start of the race; as soon as you announce yourself some of them try to knock you out of the park. That is precisely why when we discussed the introduction we minimized the opportunity for that initial objection by stating our business and going directly into fact-finding. If you get the customer talking about their baby, they are less likely to dropkick you.

At the onset, you get past the initial objection by doing the same thing you do to an objection, just in slightly different fashion. You are still acknowledging it, putting it in its place and moving on with a question, but you are doing it from a different vantage point.

"Hi, this is Vincent Scott with Scott Marketing Group. The reason I am calling is because I have a lot of potential customers looking for what you do and at present cannot find you. How are you currently marketing your business?"

"I hate your company and everything about you."

"Sure, Mr./Mrs. Customer, I understand your gut reaction is to dismiss me but I'm better than the average bear. The reason it is important we speak is because right now these people have no choice but to go to your competitors. How are you currently marketing your business?"

"Look, pal, I don't have time. Just send me something."

"Absolutely, I would love to. In order to do so, I just need to know a little bit about you. From what geographic region can you attract potential clients?"

This is a thinly disguised fact-finding question designed solely to get the customer to open up. Of course, once they tell you where they do business, you are NOT going to leave and just send something. You are going to continue your call as if they showed no resistance. Please remember that just because a customer says they do not have time for you, this does not mean their datebook will not open up when you say something interesting.

"Look, buddy, let's cut to the chase. How much does it cost?"

The lesser salesperson will answer with a price. Please, under no circumstances destroy your presentation by doing such a thing. Do not be intimidated or feel like you are under pressure because the customer put you on the spot like this. Anticipate it and meet it with the right response. Some people are tempted to give a low price they think the customer will accept just because they just gave you the ultimate buying sign but do not succumb to this temptation. Even if you do sell something this way, it is not the way to go. You can turn a bunt into a base hit but that does not mean you square to bunt with two outs in the ninth and the bases loaded in Game 7 of the World Series.

Answering the cost question is just another part of your flow on the road to the sale. Acknowledge it, put it in its place and move on to your next question.

"Great question, Mr./Mrs. Customer, and that's the beauty of it. The cost is completely up to you, based on what fits your needs best. What geographical area do you want to draw customers from?"

You deflected their intent by taking them to the next leg of the call. Granted, sometimes this works and sometimes it does not. Just remember that everything is selling and right now you have to sell them on why they should answer your questions.

"Look, I just want a price."

You cannot allow yourself to be rushed into a price. A contractor needs to know if he is building the Sears Tower or a treehouse in someone's back yard. Tell your customer that. Shut down their obstacle and get back on your agenda.

"Sure, Mr./Mrs. Customer, I get it, you are completely bottom line focused and I can appreciate that. But this isn't just some one size fits all situation. You don't just set up the butcher, the baker and the candlestick maker with the exact same program, now do you? I just need to know a couple things about your business so I give you the program that gives you the best chance at return on investment. What geographical areas do you want to target?"

Many of you are wondering if I really talk to customers like this and use these phrases. Yes I do. Never forget that you want to sound like the complete opposite of everyone else who failed before on a call with this customer. I am going to be unique to get that unique outcome. Someone once told me that if you get a customer to laugh you have them hooked, and I would say that is a fair assessment.

When the customer tries to signal your death knell at the onset of the call, do not lose your cool. Check yourself before you wreck yourself. Acknowledge, put it in its place, dismiss and move on.

It is imperative that you turn any and all of their negatives into positives. Acknowledge their objection and weave it into a sentence that turns around the nature of the factor at play. "Perfect – I understand you get a lot of referral business; clearly you are doing an amazing job with your clients! We can offer you an even bigger well for referral business. What geography are you capable of covering?" By doing this we have acknowledged the objection, overcome it and transitioned directly into another fact-finding question, meaning we obtained more information about the business but did not enable the customer to get a word in edgewise. When I talk about this, especially when I preach a steamroller of an introduction, I hear the voice of Burgess Meredith's lovable Mickey from *Rocky* advising the champ in his first fight with Apollo, "Don't let that bastard breathe!"

Another of my favorite words on a call is "courtesy." Nearly everything I do for my customers is "as a courtesy" and this is yet another way of buttering them up and making them feel special as you guide them to making the decision you want them to make. I cited earlier that people utilize gimmicks, freebies and promotions far too early in the call. Lots of people throw them out in the pitch itself, which is a waste and selling on gimmicks does not work. Besides, if you tell someone you are giving them a 25% discount on something while you are pitching it, you make it sound like what you are selling is crap. Why do you have to discount it? Do people not want it so you are having a fire sale? Remember, this whole charade is psychology, nothing more.

Discounts are best used as a closing technique after the customer has already given you some pushback. They are simply icing on the cake; they should not be and are not the cake mix.

"Well, I just don't know; I mean, it sounds good but I need to think about it."

"Fair enough, Mr./Mrs. Customer, I totally understand. The direction of your business is a very important thing. As a courtesy to you for making this decision today, I will even give you a 25% discount that our new preferred customers can enjoy. I will tack that on to the invoice and we will get you set up with this program at a reduced rate. To what address should we mail the bill?"

If you have no bullets left in your gun at critical parts of the fight you have no choice but to run. Pull the discount out as a last resort and make the customer believe you are doing them a favor because you like them. Come on, how many times have you been told by someone or some business that you are a preferred customer? How many "preferred" customers do they have and how did you get so lucky? Believe me, you are in a tie for first with thousands of others.

As you have noticed, every response to an objection is designed to move right back towards the close. The close is that ultimate apex of sales moments; it's when you ask the significant other to marry you and you wait those heart-wrenching seconds until you get the answer. Your fate lies in the balance.

It is terrifying for so many because people fear losing it even if they are nowhere near it. Few things provide the adrenaline rush that "the close" offers; it probably ranks in the top five emotions or highs in the world. It is like hitting a home run in baseball; granted it is something that happens frequently but still gives a thrill and is not always easy to do. Some people are better than others at it, some improve through hard work and some are not ready for the major leagues. Possibly the biggest difference is that steroid use has never been linked to sales prowess.

The reason the close scares so many salespeople is because many have no idea how to drop that hammer on someone. People plan a lot of elaborate marriage proposals because they do not get a second chance to make that lasting impression. The close is no different; it is a delicate part of the operation that, if bobbled, is worse than the baseball trickling between Buckner's legs in Game 6 of the 1986 World Series. Game over.

The fix is this: take the fear out of it for both parties. Yes, you are going to have to take that flying cannonball leap into the deep end of the pool and throw out the closing question. Yes, you are going to have to put it all on the line at some point in the call and get the customer to say yes or no. Yes, you are likely going to have to attempt to close the customer multiple times. But the more you focus on removing the element of fear for either of you, the better the chances at having a happy ending. The potential pain removed, the attempt becomes easier, and the customer is less timid when responding.

Rather than slamming them over the head like a mallet with your close, you want to make it sound like walking through a dewy meadow hand-in-hand. You want it to be as gentle as can be, but to the point, which you can achieve through a yes or no question.

"Mr./Mrs. Customer, based on what you told me, it is clear your marketing strategy is on the right track, however, I want to put you in a better position of strength. Having said that, my recommendation for you is our Superior Package. With the Superior Package you get additional customers looking at you from segments you are not currently exposed to. As we already established, an average customer spends $200 with you and I am putting you in front of 1,000 potential new customers per month. The price of this program is $1,000 per month meaning your 6th customer out of those 1,000 turns your profit. How would you like to put down your first installment today?"

That is what is called "assuming the sale" – you laid it all out there and asked a question that the customer must answer. That was a close. I know I am making it sound easy but trust me, do that one thousand times in your life and it gets pretty painless. You want your close to be perceived like it is walking down the Yellow Brick Road to see the Wizard. A quick, easy, to-the-point and completely painless close forces the customer to answer. You will still get objections, but that is where all of the aforementioned strategies come into play.

"No, no, I'm just not able to do it today. That is way too much money."

"OK, certainly, Mr./Mrs. Customer, I understand your hesitation. However, you do understand the concept that you just need six customers in order to make that return every month, correct?" Getting them to acknowledge

204

they understand that concept may seem redundant or unnecessary, but is quite the contrary; it is the lifeblood of what you are trying to accomplish with this line of questioning.

"Sure, I get that, it's just that I can't afford that kind of program right now."

"Sure, Mr./Mrs. Customer, I completely understand your reaction to the cost. However, with those 1,000 new customers potentially looking at you, how do you not get the six customers you need for a return on investment?"

Then you must stop talking. A huge part of working sales is knowing when to talk and when not to. Kenny Rogers' classic song "The Gambler" might as well have been written about selling as you do need to know when to hold 'em ,when to fold 'em; when to walk away and when to run.

"Right, I understand everything, but I just can't afford to take that kind of risk right now."

This, ladies and gentlemen, is where you trade down. Not before or after. The customer acknowledged they understand the return on investment model. They have also been listening for probably ten or more minutes and are interested. Price is often not a legitimate excuse, but if you have gone through this line of questioning, you have determined this customer truly means it.

Another thing you must realize when overcoming objections and negotiating a sale is that people do not walk into the car dealership to pay sticker price. People want to feel like they are getting a deal. They want to feel like they negotiated something or got something out of you that others could not. That said, you have to be flexible enough to meet some of these customers halfway. In your mind, you always want to have about three pitches ready for any given customer. Start with your dominant one while having a competitive one waiting in the wings and a last resort if worse comes to worst. Do not trade down beyond that because at that point it would just be desperation.

One thing that scares salespeople about trading down is fear of losing credibility. In fact, I have pretty much broken down fear as the reason for every sales miscue. Just like attacking any other breakdown in the sales process, analyze why you feel that way and how you can avoid losing that credibility. Sure, you pitched a great program; how do you go to something else without sounding like a fool? How do you switch gears after getting yourself and your customer all excited about the benefits of Pitch #1?

"Absolutely, Mr./Mrs. Customer, I understand you feel you cannot afford this. It is also clear you are an intelligent business owner as you understand the concept of how this makes a return for your investment. If you are not ready to be the big fish in the pond just yet, no worries. Let's just dip our toes in the pool first and get you set up on our starter package for new businesses. We can always upgrade at a later time. This starter package will still get you exposure to 500 new customers per month, involve you as a featured business in our mediums, and it is just $500 per month. Now you would only need *three* customers before pure profit kicks in. What is the address we should send the invoice to?"

This accomplishes several things; you have met the customer halfway, you yielded to their objection while still pitching a respectable program, and you may also goad them into buying Pitch #1 after all. Who wants to be told they are not a big fish? Probably not too many people. However, you softened the blow for them, used information they have provided you and showed them yet again how they will make their money back and then some. Finally, you did the most important thing: you ended the statement with a close that was designed to elicit a response. Whether it is yes or no, you go from there continuing to apply the same principles. That's sales.

Some may find sage Kenny Rogers' greatest song to be "Lady," and on a more sentimental evening I might agree. However, I invoked the fable "The Gambler" earlier, so when do you walk away and when do you run? I have always operated on a three-strike rule. While there is not an objection I cannot overcome, the truth of the matter is there does come a point when the realization hits that this customer is not going to buy. Some of them cannot understand or see your line of thinking; others have an unrealistic price expectation that would cause you to sacrifice any value in your program to give them what they think they want. For some, believe it or not, what you are selling really may not be a fit. Give these customers' objections hell; however, realize in the end you may be better off drumming up some new business elsewhere rather than kicking the dead horse.

As outlined earlier, you have three pitches in your mind that you are willing to sell. Stick to those while following the trade down strategy and you should be all set. If the customer does not buy at that point, the likelihood is that they never will.

Many statements I have made do center on the fact I believe firmly in the "one call close." While you do want to do everything you can to make that one call close a reality, there are absolutely times when you can accept a callback scenario. Not every customer can be closed on the first visit, and you have to get good enough to figure out which customers and which objections are real and which ones are just allowing you to twist in the wind. I have seen many reps chase customers for weeks that never panned out. Of course, I have also seen reps call customers ten or more times resulting in a close. Again, could they have called nine new customers in that span and closed a couple of them instead of just getting that one sale? Decisions, decisions.

206

Remember that one call closes are fun and sexy, but the customer will never beg you to sign them up. Test the waters to try to force that close on the first call, but with experience you will learn which ones are worth waiting for.

Before you settle for that callback, make sure they are legitimate and serious; there is nothing wrong with commanding some reverence for your time if they expect you to allot more of it to them.

"Mr./Mrs. Customer, I understand you are not ready to move forward right this instant. I would be more than happy to call you back if you are serious. Let's face it, we are both extremely busy people; I spend all day every day signing up customers for programs that work. What time tomorrow should I call you back so we can get the ball rolling?"

Try to gauge their level of seriousness while keeping the distance between now and the next call as short as possible.

"You won't hurt my feelings if this is not really something you are interested in. I am extremely busy and I know you are too. Are you legitimately interested or should we just part ways?"

Everything comes back to selling and closing. If you are not going to close the sale, close the next date and time of contact. You already know that the longer you allow this customer to dangle the less likely you are going to sell them. That in mind, keep the date and time of follow up as close to the vest as you can.

"Look, seriously, I am interested in this, but I absolutely have to review the budget and figure out how we are going to make it work."

"Absolutely, Mr./Mrs. Customer, I truly understand and I admire your devotion to your business. It is inspiring. Definitely review the budget and I'll touch base with you later. What time this afternoon should I call you back?"

The customer may deflect you for a day or week, but you do not want to automatically throw out a futuristic date and time. I have actually seen reps negotiate scheduling a callback for a week or month down the road when the customer gave no indication the decision-making process would take that long. Keep the next call close. Let the customer make it a longer interval if that is what it takes.

If you have someone on the fence, not ready to commit, or claims to be too busy to do business with you, acknowledge that their time is valuable but force the issue. However, do not allow them to ride the fence for too long.

"Mr./Mrs. Customer, I understand your time is valuable and you don't think you have the time right now to do this. However, for starters, you and I both know you would not still be talking to me if you weren't remotely interested and didn't see where this service will be good for you. Second, my time is also very valuable; I spend all day every day setting up solutions for customers that work. What time later today should I call you back to iron out the details?"

Force a response; close a callback for that day so they don't swim too far away.

"Once we lock this in, your part is finished. I go to work for you." Lines like this reinforce your stance and make the decision-making action itself feel really easy for the customer. Putting them at ease is one of the best ways to get them to make the decision you want them to make.

After all, you cannot close a sale unless the customer makes the decision to be closed based on what you have said and done.

If a customer is stringing you along, you cannot lack the gumption to call them on it. Be respectful, up front and honest, and command respect.

Remember, customers are not going to beg you to make them another notch on your sales board; you will have to provide the push that edges them closer to falling from the ledge of inactivity. Never forget that you cannot close them all; all you can do is push them as close to the edge of the cliff as possible. Some fall, some will not, but if you did everything you could you will get the preponderance to fall and you will find success.

People are far too scared of the word "no." Some take it personally, some take it to heart, but few realize that "no" is actually your friend. "No" does not mean "no," it means you need to press a little farther to determine what needs to be said to elicit a "yes." It means, "I need more information."

"No" is nothing more than a two-letter word; we cannot allow it to become the single most debilitating word in the English language. The word can come at the beginning, the middle, the climax or the end, but wherever you hear it you need only be prepared to rebound and bounce back from each utterance.

And to master the selling game, your handling of the pitch and the close are what turn a game of chance for some into a surefire checkmate for the best.

*   *   *

On Mother's Day 2006, Vincent Scott made an unannounced trek to Mankato to spend the day with his family. He surprised Kay and Vince, Jr., swooped in with gifts for his mother and they shared a meal. He had to make the quick turnaround after about four hours to get back to Minneapolis to rest for the sales day ahead.

He was three-quarters of the way back when his phone rang. The number was that of Gina Haskins, sister of childhood friend Eddie. "Hello?"

208

Vincent said, expecting Gina's voice on the other end. Instead, it was a frantic Kay. God love her, she had never owned a cellular phone.

"Vincent?" she said, clearly shaken.

"Mom?" Vincent asked, suddenly thrown off guard.

"Vincent, it's your Dad," she managed through tears. "He had a heart attack."

Vincent immediately pulled over to the side of the road. "Oh my God, is he okay?"

Vincent Scott, Jr. was the man Vincent will never be: patient, trusting, agreeable and accepting. Loved by everyone he comes in contact with, he was the impossible Dad to live up to. He worked hard his entire life and stayed in Mankato rather than branching out because of the ill state of his mother after his father died. He was the manager of a water softener company, member of the local golf advisory board and known throughout Mankato, typical of a small town. He was his son's hero, but his son rarely felt comfortable confiding that in him.

Kay Janice Scott, in short, was also a Scorpio. She and her son battled regularly throughout Vincent's high school and college years. Her desire for the best for her son and voicing of her concerns were often taken as attacks by Vincent when they were really anything but. They just had no idea how to communicate with each other. She was a teacher, and the fact she had seen so many bright students and so many delinquents made her adamant that her son would fit into the former category.

Vincent was far from what his parents thought should be typical. It was no fault of theirs, as they did instill their principles in him and he learned manners they taught him responsibility better than any parents could. However, in his mind, they expected the impossible: the chaste Catholic boy who studied diligently in all scholastic areas who went on to a great college and a greater job and had a perfect little family.

Were they wrong to want that? Certainly not, and Vincent could not begrudge them that. He only wished and longed for their approval, feeling he could never live up to their expectations.

Vince, Jr. was the fortress of strength – nothing fazed the man. This quick dagger to Vincent hit with brute force. It was also eerily reminiscent of the last time he started in a new department – the death of his Grandpa.

"He is in intensive care," Kay tried to speak but words failed her. "Here, talk to Duke," she managed. Duke Haskins was Eddie's and Gina's father and Vincent's Godfather.

"Vincent," Duke said as he came on the phone.

"Duke. What's going on?"

"Not long after you left, your Pops started having pain in his arm and chest. He told your Mom he thought she should take him to the hospital. She did, and it's a good thing. The doctors said otherwise he wouldn't have made it. They are putting a stent in right now."

"Okay," Vincent managed, collecting his thoughts. "I'm turning around now."

"Are you sure you'll be okay making the drive? I can come get you wherever you are."

Vincent self-evaluated for a moment, like the Terminator scanning a prey.

"Yeah, I'm on my way."

The drive back was not at all easy. He blared music and thought about everything but the situation at hand. It was the only defense mechanism Vincent had come to know: ignoring the problem so it cannot consume you. Good or bad, time had made him better and better at this mechanism.

He was greeted at the hospital entrance by Gina and Eddie who took him to Kay and the others assembled. Vincent was allowed to see his Dad right away.

"Hey, Pops," Vincent said, entering the dimly lit room.

"Vincent," Vince, Jr. said softly.

"Yeah, Dad, I'm here," Vincent said back, taking his father's hand. "How are you feeling?"

"Really, really bad," his father answered with little hesitation.

"I bet. Guess there's no question who would beat who at one-on-one now," the son attempted to crack, alluding to their legendary basketball battles. Vince, Jr. smiled.

"Get your rest. I'm going to talk to the doctor. I'll be back."

Vincent let go of his Dad's hand and started for the door.

"Vincent," he said. The son turned. "I love you, Son."

"I love you, too, Pops. I'm glad you're okay."

Vincent exited, relieved that things looked like they were going to head in the right direction. In the pre-Elizabeth days, only catastrophe could force him away from the job he obsessed over. And in the days to come, Vincent camped out in the hospital with his Mother.

The outpouring of support was staggering — visitors that used to live in their neighborhood, played basketball with Vince, Jr., and people from Church.

210

Literally hundreds of people showed up at Mankato General to show they were thinking about and well-wishing Vincent Scott, Jr.

Vincent stayed at the hospital for three days and returned to Minneapolis on Wednesday. His father was released the following weekend, bound to meds and lots of rest as he got strong enough for triple bypass surgery. The surgery took place just weeks later in Mankato and seeing his father in that kind of shape and pain was extremely unsettling. It was something that still resided within his memory bank present day.

As summer 2006 waged on, Vincent saw more of Phoebe on his floor, bringing candidates up to meet Derek or Keith, and on the mezzanine level passing by. She would stop and talk to him for ten or more minutes at a time, prompting his team and guys on other teams to chide him about her overt pursuit. Vincent brushed it off — surely this girl was just playing games.

His father's progress remained steady, rehab went well and he had dropped thirty pounds since the heart attack, now residing in Vincent's realm in the mid-170's. Kay was keeping an extremely watchful eye on his regimen, not allowing him near the greasy stuff that clogged his system the previous 60 years.

In a call center, you have to have energy, enthusiasm and originality. No workplace is fun and games but the closest you make it to that, the better.

Vincent's team gave themselves nicknames of DC comic superheroes. A team member brought in a punching bag they put at Vincent's desk to diffuse frustration after unsuccessful sales calls. Another brought in an air horn that sounded every time Team Scott landed a sale — which was over and over again. One day Vincent offered five dollars for the first person to call a karate dojo and ask, "Does fear exist in your dojo?" — a throwback to 80's classic *The Karate Kid*.

Their team became notorious for being loud, obnoxious and damn good at what they did. Any time a rep sold something, an e-mail flash went out to the department, and Vincent peppered the ones for his team with pictures of their superhero alter egos.

Every rep wanted to work for Vincent, every manager was jealous of him, and every newcomer Vincent interviewed wanted to be on his team. He was quickly making the place very aware of his presence. Vincent was in charge of managing the "library" of the directories for markets they blitzed, managed the disciplinary program, hired, coached and sold while many of the other managers just sat in their cubes.

Vincent's team numbers were amazing, topping 200% of objective regularly and he was number one on the floor all summer, save one month after someone closed a ridiculously high $7,000 per month program (the average sale was around $150 per month at this time and there was no stringency in the credit policy making sales like this possible). In early August, Derek Walters was pulled by the local office to come out and help get them whipped into shape. He was still the boss but was going to be out of pocket for a minimum of two months.

When Dickhauser solicited for managers to aid in Derek's duties, most socialized amongst themselves that the last thing they wanted was further responsibility. Vincent leapt into action – this was like a September call-up to show off and earn a spot on next season's major league roster. He was going to make the most of it.

In addition to his regular duties, Vincent jumped at the chance to handle sales tracking and send out reports, manage call-in's from their direct mail campaigns, collaborate with the vendors who designed their mailers, meet with Labor to discuss disciplinary items, put together the office mentor program and have several daily meetings with Keith Dickhauser to keep him abreast of the state of the office. In this regard, he was humble, respectful and looking for any way he could to help.

He garnered compliments galore from both Keith and Derek, and Keith started taking Vincent to lunches where he talked about the future: offices consolidating and potential opportunities as a lot of the figureheads of the business retired in the five-to-ten years to come.

As the youngsters around him saw Vincent vying for more, many made their play to hitch their star to him.

Now that Vincent's friends were all either in Mankato or married with kids or both, he found himself with a new entourage of kids in their early-20's. It was rejuvenating as he approached his 30's and was surrounded by these people even though most were only around him to buddy up to an up-and-comer.

He frequented lunches with those from his training class including Chad Willman, Jimmy Sander, Sahim Saundura and Abby, and others in the department such as Ronnie (a goof from the first classes who had a thing for Abby), his roommate Cal Riley who had just come on as a rep, Ryan, Angie and her friend Kristi.

The lunches turned into long nights at Finley's, a bar less than half a mile from Vincent's abode, which made the trek home convenient. Most lived within a mile of each other and Vincent downed buckets of beers and constant shots with them a couple times a week. They fancied themselves the best of the best and enjoyed drinking heavily trying to flaunt their greatness to anyone who would listen. The guys also liked upping their job title a couple ranks after a few too many as they tried to pick off talent at the bar.

You can always tell a rising star and Vincent definitely gave off that scent. These characters hoped that as he climbed he would throw crumbs to his newfound friends.

212

Heading into fall, Vincent's team was posting ridiculous numbers, putting up nearly 300% to goal in October. Some trying times hit, like a rep going MIA during a blowup with his wife and a cocaine relapse, another being arrested and AWOL for a few days, others showing up late or not at all, another either sleeping at his desk or attempting calls to his girlfriend in Florida during work hours, and others afraid of the phone and flat out not making calls, but a select handful kept the team rocking.

Vincent received word that Rockford had finally been absorbed. They finished September 75% to expectation, dead last in the district and second-to-last in the company with only 25 reps left on the payroll. They were swallowed by a retention department that was based in Mankato. Shelly was removed from office and given a job in a non-sales capacity with no subordinates. The fitting news proved that without Vincent and his team, Rockford's office was rendered inoperable.

While he came across as brash or headstrong sometimes, he meant well. The Rockford office did not have to fall apart like that. Those people did not have to endure that collapse. But, either way, it was the end of an era.

And the beginning of another. It was bound to happen but in late September, Vincent and Abby wound up the last two at the bar. It was late and neither wanted to part company or cease imbibing so Vincent asked her back to his place for a couple more. This turned into a makeout session until 5 AM and they had one more of those before it turned into regular sex after the Finley's evenings concluded. And all of it was unbeknownst to anyone else.

For Vincent it was the fact he was closing in on 28 and Abby was 22. She seemed exciting, was into him and was something new to take his mind off the monotony and seclusion his lifestyle brought. He naively thought he was the only one she was spending her nights with but would not find out until a year later that was not the case.

However, she quickly got clingy and would get upset when he opted to be alone after nights out with the group. At work they acted as mere associates. Vincent told no one of the involvement but Abby, ever a busybody, "confided" it in family members like her mother, and at work with Jimmy Sander. The fact she had relatives with contacts in the company resulted in rumors that certainly did nothing to help Vincent's career.

Over October and November Vincent spent several nights with Abby, going back and forth between trying to jettison the ill-advised encounters and inviting or allowing her into his bed. All the while he knew it had to end – and it did a couple of times but would always sneak back up when one or both of them were under the influence of alcohol or lonely or bored.

Vincent also found himself getting closer to something happening with Phoebe Wells; she had apparently drunkenly called Vincent her office boyfriend while in Dallas with her best friend, who stole her phone and texted Vincent sweet nothings that confused him even more. She did reveal she had talked to her friend about Vincent and told her she was going to go out with him. The plot thickened.

Times were high for a change after the health scare of his father subsided. Vincent was on top of his game in all areas – the sales arena was his, he was having regular sex with a beautiful girl 6 years younger and was on the cusp with the ultimate bombshell. He knew he had to lap up all the success because it is always only a matter of time before the bottom falls out.

Derek returned in November but it did little to deter Vincent's career plans; he was now the clear and undisputed #3. He even lobbied to become a special floater come 2007 where he would help coach all teams and be a go-to guy simply focused on driving results wherever needed. His training wheels on hiring were removed in November as he could now hire without deferring to Derek or Keith.

With things taking shape with Phoebe, Vincent jettisoned Abby in mid-November. It was for the best. They could not talk about it outside of Vincent's bedroom – or so Vincent thought – and it was, after all, just sex. Did he like the girl? Sure, but it was never going to go anywhere and was certainly not going to help his reputation or career. He had used her company to wade through a couple months of his chaotic life but Phoebe was the one he wanted.

On the last day of November there was a snowstorm in Minneapolis. They received nine inches of the powder and Vincent had joked throughout the day with Chad about grabbing a hotel room downtown and partying rather than trying to brave the fifteen mile drive home. As the end of the day neared, this became reality.

For whatever reason, Ben Friar tagged along, certainly the odd man out but on this night they thought nothing of it. First, the group went to Macy's for clothes they would don the next day at work and then got two adjoining hotel rooms. They played pool and started drinking Jack Daniel's drinks straightaway.

Into the third game of pool, Chad's phone rang and it was Abby. She was living with her cousins south of the neighborhood where Vincent, Chad and Cal all lived and was unable to get up the hill. She was trying to ascertain where Vincent was without calling him. And she had found him.

Chad, thinking nothing of it, invited her out. Vincent was already hammering back drinks, knowing full well that the office was within walking distance and neither Derek nor Keith would be there the next day. Abby showed up shortly thereafter and Vincent was determined to keep it on the level. However, self-pronounced ladies' man Ben started putting the moves on her, such as the classic "trying to show her to play pool" gesture. The more Vincent drank the more it irritated him and when they all retired for the night Vincent ensured that Chad and Ben passed out in one room watching porn while he was in the other room with Abby and a locked door.

During Pay-Per-View *Superman Returns*, the two had sloppy, drunken sex. In the morning, they repeated the act right before Vincent showered, dressed and headed to breakfast with Ben. Chad and Abby had both taken the day off work.

Vincent sauntered into the office void of many of its employees. It was a blowoff day in the making. He logged into the company instant messenger and, lo and behold, saw Phoebe logged in as well.

"Made it in, I see. What a trooper," he shot across the bow at 8:45. They traded over a hundred notes throughout the day before Phoebe departed after 3 to pick up her daughter Michelle. She gave Vincent her phone number, alluded to a date in the near future and said that her fiancé was in sales and out of town a lot. He was in the doghouse currently and she needed a "little break" from him and, while she assured Vincent he was not the break that she was intrigued by him and wanted to know more.

Vincent decided it was definitely time to distance himself from Abby and see what was what with Phoebe. This had been months in the making. Abby sensed the distance over the next couple of weeks and asked him to let her know after the holidays what their future would be. That was a foregone conclusion for Vincent and, on Friday the 22nd of December he and Phoebe had their "first date": dinner and drinks before attending a party that Gina Baker threw annually for subordinates, co-workers and friends.

They shared the same political affiliation, taste in movies and music and similar philosophies on life – and the witticisms and wonders never ceased. Phoebe insisted on buying a few rounds and tried to buy dinner but Vincent slipped his credit card to the barman while she was in the restroom. This would actually become a staple of every meal of their relationship to come: the jovial joust over who would pay the check. At Gina's party, at a sushi bar up the street, Phoebe was overly attentive and everyone got the impression the two were together. Even Abby got the impression, as she came along with enamored Ronnie.

Phoebe dropped Vincent off at the ABM parking garage where his car was parked after they left the party and they stood outside and embraced.

"So…I had a good time," Vincent said, holding her in his arms.

"I had a great time," Phoebe answered.

Their embrace ended and they looked into each other's eyes. The kissing both of them had waited months for ensued and they talked on the phone for their respective drives home. This seemed to be the beginning of a beautiful relationship. Well, modern-day, since you have to look past the fact

Phoebe was engaged and had a child and Vincent was fresh off a secret physical relationship with a rep on the sales floor.

The two talked frequently on the phone and on the work instant messenger and made excuses to disappear for makeout sessions in the stairwell between the mezzanine and fourth floor. They could not keep their hands off each other and had every intention of picking back up full force after ABM's office was closed from Christmas through New Year's.

Vincent had a leisurely vacation, hit Mankato and came back up late Christmas evening. He spent much of his week off just bumming around, gearing up for 2007. It was going to be a great year!

Saturday morning, December 30, he was playing all-time favorite game, *Final Fantasy IV*. It was a game he had defeated numerous times with characters he knew inside and out. It never got old and always managed to transform him back to the first times he played it in his teens.

His cell phone rang. He glanced at the Caller ID and it was Abby. They had agreed they were going to talk after the holiday, when Vincent would let Abby know his decision on their future, so he was unsure what she wanted. He answered.

"Hello?"

"Vincent?" Abby said with an odd tone in her voice.

"Yes?"

"I have something I need to tell you."

"Okay…"

There was a pause.

"I'm pregnant."

The sound of the words was surreal; something Vincent had only heard in television shows or movies. His mind scoffed at this information – not only had they been safe but they also had not had regular sex for nearly two months.

"No, you're not. That's not possible."

"Yes, Vincent, I am. I just got back from the doctor. I am pregnant."

There were those words again.

They had started out using condoms but, as she proclaimed to be on the pill, they had stopped. Her faithfulness at taking them at the same time every day was pretty haphazard and, there you go. Vincent had experienced "scares" before but each time the "odds" prevailed. This time, he fought the law and the law won.

Not a lot was achieved on the phone call; Vincent's professional life and his bachelor ways flashed before his eyes. He experienced total panic and complete helplessness. There was an inability to eat, leave the couch or even just feel normal for days to come. Whereas one month before he was on top of the civilized world, now his entire world was thrust into complete and utter disarray. He was terrified as to how this would play out.

Abby offered to let him walk away but he could not do that – right?

Vincent remembered just prior to leaving Mankato when Ted had gone through the same thing with his now-wife Robin. Of course, they had been in a committed relationship for a long time but the "right thing" resonated in his head – he had to figure out something here. He and Abby were going to be parents.

The sad fact in hindsight is that Vincent would have been better off psychologically, emotionally and financially in the long run had he just said, "Okay, bye, let's battle it out in court" to Abby from the get-go. But Harry Chapin's song "Cats in the Cradle" was never going to describe Vincent, regardless of his passion for his career. Hence the attempt to make it work with Abby, the fact he actually took vacation time just to be with Elizabeth after she was born and that he turned down promotion after promotion because they would have required a change of location.

In the days to come Vincent could barely move. He could do little more than lay in a state of shock or sleep and the concept took quite some time to sink into his head. In the weeks to follow, Vincent had to keep Phoebe at arm's length, just two months prior to her pending nuptials. He had to figure out how he was going to deal with this at work. He had to figure out what he and Abby were going to do. He at least did make the decision that they would try to make a relationship work.

Vincent was left to wonder: had the night of that snowstorm when Elizabeth Scott was conceived not occurred, where would the major players of this tale be today? Would Phoebe have gotten married? Would Vincent still live in Minneapolis? He wonders, but the point is moot – he would not take back the birth of the most profound figure in his life for anything in the world.

On that day, Vincent's life took an unplanned detour that has led to the greatest joys and greatest pains of his life. Holding Elizabeth for the first time, hearing her say, "Daddy", hearing her tell him she loves him, her constant learning of new things, her experiencing the world and him being able to see it, her awe and amazement and wonders – every little thing – filled Vincent's cold heart with love.

On the flip side the oil and water that was Abby and Vincent, the fights, the false allegations, the financial hemorrhaging he underwent, and everything Vincent endured at the hands of Abby left him scarred and battered. The situation with Phoebe did little to aid him. And the icing on the cake was tensions with Keith Dickhauser, treatment by ABM and the constant struggle to have the concerns of the people he worked so hard to protect be heard.

For here as November 2009 came to a close, while Vincent Scott can sit in front of his computer screen and take simple joys in moving his reps through a dialer, planning and plotting their day, tracking their statistical successes and failures and being the single biggest morale boost ABM had ever seen, he feels beaten up more and more often.

It is not unusual for him to return on a Monday with his double fists of caffeine and a head full of vision only to feel like a crowbar has knocked the hell out of him by day's end. The breakup and custody fight with Abby, the completely worthless tryst with Phoebe and the constant attacks from Dickhauser certainly beat Vincent as close to senseless as he had ever been.

Another dialer campaign loaded, Vincent refreshed the page where he had been attacked hours before. This was a case in point of the horrible things he had to deal with that no one could understand. Here was someone striking from the shadows, hitting Vincent where it hurt and he was powerless to strike back at the unknown assailant. Anonymous reports of Vincent seemed to be the order of the day for these spineless goons.

The post was still there. He read the words over and over again, in disbelief that someone would even say something so ignorant to him.

To keep his mind off it, he vacated his office again. Besides, sitting there collecting voice mails and e-mails as they arrive is not his style – he has to be out in the action.

Walking through the department he stopped for conversations with nearly every manager as he sauntered through their area.

The relationship between Vincent and the majority of the managers was a bond of true teamwork. Vincent had experienced everything they had and then some.

He finished 2006 at 233% to objective and was quickly greeted in 2007 with a 60% hike in objectives. He was also informed he was losing several of his top reps to the new inbound facet of their department. Mark Rogers, who finished 87% to expectation in 2006, a full 146 points behind Vincent, was assigned this pivotal group along with Danny Boyd. The rationale Dickhauser used was they had the most knowledge of the systems side of the business but the fact Mark was Keith's protégé was lost on no one.

Considering his top five reps were all stripped from Vincent in early 2007 to comprise part of the roster for this new super-team, it was clear the deck was stacked to prevent Mark from another atrocious performance. It was also clear Vincent had his work cut out for him.

Vincent felt the sting of this unfair movement but, like hell they were going to take his top placement from him. And what was frustrating was that in present day, he had few managers working for him that took that mentality.

Several were quick to pony up excuses when their crews were flattened daily on the report. "Oh, I had three people on vacation," "So-and-so was on disability this month," "I lost three people to the inbound group" and "I just need some new blood" were prevalent excuses for the weak amongst the managers. Vincent would never have been caught dead using something that pathetic to explain inability to do his job. No matter how down and out Vincent had gotten, he had never given up his stranglehold on the #1 spot.

He had the ability to will a situation into a win. Vincent still remembers vividly the two months he was not #1 in this department – one where Helen Johnson's rep landed that $7,000 sale in the last hour of the month and January 2007. He was #2 by $250. And the third place team was $5,000 in monthly dollars behind him. Those losses drove him to no end.

Being able to talk from experience about his days as a rep and manager helped bridge gaps between him and people in those roles and Vincent refuses to sever the roots from whence he came. He sees Keith laughed off by the people of their center because he is so removed from the job. Others make the ill-advised decision to manage through fear and ignore the fact that never would have motivated them when they sat in the same chair. Vincent has sworn to never become that person.

Every speech Vincent has delivered has contained the concession that he understands what his audience faces but that the adversity can be conquered. And Vincent had no idea what it really felt like to conquer adversity until he faced what the last three years had dealt him. Between battles with Dickhauser, squabbles with Abby and somehow still managing to motivate the masses, Vincent was headed into rough waters.

Heading into what was to be an interesting 2007, he shared news of Abby's pregnancy very slowly. The thought of telling his very Catholic parents mortified him but he was able to share it with Ted, Jack and Eddie. Vincent had seen Ted as a father over the last six years. Jack had recently settled down, having married two years ago and he and his wife Anita had just had their first child. Eddie married not long after Jack and he and wife Loren had a son who was nearing a year old. It was not a foreign concept in his circle of friends and they were full of thoughts and assessments on things he would face.

Abby moved much more quickly as she told her parents the first week she had learned the news. Her mother took it exceptionally well but her father requested a lunch meeting with Vincent. He got his wish, impressed that this kid had a good head on his shoulders, a plan for life and claimed love for his daughter.

Vincent had a million different emotions per day. At times, he was simply terrified. He had no idea if Abby was "the one" or if such a thing even existed. At other times he thought he was ready for the house, dog, 2.2 kids and wife that came along with it. While thankful this had happened later on in his life than his teenage years or early twenties, it did little to shake his fear at the potential collapse of his career.

Jack had been in Denver after moving from Mankato years ago and, after not latching on out there found a teaching gig in Minneapolis. After not able to get the job he was eventually angling for while there, Jack decided to move his family back to Mankato temporarily to plot his next attack. Vincent, as he always had in the past, helped him move and as he held Jack's young son that day, saw the gunk in his eye, touched his extremely soft skin and saw how adorably cute he was, could not wait to hold his own child. That was the day, in early February, that he shared the news with his parents by phone.

It took some liquid courage to get the words out but Vince, Jr. took it well. After garnering additional necessary guts he told Kay. She was a cornucopia of emotion and voiced her usual concerns but it went better than he thought it would. It was finally starting to sink in: Vincent Scott would be a father by year's end.

From there it was full steam ahead in many arenas. Plans to move the division to Greenfield were underway. Derek and Keith pulled Vincent in early into February to inform him that Derek was leaving to run one of the other centers that was an offshoot of the local office. Keith was going to interview Vincent to take his place. Abby and Vincent looked for a place to live together as the one-bedroom that Vincent had called home for 6 years was not enough room for a family. He introduced her to Vince, Jr. and Kay. They talked about getting married. The game was over for Vincent.

As for the job of his dreams, Vincent was ready. Interviews intimidate a lot of people but this was something Vincent had highly anticipated. He knew the field of competitors. Keith was also going to interview Danny Boyd as a courtesy and Lonnie Lawless, a local sales manager who had worked with Dickhauser for years.

Vincent came prepared with an outline that covered every topic he wanted to point out in his audition with Keith. He printed out examples of documents he covered with his team daily, monthly and weekly – showing the things he could and would implement widespread with the management team. He discussed things he would do to immediately have an impact in this new post, such as starting committees and brandishing new reports. He talked confidently about how he could get the managers to see his way of thinking, make them as successful as he was and how they already looked to him for advice. This would just be another level. And it made sense.

Vincent left feeling good. So good that he and Abby decided it was time for her to leave the company. If they learned Vincent had ascended into this new role and Abby was in his hierarchy, things would certainly not end well. Abby was excited about leaving as she wanted to finish her externship for medical assisting and she and Vincent made an agreement that he would help her financially for two months until she got a job. All was lining up well.

On Wednesday, February 28 Keith actually interrupted one of Vincent's interviews to pull him in the hall. Vincent shut the door behind him and followed Keith, noticing the odd look on his face.

"I just got out of a meeting with Lydia Rawlings. Are you…" Dickhauser began, then softened his whisper even more, "living with one of our reps?"

Vincent and Abby had provided employment verification to the apartment complex they were moving into. Could the paperwork have come across some busybody in HR's desk and they shared it with their Queen Bee? This was supposed to be confidential but he was not surprised they would breach it to circumvent his ascension. Regardless, he was not living with one of their reps. They were not moved in together yet, and Abby, as of the week prior, no longer worked for ABM.

"No," Vincent said. "What do you mean?"

"Lydia said there is a rumor you moved in with one of the reps here. Obviously that would be something I need to know, especially considering your candidacy for the area sales and operations manager here," Dickhauser said.

"I live alone and I'm certainly not involved with someone that works here." His carefully worded response was the only thing that could save his hide. Besides – why was this anyone's business?

"Okay," Keith said, with a sigh of relief. "That's all I needed to know. Carry on."

That caught him off guard. After the interview, Vincent was heading back to his desk when Derek and Keith stopped him and asked him to lunch. They must have taken the information back to Lydia, got the facts straight and this was going to be like that lunch in *Jerry Maguire*; the crowded restaurant and quiet termination away from everyone else they worked with.

When they sat down at the restaurant, both sitting on the opposite side of the table, Dickhauser said, "So, we're here to see if you want to take Derek's job, starting tomorrow."

And Vincent felt calm and triumph rush over him. Yes! Finally. Vincent Scott was going to helm a sales office. This moment made every moment he had clashed with Shelly Cheekwood worthwhile. He had finally gotten what he deserved.

It was announced to the managers after lunch and to the floor in a stand-up the next day. One year to the date of his arrival, Vincent had risen to power. Not only that, but in just the final two weeks of February he had overcome what seemed an insurmountable lead by Adam Sandberg's team ($5,000 in monthly revenue with two weeks to play) to beat them by $700 for the month. The next team down was $8,000 in monthly billing and 42 objective percentage points behind Sandberg. There was nothing like going out on top.

While Vincent knew he deserved this post, he could not believe that after all these years he finally had what he wanted. It was actually somewhat terrifying. However, it was not like Derek had ever sank his teeth in and coached managers on how to manage. That was where Vincent was going to make a difference.

It was all coming together. Vincent was working out regularly and in peak physical shape. He and Abby were finalizing their move-in to the new 3-bedroom apartment and seemed poised for happily ever after. Vincent, ever terrified of the prospect of the secret becoming public knowledge, was actually relieved after a night Abby experienced frightening indigestion when it was revealed not to be a miscarriage. It cemented in his mind that he was not just going along with the program; he did care about Abby and the baby more than anything.

However, the fights had started. Vincent was more than giving, bringing Abby what she wanted for every meal, shopping for her and being thoughtful. She was uncompromising, demanding he get rid of half his wardrobe because she did not like it and would nitpick about when he would cut his hair and called all the shots in their new apartment. When she would apologize she would blame her hormones but as Vincent would learn in the years to come, there was always an excuse. And the apologies and any gratitude became less and less frequent as time went by.

Abby blew through $1,000 of his money in 3 days outfitting the apartment with unnecessary additions and trinkets and Vincent quickly saw that this arrangement was not going to go as anticipated. If he turned to his parents or friends for advice, he did not like the generic answers of, "it will get better" or "I had it worse" or "just be strong" so he predictably turned to the bottle which only served to complicate things.

While the drink for a time washed away his fears, it did little more but bring out the worst version of him.

There was a two-week overlap where Vincent still had the keys and lease on his old apartment and he spent a lot of time there each night just to get some solitude. He looked at old pictures, listened to tapes he made with Jack and Eddie in high school and was mentally transported back to times that were, in some case, over 10 years ago. Because he did not hold back his reactions to

Abby's antics when he was drinking, she had banned him from hard liquor, so he finished off the last of the vodka and bourbon he had stashed there.

To listen to those tapes the three of them recorded in high school, talking about girls and the future, only to be thrust back into the present at the tapes' completion where Abby was pregnant and they lived in a new place together where she was sucking up his money like a vacuum cleaner, was surreal. Jack was looking to go into the Navy after not latching on in his desired profession of teaching to the degree he needed order to support his growing family. Eddie was married with a child back teaching at their old high school in Mankato after swearing he would never return home. Vincent was a budding businessman who knocked up a fellow employee. Life never pans out the way you anticipate it will.

Despite the questions and concerns, it felt right on Easter Sunday, the 34th anniversary of Vince, Jr.'s proposal to Kay, for Vincent to propose marriage to Abby. He did so after they got home from visiting his parents in Mankato, getting down on one knee in the living room of their apartment. She cried and accepted; they kissed and made phone calls to family and friends.

Time continued, the department moved to Greenfield in April, and mid-month Vincent and Abby learned they were having a girl. The initial disappointment at not having a son is now extreme joy. He could not imagine not having a little girl. She was his best buddy and his little princess.

To Vincent's chagrin, the relationship with Abby just did not feel cosmic. The more he learned about her, such as the number of partners she had before him, the history of drugs and, mostly that she was not at all innocent as he had originally speculated, did not thrill him. But there was no sense looking backwards. They were having a baby and were going to plan a life together.

As life goes on, it is amazing how things come full circle. Amidst family troubles over isolated Oklahoma City, Dick Knoll moved back to Minneapolis to helm a sales office in the same Greenfield building that Vincent now worked in. Danny Nance became a trainer in the same building. Peter Swansea had gotten a job managing a door-to-door effort locally.

Harriet Raines found out in April that her job was going to be eliminated in May. With nowhere else to turn as most of the company was slowing movement, Vincent scored her an interview with Keith and she became a manager in his department, working for him. The "teacher" became the student.

And in June, due to the still-massive hiring frenzy in Vincent's office, the company's HR team moved Phoebe Wells to the Greenfield office full-time.

Vincent was in disbelief. This was straight out of a show or movie; was this the ultimate test or a sign this was meant to be? Why, of all things to occur and at this time in his life, was this happening? Things were already tough enough with Abby as it was. Seeing Phoebe daily was not going to aid the situation.

And as the two months Abby was going to take off from having a job to complete her externship turned into more and more, strain ensued. Vincent saw his money escaping so quickly that he had to put a complete stop on contribution into his 401K. He had literally no say on anything in the apartment save a guest bedroom where he had to put his weights and computer. He had no say on his clothes or hair. Abby insisted on going out to dinner on practically a nightly basis and had no reverence for Vincent's healthy eating regimen. He actually started to gain weight to his annoyance. This was not helped by the fact he started drinking more frequently which meant he had no patience or qualms about telling Abby exactly what he thought of her growing burden on him financially and psychologically.

She was pregnant, which undoubtedly complicated her demeanor, but she was also very immature and had no idea what Vincent was going through. She made no attempt to understand, either.

Abby started spending some weekends with her parents to give them time apart as Vincent sank into depression. He would often say he was working out only to spend the majority of that time in his guest room listening to music or reading to avoid Abby. When they were around each other they bickered over practically everything. The presence of Phoebe was Vincent's last straw. He was just a man; he could not take any more.

He thought he had shaken her when he and Abby were at their high point. Phoebe got married in March and that was that, right? But now she was right outside his office, two cubicles away. He saw her several times per day and they had to communicate regularly over the hiring process in his department. She text messaged him one night while out at a bar, wanting him to meet her. He called her after drinking throughout one of Abby's weekends at her parents' and they professed there were still feelings, which he apologized for come Monday and said would not happen again.

However, the tension was thick. Just seeing each other made it impossible to stop thinking about one another and something was inevitably going to happen. Melissa Worthington did not help matters, constantly saying their relationship was "written in the stars" and talking to one about the other on a consistent basis. Vincent made clear to Abby he was not happy and hoped planting that seed would turn things around but with these goings-on, he had never been more confused in his life.

Vincent was torn; a part of him wanted this relationship with Abby because it afforded him the family he always wanted. They were going to have a child and he was already in the midst of that reality. Of course, their relationship was making him miserable. On the other hand, Phoebe, like Stacey, fit Katie

224

Barnes' description of what Vincent's soul mate should be: she floored him, she was witty, beautiful and a cut above other girls.

To attempt to take his mind off this inner turmoil, he threw himself into work. He went in earlier and stayed later. Twelve hour days kept him from having to deal with the homefront. By the time he got home he could eat quickly and disappear into his guest room. So here he was, with a pregnant live-in fiancé who tried to control every aspect of his life and with whom he fought constantly about money, day care, food, drinking, clothes – you name it. His work life was going well as he continued to destroy his own office sales records and the teams under his tutelage gained more and more momentum with every passing month. He was forming his own dynasty, promoting George Flaker and now having Harriet on his team. And he was starting to think that this time he had really found "the one." It just wasn't the one it was supposed to be.

On Thursday, June 14, 2007, neither could control themselves anymore. Phoebe was wearing a gorgeous tight black dress and they had been in a conference room together interviewing candidates all day. That would have been enough to make two people who had no feelings for each other think about mating, so the strain on Vincent was excruciating.

After hours of this and several interviews, Vincent locked the door and approached Phoebe at the interview table. She looked up to catch his gaze and he moved the papers she was holding to the side, taking her face in his other hand. With that, they attacked one another, making out profusely and running their excited hands over each other's bodies. It was unavoidable. And Vincent, while he did feel guilt and had never cheated before, felt justified in that his home life was destroying him and the move of Phoebe to his Greenfield office felt cosmic. It was the feeling he thought he had been searching for.

The hardest part was that Vincent did love Abby, but he was not gaga and he could not get Phoebe out of his head. While with Abby he was often annoyed and stressed; he wanted to chalk it all up to pregnancy but as he learned in the years following Elizabeth's birth, no – pregnancy was not the reason she acted the way she did. The things she did after their split and during the custody fight proved that. Maybe his reactions to her immaturity or thoughtlessness or selfishness just brought that out in her. Either way, they were not at all compatible.

Vincent continued makeout sessions with Phoebe behind closed doors at work for weeks. After a job fair one night with Melissa, George and Phoebe, Vincent showed up for a few drinks and there it was: an uninterrupted opportunity to talk in public.

Phoebe and Vincent were off in their own little world, leaving Melissa and George talking to each other. Phoebe revealed discontent in her marriage and that there was not a day that went by where she did not wish she and

Vincent would have gotten together and prevented her wedding day. She revealed she knew Vincent's secret and that Abby was the mother. She also revealed she was in love with him. As the group said goodbyes, Vincent offered to take Phoebe back to her car, parked at the Greenfield office. George whispered his approval to Vincent and he escorted her to his car. They held hands on the drive back, Phoebe gently stroking his, and they both knew what was about to happen. Upon arrival at the office, they both went in the building and into his office where they left the lights off and closed the door. And nature took its course.

They did not leave on a stitch of clothing. The lovemaking was intense and passionate and long overdue.

There was guilt in the aftermath, but his relationship was suffocating him and this tryst with Phoebe should have happened long ago. He was doing his part with Abby and was not getting any gratitude. In fact, he was going above and beyond the call of duty as he had been loaning Abby money for two months longer than promised and there was no job in sight. Abby did nothing but watch television, continued smoking cigarettes while with child and lied about it, and she could not even muster strength enough to do much of anything around the house. He knew she was pregnant but also knew several expectant mothers that kept jobs late into their pregnancies. Vincent was no longer attracted to her and did not know what to do.

However, Vincent absolutely had to be in every day of Elizabeth's life. That was the number one priority that governed all. And if he had to see what was going to happen with Phoebe on the side while he endured this horrible psychologically and financially draining penance with Abby, so be it. The thought of Elizabeth's arrival and this burgeoning affair with Phoebe were the only things keeping Vincent's fragile sanity. A potential happiness was on the horizon; he thought he could see it but it was still a long way off.

It was during this time Vincent started having anxiety attacks. They started slowly but soon branched out affecting his ability to drive. He found himself terrified while driving that he was going to freeze up and became petrified and breathless at the thought of having to operate a vehicle. He had to call upon Abby to drive if it was going to be on an interstate for any length of time. Short trips were still difficult but he managed to suffer through them without incident, despite the debilitating fear.

Keith Dickhauser was on constant rampages. He was well above the term "demanding" in that he would spot or think about anything on a whim and would not shut up about it until that issue was taken care of, be it important or trivial. He caught wind of Vincent mingling with Phoebe and made clear this was a cancer to his organization and that Vincent was undermining the foundation of the department. He berated Vincent regularly over his former manager Harriet Raines as well. While Vincent merely offered commentary on his experience working for her, letting Keith interview and make the decision to hire her after he was very impressed with her, her every mistake was blamed on Vincent. He could not win with anyone in his life.

While Vincent was creating all kinds of new processes and policies, leading the charge on the ascension of the office as he started to literally double the monthly revenue output of the operation, he was catching all the flak because there was no one else for Dickhauser to scream at.

There were not enough hours in the day to get everything Vincent knew he needed to get done in order to improve the business and take care of all the minutiae Dickhauser tried to throw at him. Vincent created his own job; he knew that in order to improve the managers and reps that it was about monitoring the quality of their calls, tracking efficiency and looking at sales statistics to see where improvements could be made. He received no feedback from Keith other than barked orders about cleaning up his desk or the setup of the reps' cubicles or that they were not asking for deposits often enough. Everything, big or small, was gargantuan on Dickhauser's radar. And that characteristic never improved. Instead, it got worse and worse as time went on.

If Vincent fought back with truth and unwillingness to be cursed at and talked to like a child, Keith would fold. Vincent knew this but also saved it for the fights that really mattered.

Amidst the present day ethics investigation in November 2009, Keith became somewhat cautious and started to act differently towards the managers. And "The Brotherhood," which was nearly every manager in the department, was ready to see him removed from power for his sins. The department had gotten to the point it was a nearly intolerable working environment with additional managers being prescribed anxiety medicine every month. Dickhauser, while he would not yell at a female manager had no qualms about cursing out, intimidating and humiliating males. And they were finally ready to do something about it.

George Flaker said it best, "I don't think I was hired to be a sales manager because of my impeccable ability to put together a personnel binder."

Was maintenance of a binder important? Absolutely. But Dickhauser had started to conjure up "final warnings" for everything from bad efficiency on a crew to missing paperwork in a binder and for speaking up against Scott Kinsey and his broken clerical process. He ruled with an iron fist and anyone who tried to speak up was smacked back down and screamed at like an unwanted child. He made it a habit of seeking out the most severe punishment possible despite no prior offenses or warnings. The man could not be pleased and if you angered him, watch out.

While Vincent had been fresh and full of life 2 ½ years before when he took the helm, he was now jaded, cynical and exhausted. The implosion of his romantic relationships did not help but seeing just how little he was appreciated by Dickhauser and his superiors and how little some employees were willing to try after they promised the world in interviews only to fizzle and amount to nothing in their brief careers made him realize this was not going to be where he changed the world.

And did he want to keep climbing? He wanted to climb so he could help more people. It seemed the higher he got the more he was attacked. No one deserved this abuse he had gotten from all angles.

Nonetheless, Vincent continued fighting on. He was responsible for so much that he could not take a moment's lapse to think; the department hinged on his every move.

Vincent would psych himself and others up to all time peaks in performance. They would also see debilitating valleys of horrific morale spurred by new Dickhauser rules that were knee-jerk reactions to seeing just one instance of something he did not like. Dickhauser's endorsement of Scott Kinsey's process and lulls where salespeople were not being paid properly happened too often and took their toll more each time. Those seemingly fatal blows, while causing suffering for all reps and managers, had never completely finished off their morale. However, this time, the landscape looked different. It also looked like the management team could finally oust the dictator.

The Chinese buffet up the street had been a haven for the group. They tucked themselves away at the round table in the smoking room as Jimmy, Slade, Cal and Frankie all smoked. George and Clyde tagged along today and they sat over their meal commiserating over what was to come.

"I can't wait until that bastard is gone," George said. "This place is going to hell in a handbasket."

"Seriously," Clyde echoed. "I got a call from my buddy in HR before lunch. He thinks we did all the right things. Now all we have to do is wait."

"You know what kills me," George began. "At the dog and pony shows every time we get a new boss, Keith goes on and on about how great our team is. But how many of us are on a final warning for something?"

The group laughed and everyone's hands went up except Vincent's.

"Jesus," Clyde lamented.

"For real, guys, I just want a light at the end of the tunnel," George said. "I don't remember the last time I was actually able to manage. You know – like, do my job."

228

"The other day I got blasted in front of my team," Jimmy offered up. "Keith yelled at me saying our results were awful and told me I had no control over my team."

"That's nothing, he called me at home on my day off and told me I was undermining the foundation of the department because I went out with Clyde and Jimmy on my birthday and they were hung over the next day," Frankie laughed.

"'Undermining the foundation of the department'," Vincent mused. "I've heard that one before."

"I remember when he threatened to suspend Vincent and me that time we were defending Jackson Kerr for his claims write-up," Slade chuckled. "Vincent was like, 'yes, please, can the suspension start right now'?"

The assemblage laughed. This therapy was the only way they were able to keep going. Vincent had no doubt that they wanted to be successful, yet they were being thwarted at every turn under the regime of Keith Dickhauser. Keith would walk out of his office and see a rep walking to a printer that he thought was trying to avoid doing work and he would pull the rep, their manager and Vincent into a bitch-fest no matter what duties they were in the middle of doing. His patented line in a room full of managers was, "If you can't do the job I'll find somebody who can." If it was one-on-one behind closed doors, he would add the word "fucking" between the words "the" and "job."

His sad devotion to a new computerized system called the Digital Pitchbook that allowed reps to send a slide-show via e-mail to potential customers had caused one of the most recent uproars. In a meeting Dickhauser actually told the salesforce to abort their presentation and schedule a callback if a customer was unable to view the slide-show on any given call. Vincent had to quickly tend to that fallout as anyone involved in the job knew giving up a decision-maker meant you would never speak to them again. Keith was completely out of place and made it more glaringly obvious with each passing day.

Vincent was honestly surprised it had taken this long for people to stand united against Dickhauser. One of the first big arguments he had with the man was when he did reveal not long after his promotion that he was seeing Abby. Keith framed it that Vincent had lied and that was cardinal sin number one in Keith's eyes. He brought it up hundreds of times in the years to come. Funny, the very man whose regular motto was, "I don't hold grudges," held them like no one Vincent had ever seen.

The irony was that Keith was a liar. He liked to portray himself as having people's backs and being a man of integrity, but he was a snake and a hypocrite. He constantly liked to tell Vincent that he was the only friend he had in the business, and Vincent learned over the years that this was far from the truth. Vincent had faced his own half-assed firing squad. Keith could have stood up for him then but did not. That was when he saw the true colors of this hateful and hated man.

Amidst attempts at intimidation, Keith made a habit of saying his bosses had told him to relay harsh messages to Vincent or they were displeased with his brash antics. Vincent was smart enough to call his bluff and tell Dickhauser to get those bosses on the phone immediately. Keith would always back down right away. And to sit around this table and hear manager after manager share their stories about this administration of tyranny, Vincent felt good about what was on the horizon. Everybody gets what they deserve – right? Even if it takes a long time to happen.

But the truth of the matter was that despite his status as public bastard #1, no one wanted to see Keith fired. They, as Flaker worded it best, "just want to see Keith put somewhere where he's not a threat to himself or others." He was nothing but a detriment and was so far detached from the job that he had no clue what he was doing. The other managers had made similar reports. Many had been cursed out by Dickhauser in private or public settings. They were all on some kind of unjustifiable warning. They all knew the days he was not there were their most productive. Keith had changed documentation on people to try to push his agenda. He had targeted reps and managers and made their lives hell. Now was the time for their retribution. It had to be. It was now or never.

It was Vincent's belief that, as a manager, you have earned the right to run your team the way you see fit until and unless you start to miss expectations. Keith vehemently disagreed with this philosophy. Even if a manager went to lunch a little late because they were stuck doing something, there was hell to pay if they came in so much as a few minutes after the reps were supposed to be back. His rationale was the manager had not been there every second necessary to ensure the reps returned to work on time. Of course, the dialer reports would show this, but that obvious, common sense logic was lost on Dickhauser. It was impossible to please the man. He complained just to hear himself complain.

Back to the office, Vincent had a full afternoon planned. He had a monitoring and coaching session with Randall Darwin lined up from 1 PM until 3:30 and an interview scheduled after that. Afterwards, he would finish up the day and depart to pick up his princess. Of course, as he once again refreshed the webpage featuring the blog post he had seen earlier in the day, he saw the wrench in those plans.

Vincent sat at his desk, the message board on the screen in front of him. Hours before, Vincent had casually responded and tried to put this in his past. Not only had the administrator not removed the posts but another response had been made by his anonymous attacker.

"Yeah, the fear of your pale white ass coming after me keeps me up at night. Go nail another of your employees, loser," was the response.

Vincent saw red. Livid that these posts were not removed and at this anonymous coward's audacity, Vincent did not think. His anger overcame him and his lightning quick fingers fired off a response.

"It would be one thing if you had attacked me; that wouldn't register on my radar. But if you want to talk about my daughter, we really should meet. I'm willing to bet that despite your desire to hide behind an untrue anonymous name that you bragged to a buddy about this ignorant attack. That said, I will offer $500 to anyone who reveals the identity of this coward," Vincent typed.

He read it again before submission. There was nothing he wanted to change. He sent it through, without further hesitation. He wanted nothing more than to find out who posted this crap.

Randall knocked on the door frame, announcing his arrival for their strategy session. Vincent looked up. There would be no pause in the action.

"Hey, buddy, come on in. I'm almost ready for you," Vincent said.

"Sounds good," Randall replied.

Randall entered and took a seat. Vincent was always multi-tasking whether juggling dialer movement, sending e-mails, researching sales disputes in house and out or listening to his employees vent; he somehow managed to do it all. One of his favorite things to do, despite the fact it often put him in a foul mood, was listen to calls and diagnose reps and managers. This was his forte: he could showcase his skills and knowledge on the art of the sale for reps and managers alike like no one else.

The biggest frustration of monitoring is that no matter whom you listen to, how many times you have coached or corrected someone or what you think you are going to hear, you are unpleasantly surprised 99% of the time. Good sales calls are an endangered species.

The factors that led to their status on the endangered list were often fatigue and gradual decay but what Vincent found so maddening was that even when golden opportunities were handed over on a platter for his reps to dine, they would typically fumble and make a mess of things.

Dickhauser had a general disdain for Randall, always talking about him behind closed doors as lazy and describing him as a "drive-by manager", meaning he would just walk around and poke his head in but never roll up his sleeves and do the work. Keith would chide Randall for being full of nothing more than "chin boogie" – saying he would make the necessary changes and paying lip service to them for a few days until he relapsed into his old fly-by management ways that did not work.

Dickhauser wanted to find a way to get rid of Randall, but this was complicated by his recent surge in results working for Vincent. Nevertheless, Keith had gone so far as to instruct Vincent to remove any positive remarks from appraisals and performance plans for managers like Randall, George Flaker and Steve Zimmerman, whom he desperately wanted to expunge from the business.

Vincent, however, had struck a chord with Randall early by showing him that he said what he meant and meant what he said. Vincent committed to pulling Randall's team out of the gutter with him and had stuck to his word, gaining Darwin's deep respect. Randall did relapse to habits Vincent did not like but he was committed to working with him rather than dismissing him as quickly as Dickhauser did.

After listening to calls with most managers, particularly Randall who was relatively new at actually being coached, Vincent opened it up to his managers.

"So – pretend I'm Aaron and I'm sitting right across from you. How do you critique the call we just listened to?" Vincent asked.

"Well, uh…" Randall muttered, looking at his notes. "First off, he didn't say the call was recorded."

"Okay, but that's small potatoes," Vincent said. "It matters, but get to the meat."

"Oh—okay—," Randall managed, looking again at his notes. "There wasn't enough value pitched. He needs to do a better job of pitching value."

"Good, but be specific, not general, about what you expect," Vincent coached.

"Okay…well…he talked about our search package but he never really recommended it."

"Randall, here's the thing. You're right. Yes, he failed to mention the call was recorded. Yes, you hit the nail on the head, he pitched no value. But the trick here is you have to get that across to him in a way he is going to understand it and is going to fix it walking away from your coaching session."

Vincent was always careful to point out something the manager did effectively and then move in to the real techniques and methods he wanted instilled in them.

"You are glossing over the surface of your diagnosis," Vincent continued. "Yes, you are pointing out something true about the call, but you are not hitting them between the eyes with the real problem and then showing – not telling – them how you expect it to be done. You have to sell them on why they have to do it your way. Go get him."

"What – Aaron? Right now?" Randall asked.

"Yes."

Randall exited to retrieve Aaron Jameson, a linebacker-sized rep who was actually pretty timid in person and on the phone. The kid had never really amounted to anything and was three months away from a retention decision in the current job.

"Aaron, how are you?" Vincent asked, standing to shake his hand.

"I'm okay, how are you?" Aaron asked. When reps entered Vincent's office they initially showed signs of nervousness. Vincent knew how to immediately put them at ease.

"Aaron, the fact that you're here is actually an honor for all of us. It means I care enough about your well-being and your future to take time out of my day to make you better. Have a seat," Vincent said, outstretching his arm to signal to an empty chair. Aaron sat and Randall sat next to him, both across the desk from Vincent. "Aaron, Randall and I listened to a call you made not long ago to Minor Construction. You spoke to Julius. Remember the call?"

"Yes," he replied.

"Randall, you want to lead us off?" Vincent prodded.

"Sure," Randall acknowledged, hesitantly. "Aaron, we've talked in the past about your value presentation. You are talking about our products and you do a good job offering our full suite but you are not proving enough value to the customer. You need to do a better job of making sure the customer understands how this is going to work for him."

"Okay," Aaron said. Vincent felt frustration build. Randall was spouting generalities. Aaron was not being reached. It was about time for the doctor to operate.

"You did a good job of fact-finding and finding out about the business," Randall proceeded. "You talked to him about our directory, the online portion and our search package. But you did not show the customer how this was going to benefit him."

"Well, I talked about the searches we provide and where he would be placed," Aaron stated, still not fazed by this session.

"Yes, but the customer does not deal in our products every day. You want to make sure you do a better job of articulating exactly what comes with our program. In addition, you did not announce the call is recorded. And when the customer said he needed to go, you went in to schedule a callback."

"Yeah, I probably should have pushed him a little harder there at the end. I just didn't want to piss him off."

"Sure, I hear you. But you should at least overcome his objection a couple of times. Okay?

"Yes," Aaron said.

Randall, unsure of what to do next, asked, "Vincent, did you have anything to add?"

"Absolutely. You know me," he responded, moving his feet from his desk to the floor and sitting up in his chair. "Aaron, here's the deal. You're a smart kid. As Randall pointed out, you did an admirable job of fact-finding. But here's the way I want you to approach this: your call is a puzzle. You put a few pieces in, but without all of it, it's incomplete. Period. Randall mentioned you did not point out value. What is this customer's weakness? Why does he need your service?"

There was silence before Aaron answered, "I—I don't know."

"Exactly," Vincent continued. "You went in and you talked about everything we have to offer, which I am proud of. Awesome job talking about benefits of our programs. But you did not diagnose this customer's weakness nor did you show him why he absolutely must get our package. How does he market his business right now?"

"He said he did fliers and newspaper."

"Right. So the most important thing for you to do is pounce on everything you learn and drop little bombs the whole way that show he is missing out on something great. 'Mr. Customer, right now you are advertising in fliers and newspaper. It's great that you are actively marketing your business. How are they working for you?' Get the answer to that because you'll need it later. Even if it does work for him, it still can be used to your advantage. 'Julius, here's the thing: you are kind of throwing your name out there like bait hoping that someone will come along and bite. We put you where people are actively looking.' What is this guy's average sale worth, Aaron?"

"He said it could be thousands of dollars."

"Yeah, so making back his investment is a no-brainer. What did you pitch him per month?"

"Eight hundred dollars."

"Okay. Kudos for starting relatively big. However, you spent far too much time just giving him a book report on how our products work. He doesn't care. This guy cares about one thing: making a return on his investment. Your pitch should be short and sweet. 'Julius, to give you the best probability at return on investment, I'm going to put you everywhere we have potential customers looking. You will appear in the 700,000 bound directories we publish in your area, online on our site and our sister sites and you will also get one hundred searches from the major engines per month. With all that, you need just one customer per month to make a profit. Make sense?' Then gauge where his head's at and attack. Does that make sense, Aaron?"

"Yeah, yeah, it does," Aaron said, starting to become engrossed in the session.

"Aaron, what I just described is not a major change for you. It is a minor tweak. Do you see that?"

"Yes, I do, boss."

"The bottom line, Aaron, is you are spinning your wheels and wearing yourself out doing the same stuff that flat out isn't working all day long. You know the difference between you and Kyle Carver?" Vincent asked, referencing the top rep on the floor. "He closes forty sales per month and you probably get five to ten. Both of you make thousands of calls. Do you understand that the margin of difference between those two close rates is minuscule? That it's just something minor separating the two of you? And this is it. You've got to hit the customer with facts that are directly pertinent to his business. Make him feel like his methods are inadequate. Don't insult, but show him why his method is weak and yours is strong. Make it make sense. Make it a no-brainer. Make sense?"

"Yeah, yeah," Aaron said, still gaining excitement.

"Good. The other thing is you may go out there and hammer out calls the rest of the day and try what we just talked about. Even if it doesn't go as planned on the first ten, twenty or even one hundred calls, it doesn't matter. If you do the right thing every time out, the law of averages dictates that you will come out victorious in the end. Can you do that for me?"

"Yes, I can do it. Thanks so much," Aaron said.

"What do you want out of life, Aaron?" Vincent asked him.

"I just want to find something to do that makes me happy. I want to make money. I help support my Mom right now and so I just need to make as much money as I can."

"I don't want you to focus on where you stand on the sales report or how much revenue you have on the board at any given moment. I know it sounds crazy, but don't think about that," Vincent directed. "I want you to look back on every call and be able to tell me the specific reason that customer didn't believe your program would work for him. If you do that – if you know the answer to that question on every call – you will be a star. I promise."

Aaron nodded.

"Anything else you need from us, Aaron?" Vincent asked.

"No, I'm ready to get back out there and do it."

"I know you are. Randall – anything else?"

"Aaron, Vincent and I believe in you and know you can do this. Make us proud!"

"Will do. Thanks, guys," Aaron said before dismissing himself and closing the door behind him.

"What do you think?" Vincent asked Randall.

"I think he could just be so good if he applied himself."

"Something I want you to pay attention to, Randall, is that you told him at the start of the session that you guys have talked before about pitching value. You've got to ask him how he would diagnose himself. You've got to ask him how he has been progressing with the things you guys are working on. You want to have a steady progression, always have an improvement plan in place and a goal you are trending towards and working on. Do you know what the biggest thing I found out about this kid was?"

"What's that?"

"He is helping support his Mom. I found his motivation. You've got to find everyone's motivation and use it to your advantage. I gave him all the tools in the world. I spoke in his language. I got through to him and he is going to walk out of here and try something new. But follow up is the key for you. And it is important that you give everybody on your team a daily touch of some sort with whatever you are working on with them. With Aaron, it needs to be logging his pitches and keeping track of why the customer did not believe it would work. Remember: work smarter, not necessarily harder, Randy. Make him jot these things down and touch base with him a couple times a day to see what he's got. It takes little effort on your part but it is you affecting process. I can't tell you how important that is. It's your job as a manager to have an effect and an impact on every call this kid makes going forward. You could sit there on a call with him and impact one call. Or you can put process checkers like this in place that impact every call he makes until the end of time. Which do you think is better?"

"This. Definitely. I see what you're saying," Randall acknowledged.

"Good. I know you do. I don't want you putting your effort in the wrong areas. I want you figuring out what makes these guys tick and what makes them fall. Then give them each a little check and balance method to keep their falling in check. Then touch base with them regularly. Listen to calls with them. Chart a course for them and work towards it. Give them the benefit of the doubt with exercises like this until they show they don't deserve your trust. You can't expect them to wake up a superstar overnight but you can chart the course and steadily make strides towards it. Make every goal seem attainable, even for yourself. Got it?"

"I do, Vince. Man, I will follow you anywhere." Randall stood up and the two did a semi-embrace and shook hands. "Thanks, Vincent. You make me feel like I can do this shit."

"You can, Randy. We're going to get there. I told you that Day 1 and I stick by it now."

"Thanks, brother," Randall said. He dismissed himself. Vincent sat down, felt good again and re-immersed himself in the e-mails, the dialer functions and the rigmarole. And his day was more complete: he had impacted these two like no one ever had. He instilled the sense of belief in them with direct marching orders pertaining to tweaks and developments they needed to make in themselves, all while making them sound so attainable. He sold them both on why they should do it his way.

Diligently typing away, Vincent saw through peripheral vision that Phoebe had walked by and dropped an interview packet in the inbox outside his door. She had not so much as come into his office since he had given her a final blasting nearly five months before. What a difference a few years had truly made in their relationship.

As summer 2007 wound down, Vincent and Phoebe continued sporadic sexual encounters in his office, her office and the conference rooms after everyone left for the night. Vincent's relationship with Abby continued to have its occasional ups and far more frequent downs. Somehow, while anxiety attacks plagued his life, Vincent was holding it all together at work and continuing the steep upward trajectory the department was enjoying under his control. As for Phoebe, he longed for a future where this would all make sense and turn out to be worthwhile.

It was at that time on a night out with Abby that Vincent encountered Ryan Kish, a waiter at Olive Garden who was extremely personable, attentive and courteous. Trading comments with Abby through dinner, he decided he wanted this guy on the sales team. For Vincent to see that in someone in the outside world was saying something – he tried to never refer anyone to the job because he did not want to be saddled with or associated with their failure. Harriet Raines's extremely quick descent to the bottom of the crew standings and her team's complaints of her ineptitude were something Dickhauser never let Vincent live down. But this kid could be something special and Vincent was willing to take that chance.

Rather than embarrass Ryan and solicit his services while he was on duty, Vincent slipped his business card into the receipt holder, scratching a note on the back. It read, "Ryan, thanks for a great dining experience. If you are interested in a sales job where you can make some serious money, give me a call. Vincent Scott"

A week later, Ryan called him, intrigued. And two weeks later, he started training. Vincent got all kinds of visions of something he had always wanted: a protégé. This could be another birth of a salesman.

Finally, and fortunately for the relief it brought, the rumors starting making the rounds that Abby was pregnant with Vincent's child. Keith actually learned from Mick Farmer, one of his many confidantes scattered throughout the office, and he approached Vincent with his knowledge of the situation. Surprisingly, he seemed to take it relatively well. And on Monday, August 27, Vincent began a week of vacation, as Elizabeth was due that Wednesday.

However, Elizabeth had other plans. Abby and Vincent awoke that Monday morning and Abby turned to Vincent.

"I think it's baby time," she said.

Vincent, still half-asleep turned to face her. "For real?"

All the anticipation, the wonder and the rollercoasterish episodes of their volatile relationship had led to this moment. The excitement hit Vincent: he was about to be a Daddy. "I think so. I feel what they described the contractions would feel like and they are about ten minutes apart," Abby said.

"Well let's get to the hospital," Vincent said.

"But what if it's not the baby?"

"Then let's let them tell us that. It's no time to be cautious."

Vincent grabbed the bag they had packed and he and Abby got in his Accord. He drove her to the hospital, parked and they entered in an attempt to check in. Initial tests around 7:30 showed Abby was not dilated enough to be admitted but after the recommended stroll around the parking lot, they admitted her at 9 AM.

Vincent still has hundreds of pictures from that day on his home computer: of Abby in her hospital gown, sitting on the birthing ball and in bed prior to giving birth. There were pictures of Vincent sitting by the window smiling beforehand, of their families coming together for this most joyous of occasions and of Vincent holding his baby girl for the very first time. Memories like this were what made it so hard for Vincent to eventually walk away.

At 7:51 PM, Elizabeth Marie Scott was born. She was 7 pounds, 20 inches long and had blondish-red hair – the spitting image of Vincent when he was born, as Vince, Jr. and Kay marveled upon first sight of her. Vincent had often found it humorous how parents seemed to be so blind to the degree of attractiveness of their own offspring. But there was no doubt about it: Elizabeth Scott was absolutely beautiful.

This was the apex of the relationship between Abby and Vincent. It went completely and uncontrollably downhill from there but if there was a shining moment of unfettered goodness it was the moment their amazing daughter was born.

Vincent returned to work the following week and announced to the management team that pretty much already knew anyway about his special arrival.

Abby's insistence on calling all the shots, trying to impose her way of everything on Vincent and constantly berating him for not spending enough time reading "What to Expect When You're Expecting" after his 12-hour work days frustrated him a great deal. To talk to her, she was the expert on all things parenting. While she had every right to feel a strong bond with her daughter, she would hastily dismiss Vincent's thoughts or feelings or opinions on anything and everything relating to Elizabeth. It drove him crazy. It also drove the pendulum very much back towards Phoebe.

Vincent's reluctance to discuss marriage began to finally make it clearer to Abby that he meant it when he said he was unhappy. She actually relinquished her ring at one point in September. Phoebe and Vincent continued their secret work meetings and the more Vincent ran over it in his head he came to realize that he and Abby were going to crash and burn.

The love triangle could have easily been ripped out of a soap opera. Despite the fact Abby had promised to have a job in April the months kept piling up and she refused to get one. She actually made mention at one point that she was considering being a stay-at-home Mom. Vincent laughed, saying he too would love to stay home and watch Elizabeth all day but it was neither feasible nor what they agreed upon.

Every time Vincent paid bills would turn into a fiasco as he tired of shelling out $1,500 per month just for Abby and all of her personal expenses, insurance, student loans, car payments, wardrobe, gas, drinking and cigarettes, etc. And if he made mention that he may stop paying, Abby threatened to move back in with her parents and said Vincent would not see his daughter. It was like ransom; he was trapped. And it did little to aid his anxiety attacks.

In the first nine months of living together, Vincent had loaned over $20,000 to Abby. He paid off $6,000 of her credit card debt, moved out of his apartment for her into a more expensive one, saw her throw away half his wardrobe, bought unnecessary new furniture at her behest, paid $600 per month for her insurance and forked over money for every bill and for the "allowance" she demanded. He would return home from 12-hour shifts to her drinking daily either alone or with her mother on his dime.

As for Vincent and Phoebe, it ran hot and cold. Vincent grew weary of the fact other men were around her all the time combined with her apparent restrictions to spending time with him, causing him to frequently pull back emotionally from her.

On his 29th birthday, Vincent finally succumbed to something he had known for months he had to do: he went to the doctor for the first time in his life. His blood pressure was through the roof and anxiety attacks were destroying him more and more quickly.

Thing is, with the beatings he was taking on all fronts and the antidepressants the doctor prescribed, Vincent became numb. He had no desire to be intimate with Abby. He was fazed by her antics less than before and avoided or walked away from most of their confrontations. It angered her even more – she could no longer register an emotion or get a reaction out of him.

Both sets of parents had relationship interventions with them as their rift became obvious, which pissed Vincent off because he knew he was doing the best he could. Any foundation their coupling once had was quickly crumbling. Vincent announced to Abby in November that he did not want to hear the word marriage again.

Thanksgiving was ruined after a morning argument and Vincent ended up having a turkey sandwich and some of his mother's apple cake with his parents while Abby swept Elizabeth off to her aunt and uncle's.

Abby sought the most expensive day cares possible and at first was adamantly against Vincent's inexpensive alternative of the same sitter that sat for buddy Jeff Mason's children. Anything possible Abby could do to annoy Vincent or maximize usage of his money seemed to be exactly what she did.

However, any time their screaming matches ended with the consensus to split up, someone reneged the following morning. Vincent stuck with it because he could not make the decision not to see Elizabeth every day. As for Abby, she knew an attempt to retreat to her parents would not go over well with them or as lucratively for her. And, in some weird, demented way, the two loved each other.

Vincent tried to get Abby to return to work in his department in a different office, now that the controversy over their relationship had subsided and Abby's dad had lamented his displeasure with her having left in the first place. Her returning would have left her no worse for wear, yet of course she declined. She finally got two other interviews, one that Vincent scored for her, but found reasons to decline them as well. It was becoming far too much for Vincent to bear.

He continued to throw his energy into work. Vincent managed to pull off the greatest sale of his career by framing Harriet Raines as a savior to the head of the other department in their building. Thanks to Vincent, she got a job running an office, which was what she had always wanted and he was finally rid of her.

He promoted Maria Fernandez and Johnny Slade. With Keith out of town, Vincent stepped up to give the presentation at a Career Fair for ABM and blew away the room. He closed out his first year at the helm in grand fashion and set himself up for a huge bonus. The career arena was reaching its peak.

240

Over Christmas, Abby went with Vincent and Elizabeth to Mankato for Christmas Eve and the beginning of Christmas Day. Of course, she whined about the fact they were not waking up on Christmas Day with her parents. She was bossy about everything related to Elizabeth. They got into an argument about bills, her job status and daycares. All of it sent a resounding message to Vincent: it was time to end this.

They agreed to split – and did – and the engagement ring never made its way back to Abby's hand.

When Abby left, taking Elizabeth with her to her parents', Vincent broke down. He cried fiercely into a pillow on their bed, striking it with his fist. A two day bender ensued featuring Jimmy and Chad. Vincent drank himself to the point of barely conscious; their assemblage got thrown out of Finley's and he sobbed himself to sleep.

Vincent was genuinely happy when she returned two days later. They seemed to reignite initially, making passionate love together for the first week of their umpteenth attempt to make it work. They were fine the first couple of days. They got nitpicky with each other the next couple. Over that next weekend, at the hospital in the wee hours of the morning with Elizabeth over a viral infection, Abby was particularly cantankerous and cranky. And the downhill slide started again.

January 2008 was quite eventful. After a few weeks of fighting and debating, Vincent sleeping in the guest room, getting in arguments that involved screaming, her actually physically hitting him repeatedly in the arm one night and even one where she got the police to remove him from his own apartment and take him to a hotel for yelling at her when *she* barged into *his* room, Vincent told Abby it was time to go.

This time, there was no going back. He was 100% sure this time. It tore Vincent apart as he thought about Elizabeth's smile, her laughter, the excited sounds and looks she gave when he would hold her up like she was standing on her own – they were the most precious things he had ever encountered. But for the sake of his well being, he had to move on without Abby destroying and attempting to control every aspect of his life. He deserved better than this constant misery and, although the choice was difficult it was the right thing to do for Elizabeth and for him.

Abby did not go quietly. Initially, she tried to take blame for their downfall and promised she would change. Then she would use Elizabeth as a tool to spend time with Vincent in the apartment. Later she used Vincent's time with her as a weapon when she did not get her way. Vincent quickly sought an attorney as he knew where this was headed. Abby had no qualms about trying everything she could think of to call the shots where Elizabeth was concerned.

She would condescend to Vincent calling herself the custodial parent and threatened that if he was not "nice" he would never see his daughter.

Whereas when he split with Julie, Vincent actually missed having a companion in his bed, he quickly took down all pictures of Abby and removed any reminders of her from the apartment and the portrait scrapbooks. His time there when Elizabeth was not with him was spent playing NBA Live with Chad or sipping on a few brews with Jimmy rather than fighting constantly with Abby. He did not see Elizabeth as much as he wanted to but it seemed like the overall quality of his life was finally going to rebound. He could not remove Abby from Elizabeth's life but he sure could try to remove her from his own.

Vincent wasted no time making it known to now-separated Phoebe that he was ready for an exclusive, committed relationship with her. She had not left his mind to date and, despite everything they had been through both together and apart to that point, they were still seemingly crazy about one another. Abby's absence in the apartment meant they could finally graduate to a bed. They talked about marrying once her divorce became final. They bandied around the concept of having a child together. They took vacation days together and stayed in, ordered pizza, watched movies and made love all day. It was bliss. The upswing seemed to be in effect.

In the professional realm, Mark Rogers was promoted and became Vincent's peer; a clear move by Dickhauser to advance his protégé into an undeserved position of power. Mark was a nice guy but a manager of managers he most certainly was not. He had never had success as a manager much less could he bring about success in managers and, while everyone could see right through the move, nothing could be done to stop it. The three downtown outbound teams were announced shortly thereafter.

No matter. Vincent proceeded with his agenda in mind. He promoted Jimmy, Dean Yamnitz and Cal– a strong crop – and made it through his first real test in February leadership-wise.

Initially he lost his cool when they sat mid-month on pace for 50% to office objective and Vincent was openly disgusted and spiteful about the results to compensate. However, one day on a lark he just decided to start being nice, ignore the slump and just give an uplifting message day after day to wade through the murk. And it worked. They ended up achieving the unthinkable of February objective despite the poor start and Vincent never came close to missing again. In fact, March saw them hit yet another new record of 145% of objective.

Vincent thought he was on top of the world at this point. Abby gone, seeing Elizabeth about half the time and getting to call Phoebe his girlfriend all while sitting atop a department and surpassing all expectations as its leader, Vincent Scott was ready to settle in for the long haul at the summit.

"The Selling Game" by Vincent Scott
Chapter 6:
HODGEPODGE

There are a lot of topics in this cornucopia of sales greatness that do not necessarily fit into the chapter outlines yet by no means can forget about them. I would be negligent to graze past them. This chapter is the potpourri of the outlying themes; general sales stuff you will want to know in your plight for excellence.

It is important to remember that sales tips that work can be found anywhere at any time. Be ready for them in all of their forms. When I was on the phones, I picked up from my cubicle neighbors, occasionally from managers and also from just trying constantly to put a different spin on my spiel. I was relentlessly in search of the perfect version of myself and you should be, too.

Someone that worked for me once said he felt like a conglomeration of all the good sellers he worked with; he latched on to things he liked that other people used successfully, made them his own and perfected them in putting together his approach. I thought that was a very good analogy. Greek philosopher Aristotle broke several different facets of life down into a series of seven, such as the presence of only seven original plotlines in the world. That analogy would substantiate his theory; while there are a limited number of original themes, there is a multitude of ways to execute them effectively.

We have talked a bit up to this point about finding the right words to say with customers and not over-using information to sway someone to your line of thinking. The best bet is to latch on to what the customer's weakness is and try to bait them by showing how your solution solves their puzzle. That said, a mistake that often befalls us is the over-use of statistics; too many facts and figures muddy the sales water.

Don't get me wrong; some effectively placed statistics can go a long way because they are food for thought. They make your customer sit up and take notice if you pepper your spiel with the right ones. However, too many tasty morsels will turn even the most savvy and thoughtful customer off and make them flee from the table.

Pretty much any sales occupation you land in will provide you collateral pieces and facts and figures that support usage of their product or service. You should have at your disposal many positive attributes of what you are selling, testimonials of success stories or ratios and the numbers to back up what you spout in your presentation. While these things can and should be used in your pitch, you must resist temptation to read off every one of them like a laundry list lest your customer will become buried and the effectiveness is minimized.

There is a huge difference between spouting out every statistic you know or have heard and strategically placing them in the mix. This is much like picking and choosing the words you use to effectively guide your customer to the close. Pick the ones most applicable to the situation at hand and stick to them. If you are talking about a particular product or service, pick the stats that most effectively articulate the benefits that correlate to the customer's situation. Inundating them with unnecessary facts detract from the quality of your argument.

These product or service-related statistics can go a long way in aiding you in your quest to ice the deal but, like anything else, ill-timed words or statistics inhibit progress. Put yourself in your customer's shoes; is it easy to pay attention to the task at hand when numbers and facts are whizzing by your face a mile a minute?

We have spent a lot of time trying to pinpoint and analyze the most effective means by which to do pretty much every aspect of the sales flow. The back end situations or behind the scenes processes can also go a long way in furthering your cause and anything you can do to give yourself a leg up versus competition, customer objections or just the odds at work in your version of the selling game can provide a healthy push.

I have alluded to this before but I am a big proponent of leaving professional voice mails when your customer is not available and your attempt to squeeze in their door is turned away. In various worlds of small to smaller conversion rates, we have to do anything we can to give us the best chance. To give yourself the best shot at closing an account, it is imperative to find methods that take little to no time that can further your cause. This is why I like the voice message.

If you're already calling, it is no additional skin off your nose to leave some pearls of wisdom that could elicit a callback. Even if only 1% of your messages result in a customer returning the call, that is success; especially the smaller your typical close ratio may be. What would you have said in your introduction? Say it to the machine, say it quickly and remember to set yourself apart from typical sales voice messages so you have a shot at the callback. If and when they call, the lead has transformed from cold to warm.

Make it short, sweet and compelling; give that customer a specific reason to call you back. Is it that you have noticed a lot of their competitors getting business from what you have to offer and you wanted to give them some of that opportunity? Is it an impressive number of people using and enjoying your product? Most importantly, whatever you say, would you as the recipient of that message have responded or deleted it after five seconds?

244

For, ultimately, a lot of finding sales success is putting yourself in the customer's shoes; asking yourself what the customer would need to hear or see to allow themselves to give in to the temptation of the close. When reviewing our personal voice mail and the first 3-5 seconds of any given message fails to get our hearts to skip a beat, the remainder is already in voice mail purgatory – cut off by the "delete" button. To prevent that fate from befalling your message, leave something compelling – likely what you would have said in your introduction had they answered – and make it short, sweet and to the point so it gives you the highest probability at a returned call.

In sales trenches where getting decision makers can take several calls or visits, irritation can run rampant and the lengthy dry spells between live bodies can lead to mental lapses. Leaving energetic and off-the-wall voice mails can serve to spell your dreary day. It's easy to leave a message saying, "Hi, this is Vincent with Scott Services. I was calling today to talk to you about our line of appliances. Please call me back at your earliest convenience at XXX-XXX-XXXX. Thanks, and have a great day." Those are the messages that wind up deleted before the words make it off the recording. If you want a callback, change it up and be different than everything else out there.

Here is an example of something that gives you the best shot possible at a callback, "Hi, this is Vincent Scott, with Scott Services and I'm beside myself with excitement after looking at your account. The reason I'm calling is you actually qualify for some outstanding new services that would give you a leg up against the competition. Call me back so you can seize the opportunity before your neighbor beats you to the punch. I can be reached at XXX-XXX-XXXX. Thanks, and I look forward to speaking to you – have a great day!"

While that was wordier, it is not your typical message, it gives direct applicable benefits and cause to the customer to call back and it is insightful enough you would be more likely to listen if it was on your machine. Think about how you can apply those same principles in your job; step out of the mold that everyone else seems to be a part of and leave something compelling that gives you a better shot at getting that warm lead calling back.

Keep these philosophies in mind as you look for new ways to better your approach; if something can be done that takes up no additional effort or energy, it is worth pursuing. Inflection of your voice may not sound like a big deal to you, but sounding excited can make all the difference and takes no extra effort (well, unless you went out partying the night before – then it might).

There are all kinds of factors that weigh significantly into the end result. This is the reason you do not wear shorts and a Hawaiian shirt to a job interview (unless you are looking for a summer gig at a beach club like the cast of "Saved By The Bell") – because you may possess the greatest sales skill in the universe and may be the best fit for the job, but many variables are used to determine your perceived value and professionalism is one of them.

Professionalism is huge when it comes to surviving in any occupation for that matter. Newscasters can wear shorts under the desk while they talk through your boob tube but there is something about looking good, even while you sit on the phone. The station in life clothes can elevate you to – whether dialing or door-knocking – makes a big difference in your presentation, persona and projection of confidence.

You have likely heard, "the clothes make the man (or woman)" and this means you act a certain way based on the way those clothes make you feel.

Wearing jeans and a t-shirt will likely not inspire you to act like the CEO of a big company or even a supervisor of staff. A shirt and tie or suit whether you are an entry level staff member or a bigwig can make you feel important, sexy and super-confident, and we have already established the importance that plays in your sales game. As you contemplate the clothes you will don when you walk into your place of business, just remember: status quo will lead you to be average. Going above and beyond, even in picking out a wardrobe, can help catapult you to being noticed for the right things and the attitude of success and professionalism you desire.

In addition to wardrobe choices, professionalism needs to exude from every expression you make. We have spent time looking at how to approach the call or visit but have talked little about other expressions you may make (aside from not sending proposals). Communication outside of the spoken word will eventually become vital; you will have to resort to it from time to time when unable to speak to people when and how you want to, and it can be a helpful supplement to your arsenal.

If you expect someone to purchase and are trying to gain respect so they are more inclined to do so, showcasing horrific grammar or inability to put two sentences is not going to further your cause.

Concocting a professional e-mail is a science all its own. If you are managing people, do not take for granted that your employees have any idea how to do it all by themselves either. Remember your goal is for someone to see it, read it and be captivated by it, but, like many facets of a call, it cannot overstep its bounds or fall short of its purpose. It cannot underwhelm, over-use statistics, words or benefits and cannot look like it was written by a kindergartner.

When putting together an e-mail or memo to someone you want to turn into a client, there are factors to consider ensuring it helps rather than hurts. The most common mistakes and cures for the improperly constructed business e-mail are similar to the ones applicable to call flow. Overabundance of words and statistics and facts and figures need to be avoided. Trimming the fat of everything you feel compelled to include and proofreading or having someone review your correspondence before you send it to an unsuspecting customer are good ideas.

Such an e-mail should always lead off with a "thank you" for their time referencing the occasion you spent together discussing your product or service. It should be succinct and should end by acknowledging the next time you intend to speak. For instance, begin the note by saying, "Mr./Mrs. Customer, I wanted to sincerely thank you for your time today. Per our conversation, I am sending you information that will aid you as we discuss you coming on board with Scott Services. Please review the attached information. As we agreed, I will call at 9 AM tomorrow morning to review."

I know you have likely sent notes that are much longer. I have seen some that seem to go on forever. The wordier you get and lengthier yours drags on, like a sales call or voice message, the less likely your audience will pay attention. Keep it to the point and keep your attachments, if any, pertinent.

I highly recommend a template for just such an occasion. You should keep it 2-3 paragraphs maximum so it does not linger on like an unwelcome houseguest. Put yourself in their shoes; would you rather read a several paragraph article or straight-to-the-point highlights? The epic novel or the CliffsNotes? No one will read a lengthy letter unless it comes from a relative. Even then, they may skim for the pertinent stuff. Keep it to the point, professional and precise so it serves its purpose. If need be, have someone proofread and give it a stamp of approval as well.

It is sad I have to say this, but if you send a potential client an e-mail strewn with grammatical errors that would take them 20 minutes to read, the likelihood of it doing you any favors is slim to none. Terrifyingly, I have read e-mail correspondence from *managers* that leaves a lot to be desired. Your first grade level writing skills may go unnoticed when you vie for a promotion but there is no hiding it when you are called upon to guide someone in writing memos to clients. Find someone who is articulate and well-versed in this sort of thing to lend a helping hand and save the template in your "drafts" folder for regular use.

Akin to the game of life, the sales game is about taking occasional gambles. We will be called upon to defend our products, services and ourselves, and we have to be willing to do this at the risk of "losing" a sale. I use that terminology loosely because you cannot lose something you never had. That is where risk comes in.

If someone falsely accused you of spray painting graffiti on your neighbor's home, you would defend yourself with tenacity– am I right? The same needs to be applied when someone claims they will not benefit from your arsenal of goodies. Your product deserves your passion and defense as well. Your reputation and good name are at stake.

The common mistakes in sales are made due to fear. If you do, say and ask the right things and stick to your guns, you have little to worry about.

Where would society be without risk-takers? Columbus discovered America, Babe Ruth gave up pitching to become a home run hitter and the 300 Spartans stood their ground against the Persians in 480 B.C. (both historically and cinematically). Remember when two-sport superstar Bo Jackson took the risk of returning to baseball's Chicago White Sox after a football injury ended his career? He hit a home run against the New York Yankees in his first at-bat back. It was a risk that paid off. Yours can too.

Risk in your world could come from a variety of facets, be it risking life and limb swerving through construction-laden streets en route to your sales destiny or just standing tall on your pitch, recommendation and knowledge. In order to close down the dollar amount you want to close down, you often have to start 2-to-3 times higher.

Do not be afraid to lose a "sale" you do not have. Do not be afraid to gamble with results that are less than spectacular. If others are succeeding where you are failing, you need to up the ante, take a chance and roll the dice. You can't win if you don't play. Failure to step out of the box in any instant does not give you the experience you need to be able to do it the next time and the time after that. Failure to dabble in the unknown will keep you unknown. Failure to step outside your comfort zone will keep you confined to the "comfort" level of being just another salesperson.

Heroes are typically determined during moments of great consequence and greater risk. Stocks rise and fall but if you bet on yourself and you give it your all, you can be a sure thing.

If you have not produced revenue for the company greater than the sum you've been paid, do you think anyone should be satisfied with your performance? Would I even be in a position to write a book about this topic had I not accomplished a few things in my day as well? Analyze your end result and when it is not what you or your superiors want or expect, it is time to change the variables that got you there.

* * *

In January 2008, Vincent's star was on the rise. By November 2009, just 22 months later, he had been dragged mercilessly all the way back to Earth.

It was time for him to bring another unsuspecting victim into the company. These poor candidates actually wanted a job with ABM; little did they know they would slave away and never get paid properly and if they complained

248

would be targeted and removed from the business somehow by Keith Dickhauser.

He glanced at the candidate's name and briefly skimmed to find their last place of employment so he would have some springboard into conversation once his standard questions began. Aside from that, Vincent did not care about what the résumé had to say. He was looking for killer instinct, competitive fire and oozing confidence. In short, he was looking for himself.

This candidate's name: Phil Sax. His last job? Director of sales for a small marketing company. He was overqualified, but in this day of questionable economy and massive layoffs, that was not uncommon. Vincent opened the door to the conference room, sized up the middle-aged, snappily dressed gentleman and greeted him.

"Phil," Vincent proclaimed. "I'm Vincent Scott."

Sax accepted Vincent's outstretched hand.

"Mr. Scott. Great to meet you."

"Please – call me Vincent," Vincent said.

"Vincent," Phil repeated.

The two took a seat.

"Phil, I am sure the ladies gave you a blow by blow of what we would do here today. First we will do a brief sales role play and from there I will ask you some questions about your relevant experience. Hopefully from that conversation we will both get a feel for whether or not this is a good fit for you. Sound good?"

"Yes, it does," Phil responded.

"What are you going to try to sell me today?"

"I'm going to sell you an online advertising program," Phil said.

Vincent smiled. "A novel idea. What questions do you have about the process?"

"None."

"Fire when ready."

The role plays always followed the same general outline. The candidates were given a rough call flow but they were on their own as far as improvising each step of the process. Vincent did not buy. The only exception was if he was tired from a long day and did not feel like going through six or seven attempts at overcoming objections from the eager beavers he encountered. After rebuffing Phil a couple of times, their flow ended.

"Phil, thank you for your participation in the role play. What prompted you to apply for this position?" Vincent asked, making a segue into the interview.

249

"Vincent, I'm going to shoot straight with you. I was laid off from my last position. I have been in the sales game for twenty years. I have a wife and children. I need a job. That's why I'm here."

"Makes sense to me. Why would you be successful here?"

"Vincent, you name it, I've done it. I have sold furniture, sold insurance, done cold calling and inbound. I understand what this is: calling on businesses and getting through to the decision-makers. That is something I did for several years. In short, this is right up my alley," Phil responded.

"How are you going to react to dialing two hundred customers daily and yielding very few decision-makers, hoping to achieve one sale per day?"

"You have people that are successful at it, I assume. That said, I know I can be one of the best," Phil responded. "I know what I'm getting myself into. Sales involves a high level of discipline, tenacity and a thick skin. I'm your guy." Vincent could not help but smile.

"The job requires toggling back and forth through multiple computer systems and screens. What have you done that leads you to believe that will come easy to you?"

"I have actually built computer programs from scratch for a prior company. In many of my jobs I have had to utilize multiple programs; probably as many as five or six."

This was easier than Vincent would have dreamed. A few more questions and he could go visit the floor for a while before departure.

"At the end of a day cold calling prospects, your energy level is noticeably different than it was at the beginning. How do you keep your energy at a relatively high level?"

"Caffeine."

Both men smiled.

"Seriously, Vincent," Phil continued, "I am not here to waste anyone's time. I have been a professional for many years. I have discipline. I know what it takes to be successful. I'm here to work."

"Fair enough," Vincent said. "What do you feel will be your biggest challenge transitioning into this situation considering the mobility you have enjoyed in recent positions?"

"Well, like I said, I have discipline so I will adapt. That said, yes, it will be a change of venue that will require some adjustments," Phil acknowledged. "But when you know what you are working for and who you are working for, you force yourself to make those adjustments. I have matured in the workforce over the years and will quickly do what I need to do in order to be successful here."

"What questions do you have for me?"

"How long have you been here?"

"I have been with the company for over 8 years," Vincent answered.

"Do you like it?"

"Let me put it this way," Vincent answered, "I have gotten everything I want out of it so far. It has not been easy but it has been rewarding. I have met some good people. And what's best is being a part of the business that is growing while other parts of the company are laying people off. I have a hand in making policy every day. That is an experience."

"That's good to hear," Phil said. "I would like to think this will be where I retire from."

"And that's good for me to hear," Vincent responded. "Any other questions?"

"Just when do I start?" Phil inquired, grinning.

Vincent smiled and chuckled. That was always his favorite question to hear in an interview. He was surprised he did not hear it more often.

"Excellent question, Phil," Vincent responded. "Basically, what I do is go through, score the role play, score the interview questions and our Human Resources team gets back to you within the week. I'll walk out with you so you don't get lost in the maze out there."

"Sounds great, Vincent. Thank you," Phil said. The men stood and shook hands.

"My pleasure."

The interview. We have all been there at some point, some more than others and some on both sides of the coin . No matter the situation, there are fundamentals you must remember to achieve your goals regardless of what side of the table you are sitting on. What should we say to have the maximum probability at success? What is the interviewer looking for? And if you are the interviewer, what should you be looking for? The answers to these and other questions will soon be revealed.

It is always most logical to begin at the beginning; you will be or have been interviewed by someone banking future sales greatness on you. I have interviewed over one thousand people in my career and my expectation of potential candidates has changed dramatically over the years. I started out thinking sales experience was the primary thing to look at but came to realize over time it should take a backseat to personality and charisma. I started out thinking intelligence and professionalism and being overly articulate or analytical were heavy positives but wound up realizing that if you want someone with sales potential, you want someone a little zany.

Something I feel compelled to throw in here is never turn down the opportunity to interview for something. It may not be a job you are interested in or something you deem as beneath you, but any time you sit in front of a professional who is asking you questions and keeping you sharp, that is a good thing. You can make connections in the interview that can benefit you for years to come. They may create a position for you someday, keep you in mind when something better opens up, or just give you positive press when they talk about you to someone that matters. So, you are headed to the interview for a position in sales. Dress for success and arrive well ahead of the scheduled time. Being late means you are pretty much toast. You want to do anything you can to impress the interviewer; anyone can show up on time. Why not show up early?

As for attire, you likely have no idea going in what the dress code for this position will be. If you show up wearing less than required, it is doubtful to earn you any additional points. Giving yourself an excuse to break out the old suit is never a bad thing; I like standing in front of the mirror reciting James Bond quotes when I am wearing one. Granted, I wear one practically every day but, that's not the point...

For men, it is a good idea to at the very least wear slacks, shirt and tie; for the ladies, they should wear something their father would approve of that exudes a professional business look. Never take the risk that showing skin is going to help you in the interview. It will not impress a female interviewer and even the guys shouldn't be looking for that revealing look. Believe me, I have interviewed some females that seemingly dressed to appeal to a different side of me than my interviewing persona. However, I never made hiring decisions with any part of my anatomy other than my head or gut. I promise.

Be polite; everything you say should exemplify that them taking time out of their busy schedule to talk to you is an honor. Thank them for their time. Wish them a good day. Ask how their day has been. Whatever you can inject to sound and be personable is a good thing. A little bit of small talk, such as how busy they must be or something flattering to their work ethic can do nothing but help.

Nervousness often plagues candidates. Why be nervous? Heck, they should be nervous about meeting you, right? You are the future of their business! You could someday take their job! Regardless, in all seriousness, you want to act the part of a successful salesperson. The way you project yourself will make or break you and will also make up for any shortcomings that may appear on your résumé.

You will hear several schools of thought on the résumé itself, so here is mine: I never paid them much mind. These days, your résumé mostly serves as a keyword-searchable tool to see if you have some basic requirements to get your foot in the door. Unfortunately, most staffing sects these days are overworked and shorthanded, meaning you could be the most qualified person in the world but never get a call.

That said, your interviewers will have various levels of devotion to utilization of the résumé, your experience and the circumstances surrounding any departures. Your résumé should tout what you have achieved and accomplished for previous companies because the interviewer will want to envision you being able to do those things for their company. That is what they will likely be looking for in you. That is also the picture you should focus on completing in their mind when trying to sell them that you are the right fit for this position.

I recommend you have answers to a lot of the most frequently asked questions, which could center around your job history, why you have left jobs and under what circumstances, and what your biggest strengths or areas of opportunity are. Have a positive spin to put on any negatives and you want to – like overcoming an objection – anticipate any apprehension a potential employee may have before you even arrive.

If you have a history of disciplinary problems, obviously you want to show some kind of personal growth when explaining this as your area of development. Always explain that as part of the evolution of your character, you are working on being as professional and respectable as possible and you learned a lot in your previous position. Remember that an interview, like the job itself, is selling yourself. They have to be sold that you can do this better than the other people they have seen or will in the time to come.

Lots of questions in interviews will be situational. The interviewer will ask you to describe a time you dealt with a characteristic or work scenario you could very well face regularly should you be chosen for the position. Stay away from generalities; give them, to the best of your recollection, a concrete example of what they are asking you about. They are looking for your level of experience dealing with the things you would deal with performing the job in question. If you do not have the experience, and someone else does, it is likely they will skip right over you.

Like a first date, you put on somewhat of an act, hide your flaws and only talk about the things you think will impress the other person. Reliance on wit and charm are pluses and yes, they can help overcome any shortcomings on your résumé. However, keep in mind it will be the candidate who perfectly balances experience with personality that is the ideal one.

The people that impressed me most in job interviews over the years have been overflowing with confidence and there was nothing I could ask that they did not meet with a decisive answer. Previous experience is fine to draw upon but, for me, the charisma on display was the determining factor.

Think about the job you are applying for. What are the tasks required of the incumbent in the position? Then think about what it would take for you as a potential customer in these settings to be impressed. Then become that person. You have to become the person they are looking for to win them over in. Convincing them you can win at this job will ultimately ice the deal. Like the art of the sale, anticipate the answers they want and give it to them with finesse. Give the people what they want.

It is acceptable to brag about what you have done. I was never looking for much in the way of modesty, but even if you encounter an interviewer who is, showing you have some swagger is a plus. Do not ask how quickly you can become a manager or move to a different level or job. While you may think that showcases ambition or desire to succeed, the interviewer wants you for the position you are discussing. They do not want to talk about you conceivably taking their job and you are not interviewing to be the next step up yet. Until you master the path ahead, keep your mouth shut about it.

The interviewer will likely also ask you things that are difficult to answer or talk about. Anticipate it and come up with the best, most truthful answer to any such scenario. Honesty is the best policy and even if you had a difficult termination or an attendance problem in the past you want to show you learned from the mistakes and are a different person now. Those were not necessarily nails in the coffin during an interview with me, provided there was sincerity and

254

clarification. Someone who tried to cover up something or still seemed too immature to work in my environment hammered those nails all by themselves. Be upfront, address the concern and bridge the conversation back into your realm of strengths that make you a perfect fit for the position.

Also ensure you have questions of your own to ask the interviewer. Doing so shows that you are not just going through the motions, you have put some thought into being there and you have legitimate questions about the position. These questions can also provide a lot of insight as to what the interviewer thinks your chances are.

A question some are unsure about asking concerns salary, yet now is the perfect time to do so if you have not already. This is far from out of bounds. In fact, one of the last things you want to do as a job seeker is to give off the aura that you are going to be a pushover to take the job no matter what the terms. Yes, you are interested and yes, you will do whatever it takes and yes, you studied information about the company from their website or other materials, but you do need to support your family in the manner with which they have become accustomed. Asking what expected, low-end and high-end earnings are can help you figure out where you will fall and if this is going to be a fit from your vantage point.

Ask what type of candidate they are looking for to fill the role and based on their answer, draw from something you have already said or something new to address any deficiencies you may have identified. If they say they are looking for someone with sales experience and you have very little, greet that hurdle with, "Absolutely, experience is great. Lots of people can get hired for sales jobs but I know a lot may not fulfill the promise they originally showed. You won't have that problem with me. Teach me your products and my personality, can-do attitude and will to win will finish the job."

Another question I recommend is asking that, with the knowledge they now have of you, what they think would be your biggest challenge(s) transitioning into this new role. Getting answers to questions like these are self-fulfilling; while you come across as conscientious and interested, you also get a window into what the interviewer thinks of you. Gleaning what they think any potential obstacles for you would be also gives you the opportunity to once again turn a negative into a positive; take the constructive criticism, acknowledge it and show them how you would be able to tackle that hurdle.

Finally, once you have made a statement showing why you are perfect for the job, bridge directly into asking the interviewer when they want you to report to work. I'm serious. This was always my favorite question that a candidate could ask. Like any sales opportunity, you have to close the sale and nothing does it better than this. Something along the lines of, "Well, that said, when should I report to work?" effectively segues from your statement of confidence in your abilities into an assertive close.

Likely, this will elicit a laugh from your interviewer, which is always a good thing. Coming across as the person they want to be around in their place of work is what you are shooting for. Make them laugh, whichever side you find yourself on – the interviewed or the interviewer. It puts the other party at ease if they are being interviewed and it shows you are fun to be around if you're the one fielding the questions.

Think as you prepare and execute the process of being interviewed: what would your detractors say about you? No interviewer is going to be a pushover; they have every intent of ascertaining if you are a fit but they are also going to look for potential weaknesses. They mask questions designed to see if you are going to stack up against what could be a stringent regimen required to work there and be successful. Every answer you provide needs to be delivered with the utmost confidence in yourself to do the job and do it well.

Find out what the next step is and talk future tense about the next time you will be in contact. Express gratitude towards the interviewer and confidence that when the dust settles, you'll be the one standing. Likely you have contact information of the interviewer or someone in Human Resources, and you should always utilize this afterwards to send a note of appreciation. If you do not hear anything, it is prudent to follow up to reaffirm your interest. If you are declined, it is also not out of bounds to inquire as to what you could do to better yourself for future interviews with either their company or another because you "value their opinion."

As I move into talking about the role as interviewer, I will say this: realize at whatever stage you are in your job search, be it filling out applications, getting ready for an interview or post-interview hoping to hear the good word, most human resources staffs are up to their ears in their process. Many are overworked with way too many applicants and requisitions, meaning you may not get an answer that satisfies you. You may be looked over despite overwhelming qualifications and charm. You cannot take any of this personally; it is the nature of the beast. Like anything else, go out there and give it your all and stand tall. You're a winner.

Looking for the right candidate is a science. Just like a chemistry set, the wrong combination of personality traits and experience levels can lead to volatile explosions while the right cocktail adds the winning touch to your sales team. Experience is nice and all but it takes individuality and oomph to excel at the level of consistency required to make you successful. I have seen people come and go that had been in sales for years but could not master the trade. I have seen people with no sales experience and no degree ascend to the top of the charts.

As an interviewer and sales manager, do not overcomplicate things. Would you want this person working for you? Would you pick them to be on your team? I have seen hiring managers lower their guard and hire somebody because they think under the right circumstances the person might pan out in a positive fashion but these are the people who are unsuccessful.

If you are hiring, you cannot be stifled by the prospect of delivering rejection to a candidate. For whom are you doing a favor if you hire someone who has not convinced you of the job match between themselves and the company? They will find their calling elsewhere; do not worry about or lose sleep over them. You are doing them a favor by not putting them in a job where they would fail and you would later have to put out of their misery. If you are not convinced they would be a fit, and you gave them every opportunity to sell you on why they would be, move on to the next candidate.

Seriously, I have interviewed so many people that have "been in sales for twenty years" who sold any number of different things but had no personality, did not excite me and did not convince me they could sell my product. Your product or service is a different animal than the others and you are not wrong to hold your job qualifications in high regard. Make your job out to be an elite trophy because that is how you attract the candidates you want to attract.

The résumé, the document designed to trumpet their experience and describe past occupations, does not tell the whole story. If it did, there would be no need for the interview. Presumably, if the candidate has passed a screening process, they have been deemed worthy to meet with the hiring manager. Then, the mission of the hiring manager is to determine if this candidate has the right stuff.

You think you are looking for the perfect candidate but the important thing to realize as an interviewer is there is no such thing. Sometimes you have to go with your gut. Some people are worth the gamble. I have had people I turned down who probably could have done a better job than some people on my payroll. I have hired people who had no business being there because I thought I saw something in them. However, for every one of those there were five more that I rolled the dice on and won with.

Never take it all too seriously. Yes, you are filling a position that is responsible for generating revenue. Yes, you are in need of someone with the right tools, work ethic and smarts to equal a winning combination. However, you are (hopefully) not making a decision that will determine if someone lives or dies. A lot of these jobs that you may be hiring for are entry level positions. If you make a mistake, it will not be the end of the world.

It is likely you have standardized questions you are supposed to ask potential candidates. As you can probably guess, I did not follow those questions; I came up with my own and my own style of interviewing. Of course, no matter what methods you choose to use, you have to stay away from politically incorrect topics like age, race, gender or anything that could be traced back to them. That is why for most it is probably a good thing to stick to the script.

However, the types of questions you ask need to mentally put the candidate in the driver's seat of the job you are filling. How would they handle the pressures, the stressors and deadlines? What did they do when a similar situation was staring them down in their last job? What are their favorite and least favorite things about working in the type of environment your job takes place in? The questions you ask are designed to give you the chance to see how they will react to being in the job post they seek, what they will do in common situations and if they can take the wear and tear to become the best.

Do not be fooled; practically everyone is going to tell you they will be #1, they were top dog in their previous sales job incarnation, and the like. You cannot believe all of these things or be sucked in; if it all seems too good to be true, it likely is. You definitely want to picture them doing the tasks they would be required to do and if that seems like quite a stretch that should be telling you something.

While you want to challenge them at every turn and see what they are made of, be personable and put them at ease. Scaring someone is not going to bring out their best. At the end of the day, this process is having a conversation to figure out if you are going to work well together and if making them a part of your team is going to be a wise investment of your time and your company's money. As for hiring managers to work for you, it gets trickier but this really does come down to experience. You need to see or hear what this candidate has done in predicaments similar to those they will face when managing in your department. Just because someone can sell does not make them a great leader; we have discussed this already, but people who have experience supervising effectively or have taken on projects to showcase such skills can often have the leg up in a management opportunity.

I could write a book on how to manage (in fact, I may someday do that) but it is the commitment and execution of the person seeking that higher command that will determine if they are ready for the next level.

Experience is a plus but not everything. Whether being interviewed or conducting the interview, remember your place, remember what you are looking for and what is expected of you. Meet those needs and you are already way ahead of the curve.

*   *   *

258

Vincent opened the door and led Phil Sax out of the conference room, into the hall and towards the exit. Keith Dickhauser's secretary Marla Mooney was in the hall waiting for Vincent.

"Vincent, Keith wants to see you right away," she said with a concerned look on her face.

"Okay, tell him I will be there in a few minutes," he answered, not thinking much of it.

"He said it's urgent," Marla said, not smiling. "I can walk the candidate to the door for you."

Then it registered: the blog post.

"Thanks, Marla. Phil – thanks again for your time," Vincent said, shaking hands with Phil again.

"Hope to hear from you soon," Phil said.

Vincent walked down the hallway, back towards Block 3. It was a walk he had dreaded hundreds of times. Vincent entered the office and waited for Keith to signify if this was a closed door session or one he would allow the door to remain open for.

"Close the door," Keith said, motioning with his hand. Vincent shut the door and sat down.

"Vincent, it came to my attention today that you posted a threat and offered a bounty on an employee online attached to an article about our company."

"Whoa, whoa – a threat? Bounty? An employee? What the hell are you talking about?" Vincent shot back. Used to being on the defensive in conversations with Dickhauser, he was ready to fire.

"Are you denying that you made an online post attached to an article about our company?" Keith asked.

"Keith, I have no idea what you've heard. Here is the actual truth: I was made aware earlier today of some random blog post about ABM that wasn't even factual. In fact, it had stats that weren't accurate and made claims about the company that were not true. It cited a 'source' that doesn't even work for the company!" Vincent said rapidly. "Below the post, in the message board section, somebody attacked my kid and me. I immediately wrote the blog administrator to have the libel removed. I made an initial response just saying that only cowards hide behind anonymity—"

"Right," Keith said, cutting him off. "That is not the post they had a problem with."

"Okay, and what I was going to say is that I checked again hours later and not only were the comments not removed, but the jackass attacked me

259

again," Vincent continued. "This time, I simply responded and said something about I am sure he bragged to buddies and would offer a reward to anyone who told me the name. I said if they want to talk about me, I don't care but when you talk about my kid we should meet face to face. That is exactly what I said."

"Well, our legal team views this as a very serious offense," Keith stated.

"A serious offense of what?" Vincent retorted.

"Well, they are calling it a threat. They referred to it as you putting a bounty on someone."

"That's ridiculous! I didn't threaten anybody! Read the damn thing!" Vincent raised his voice passionately. "Keith, do you have any clue how this made me feel? Any father would have done the same thing in my shoes, if not worse."

"Be that as it may," Keith began, picking up a piece of paper from his desk, "this is very serious by company standards."

Vincent knew what the paper was before Keith gave it away. It was the infamous confidential record of discussion, meaning some kind of warning was coming his way. Oh, well. It would be some formal warning and he would move on. The only disciplinary action in his career had been retracted the next day so this should more or less be a formality.

"I have to suspend you," Keith said, handing the piece of paper to Vincent awkwardly. The person delivering the speech to the disciplined employee was supposed to actually read from it. Keith did nothing of the kind.

Vincent quickly scanned the document and smirked with disgust. "You're kidding me," he spat. "This is outrageous. What are we going to do about this?"

"You don't think I tried to defend you?" Keith asked, his typical deflection.

No, Vincent thought, *I know you didn't. This bastard has never had my back on anything.* Any sympathy he had towards the unsuspecting soon-to-be-ousted dictator was next to zero.

"So, no investigation – nothing?" Vincent asked. "I don't get an opportunity to defend myself?"

"My hands are tied on this one," Dickhauser answered.

"Who do I talk to about this?" Vincent asked, not relenting. "I'm not going to take this lying down. I want to talk to Gil."

Dickhauser suddenly perked up and it was his turn to go on the defensive.

"Vincent, Gil is disgusted with you at this point," Dickhauser boomed. "These guys wanted to fire you. I saved your job."

"Saved my job? That's bullshit, Keith," Vincent scoffed. "This is the first time I have been written up in 8 years. Are you kidding me?" Vincent cried in disbelief. "So how long am I suspended for?"

"It's on the document," Keith said. "Two days."

"Two days? Jesus Christ," Vincent said, shaking his head. "This is ridiculous."

"You are your own worst enemy, Vincent. Upper management is tired of the drama you bring."

"Tired of the drama?" Vincent shouted. "Tell them to put me out of my fucking misery! Are they tired of the millions of dollars I have made them? They don't even know what the fuck I do every day! Nobody could do this job or put up with the shit I put up with. Tell them to walk a mile in my shoes."

"Yeah, that's the attitude to have. I stood up for you. I tell them all the time how great you are."

"Yeah right, Keith. You won't even publish a sales report that shows the difference between my teams and Mark's in revenue because it would make your golden boy look bad. You just let me fry when Lydia and Agnes were investigating me You don't have my back."

"What?" Keith said, coiling in surprise. "I'm the only friend you have in the business."

"I don't believe that anymore."

"Who do you think goes to bat for you all the time?" Keith raised his voice, his face turning red.

"Nobody. I'm a man against the world. But, you know what? That's fine. Thanks for the vacation," Vincent shouted, standing. "Can I go?"

"Before you leave, can you make the dialer schedule for tomorrow?" Keith asked, almost timidly at that point.

"No," Vincent answered after a split second of hesitation. "I'm suspended." He reached the door, then turned to face Keith again. "And, one last thing. If you supposedly go to bat for me all the time, you won't mind if I send Gil my side of the story and request a meeting, right?"

Dickhauser stuttered and his face turned red. "Uh, no, but I want you to send it to me first."

"Sure thing," Vincent said, opening the door and exiting the room.

Vincent walked out of Keith's office onto the now empty floor, back to his office and did not even unlock his computer to see what was sold for the day.

He grabbed his jacket and walked out the door, leaving the Greenfield office to pick up Elizabeth – the only thing left in his life that did not let him down.

This was a deep wound – a two-day suspension? That was barely a tier under termination. Had he done something somewhat brash or stupid? Maybe, in hindsight, challenging someone somewhat publicly was letting his guard down or letting someone see him bleed. He was just so tired of all of these anonymous attacks. Every attack on Vincent his entire career had been anonymous. Just once he wanted to call whatever coward out of the shadows and see if they could talk like that to his face. No one had ever given him any kind of preparation for this type of thing.

But it also became even more glaringly obvious that Keith did not have his back. The man played golf with all the bigwigs but could not stop his suspension? And he actually said they wanted to fire him over it? With no investigation? Unbelievable. This was basically the first disciplinary conversation he had encountered in over 8 exemplary years in the business and he was sent packing for two days. It was highly illogical and outlandish.

As Vincent drove to the sitter's, he realized the day had been the culmination of the last two years of his life; a continuing downward spiral that surely must end soon – right? Vincent was suspended for unprofessional behavior regarding an online blog forum, offering a "bounty" on an "employee." What forensic expert had identified this person as an employee, anyway? The timing was also peculiar; whoever did it planted it right in the thick of the Dickhauser investigation like it was baiting him intentionally...

The spiral began when things hit the skids with Abby and he made the decision to kick her out of the apartment. While there was an initial spike in his happiness, rockier times were ahead.

In March 2008, Vincent was announced as one of ten recipients of the Top Gun trip to Las Vegas. Against better judgment, he lobbied to get Abby a job as a clerical staff member downtown for his department. He figured the distance would be enough, as Keith naturally did not want her working with him in Greenfield, and was just glad he was no longer paying for every one of her whims himself.

Word of his relationship with Phoebe was very quickly making the controversial rounds. Not only did reps and managers pick up on or hear about Vincent and Phoebe's involvement but the news reached Abby and Keith as well. Neither was thrilled and both decided to act out in different ways.

Keith made clear to Vincent he did not want him involved in any way with her; it was a needless distraction that undermined the department, was unprofessional and he did not want to hear anything further on the topic. Abby used a different tactic: revenge, with Elizabeth as the weapon.

Slated to leave for Vegas at the end of March, Vincent knew the trip would coincide with the days they agreed he would get to be with Elizabeth. On a Sunday afternoon, while he played NBA Live with Chad Willman and Elizabeth played in her playpen, the whole situation came to a head when Abby came to pick her up and vehemently refused to renegotiate days. Her refusal meant Vincent would needlessly go ten days without seeing Elizabeth. He begged her to reconsider, but Abby coldly refused to budge. She left with Elizabeth and, after switching from the Heinekens he enjoyed while Chad was there to vodka and soda, he made the ill-advised call to Abby's parents' house to try again to persuade her otherwise.

Alcohol thrown on any flame is never good. Abby, of course, still refused to let Vincent see Elizabeth, as if it was her right to do so to begin with.

From there, the conversation took a turn for the worse. While Vincent would never threaten her, he came as close as he could by telling her he wished she was a man so he could punch her out instead of putting up with her. She hung up. He called back and her father answered. Abby was not only a liar but she also did her best to poison everyone against Vincent, telling people he was a deadbeat father that did not give her money and was mean to her. Abby's father acted on these falsehoods and it led to a heated conversation between the two.

Dan Winters started talking condescendingly to Vincent, who, true to character, did not sit too well for that. He in turn challenged him to settle it like men and Dan hung up on him a few times before letting it go to the machine. Vincent left foolish drunken messages that he was more than ready to fight Dan for what he said to him and would put him in the ground. In the week to come, both sides filed restraining orders. Abby refused to let Vincent see his daughter and defamed him to everyone, even slandering him to Vince, Jr. and Kay for purely selfish reasons. The derailing of Vincent's life jolted forward.

Las Vegas, Nevada. It was an escape for Vincent and much-needed one at that. Cal Riley had earned a trip there, as had Yamnitz, Maria Fernandez, and Johnny Slade. Barred by Keith from taking Phoebe as his guest, Vincent took his father for some father-son bonding. Vince, Jr., while not partaking in the partying many enjoyed, had a great time sightseeing and taking in shows while not with his son.

Having not seen Elizabeth in a week and a half, aside from a quick visit he made to the sitter's the day prior to departure, Vincent was drunk before the plane from Minneapolis landed in Vegas. Needless to say it was a long night. The company had hired an entertainment group to put together a package that included shows and sights but also included unlimited drinks. And once they had your drink order, they force fed refills to you. Vincent felt nothing come touchdown and remembered nothing from about an hour later. He got lost trying to find his room in the Stratosphere and was later told that at some point he knocked over a prominent manager from Texas. It was not his finest hour.

The rest of the trip was mostly subdued for Vincent. He got sunburned on Day 2 playing golf with his Dad and spent much of the rest of the trip in seclusion drinking alone in the ice cold tub in his room, only reappearing for the dance the final night. Aside from draining a 27-foot putt, the trip was mostly spent trying to drown out the pain of missing Elizabeth in the longest two weeks of his life. But the damage was done. The whole civilized world had seen him at his worst, drunk, stumbling and knocking over an unsuspecting sales manager. That image could not be erased and no one cared about the justification.

The hits hardly stopped there. Back in Minneapolis not long after, someone actually wrote an anonymous letter to Human Resources Vice President Karl Farr damning Vincent, stating he walked the floor talking on his cellular phone (though the only instances of this were Keith calling him), citing his child out of wedlock, touting his "illicit affair with a staffing manager with initials PW", and claiming that he purportedly lied to salespeople. It was written haphazardly and typed in a way it could never be linked to anyone, but the attacks were baseless and anyone who knew Vincent would know that. Furthermore, the anonymous packet included one of Vincent's recent newsletter columns that circled in red the word/letter "I" everywhere it appeared, trying to frame him as an egomaniac. Of course, they picked the one where he was asked to talk about his career-to-date and his successes.

This type of attack on Vincent was foreign to him. He knew when he sat atop the Rockford charts that Bambi Jennings and others would speculate as to how he got there but he had never experienced hatred on this big of a stage. The anonymous letter earned him enough notoriety that it bought him his first trip to Lydia Rawlings' office just days after its postmark.

Lydia questioned him about the nature of his relationship with Phoebe. She asked about the items in the letter. And while they found him not guilty of any conduct violations, the sting of this was just the beginning.

As this was all occurring while Vincent was being considered to take over an additional office in San Diego, the chain reaction led to a meeting with Keith's boss Monty Mills. Monty was easygoing and merely alluded to the fact that his womanizing reputation would not help him get promoted if they had to worry about him having relations with others. Vincent deflected it by saying he was in a relationship with one person that he intended to stay with. This, however, did not help him when he was next summoned to the office of Gil Walker, Senior Vice President of sales and Monty's boss.

Vincent marveled at the setup upon entrance as Gil's desk was thirty feet across the room from the table where their meeting was to take place. This was the true office of an executive; there was a leather couch and beautifully upholstered chairs, artwork adorning the walls and enough room to have a putting machine.

At that point, it was actually a surprise to Vincent when Keith made no attempt to deflect any of the assault on his character. Gil cited one allegedly ego-drenched newsletter column that Vincent wrote , his reputation as a womanizer and told him he needed to get his personal life and the reputation of the department out of the gutter. Keith just sat there.

This, of course, came after Vincent's best results month ever and while he was riding high with the support of his reps and management team. But no one would know this, as Keith only published all-in results and the inbound group – struggling mightily under Mark Rogers – diluted the reported numbers. No one would know what Vincent did for the department because, to cast Vincent as the department's Messiah would attract attention to the fact that Keith Dickhauser was utterly useless.

Vincent took the lashing from Gil like a man. He was told that the department was run like a fraternity, a charge that he, Johnny, Jimmy and Cal actually took a liking to in subsequent conversations, dubbing themselves as such. He was told that the Labor department had complained about Vincent's combative disagreements with their practices. Vincent had to bite his tongue; buffoon director Ed Michaelson and his clueless pawns had no idea how to do their jobs, changed their opinions multiple times and no one policed their incompetence.

How dare Gil question him when he had no idea what was going on? He had no clue what he and his managers contended with on a daily basis, and for Keith to sit idly by and not be chastised for what he did or did not do was disheartening to Vincent. But like everything, Vincent took his beating and got up from it. He made the decision to turn the negative into a positive, which was never more evident than the day and a half to come.

Upon return to the office, Keith conducted a meeting with the entire management staff. He referenced the fraternity comment. He stated there were "fatal flaws in this management team." He also said, "And if this isn't for you, that's fine. There's no shame in that. Come and let me know, because if you can't do your job, I'll find somebody who can."

Vincent's job, on the other hand, was to pick these people up, regardless of his opinion of the message from above. Vincent's job was to give them the message they needed to hear in able to work and do their best. The fact this was clearly lost on Keith and apparently lost on Gil was not his fault or his problem. As long as Vincent was in this position he was going to do things the way he saw fit: the way they needed to be done.

The following morning, Vincent woke up around 3 AM as he always did when he could not control his excitement for what was to come. He jotted down notes for the speech he would deliver on a notepad by the couch he had woken up on. Come 8 AM when the managers gathered in their conference room not knowing what to expect, they got this:

"Good morning, team."

"Good morning," they replied in unison.

"Team, I am going to cut to the chase. I am going to reference the conversation that Keith had with us yesterday – that this place is a frathouse and that there are flaws in the leadership of our department. As your leader, that reflection is on me, and I alone will take responsibility for that image," Vincent announced to stares he had never seen this attentive. "I have as many chinks in my armor and weaknesses, if not more, than anyone here. They say a team follows the lead of its boss, and if there is an attitude that we are high on sales but have a cavalier attitude towards everything else, I am as much to blame for that, if not more, than anyone else.

"I want *everything* that comes out of this department to be the picture of excellence, not just the sales. If there is a problem around here – I don't care if it came from Gil Walker or from Luke *Skywalker* – we're going to fix it.

"I know that as every day winds down, we feel like we have literally been beaten to a pulp. We're spent. Like we can't do anymore. I feel like that, and I know you do because I have done that job too and know what you guys put into this place. But if there is a problem with us and our Labor team, let's fix it. If there is an issue with our contracts getting in on time or their accuracy, let's fix it.

"When I feel more beaten down than usual, nothing inspires me more than the words of the great sage, Rocky Balboa. 'The world ain't all sunshine and rainbows, it's a very mean and nasty place and I don't care how tough you are it will beat you to your knees and keep you there permanently if you let it. You, me, or nobody is going to hit as hard as life. But it ain't about how hard you hit, it's about how hard you can get hit and keep moving forward. How much you can take, and keep moving forward. That's how winning is done! Now if you know what you're worth, go out and get what you're worth, but you've got to be willing to take the hits. And not pointing fingers saying you ain't where you want to be because of him, or her, or anybody! Cowards do that and that ain't you. You're better than that!'"

Vincent stopped for a moment for effect. His managers were nodding and smiling. He had them right where he wanted them. It was time to bring this thing home.

"Guys, nobody can take away from what we've got or what we've done, but we need to put the stamp of quality on *everything* we do. That's what we get paid to do. Everything that's in the past is gone and the future is up to us. There's nothing to it but to do it. Let's get out there!"

Vincent stood and his managers stood with him, cheering loudly. It was the best management meeting of his career. He opened the door and they marched out, high-fiving him and each other, whooping, hollering and patting him on the back en route to making another magical day happen.

As for Vincent Scott, he was exhausted, more than ever before. This was the first time in his career he physically broke down; slinking into his office and drawing the blinds, he sat there, breathless with his heart racing and he was not sure if he could go on. Not only had he been beaten to a pulp by Gil Walker but ensconced in this custody battle with Abby, unable to go public with his relationship with Phoebe but still being put through the ringer over it, being harassed regularly by Dickhauser and being the lone buffer between him and the managers was taking its toll.

He took a half day off and spent the rest of it with Elizabeth.

The following week, he took a day off with Phoebe and Elizabeth to again clear his head. They left his apartment after Elizabeth's nap and took in a day Twins' baseball game. Unbeknownst to them, they were spotted together by someone who worked in the downtown office, of all places, and was also on a day off. By the end of the day, news of their public appearance and relationship was all over the place.

Things did not get easier. With Vincent in the spotlight for the wrong reasons, upper management in Phoebe's group like Karl Farr made clear to her that involvement with Vincent would be nothing but detrimental to her career. From there, rather than stand by her man, she slowly started distancing herself from him.

Their time together was sporadic already, as Michelle was playing soccer and Phoebe was not ready to bring Vincent around that scene, Phoebe was still under the same roof with Nathan, and many other reasons she gave any time Vincent asked her to be with him. Vincent left one day to help her at a job fair but when Dickhauser caught wind of it, he screamed violently and threatened to terminate Vincent if he ever heard of him being around Phoebe again.

Keith had come to the realization he could not replace Vincent but he also could not control him. Those threats were the only thing he could think of to keep him in check.

For as spring continued its trudge towards summer, Vincent's teams pummeled Mark's by huge margins. He was the one keeping the place going and that was all too clear to everyone, regardless of their feelings towards him. Vincent's outbound group in Greenfield was on such a high – both sales and morale-wise –people even stopped making the defection to the inbound group which had been considered the elite job in the department.

And now, as November 2009 ended, as Vincent sat in his car departing work post-suspension, his tumble from the top of that mountain (hopefully) complete, he would not have changed what he did if given the opportunity but had to find some way to move forward.

He was certain the powers that be had waited a long time to enact this on him; why else would they have skipped steps of discipline and gone straight for a suspension? He had been cleared of the investigations from the past because there was nothing they could pin on him. They couldn't discipline him for Abby because she left the company before she was his subordinate. They could not discipline him for Phoebe because she was not his subordinate. Keith did nothing to quell this suspension, as no investigation was even done. *Oh, well,* he had to say to himself. Considering everything else he had been through he supposed he could take this, too.

For 2008 had continued to bring the hits. In late spring, he got a call from the apartment complex to tell him water damage from a third floor fire had rendered his first floor apartment uninhabitable. Vincent did not panic or even leave early to tend to the matter; he came home at the regular time and ate take-out sitting on a chair in his sopping wet and dark living room while water spouted like a fountain from the light fixtures.

Abby came to pick up her belongings unannounced on the day he was moving out, despite being specifically told to stay away and Vincent had to call the police. He had to take Jimmy with him to one of Elizabeth's doctor appointments to keep from having communication with Abby. However, after opening lines of communication by being the bigger person and texting Abby to have a happy Mother's Day, she started wanting to meet for family dinners. Since this was a relationship that was not going away anytime soon, Vincent obliged.

Very quickly her conversations would evolve around the fact she was willing to break up with her new boyfriend, an overweight hillbilly named Ricky, if he would break things off with Phoebe. While Vincent was enjoying seeing Elizabeth more, Abby would always make some condescending comment signaling she parented in a superior way, she had no intention of paying back the money Vincent loaned her or that he should just settle on a less-than-50% custody arrangement because if he didn't, he would be worse off. Needless to say, that was all it took for Vincent to realize he would rather not see Abby anymore.

His top priority was no longer being Mr. Popular, it was being "Dada." He was making the final descent on age 30 and was just working hard, dealing with the rollercoaster that was ABM and seeing Elizabeth and Phoebe as much as he could.

Phoebe promised that come summertime they would have lots of time together but none of that time came to fruition. They started to get into it over Phoebe's quelled frequency of communication with Vincent, brought about by

268

the prodding of her department's vice president to steer clear of bad boy Vincent Scott. Phoebe's daughter Michelle met Elizabeth. The four spent time together once a month at Chuck E. Cheese's or at Vincent's apartment. And it seemed like it would eventually come together, when the work drama ceased and Phoebe's divorce was finalized. Vincent was trying to be patient.

Vincent wanted to come home at night to Elizabeth, Phoebe and Michelle; he wanted to have dinner together and talk about their days. He wanted to sleep in the same bed with Phoebe. He wanted to get up and have lazy Sundays together watching football as she rooted for her Vikings and he rooted for his 49ers. He wanted to be on the sidelines with her at Michelle's soccer games.

But there was always something standing in the way. First it was Michelle's soccer schedule. Then it was an inability to divorce Nathan at the time because of the debt it would bring. Then it was her going out of town for a trip. Then it was her going to dinner with her Dad and stepmom. There was always something. Vincent could only ignore the obvious signs for so long.

Being with Elizabeth was all that kept him going; she was starting to pick up on more and say more words. She was exceedingly interactive as she developed quite the personality. And giving her up, even for a day, was like a punishment equal to death. There was many a night Vincent would drop Elizabeth off at Abby's only to have tears streaming down his face as he pulled away in his Accord. He dreaded the exchange from the moment he woke up that day and, once completed, the typically emotionally unexpressive Vincent Scott would hurt uncontrollably as he drove home.

Abby was telling Vincent she still loved him and she had changed. He wanted three things from Abby: for her to stop making false accusations about him to friends and family, to let him see Elizabeth the fair 50% of the time and to stop going after more and more of his money just to turn a profit. She was clearly not willing to comply.

She was gunning for $1,000 per month while she could name no reasons that would amount to more than the $400 it cost for the sitter. She said Elizabeth belonged with her mother. She told cousins and co-workers (at the job he had gotten her) that Vincent was not giving her enough money. The most classic moment was when she annihilated his cell phone and left several messages while he was at work accusing him of getting Elizabeth's hair cut for the first time without her. Especially amusing in a sick and twisted way, was that he never did, meaning the police once again had to get involved and tell her to leave him alone.

Vincent had turned his back on Phoebe before and did not want to do it again. They had been through so much – her engagement and marriage, Abby's pregnancy and their engagement, a work affair, both of their careers being raked over the coals, her limited availability – it all had to count for something, right? It had taken this long to come to the realization there would always be haters who make haughty assumptions about him based on snippets and falsehoods. There would always be bosses that did not have his back and peers who were jealous. Only God, Elizabeth and he needed to know the truth. He couldn't walk away no matter how stressful it became because he was too good. He would miss parts of it that he could never recreate elsewhere. He would miss the control, the ovations and the sentiments from those who respected him.

Vincent gave speeches that repeatedly earned him standing ovations. He continued to sell people every day on giving their all in a job where they were not being paid accurately and the commission supervisor talked to them like they were two years old. He continued to take beatings from Keith, who just got worse and worse.

If there was one thing that could be said for Dickhauser, he was extremely adept at the dirty political game. Keith was chummy with the other district managers, most of whom had been in the business for 20+ years like he had and had typically been promoted for political reasons or because they were the last men standing. Because of this, Keith did a lot of favors for them despite the negative impact they could have on his team.

On September 10, 2008, Keith agreed to call the absolute worst leads in Houston: customers that had not been called for over five years because they had no value. When Vincent had dialed through leads of their caliber in the past, they had a 0.008% conversion. Of course, with their department treated by many like the junkyard of the company and politics more important in a big company than people's well being, Keith ordered Vincent to dial these leads for three hours that day.

Not to mention a decision like this cost Vincent and his unit hundreds of thousands of dollars in annual revenue, but, with Hurricane Ike ravaging the region another potent variable had entered the mix. Very quickly after beginning the campaign, reps, managers and even Mark Rogers called or e-mailed Vincent begging him to move out of calling these poor business owners who were fleeing or boarding up their shops.

With Keith out of pocket in Atlanta in a meeting with his new boss César Fiorentino and the well-being of his office's results and reputation at stake, Vincent made a decision. That is why he was in the position – right? Apparently, from the volcanic catastrophe that ensued, he was dead wrong. Seeing the e-mail from his company BlackBerry that Vincent was moving the team due to the natural disaster, Keith called Vincent immediately upon learning he had stayed in Houston for only one-third of their 6,000 leads (of which they predictably sold not a penny).

"What the fuck do you think you're doing?" Keith roared upon Vincent's acceptance of the call.

"What are you talking about?"

"Are you a fucking idiot? I told you to call Houston," Keith yelled. "Why can't you do a Goddamn thing I tell you to do?"

"Whoa, whoa, hold your horses," Vincent hollered back. "Everybody, including your golden boy Mark, the managers and the reps, is telling me these guys are boarding up shop because of the hurricane. I don't bother my boss when he is with his boss out of town. I thought I was in this job to make decisions and I made one based on all the facts."

"I gave you a basic instruction," Keith snarled in response, clearly not listening to a word Vincent said. "Who runs this fucking department – the reps or me? If I can't trust you to do your fucking job, how can we work together?"

"I am doing my job. I made a decision based on the best interests of the department. If you don't want me in this job, that's your call," Vincent fired back hotly.

"Fuck you."

And Keith Dickhauser hung up the phone.

Vincent, stunned and livid at this point, sent another e-mail to the floor, informing them he was ordered to dial these customers regardless of any personal tragedies they were going through. They dialed Houston's worst leads for another hour, selling absolutely nothing and unnerving many business owners who wondered why ABM had such little class.

When Keith saw Vincent next, he first attempted to cop an attitude and chew him out. Vincent immediately went on the offensive and made clear to Keith that he would not be spoken to in that fashion, would not be cursed out, would be respected and would make decisions based on what he knew needed to occur for the needs of the business. He blasted Keith for having the audacity to condescend to the one man keeping them in business. From that point until late 2009, there were no further problems to this extreme.

But after Keith's investigation sprung up, he treated everyone differently, including his most valuable yet unheralded player, Vincent Scott.

The two days off without pay to lead off December 2009 meant to be his penance were sobering for Vincent. He ignored the inevitable calls from managers wondering where he was, and Keith wanted to uphold some lie that he had just taken unannounced vacation. He claimed he did not want negative press for the department. As Vincent routinely lost 1-2 weeks of vacation annually, managers did not buy it. They knew something was up.

Vincent finally read the document intended to deliver his suspension, taking exception with the word "bounty," that there had been "several" conversations with him regarding unprofessional behavior in the past (where was he during these times?) and that he had "attacked" an "employee" on an "article" about the company. These hefty fabrications were obviously woven by some legal mind to make him look like an unstable criminal when he was anything but. Guilty until proven innocent, just like the ABM way.

He put together a response document that he wanted alongside the original in his binder –his legal right – and a lengthy note featuring his side of the encounter and a request to meet with Gil Walker in person so he could own his actions and show Gil he was serious about his career. Despite statements that he would allow Vincent to contact Gil, he immediately shot down the professionally written note and said they would discuss that and his revised document upon his return. Neither request was carried out. Vincent was forced by Keith to accept this punishment as written and, while Keith could have allowed some positive public relations for Vincent, he vetoed that opportunity as well.

After he put Keith in his place after being cursed out and hung up on over a year prior, Vincent realized Keith hated confrontation; no matter how Keith came at someone, if they held their ground and fired back, he would retreat. Vincent swore Keith spent all his time bitching and refused to retire solely because he would be bored without terrorizing employees and would have no one to scream at if he was at home all day.

The accusations and agony in the custody fight became worse, with Abby attempting to come up with some kind of new attack on practically a weekly basis. Dealing with the feminist Abby-sympathizers in the court system was difficult for Vincent to handle. The forced "therapy" sessions with the court-appointed mediator went nowhere, as Abby spouted lies, claimed Vincent was mean and threatening to her and failed to acknowledge he had gone above and beyond for her in a way no other guy would have. Vincent's truths fell on deaf ears and it became clear he would have to fight to get anything close to fair.

She brought up his drinking and he brought up hers. She started into her lies about "threats", despite the fact he had never threatened her. He talked about her refusal to get a job, the fact she owed him thousands of dollars and that she had even hit him, but she turned on the waterworks and these biased social workers bought it.

In mid-December, Abby even withheld medicine from Vincent meant for Elizabeth and tried to claim he let the medication run out. Things like this would result in wretched claims from her attorney that Vincent should not even be allowed to see Elizabeth because he was an unfit parent. He could not keep his blood from boiling anytime the Caller ID announced her call or a letter from her attorney arrived in the mail.

These defamatory letters sent Vincent on a drunken spiral that culminated mid-December at a happy hour. Depressed, and tired of watching Phoebe talk to and dance with every guy there but him, Vincent started drifting off at the bar and later made a spectacle by kissing her in front of people they worked with to mark his territory. It was not that their relationship was under wraps, but any heat she had already gotten from her hierarchy intensified and she accused Vincent of not respecting her position in the company.

How was he supposed to know what was okay and what was not when she was telling reps on his floor about their sex life? Everything she said and did was a contradiction and Vincent was tired of waiting for a day that would obviously never come.

They were on life support from that point forward. Vincent, stubborn as can be, backed away and ignored her when they ran into one another in the hallways.

The most irritating thing was the lying and 180 degree turnaround Phoebe had undergone. Every time she told him she would stand by him through anything was a lie. She tried to say she had supported him through the fallout of his relationship with Abby but what had she done? She had never been available, had promised they would be together forever but now that he could have used her support it was nowhere to be found.

The most hypocritical of all was her statements to Vincent when Keith threatened to fire him over their relationship: that it was none of the company's business and that they could never stand between them. But with the shoe on the other foot, she folded. And Vincent got yet another classic lesson in betrayal and disloyalty.

Heading into 2009, Vincent vowed to be cool, calm and collected. He held out some, albeit little hope that Phoebe's continuous and repeated promises to be with him forever would come to fruition, but his now only occasional requests for time together were ignored and promised phone calls never placed. She made time for lunches with now-retired Melissa Worthington, for her senior management when they wanted her for dinner or drinks and for pretty much everything but him.

This farce had dragged on for nearly three years; people make their most foolish decisions out of loneliness, but not Vincent Scott.

Vincent would give her the opportunity to tell him she wanted nothing to do with him, but she would instead say she had faith they would be together forever. It would have been much easier for him had she just told him she had used him for the notoriety and thought he was an idiot; it would have had the same ending. But no; Vincent got yo-yoed for much of the year and it was not one of his more pleasant experiences.

Much of Vincent's latter years have been a seesaw between Phoebe and Abby, and back again. As the distance between Vincent and Phoebe became a seemingly insurmountable chasm at the onset of 2009, it resulted in Vincent inclined to test the waters with Abby and Elizabeth as a family.

Despite what she had done to him, Vincent had the hardest time abandoning the concept of ever having a family. The flirtatious banter was something they easily slipped back into. Abby did not have a boyfriend anymore, as he cheated on her after moving in with her and apparently proposing to her. Vincent wanted nothing serious, as it would be very difficult to forget or forgive what she had done to him. However, Abby was somewhat tolerable in very small doses and he took what extra time with Elizabeth he could get.

Vincent spent the rest of countless hours wondering if and when he was ever going to hear from Phoebe. She rebuked him for basically everything possible. Compared to that, Abby was sadly a bargain. Facts were facts: Vincent had flashes of brilliance with Phoebe but they faded quickly and had lied dormant for intervals far too immense.

The beginning of the work year was a different story. On Day One, January 4, Vincent laid out his new scheduling plan to Keith.

Vincent had devised a new scheme that was the epitome of his living-on-the-edge mentality but also made perfect sense. The plan was to dial the lowest propensity-to-buy leads first, racking up a few days of calling the coldest leads and getting their obligatory campaigns out of the way so they could leave the rest of the month to gradually accelerate to the better leads. Vincent would slowly wean them onto warmer leads based on the statistical history of their conversion rates.

"Let's force them to be sharp," he explained to Keith and Mark when he told them about it. "Let's put ourselves behind the 8-ball on purpose. Everybody loves a comeback."

Vincent lobbied hard against Keith's disapproval, won, and made Keith agree that the schedule would stand until he missed objective. He also made Keith promise to call him on the last day of every month they did hit objective and tell him he was a genius. Not only did Vincent hit objective with the schedule, he was having months over 130% or so at that. And if he did not get to the phone in time, he saved the messages of Keith telling him what a genius he was.

Quickly following, the department's customer research team was re-assigned to Vincent as well. This group contacted new advertisers after their programs were activated in an attempt to run through the details and fine tune them prior to billing. They were designed to upgrade programs, but sadly this priority had hereto now taken a backseat. When the team had formed in early

274

2008, they were managed by Haley Jones under the Mark Rogers hierarchy but had struggled to achieve 70-80% of their objective.

Their lack of success was always puzzling to Vincent as his own teams converted existing customers better and the customer research team's efficiency was mind-bogglingly terrible. With them in danger of being shut down, Vincent was assigned the team. This did not set well with Haley, who complained to Keith and Mark that Vincent was nothing but a gunslinger with little but contempt for building customer relationships and that his devil-may-care dialer methods were not right for these subscribers.

In reality, she just did not want Vincent taking the reins of her baby. But he did and, of course, they finally started not only hitting but blowing out objectives once re-assigned.

Vincent's meetings took on a new tone as he was intentionally putting them behind the 8-ball with lesser quality leads early in the month. He refused to recognize that they were calling tough leads and that was the point; every report, meeting and speech emphasized where they stood on pace for their objective. Keith started sweating after just a couple days of poor results but Vincent was steadfast. Rather than relenting, Vincent forced his managers to spend the entire day on the phone to drum up business.

"Team, as you know, we cannot afford another day like yesterday," Vincent said, his team gathered around. "And I know we won't have a day like yesterday because today I am doing you a favor and freeing you of any paperwork obligations. I am going to even cut this meeting short because, come 8:30, you are not allowed at your desk. If I see you there, I will shut off your computer myself. You are to be on the floor all day with your team and I want you to tell them to flag you down if they so much as get a decision-maker on the phone. That's your tag into the game. Get it? Got it? Good."

Despite calling the coldest of the cold leads in the midst of a recession and to business owners in Michigan, the team posted 110% of daily goal.

On Wednesday, January 14, Vincent gathered the sales floor for a morning stand-up and they were expecting the worst. With January slow-starting and the team on pace for 47% of objective for the month, it looked like Vincent's plan was a failure. At least, it looked like that to everyone but Vincent.

"Good morning citizens!" Vincent Scott boomed, no strain in his voice. He held a stack of papers, clearly sales reports, in his hands.

"Good morning!" came the reply.

"First off, thank you for coming out today. I appreciate you. Second, I want to thank those of you who are making it happen this month despite calling nothing but zero dollar customers," Vincent announced. "First off, with ten sales in this young month which is more than some whole teams have, Kyle Carver! Great job Kyle!"

There was boisterous applause and Vincent pointed to Kyle in the crowd.

"Next, with objective in just seven sales days as well, Karen Kennedy! Nice work, Karen!" Vincent shouted. Another thunderous applause ensued. "And finally, our slim pickings of decision makers has not equated to slim results for Mick Sasser. Solid performance, Mick!"

The crowd cheered again and Vincent pointed to Mick, who smiled and nodded.

"Okay, I could sit up here for the next ten-to-twenty minutes and talk about the rest of these results. But I have a feeling you have already been beaten up about them in your crew meetings and you can read. So…" Vincent trailed off. With that, he flicked his wrist and the stack of papers went flying to the ground in several different places.

"Let's face it, folks, we are not where we need to be at this point in the month. We have called some zero advertisers, some one-tier and two-tier advertisers," Vincent continued. "But I'm not going to talk about results. You know why? Because today is the first day of the rest of our month. What's past is past. It does not matter. And if I dwell on it, if your manager dwells on it or God forbid you dwell on it, what does that accomplish for any of us? Nothing."

Usually boisterous Lloyd Meridian quickly spoke up, "That's right! Boom!" Several others began to chatter.

"Team, I'm not going to pull punches. Our efficiency for the first week and a half has left a lot to be desired. It's sad to say that we have yet to start our month or our year. But, you know what? Today's the day. And today's the day because, quite frankly, I said so," Vincent said, again having his speech met with some applause and laughter.

"I know when you are strapped to a desk every day and you come in and leave with nothing to show for it…well, let's face it: it sucks. Right?" Vincent asked, holding his hand in the air and playing to the crowd. It was met with the expected affirmation.

"Right. It's tough to bring yourself back every day to take another beating.   It's tough to bring yourself back every day and be mired in self-doubt. Now, I don't know much about self-doubt," Vincent chuckled, pausing for the laughter that followed, "but I do know something about the grind that you guys go through every day. And I love you for it."

"We love you too, baby!" Lloyd shouted. Others signified their agreement and started clapping and clamoring.

"But here's the deal. Today, I have 6,000 brand new ECL leads," Vincent announced and then stopped, again putting his hand in the air to play to the crowd and the applause was the loudest of the young day. "Yeah, that's right, guys, because while you were giving it what I hope was your best on these leather-tough leads, customers were still coming to our site to sign up for listings. And today, we are going to call them."

The team started clapping and screaming again. He had them right where he wanted.

"Okay, team – I am not going to waste another second of your precious time because these scalding hot leads are waiting and are going to be in the dialer the second you log in," Vincent said to the eager salesforce. "All I'm going to do is leave you with a quick message that I had to use to remind myself of my mission every single day when I was a sales rep in your shoes. Don't ever forget it, team. You can always be a champion if you *don't stop believin'.*"

With that, Vincent pointed to Jimmy, waved to the crowd who immediately started cheering excitedly and with a press of a button, Jimmy filled the room with the booming sounds of epic anthem "Don't Stop Believin'" by Journey. It was yet another classic Vincent Scott stand-up. And the 312%-to-daily-objective sales day put them well back on the path towards January objective. How sweet it was.

Ten-and-a-half months later, as December 2009 began, Vincent sat on his couch in his pajamas, suspended from work, Elizabeth in her bed and a vodka and soda at his side. He started to question if he was cut out for Corporate America; he could never conform to the standards, could never just sit back and watch bad decisions being made that crippled the salesforce and he could not sit down and shut up when his reps were not being paid properly, were suffering for mismanaged clerical work and were having their morale beaten down by Keith Dickhauser, Scott Kinsey and Danny Boyd every time he and his managers lifted it to the top of the mountain.

Keith never did anything to provide positive public relations for Vincent. Letting out that Vincent was the primary bright spot holding it together would have detracted from his Boys Club and reflected poorly on Mark Rogers. Requests Vincent made to differentiate his results from Mark's on reports to upper management were denied. Disparities in results from location to location were explained away with excuses that had no basis in reality.

Vincent again won Top Gun for 2008 and was the picture of discipline on the trip to Vegas in March 2009. However, rumors apparently reached Gil Walker that he had been loud and obnoxious poolside at a time he was not even there or that he had been drunk and belligerent at a bar he was not even at. It was unbelievable.

The senior leadership of ABM had no idea how good Vincent was; they never got that picture of him and certainly were not allowed to see his impact on results. Gil had supposedly been invited to the department's monthly division meetings where Vincent reigned king and was among the most energetic emcees in the company yet he never attended one. Vincent's dog-and-pony-show quarterly meeting showoff sessions became great but during 2009 Keith was shuffled to three different bosses so it became moot. The rare chance Vincent had to showcase this was when César Fiorentino, who really took a liking to Vincent and requested his services in an Jacksonville office he had to decline, got to see the January 2009 event honoring performances from the year prior.

Vincent was one of the last people to the stage, coming on after Keith and Mark. Disgusted with the boring start, Vincent requested music and got the audience going, got César chuckling and got a standing ovation upon entrance. Vincent was energetic, enthusiastic, called many of the reps and managers by nicknames and told stories about half his managers. He put on a show.

The unsettling revelation was that, for the third year in a row, Keith snubbed Vincent for the departmental MVP award. Year one, it was given to Scott Kinsey who had been there half the year. Year two it was Eric Aames, who actually deserved it. This year, to everyone's surprise it was given to Danny Boyd. Unbelievable.

Once every 2-to-6 months, Keith, behind closed doors and typically peppered in after reaming or cursing him out for something, would tell Vincent he was the smartest person he had met in 27 years in the business or he would one day run the company or was the biggest reason for the department's success. However, this sentiment never made it to the public ears or eyes, which was really all Vincent wanted. Any time Keith had the chance to publicly thank or laud Vincent he would rave about someone else that paled in comparison.

With full realization of how thankless this was for him, how the powers that be had no idea he was running the department and was a hero, the custody battle with Abby waging on and his "relationship" with Phoebe circling the drain, Vincent was headed downward. When Vincent was announced as a Top Gun, he lobbied to take someone else's intended guest so Phoebe could go with them. Seemingly excited at first, when time came to submit the names she backed out, saying only that her hierarchy did not approve. She could sure put up a hellfire of an attack standing up for herself anytime the person on the receiving end was Nathan or Michelle's father or Vincent. She sure could talk a big game when Vincent was under heat for their relationship but she could not stand up for herself or their relationship to her own superiors at the first sign of adversity.

Interesting also that Michelle wanted her to stay single for so long just months ago and now she was already hot and heavy with some stooge of a sales rep. Apparently her hierarchy approved of her dating down to people she hired and could be called upon to release.

Vincent contacted the coordinator of Top Gun withdrawing his name from attending but Keith blasted him and told him he was going whether he liked it or not.

Vincent's February project was monitoring 5-10 calls on a team with their manager in the morning and welcoming them back from lunch with a furious but sensational team meeting. By the end, he would uplift them as only he could and walk out, leaving them to their manager and peers to decide they were going to take it seriously and get back to where they needed to be. After one week of this, Vincent gained another 12% on Mark's downtown teams before concluding February at his usual 25% margin of victory. These were the types of constant reinventions required to keep Vincent coming back month after month at such a high level.

Sadly, after one of the sessions, a member of the team came to him with manager Frankie Rivera in tow. It was Ryan Kish – his success story.

Frankie knocked gently on the frame to Vincent's door. He looked up and saw the two standing just outside.

"Come on in, guys," Vincent said, welcoming them. He sat back from what he was doing and the two took seats. "What can I do for you?"

"Ryan wanted to talk to you," Frankie responded.

"Sure," Vincent said, turning to the concerned and seemingly defeated rep.

Ryan had come out of the gates slowly when he came on board nearly a year ago but picked up momentum and earned a berth into the inbound group due to above average results. He had a solid start there and was one of Mark's and Danny's favorites for his effort and exemplary paperwork. Unfortunately, after two tours in the group he had not been in the top 60% of the standings and was returned to outbound. His confidence shot, he tapered off and had a hard time getting his bearings. He had reached out to Vincent for help a couple of times and Vincent listened to his calls and liked what he heard. He was just having trouble consistently closing and overcoming his self-doubt.

"Vincent, I just can't do it anymore," Ryan said, tears in his eyes.

"Hey, it's OK, man," Vincent said, hesitating, not typically dealing well with situations such as this. "Tell me what happened."

"I have been doing everything you guys have been telling me to do. I just don't have it anymore," Ryan said. "I really, really wanted this."

"Ryan, there's no shame in it. This is just a different animal than anything else out there. Trust me. I told you that when I first met with you. But what you've got to understand is that this isn't for everybody. Honestly, the fact that it isn't for you probably is a good thing – it means you're above it," Vincent said.

Ryan looked at him and smiled slightly. "Vincent, I just wanted to thank you. Seriously. Your confidence in me meant a lot and I made more money this last year than I had in my entire life," he said sincerely.

"Ryan, don't mention it. You earned it. I feel bad that I brought you into something that didn't pan out for you," Vincent lamented.

"Don't feel bad at all. This was a good experience for me. I just can't do it anymore. I have talked about it with my wife and I just have to go," Ryan said.

"I understand 100%," Vincent said.

"I didn't want any hard feelings. That's why I wanted to talk to you and just say thank you. I couldn't leave without saying that to you," Ryan said.

"That means a lot," Vincent said. Any idea what you're going to do?" Vincent asked.

"I have had some offers to come back into the restaurant business as a manager," Ryan answered. "My experience here helped me parlay it into more money."

Vincent smiled. "Good for you, Ryan. And seriously, stay in touch. I wish you the best."

The three stood and Ryan and Vincent shook hands.

"Best of luck, Ryan. Don't be a stranger," Frankie said. Frankie looked at Vincent, who nodded, and Ryan and Frankie departed.

This fairytale story was not meant to be. Reality always set in and, in this case, it crippled what could have been the birth of a salesman.

February 2009 closed out with another bang and "You're a genius" call from Keith Dickhauser. Of course, Vincent had to remind him mid-day on the last day of every month to call to begin with, but he did not mind. It was nice to get a compliment from the man even if he had to ask for it.

Vincent and Abby had a few more dinners, spent time at their respective apartments as a family and talked on the phone and texted. They shopped together. They watched movies together. Abby would leave Vincent's apartment at night and reveal later her feelings were starting to warm up. Some nights when Vincent had Elizabeth, Abby would not contact him and he thought nothing of it. It was not until a mid-month conversation that he pried out of her she was having regular casual sex with a guy in her apartment complex named Chris. Not only that, Chris had met Elizabeth. Those two things dealt another blow to Vincent and he backed away from Abby yet again.

Keith continued his torrential downpour on Vincent for anything he could find; yelling one day because he supposedly prematurely socialized their 2009 objective to the managers (in a conversation where he did nothing but speculate on numbers Keith had given them) or another for alluding to a rep in the inbound team that if he had his way he would totally revamp the hapless group. Keith threatened to fire Vincent, probably for the tenth time in their years together.

The trip was the final week of March and, on the Friday before, Phoebe finally made some attempt to speak to him, dropping off an interview packet and asking if he had liked the prior candidate. Vincent got up, took the new packet and said simply, "Fortunately for both of us, if you read my notes you don't have to ask and you can just go on ignoring me," before walking off and leaving her in stunned silence.

Before the next interview she asked what that meant and he laid into her. She fired back. She had not closed the door to his office before their tirade so the entire front few rows and busybody Marla Mooney heard every word.

His attack included her sporadic affections, infrequent communications and the fact she promised him the earth, moon and stars and did not even give him a pebble. She countered with what was going on with Nathan, her Dad's health, her bosses, Michelle and the like. Vincent closed the door.

"Look, I understand you're going through a lot," Vincent said. "But the thing is, I have asked you for literally nothing. And I'm getting less than that."

"Vincent, I can't give you what you deserve right now," Phoebe said. "I'm just going through so much. And the kicker? Karl and Moira want to move me to Birmingham to hire classes for them."

"Birmingham?"

"I suspect it's because of us."

"I see."

"Vincent, I love you. But the timing is terrible."

"It always is," Vincent said.

"I just can't take on a relationship right now," Phoebe said.

"And when you can?"

"I promise it will be with you."

Vincent looked at her for a moment and forced a smile. They kissed for the first time in over a month.

After the following Monday, Vincent was in Vegas the rest of the week. Anytime he and Phoebe were back on better terms than not, he would saunter into her office in the mornings. On this one, she was clearly flustered and rebuffed a kiss attempt, telling him she just could not deal with it right now. Once his last interview of the day concluded at 4:30, he dropped off the interview packet himself and did not attempt to go near her. He stood in the doorway, ready to depart.

"Have a good rest of the week," he said.

Startled, she looked at her watch. "You're leaving now?" Phoebe asked, awkwardly.

"I am."

Unsure of how to react, she managed, "Have a good time. Be careful and stay out of trouble."

"I'll try," Vincent said and he split.

Abby called at 8:15 that night and told him she would miss him. As the world of Vincent Scott turned.

Vincent got up the following morning at 4 AM, left for the airport and was headed to Las Vegas, Nevada. The escape from Keith, Abby and Phoebe could not have come at a more opportune time.

Upon arrival in Sin City he met up with everyone for drinks. The assemblage included Jimmy, who had taken Phoebe's spot as Vincent's guest, Gina Baker and her husband, Haley Jones and her husband, Johnny Slade and his wife, and six of the reps and their significant others.

This trip was much more subdued but the rumor mill did not tell that story. Be that as it may, he used the time to forget about what was at home. He stole the show at an Elvis-themed karaoke dive bar, singing all the classics. He accompanied the gang as they went up and down the Strip through the Vegas nightlife, gambled, drank but not nearly as much as the year prior and he sent texts to Phoebe and Abby. Phoebe never responded. As for Abby, they talked a few times through texts and calls and he picked her and Elizabeth up some souvenirs. But it was clear she was more serious with this Chris character than she had originally let on.

He returned to Mankato with zero fanfare. No one was waiting for him at the airport, where he saw couples reuniting after journeys. No one was waiting at home. No one called to see how his trip was or if he got home safely.

He returned to work to the final sales day of March with enough time to lead them to, again, the best month in history.

Starting April, Abby revealed she and Chris were relatively significant; they were starting to talk about being a couple. Vincent decided to back off completely. Phoebe, on the other hand, asked Vincent about his trip and the custody battle, the first time she had asked about the court situation for months and Vincent gave her a chilly reception, saying not to worry about it.

And when he went to her office later to apologize, there sat Denny Price.

He had no idea who this peculiar looking guy was but he could tell it was not his first time in this office. He looked like he had no intention of leaving and pretty comfortable sitting casually in the chair Vincent had sat in so many times. Vincent saw the look on Phoebe's face as she stopped laughing at whatever they had been talking about and looked surprised to see him.

"Sorry to interrupt," Vincent said. "When you get a minute, let me know."

"Okay," Phoebe said as Vincent walked out the door.

Phoebe went on to explain that Denny was just helping her with a loan. What Vincent found interesting is that he started to see him walking in and out of her office multiple times a day; amusing considering Vincent was a busy guy and just happened to be in the hallway enough to notice. It must have been a pretty intense loan.

The custody battle ended the first week of April. Once Abby learned the ruling was not what she wanted she tried to get Vincent to make some kind of alternate deal but he did not budge; he got the 50/50 arrangement he wanted. Despite having to pay an absurd $700 per month in child support, meaning Abby would never spend a dime of her own money on Elizabeth, his attorney advised him this was likely the best he would get at the time. He took it.

Celebrating the ruling over a drink with Chad Willman, the conversation touched many topics. Chad had proposed to his girlfriend Jamie and was bending Vincent's ear about wanting to be promoted – a regular topic in their conversations. He also told Vincent that while he had been in Vegas, Chad had talked to Phoebe roaming the halls and she said she very much wanted to work things out and be with Vincent. The news came as a surprise as that was a stark contrast to her actions over the last several months.

Acting on the news from Chad, he sought her out the following week, proposed an out-of-town trip to get away from the drama and fall in love all over again. She said it probably was not a good idea and she denied saying those things to Chad. Why would he make them up? She said she would call him about spending time together during the upcoming weekend. She never did. While it was utterly confusing, it was not surprising.

Vincent mailed Phoebe a card for Mother's Day that was heartfelt and contained sentiment that their relationship and chemistry was past tense. She thanked him in a closed-door conversation in his office the following morning and kissed him for the last time. She was off two days midweek and hinted she would call so they could spend time together, go to lunch or dinner or anything. The call never came.

Vincent allowed too much before he walked away. Everyone has been there: that fine line between hanging in there and moving on. On the last day of May, Vincent was dealt what was beyond the death blow.

He had asked Phoebe to spend time with him many times lately but it was always a different excuse. They closed the month down on a Friday and he, once again, cleared his 125% target barely after a rollercoaster month.

Celebrating afterwards at Cullen's, the bar across the street from the office, Vincent was sitting at the table with Jack Franklin, a longtime friend whom he had met years before through Eddie while they were all in college. He was visiting Eddie at college in Rochester and Jack was in the same fraternity. When Eddie called it a night, Vincent and Jack had taken the town by storm and had been friends ever since. When Jack had been on the job hunt in recent months, Vincent brought him on board, but only after giving him a full briefing on how undesirable the job was.

Not fifteen minutes after Vincent and Jack had walked into the bar and started their beers, Denny Price entered and he was accompanied by none other than Phoebe Wells.

Vincent froze in disbelief. Denny looked away, intentionally not making eye contact with Vincent and he went to join co-workers. Phoebe slowed and went to Vincent's table.

"Hi," Phoebe said.

"Hi," Vincent responded, looking away and taking a drink.

"So how was your day?" she inquired.

"You don't have to make small talk with me" Vincent said coldly.

"Did I do or say something wrong?"

"It's nice to know who you make time for."

With that, Vincent turned to Jack, and merely said, "Sorry, I'm not thirsty anymore."

He turned and walked out; some arriving folks like Johnny Slade and Frankie Rivera tried to stop him but he made a beeline for his car and screeched out of the lot. How dare she show up with this clown after what she had put him through over the last couple of years?

His phone rang incessantly over the hours to come: Johnny, Jimmy Sander, Frankie, Jack. Of course, everyone but Phoebe.

Vincent found solace that night in a fifth of vodka. Phoebe was obviously playing games and clearly not going to issue a decree of their breakup but was doing nothing to foster a healthy relationship. He had to quit her cold turkey. And he made that his resolve.

One of the sales reps, Jackson Taber, had a VIP membership and room every weekend at the Mystic Lake Casino and had often spent weekends there drinking with his manager Cal Riley and other reps. Vincent awoke that Saturday morning after drinking away the sight of Phoebe with another man and decided to throw himself headfirst into the decadence. He called Jackson and made his way to the casino where they had a comped dinner of steak and lobster and a night on the town followed by a leisurely Sunday poolside sipping margaritas.

For months, this is where Vincent spent the weekends he did not have Elizabeth. There was drinking, swimming, gambling, drinking, girls and more girls; first Keri, then Lisa, then Gina and then Violet. Jackson's roommate Kevin Kessler made regular appearances, Cal showed a couple of times and they also hung out with an older guy who practically lived there named Timmy. It was an excuse to go out, blow money, drink and eat like kings and meet women galore. They would end up at the downstairs breakfast joint or playing quarters in their smoke-filled room at 4 AM, followed by a day of easy living Sunday poolside. This was the life: a vacation without leaving town. It was also the only therapy that could ease the pain of Vincent's wounded psyche.

All the booze, good food and girls in the world could not wipe away his memory of Phoebe, but he sure as hell tried.

She slipped a Father's Day card to Vincent in mid-June and tried to talk to him a smattering of times during the month but he ignored her. Jimmy revealed to him that Phoebe asked how Vincent was resisting talking to her and said it upset her a great deal, but he was not going to bite this time. June was difficult seeing more of Denny going in and out of Phoebe's office and the sales results were not coming as naturally as they had before. The reason was because Dickhauser decided to crack down on claims that were coming in from customer service and took a "guilty until proven innocent" stance on anything a customer claimed was unauthorized. Keith played judge and jury and suspended or terminated everyone he could. Many fell victim to his wrath— a couple of them deserving it and 90% of them not – but no matter; Keith made it clear in times like this that no matter how much he tried to say to Vincent and Mark that their input mattered, he called the shots.

Morale took a heavy hit so Vincent was relieved to hit 120% of his expectation; it was his most difficult month of the year but he would live with it. It also prompted his first hiatus of the year: a weeklong vacation to kick off July.

Vincent gone, Keith took it upon himself to investigate the Internet usage of Vincent's friend and neighbor Chad Willman; Chad had been a thorn in Keith's paw filing grievances over clerical and commission gaffes, questioning procedures and, like anyone that stood in Keith's way, he had a target on his back for quite some time. Keith happened to be walking through the center one day and saw Chad on a sports site (probably one of 150 reps currently surfing the Internet) and had company security run a full scan of his Internet usage.

Keith not only removed Vincent from the process by waiting until he was on vacation, he brought Mark in from downtown to preside and even lied to the Labor department saying there was past history of warnings with Chad regarding Internet usage. Chad never stood a chance. However, Keith waited long enough to carry out the termination so he could read the document himself – the first time he had ever taken part in any type of discipline – and, in a shockingly overt vindictive move to make the act of retaliation complete, he had Vincent walk his own friend out the door.

This was when Keith went outrageously too far, breaking the law and lying to get someone fired. Labor had even recommended suspension, yet left the decision of Chad's fate in Dickhauser's hands. Needless to say, he eliminated Chad dispassionately.

Vincent was no-nonsense upon his return. They had missed their 125% goal in June and he was on a mission. He also made the decision he had finally had enough of Phoebe. They traded some e-mails at the beginning of the month regarding her issues with his complete apathy towards her, the fact he was returning interview packets to Marla instead of to her, and his disgust with her lies, immaturity and lack of loyalty.

On July 9, Vincent fired off one calling out her extreme inconsistencies, blasting her selfish behavior and telling her not to speak to him again under any circumstances. In the next several months to come, she did try a few times but he never acknowledged or spoke to her. She responded to his final e-mail but, for the first time in his life, he neither wanted nor cared to pursue the final word. It was irrelevant. He had heard it all before and it was a load of crap.

Vincent re-focused on work and July became yet again the biggest month in department history.

The sales were great but tensions got high between Vincent and Keith again as they battled over Keith's desire to deviate from the company's credit policy for their department. Not only did this seem to violate company policy but the way Keith force fed it down the throats of the reps and management was not helping matters. The fact Keith had created documentation to execute Chad Willman did not sit all that well with Vincent either.

In mid-July, Vincent timed a day off to spend with Elizabeth and fielded a call from Jimmy, who was on his way home.

"Hey buddy," Vincent answered.

"Hey. Dude, I don't really know how to tell you this so I'm just going to say it," Jimmy prefaced. He was often a pretty emotional guy but this did sound ominous.

"What's the deal?" Vincent asked.

"There are calls going around about you from HR."

"What about?"

"You remember that meeting where you said something about your conversion rates report and that if people were ignoring it they were damn fools?"

"Absolutely."

"Yeah, that's what it's about. I didn't get a call about it yet but Slade did today."

"Who was the call from?"

"Agnes Landry."

"Jesus Christ. This is ridiculous."

"Trust me, man, we've all got your back."

"I hear you, but obviously somebody threw me under the bus."

"I hate to ruin your day off but I knew you would want to know," Jimmy stated.

"Absolutely. Thanks buddy. See you tomorrow."

Investigations of this sort were supposed to be anonymous but in the three days to come, over half the managers came to Vincent and told him the details of the calls they were getting. By the end of July, Vincent was summoned to Keith's office for a conference call with Agnes and Lydia Rawlings for the reading of his purported crimes.

The bright spot was that of the 20 people in the room when Vincent gave that speech, only 6 admitted even hearing Vincent curse and 4 stated they could see where, at times, Vincent could be overbearing in his tenacity. Everyone conceded that Vincent was an amazing leader who had their backs and was very passionate about his job.

Lydia's condescending statements of Vincent needing to work on being a more effective leader, offering to send him some online courses he could take and her self-righteousness over Vincent's use of the word "damn" in a meeting made him want to vomit. These people had no idea how to run a sales organization. If it was not for people like Vincent that actually earned revenue for a company that was bleeding it, people like her would not even have a job. A well-timed curse word in a meeting can be a good attention-grabber.

It was through Brotherhood tipoff he learned this was the doing of Scott Kinsey, but just because he wanted to take Vincent down for whatever purpose in his agenda, Vincent had to listen to this tripe?

The most gruesome moment came towards the end when Lydia asked Keith where they would go from there.

"Well, Lydia, obviously we take this very seriously. I have to have tough conversations with these managers on a regular basis but I always do it behind closed doors in a one-on-one setting. I will commit to coaching Vincent to do the same," Dickhauser lied.

Vincent glared at the man. Keith had told Vincent on countless occasions that he always had his back, supported him and claimed he sang his praises when he was talking about the department. Now, in front of him and when he could have given him the first tangible sign in their history working together of support, he lied and in no way had Vincent's back. Vincent was flabbergasted. Keith was notorious for screaming and threatening managers in open forums!

Lydia then asked, "Vincent, do you have anything else you would like to add?"

Keith tried to cut him off by signaling with his hand across his neck but that did not deter Vincent.

"I absolutely do," he announced, a firm resolve evident in his voice. "It is clear that a few people here are attempting to make me out to be the scapegoat for the perception there is a hostile work environment here. I can tell you this: the managers love me and that is why when you did your investigation they all jumped to defend me. We are a team here. Someone decided to take an anonymous potshot at me yet again and they have failed yet again."

"Vincent, let me make clear," Agnes chimed in. "The managers are very supportive of you. They know you work hard for them and are very passionate about your job. We want you to be successful and be as effective a leader as possible. We are not going to put any reflection of this investigation in your personnel binder."

"Fair enough," Vincent said, satisfied with that result. "That is what I wanted to hear. Thank you, ladies."

After the call concluded, Dickhauser tried to make some kind of comment that it was a relief this was over; Vincent merely nodded and walked out. Lesson learned: Keith Dickhauser was no friend of his.

The redeeming quality of this latest ordeal was that both Lydia and Agnes made mention of some complaints from managers about Keith's antics they had made in this call-around process. It was nice to have that on the record. But the question for Vincent was how much more could he take of this?

To complicate things, Vincent found out the first week of August that Abby was about to be laid off from her job as a clerk but he was under gag order. He knew she would come begging for his help upon receipt of the news and it furthered the fact he should stay away from her dependency.

While it stung that he could not forge any bond with Abby he came to a realization: it was his own ego that made him obsessed with wondering why these women could be with losers like Denny or Chris. That ego was what kept him throwing his hat in their rings over and over. In the end, these girls were with these clowns because they felt superior to them and inferior to him. They wanted to be headliners of their relationships, as opposed to being with Vincent who, coupled with them was certainly the lone star.

August was a ho-hum month; he posted his 125% sales goal and, finally, Mark Rogers' inbound team hit expectation for the first time all year. September brought a different challenge to Vincent, an ultimate gamble but the only thing left to tackle.

The pot was boiling with jaded salespeople who had finally had enough of not getting paid properly, sales charging back to them through no fault of their own and Scott Kinsey copping an attitude when they rightfully inquired about their mismanaged commission.

Vincent had made these claims to Keith before, however it was always met with, "I deal in facts, not hearsay. Get me examples." That generic response was designed to deflect something he never intended to get involved with anyway. Rather than take the chatter to Keith, he decided this time he was going to take matters into his own hands. If Keith wanted examples, he was going to bombard him with them.

Vincent crafted an office-wide memo that acknowledged these problems had gone on long enough.

The memo read as follows:

Team:

It has come to my attention that in recent days and weeks, the perception of rampant commission and paperwork issues has grown.

I want to first assure you that I take these concerns very seriously. The company pays me to support you; without you, there is no need for my presence. In addition, I have a great deal of respect, as should you, for our hard-working clerical team. They have limited resources and are doing the best they can under the current circumstances to support us.

Going forward, I wish to be included on all e-mails regarding commission and process questions, concerns and complaints. I am open to any and all suggestions as we look to improve the processes to best meet your needs. We are a team and in order to function as one it is going to take all of us on the same page.

I will not stop or rest until this situation is no longer perceived as a problem. I have not gotten involved in this in the past but it is clear I have no other alternative in my constant quest of deciding how to serve you best.

My only simple request is that you investigate a situation yourself before deeming it a problem. We do not need the rumor mill festering this into a bigger problem than it actually is.

Thank you in advance for your attention to this matter.

Vincent T. Scott

Vincent's intention was, as usual, to eliminate any and all excuses, barriers or obstacles for his division. Of course, he was also deliberately slapping Kinsey and Danny Boyd in the face for their inability or unwillingness to fix the problems that had plagued the department for four years.

He also intentionally left Keith, Scott and Danny off his office memo. Several managers dropped by to comment that he certainly had brass and they warned him Keith would be pissed. To be sure, within the half hour he was summoned via Marla Mooney phone call to Keith's office. As Vincent emerged from his office, cheers erupted across the sales floor. Shouts of, "You the man!" were heard. Vincent waved and acknowledged them. His e-mail inbox was flooded with letters thanking him graciously for taking on this mission, detailing issues that had been going on with them for months. They recounted losing sales because a clerk lost a payment form and they looked like buffoons when they were forced to call the customer and try to get payment again. Many contracts were inexplicably never worked. There was a litany of horror stories a mile long.

Shutting the door to Kinsey's office where Keith and Scott sat waiting for him, he took his seat and prepared for the abuse.

"What the fuck did you just do?" Keith erupted.

"About what?" Vincent said, nonchalantly.

"I just received a copy of an e-mail you sent to the floor about commission issues. First off, why did you send this and not include us on it?" Keith interrogated.

"I don't include you guys on every e-mail I send to my subordinates. I knew you would want examples of issues they are facing so I am going to get them before presenting the problem," Vincent responded coolly. He had Keith's number.

"It isn't your place to do this. This is Scott and Danny's job," came the retort. Vincent wished he could respond by asking why they were not doing it.

290

"And we're all busy guys. I know Scott works his 70 hours a week and we are all thankful to have him," Vincent said, spinning his sales magic with the obvious undercurrent of sarcasm. "But let's face facts: this is still a huge problem, we're all on the same team, and this is me willing to help and investigate so I can alleviate some of the strain from their backs."

It was incredible how quickly Vincent manipulated Keith on the topic; his tone suddenly shifted and his voice dropped an octave.

"Well, uh—," Keith stammered. "Well, bottom line, I want to be included on all correspondence to the floor."

"No problem, I will make sure you are going forward. Anything else?"

"Vincent," Scott began, trying to control his anger towards what he viewed as a pompous, arrogant kid sitting in front of him. "In any given day, the reps will throw 20-to-30 different examples of what they perceive to be clerical or commission issues at me. The majority of those, after I investigate them, turn out to be self-inflicted. Maybe they waited to turn in the contract; maybe there was an outstanding item to be handled on the account, whatever. But I would say eight out of 10 times everything is done correctly from a clerical standpoint."

Keith started nodding, sold once again by Kinsey's methodology.

"With all due respect, how can we be okay with that? I'm sorry, but this is a big company and we are satisfied with 20% of our processes resulting in my reps suffering? If a rep screws up, absolutely they should and do suffer for it. But if a clerk doesn't do their job or loses a contract or never keys a contract, why do my reps continue to suffer for that? There is no accountability. I just want a process in place that holds people accountable. It's that simple. If I wasn't doing my job properly, I would want and need to know it. But what process is in place to deal with clerks who are not doing their job?" Vincent fired back, ready to go on the offensive.

"Well, if I notice a trend with issues stemming from a certain clerk, I will address it," Scott said vaguely.

"Exactly, but a process in place that tracks it, like the claims and errors process for reps and managers, would make it easy for us to identify strengths and weaknesses in our clerical force," Vincent said, making clear he came to play. "That's all I'm asking for. I am tired of my reps suffering and losing their hard-earned sales and commissions because someone else dropped the ball. We wouldn't like it if we weren't getting paid properly and it's my job to make sure my people are. And when these guys see literally no hope for themselves, it's my responsibility to act. It's my job to give them hope."

Enter Dickhauser's diplomatic conclusion where he would try to divert attention from the issue: "Well, uh, sure, Vincent, and we understand. But it all comes back to the reps turning in their contracts on time. They have a 24-hour window to do it. Then it comes down to the managers managing their missing contracts report. This is a management problem. These reps aren't getting deposits to protect their commissions, either. We're all responsible for that."

"Keith, 80% of the contracts on the missing contracts report are already in. We have had this conversation." He quickly realized this conversation was going nowhere. "Look, my intention was to get the issues sent to me so I could deem them worthy or not before Scott or Danny have to spend their valuable time looking into them. The reps work for me and I just want to show them that I take this issue seriously. That's all."

"Oh, well, okay," Keith mumbled. "That makes sense. Just try to keep us in the loop better going forward."

"Sure thing," Vincent said, excusing himself and shutting the door behind him, sure that Keith and Scott were cursing him behind his back.

Vincent had done exactly what he set out to do: he aggressively forced this issue onto the radar, stood his ground when called on it, and the people got to see firsthand that he has their backs and will take literal beatings for them. It accomplished what it was meant to accomplish. In the days to come, the sides quickly aligned. It was the reps and managers versus clerical, Scott and Danny. This was never necessarily Vincent's intent but it had to be done; the issues were too prevalent and they were ripping the department apart at the seams.

And finally, a day Vincent Scott had waited for and had wondered why it had taken so long arrived: the managers started plotting to overthrow Keith Dickhauser.

Perhaps the seed was planted when HR calls were going around about Vincent; the managers realized that one anonymous call would be all it took to start the same thing on Keith. It started as the brainchild of always-plotting Clyde Barton after everything he had endured from Keith and the aforementioned attempt to suspend him.

Additional motivation for Clyde was Keith's constant attacks on his missing contracts report. Clyde's team, while their average sale was lower than most, had 20-to-30 more sales per month than any other team. This would obviously result in more claims, more contracts being out at any given moment and higher dollar totals of chargebacks. While Clyde maintained this stance with Keith and Vincent agreed, Keith dismissed it as irrelevant and vocally questioned Clyde's competency as a manager. Clyde did not take kindly to this constant harassment and after seeing Vincent raked through the coals unfairly, he began to socialize the burgeoning idea with his growing inner circle.

It started as talk and big dreams. Clyde would paint the picture of a world without Keith and slowly sold other members of the team that it was feasible. He had in-confidence talks about it with the people he felt could be trusted with the intel: Gina, George, and even typically reserved Randall and

292

Helen. They all had their own bone to pick from their various negative encounters and run-ins with the tyrant.

Vincent knew that his own name had to be off of this revolution but at the same time he was vital to the cause. As time went by, Clyde had conversations of some sort or another with everyone except ultra-corporate Dean Yamnitz, Cathy Schumer because she was new enough she had not seen as much heinous activity as everyone else, Steve Zimmerman because he was an outsider and had been politically placed by Dickhauser to being with, Adam Sandberg because of his close ties as Mark Rogers' best friend, and the obvious omissions of senior staff like Betty Cross, Kinsey, Danny Boyd and Mark. Everyone else was part of the brigade.

The conclusion of September was especially upsetting to Vincent as they had their worst month of the year at 110% of the budgeted target. He was glad there was cushion in the numbers but this was a loss and was a direct result of Keith's and Scott's inept operations management.

Livid, Vincent started feeding all of the examples and details of clerical and commission complaints directly to Chief Union Steward Terry Fontana. As neither Keith nor Scott had done anything to address the nearly fifty complaints he had provided within the first couple weeks of his experiment, he had no choice but to feed the wolf that could hopefully do something about it.

Vincent took his team out of the gates stronger than ever in October, scheduling four crew monitoring sessions per day that first week. The most he had ever done was two so this was daunting, but he did not care. It had to be done. He cracked down in open forum on reps playing phone games like plugging in fake numbers to elicit a busy signal or dead line. He stressed to them that the managers and he were giving them everything they had but not seeing reciprocation. He also let them know his anguish over the fact they were doing everything they could to fix the fractured processes and had delivered better sales coaching and training than anywhere else but people still refused to do the job properly.

With more monitoring than ever before, Vincent was worn more thinly than ever before. The most difficult experience for a sales manager is listening to calls of those who refuse to follow protocol; those who have been instructed to do something a certain way time and time again but refuse to listen to the guidance. Vincent was, at this point after years of this agony, growing to despise the work.

This was further complicated by Dickhauser's ridiculous antics throughout the month, taking on a new direct mail project that had no business in their department, scheduling refresher training for three products when the training was unnecessary and actually having the team participate in a corporate project that did not even generate revenue. Vincent did everything he could to sell the managers on the importance of these things but even they could see he had to strain to cover up Dickhauser's incompetence. Even they could see that the place they had worked so hard to build was making an inevitable and tragic descent.

Vincent would deliver stand-up's for the team nearly daily, somehow continuing to sell the reps and managers on a thankless occupation. Dickhauser would schedule training sessions on a whim because he happened to run into someone in the hall who said they were struggling on selling a particular product. The next day he would lay out plans to pull the entire salesforce off the phones to retrain the product because one rep stated they struggled. It was getting to be too much.

If Vincent tried to speak to Keith about it, he would be labeled as defiant. Ironic that when 2009 started, Keith had dubbed Mark, Vincent and himself the three business owners that would make decisions together to grow their unit but more and more often it was simply becoming Keith's way. And Keith's way was leading to departmental turmoil. The more Vincent, and now, oddly enough, Mark, would disagree with Keith the more belligerent and unbearable he would become.

That said, Vincent finally made a firm decision from which there would be no turning back: he was going to do whatever he could to aid in the removal of Keith Dickhauser. It was for the good of the people and was the only resolution that could save them all from certain doom. Whether at breakfast, lunch, Vincent's office in closed-door sessions or in the bars after work, the Brotherhood heated up and became fast and furious in laying out plans to complete its dire mission.

Keith had forced the third and fourth quartile reps to undergo specific product refresher training during the first two weeks of the month. As brutal as the first half of the month was for Vincent and the managers, they were trending 20% better than September and Vincent convinced them they were going to march to clear victory. That was until Keith announced mid-month he was going to have the second quartile reps do the refresher (because *one person* out of the training had gotten two sales, so Keith's deduction was that immobilizing the department for a single victory would be a huge success) during week three when Vincent unveiled the ECL leads. Not only that, but he was going to have the managers with the lowest product results attend the training as well, regardless of their knowledge of the product.

Needless to say, reps and managers alike were infuriated. Keith and Scott made a habit of sending out these announcements around 4:29 PM and then disappearing, so Vincent called and had to leave a message on Keith's voice mail when he did not pick up the phone. He pleaded with Keith not to wipe out their momentum. Keith's return voice mail, which Vincent saved and played for all managers in the Brotherhood to hear, announced very clearly, "Vincent, this training is not an option. I don't give a fuck if the managers think they need it or not. Fuck them. They don't know what the fuck they are doing anyway. I don't care what leads we're calling. Have a schedule ready to roll out tomorrow."

If there was any lingering doubt on the minds of managers riding the fence as to whether or not Keith Dickhauser needed to go, that voice mail eliminated the doubt.

October ended with a much improved month: 124% of expectation but Vincent fell short of his stretch goal thanks to the obstacles from Keith.

Abby had been informed in September of her clerical job being eliminated in November based on layoffs throughout ABM and learned with a week to spare in October that they were unable to place her in another job in the company. She would be out of work in mid-November. Of course, in Abby fashion, she did nothing to find a job outside the company and called Vincent asking for help.

He blasted her disappearing act over the prior couple of months, correctly presumed she had let unemployed Chris move into her apartment and live off his child support payments and chastised the fact she only called him when she wanted something. Abby tried to pin the distance between them on Vincent's commitment issues that surfaced when last they spent time together and stated she would have been with Vincent instead of Chris had he seemed more interested. Not buying it, but also not wanting to pay even more child support that Abby would squander, he agreed to help.

Vincent scoured the countryside for potential positions to no avail. Keith, however, came to him and offered to interview her for an online rep in their department; quite unorthodox considering the nature of Vincent's relationship with Abby. Nonetheless, he interviewed her himself, taking it out of Vincent's hands, and offered her a job to return to the position she came into ABM to perform. What an interesting twist of fate.

In the wake of every month, regardless of the day of the week, Vincent would reflect on the month past. With the scoreboard set back to zero the following day it is a feeling of relief at the accomplishment. However, the relief is fleeting before the team is thrust headfirst into the inferno of a new month where they do it all over again.

Vincent knew he would have blown out his number had it not been for Keith's ignorance as to how to run a business. In addition, as soon as November began, Keith was whining that he did not think his department would achieve their annual budget. Vincent's teams were 123% for the year. Mark Rogers' downtown inbound team was 89% and because their objectives were much higher since customers were calling in asking for advertising, they single-handedly dragged down the entire department. Why Keith would not wake up and allow Vincent his wish of managing them as well was beyond him. The request was always met with, "Well, what would Mark and I do?" Vincent's answer, "Count your money."

The decision had been made in early 2009 to count their all-in money in calculating the bonuses for Keith, Mark and Vincent. As it stood, the inbound team Vincent was not allowed to help with was on target to cost him $10,000 in bonus money. Just like when Keith refused to pay any attention to the clerical and commission problems, Vincent decided to take matters into his own hands.

Vincent kicked off November with several changes to kickstart the department. He informed the salespeople he would no longer authorize a couple of the low-end product offerings, meaning the cheapest packages were eliminated. In addition, because oustanding contract items and commissions had gotten so much attention, Vincent granted built-in closed time for the reps into their schedule so they could look into issues and not be dinged for efficiency numbers. Finally, he had Eric Aames put together a report for him that combined the results of inbound and outbound reps, comparing them to one another and making it glaringly obvious that the inbound team was failing miserably in cutting the mustard.

Vincent lobbied Mark and Keith to allow him to go downtown once a week and to try to help out since "clearly you guys are busy and maybe I can lend a helping hand." His tactics of selling others on his agenda knew no bounds. And he finally won the argument, after two years of fighting.

He made haste to get downtown to observe on inbound, meet with managers and reps there and try to figure out very quickly (just as he had with Haley's formerly customer-service-only team) how to get them on track. It was really pretty simple: there was no accountability and no one pushing them to meet the expectations. The attitude was defeatist in that no one viewed the goals as attainable because no one was striving to reach them.

Within the first couple of visits to the downtown team, Vincent had already put through an order with Marla for recording devices for every rep station, had re-trained the managers on the call grading process they were not using and pulled several reps in the office he was borrowing and showed managers how to have a coaching session – tragically, as they reported, the first time they had gotten this type of coaching effectively. Also nice was that when Vincent was downtown, they had their best days of the month; unfortunately, his Greenfield office posted lackluster days in his absence.

The Brotherhood continued full-force. With Keith and Mark downtown one day meeting with Gil Walker concerning the struggling inbound group, both Jimmy and Clyde made anonymous calls to the ethics hotline from Vincent's office. They detailed to great degree the harassment and hostile work environment that Keith Dickhauser created and fostered.

296

As November trudged forward, Keith was even more overbearing, threatening to write up managers if their teams did not have 40 uses of the unnecessary Digital Pitchbook slideshow per week and he continued his belief in the fraudulent missing contracts reports. He would not let up. Fortunately, however, for the cause of the Brotherhood, this made it very easy to drum up support to oust him once and for all.

Finally, mid-November, the calls investigating Dickhauser began and they happened quickly and in bulk. Jimmy got his, then Cal, then the training managers. Finally, something was going to be done.

Pretty quickly after the initial call rang through, Keith called Vincent into his office and revealed both Scott and Mark had informed him about their calls. Vincent played it off and acted aloof but found it amusing that Dickhauser was sweating this immensely.

Finally, mid-month, Vincent got his call from Agnes Landry. It was one of the most empowering and gratifying hours he had ever spent in his life.

Of course, Vincent prefaced it with genuine concern for his well being. When Agnes assured him with the obligatory statements about how he could not be retaliated against and that his statements would be anonymous, he sprung forth like a fountain.

Vincent expressed he understood why this was happening, as people were at their boiling points. He answered everything truthfully and buried Keith Dickhauser. He coughed up e-mails, voice mails, and bore witness to Keith's creation of documentation to take out people he had targeted in the past, his vengeful and retaliatory ways and the hostile work environment he had turned their department into. It was a serious load off, like a church confession.

The call ended with Agnes asking what should be the outcome of the investigation.

"Agnes," Vincent stated, "this is a critical time for our team. Truth be told, if this department is going to stay open, which I believe it should because we add a great value to the company, Keith must be removed from power. I am not going to tell you to fire him; maybe he could bring value to the company in some other job, I don't know. But if he is going to stay in power here, this department is headed for certain doom. Once he is gone, there is really only one person that can take his place, but I am sure you will learn or have learned that from your conversation with the managers."

The Brotherhood lunched that day on the patio at the Asian restaurant down the street that oversaw the highway; eating, talking, laughing and wishing that drinks were flowing. It would have been the icing on the cake. Keith Dickhauser was going down.

Vincent had to make the decision to keep lying to Keith that he had not received the call. Only when the investigation was winding down would he cop to it; right now there was too much at stake.

Abby began training in Vincent's office again for the sales rep position. She dropped by his office and invited him to buy her lunch a few times and the spending time together at work parlayed into spending time together after hours as well. She claimed she had kicked Chris out of her apartment and they were history. Others in the office, including Keith, got the impression the two were potentially rekindling. Keith had the opposite reaction from when Vincent was involved with Phoebe; he actually seemed glad at the prospect of Vincent and Abby together despite working together.

November continued and good sales days were plentiful. The month was a shortened one with just 19 sales days but they looked good, ahead of pace on the tough leads and they moved into the good leads and got the needed results.

It was believed through rumors, helped by Helen Johnson who was best friends with Agnes that Keith would be removed at the beginning of December and moved to a staff job where he could not hurt anyone anymore. The end of the oppression was nearing.

*　　*　　*

Suspension. He spent the time with Elizabeth, who had just started doing an adorable new thing where she would say, "Do you know what?" and when he asked, "What?" she would answer, "I love you so much." Without her, he would not have made it this far.

Vincent also wrote, starting to hammer out a book that would teach others how to sell at his level. After everything he had accomplished and endured, he still clung to the belief that life was about an ability and an attempt to reach out and touch other people's lives. His excellence in the selling game and leading others was his gift to the world and he wanted to share it with other people.

Vincent had wanted to be a writer since Kay put him in front of a typewriter at age 3. In grade school it was stories involving his classmates and him in precarious situations, whether at home or in outer space. In college it turned into writing movie scripts. Now, he wanted to impart his knowledge to a broader spectrum of readers that could learn from his steps and missteps.

Upon his return, Vincent arrived early and Keith was in his office before anyone else arrived, drawing the blinds and closing the door. He sat in the chair

298

opposite Vincent, his trademark trembling, quivering lip in moments of anger in full effect.

"Are you out of your fucking mind thinking you are going to send Gil an e-mail that basically says you are going through the motions here and you should be promoted?" Keith blasted.

"That's not what I said," Vincent corrected him. "I said I am ready for a new challenge."

"And you basically went on and on defending yourself and saying how great you are," Keith continued.

"Nobody else does," Vincent fired back.

"I can't believe you. You are lucky to have a job."

"Then get rid of me. I'm tired of the attacks; I'm tired of giving everything I have to this place only to have the shit kicked out of me for nothing. I was defending my kid for Christ's sake, and the company can't even do me the courtesy of an investigation. They just suspend me. They don't give a damn about what I have done for them and I'm sick of it."

"You don't think I had your back?"

"Like you couldn't have made this go away. You always tell me how tight you are with Legal and with Gil."

"Your behavior just caught up to you."

"My problem is that I am treated like a criminal while my concerns are ignored. After everything I have done for this place over eight years, you'd think I would be treated like a king."

"Jesus Christ. You're unbelievable. You are the most arrogant and reckless person I have met in 28 years in the business."

"Thank you," Vincent said cockily and unafraid of repercussion.

"I'm serious. I think you need professional help. For fuck's sake, 95% of the things you do are perfect. They are better than anyone could ever dream of doing. But the other 5% is your undoing."

"That's a pretty good ratio."

"You know what? This isn't going to work between us anymore. Are you here to be a jackass or are you here to do business?"

"Trust me, I wouldn't have walked back through these doors to put up with this shit if I wasn't here to do business. Have you ever known me to do anything half-assed?"

"No," Dickhauser backpedaled, his tone even softening.

"Then believe me when I say I won't now. I'm here to do my job, which I do better than anybody else. I'm here to make this place go and hold it together like nobody else can. Is there anything else?"

Keith was unsure what to say after dealt that blow.

Vincent, hot at this point, sat in silence. From there, Keith did his trademark fumbling and started talking about random goings-on in the department. Vincent's mind was made up: he was going to be on his best behavior from here on out, do what could be done to get Keith his much-deserved departure and figure out his own exit strategy. To warrant a suspension after one alleged gaffe clearly meant this was not going to be where Vincent made his next big move.

In Vincent's manager meeting and office stand-up, which he had carefully planned in an attempt to take as many subtle jabs at Keith and ABM as possible, he reiterated his purpose and the importance of trust. He said over and over how he had their backs, that he would walk through fire for them and he would never falter in that charge. Both were far from typical because Vincent did nothing to mention sales statistics, he talked simply about how proud he was to work with them and that he would have their back until his dying breath. Vincent knew it affected Dickhauser because Keith pledged later in the day to work on "rehabilitating" Vincent's career. Of course, it was not lost on Vincent that this was too little, too late.

The week of his return Vincent came up with a well-mapped out idea to fix clerical, commission and contract problems and sent it in e-mail memo form to the entire management team to obtain their opinions. This was strategic because he wanted to build momentum for it and knew Keith would shoot it down if he tried to make any suggestion about Scott Kinsey's baby, despite its deformities.

The team loved Vincent's idea, which put several tracking measurements in place for each contract and allowed constant updating on where a contract was at any given point from inception to execution. It was also something that would not take up too much precious time for any person during any of the checkpoints.

Scott, taking his opportunity to show just how much of an ass and impediment to progress he was, responded after ten or so managers praised the idea and put in big red letters, "STOP." He detailed that there was a plan they were looking at implementing for 2010 and that he would share details when the time came. Vincent's idea could be implemented immediately which begged the question, why is Scott Kinsey so afraid of the prospect of these problems finally being solved? Was he or anyone else benefiting from improper payment of reps and managers?

Vincent voiced that frustration, putting in big green letters, "My apologies, I assumed we would want to GO forward with fixing the issues that are crippling us immediately rather than to put it off." It was a pointless skirmish with no end in sight but he could not resist getting in that cheap, parting shot.

November had once again been a 124% finish which was good on 19 sales days. Vincent shifted his schedule to warm leads all month in December to give as good a sendoff to 2009 as possible since many were vacationing and heads were not in the game. After the year he had been through, he was limping to the finish line.

Mentally, he told himself this would be the last full year he could tolerate this position.

Keith called Vincent on the Friday ending the week of his return to work and revealed he merely got a slap on the hand from ABM. Sure, they used tough wording and put him on a final warning of some sort, but he was staying in power. The Brotherhood had failed.

Dickhauser had apparently been told to manage Vincent and Mark rather than the managers, which just meant he was declawed from their vantage point but Vincent was going to have to put up with him just as much if not more. Lovely.

Over the weeks to come, Keith referenced the warning multiple times daily as he constantly speculated as to who was behind it. Rather than take it seriously that his entire management team thought he was a vengeful prick, he never took it to heart; he just sounded like he wanted revenge. He had been made fully aware that practically everyone interviewed had said nothing but damning things about him and his horrific leadership style. Instead of inspiring him to turn over a new leaf it was clear Dickhauser was on a personal vendetta to uncover a culprit.

Amidst a power struggle with his boss, César left the company and was replaced in December by Gerald Murphy. Gerald visited the office mid-month, meaning Vincent had to put on his well-rehearsed routine, and the new boss seemed impressive and serious about the task. As usual, he was impressed with Vincent and asked Keith about his mobility and if he would be available to take over a struggling office in Atlanta.

Vincent and Abby continued lunch sporadically and spending gradually more time together after hours. It was only a matter of time before they slept together again and they did so after a day out as a family after Elizabeth went to bed. The next day, however, while Vincent was at his apartment with Elizabeth, Abby showed up unannounced not feeling well wanting Vincent to order and buy her dinner, and brought her laundry over to do at his place. Needless to say, this did not turn out well as they ended up shouting at each other in front of Elizabeth and Abby took off.

Come Monday, Abby came to Vincent's office and wanted to go to lunch. During the meal Vincent pried out of her that she had been with Chris the night before. He assumed they had kissed, and was correct. Abby swore nothing else happened but Vincent was still ticked off.

Later that night on the phone, Abby came clean; not only had they kissed but she had slept with him. And that was that. For good.

Vincent hung up on her. Considering her promiscuity he was not at all surprised, but he needed this to happen to be 100% ready to walk away and never look back. The sting was that this put the nail in the coffin of any hopes he clung to for a normal family and a future like he had pictured since he was younger. This was the end.

He ignored 17 phone calls from Abby that night and countless text messages. He disregarded her at work but, with the Christmas holiday it was a shortened week. And while he had gone to great lengths to make her a Christmas present that would blow her away – a poster collage of 30 of Elizabeth's pictures from birth to now – he dropped it off when he dropped Elizabeth off mid-week and did not stick around for the reaction.

Whatever Vincent had for Abby fudged the line between love and hate; it was an intense passion that swung dramatically both ways. But this event pushed the pendulum permanently to the negative; there was no rebound from this no matter how she tried to spin it. It was great to see more of his angel but not if it put him in bed with the devil.

Abby did not relent, texting throughout the week, calling twice and again on Saturday night before Elizabeth went to bed. Vincent answered that call so he could say goodnight to his princess, but when Elizabeth actually said Chris's name towards the end of the call, it set him off. He went for the nearest bottle, and when later that night Abby tried to text again, he had finally taken beyond enough.

He unloaded on her via text message, saying he never wanted to speak to her again about anything other than Elizabeth; citing the $25,000+ that she owed him, that she had cheated on him with a loser with no job, and had blackmailed, lied about and demoralized him all while spreading her legs for everyone under the sun. She slinked away like he had done something wrong, saying if he was going to talk to her like that to leave her alone.

Vincent did not let up; he had told her to leave him alone after she bunked down with her ex and lied about it, and he had no respect for her. He called her every name in the book – a whore, a slut and a cunt (making her the first female he used that word for) – and told her karma would give her what she deserves in the end.

Vincent bottled everything up – the anger, the hurt and the pain – but when someone triggered him while his cup was about to runneth over, he was a prime candidate to explode. Abby was the scourge of his life and he finally got to tell her exactly what he had wanted to for years.

The vacation week in years past had been enough for Vincent to recharge his batteries, but this year it was not; another clear indication it was time to go. His first day back in the office was slow-starting; Vincent had compiled a 3-page plan for Keith, Mark and himself to peruse to get the year off to a successful start and proposed many changes in the floundering inbound unit. They met for lunch to discuss but Keith's ability to stay focused on the plan was nonexistent; he kept getting caught up on minor points that amounted to nothing and it was clear this was a hopeless cause.

Regardless, summoning strength he did not know he had from within, Vincent came back on Day 2 energized; he arrived at 6, ran several reports, put together his agenda for the manager meeting and office stand-up and both gatherings ended up blowing away their respective rooms.

By end of day, however, Keith had once again managed to derail the Vincent Scott express, calling for a 2009 revenue audit that would wipe out any and all missing contracts from the revenue and manager bonus totals for the previous year. Considering Scott and Danny's clerical team was 700 contracts behind in production (nearly three weeks' worth) and their missing contracts report indicated another 700 missing contracts (of which, historical data dictated probably 70-80% were already in), this sent the reps and managers into an uproar that even Vincent could not contain.

This revenue audit consumed nearly every working day of January and about every last ounce of the patience of the entire organization. Dickhauser's incompetence was going to cost hundreds of people their jobs when this department came crashing down over the horrifically fractured processes.

Vincent's cries fell on deaf ears. He sent memo after memo to Keith explaining just how wrong this audit was on so many levels, how frustrated everyone was with these processes that had not been fixed in four years, and he offered solutions and to fix the problems himself. Vincent likened this to the doomed *Titanic* headed for certain peril against an iceberg; however, Vincent had the foresight to see the iceberg and warn the captain but those warnings were never heeded.

On Wednesday of that first week, Abby was a witch about demanding Vincent stay home with a sick Elizabeth despite the fact he was up to his ears in this nonsense and she had just gotten a fresh batch of vacation. Not even wanting to put up with her attitude, he agreed, and scheduled many of his meetings to occur via conference call so he could take them from home. However, one call he was not expecting arrived mid-day from Lydia Rawlings. On the line in attendance: Keith Dickhauser.

"Vincent, recently a situation has come to my attention where you sent some text messages while on break to Abby Winters. The text messages contained vulgar language. Do you know anything about that?" Lydia asked.

Unbelievable, Vincent thought. *What on earth was Abby thinking? Why is she biting the hand that feeds both her and their daughter?*

"Absolutely, Lydia, as you know she and I have an extensive history and she is the mother of my daughter. We had been spending time together and had discussed reconciliation until I learned she was cheating on me and lying about it. She then proceeded to ignore my requests to leave me alone, continued harassing me and I finally had enough," Vincent stated. "After a week of her refusing to respect my wishes of leaving me alone, I finally got sucked in."

Lydia read one of the texts to Vincent. "Does that sound like what you sent?"

"Yes it does."

"Yeah, you know, I should have had the foresight to think her reporting to you was a bad idea," Keith Dickhauser chimed in.

"Actually, all reporting in our department is ceremonial," Vincent corrected him. "Keith made that clear last year when he changed the bonus structure. She and I are not even in the same quadrant of the building and have no contact, nor would we under any disciplinary circumstances. Not only that, but this is a personal matter and has literally zero to do with the company."

"Be that as it may," Lydia continued, "she is a fellow co-worker and you are a manager in the company. These text messages were brought to my attention by Danny Boyd and it is my responsibility to investigate."

Brought to her by Danny Boyd? What the hell is going on here?

"Lydia, I can assure you, I take my responsibility to ABM very seriously," Vincent began, thinking quickly on his feet. "In no way did I abuse my power as a manager, threaten her job or her in any way, shape or form and this is a domestic issue. I have voice mails she left during the week where she also used curse words, calling herself a bitch and saying she knew she fucked up. I have my phone records showing the repeated calls and texts throughout the week. I also have three years' worth of documentation of what this woman has put me through, not to mention issues of when she harassed me on company time and company computers and I had to report it to Danny Boyd, Mark and Keith and nothing was done about it. Now, I don't know what on earth is going on here, but this has nothing to do with my career with ABM."

"Vincent, I understand where you are coming from. I have to report back to our Legal team, but I will go to them with that stance; you probably had no idea you were even doing anything that could be brought into the company, did you?" Lydia inquired, softening her tone substantially.

"Absolutely not. I have been on my best behavior and, while I disagreed with how the blog post incident was handled, I take my commitment to ABM very seriously," Vincent repeated.

"I understand. Actually, I have been through very similar situations with my daughter and with her estranged husband," Lydia said, now sounding motherly in tone. "I know these situations are difficult. Just always remember, you have a beautiful baby girl and she is the number one priority. I will contact Legal with the stance you two were simply having a domestic dispute and will get back with Keith if we need to discuss this further."

"Sounds great, Lydia, thank you."

"Keith, do you have any other questions?" she inquired.

"No," he answered flatly.

"Okay, thank you both for your time," Lydia concluded.

Keith stayed on the line.

"Wow, why would Abby throw you under the bus like that?" he inquired.

"How should I know? She would not stop harassing me and I fired off at her."

"Well, don't talk to her about this. I will talk to Lydia and see where we go from here."

"Okay," Vincent responded, still formulating the thoughts in his head.

The next morning, Vincent knew how to proceed and went to Keith's office directly following his morning meetings. He rapped on the door frame with his knuckle.

"You got a minute?" Vincent asked.

Keith looked up, startled, as Vincent rarely came to him for anything. "Sure," he replied.

Vincent came in, closed the door and sat down.

"Why did Danny take those text messages to Lydia?" Vincent asked, as serious as he had ever been.

"Well, uh, I don't know," Keith responded, turning beet red and stammering. "I, uh, had a conversation with him about it and asked him why he did that because I didn't appreciate it. But don't go talking to him about it because I don't need two of my top guys fighting."

"Uh huh," Vincent said, processing the information. "So did you hear anything back?"

"No, just that Lydia called me afterwards and said she had your back," Keith said.

"Good. Whatever this nonsense is, make it go away," Vincent said. "This is preposterous and I am tired of being under fire for nothing on a monthly basis."

"How do you think I feel?" Keith retorted in his patented way of making everything about him. "I have to constantly come to your defense."

Vincent half-laughed. "Come to my defense? Whatever is going on here is just more bullshit and you know it. Besides, even if that were true, I'm well worth any defense you may have ever done on my behalf. Make this go away."

"I don't want you talking to anybody about this," Keith advised. "Let me handle it from here."

"As you wish," Vincent said. "You find out how to make it go away."

Okay, good to have this settled, Vincent thought. For crying out loud, now he was being run through the mud for personal, off the clock, non-threatening and non-company related text messages to his ex-fiancé and daughter's mother? Wonders never ceased in this place.

Vincent tried to re-focus on business but with the entire workforce up in arms about the contracts and commission fiasco and the one man who had to deal with it not willing to budge, he had to finally embrace the fact that his time in this department was over. He continued regular therapy sessions with Gina, sometimes camping out at her desk for a half hour as the two tried to console one another and strategize as to what the next move was. Neither had anything left to accomplish in their respective positions. They were fried.

The breakfast and lunch conversations shifted to all of the managers in attendance talking about finding their next big project together or having a mass exodus. There was no shame in leaving a sinking ship, they reasoned. What was even odder is that Vincent started to get even brasher in his dissenting opinions to Keith, Danny and Scott on the impending collapse they were leading the department into but they only went ignored.

Mark Rogers even found a huge sale of $2,000 per month in advertising that was marked as missing and was seconds away from being removed from 2009 numbers until he went to the clerk's desk personally and found it buried under a stack of papers – it just had not been marked off yet. Had he not found that contract, the sale would have been removed from everyone's results, commission would not have been paid to the rep, costing them over $3,600, and the customer may or may not have ever gotten their advertising. This was just the biggest of hundreds of such mistakes and no one would do anything about it.

Vincent did something he had never done: applied for jobs that were not promotions in an attempt to leave. Keith's reaction when he found out?

"What's your problem?" he barked over the phone, calling Vincent's work line.

"My problem?" Vincent responded. "What do you mean?"

"You've never hit on lateral transfers before," Keith responded.

"Just looking for a new challenge. That is my right," he answered.

The following Monday, he got a call from an executive director in the business-to-business sect of the telecommunications portion of ABM, Vincent's former home. The fellow's name was Cameron Cole, the position paid $15,000 more per year than Vincent's current post and they set up an interview for that coming Friday. Vincent breathed a sigh of relief; once again he was seemingly at a dead end and from nowhere an outstretched branch appeared to potentially save him.

Vincent knew he would be sad to leave some of the people he worked so hard for and with, but he knew this was the right step and the right path. He sent Keith an e-mail with the job information and description attached, asking if a Friday interview would pose any problem and Keith simply responded with a one word answer: "No."

Thanks for wishing me luck and have a great day to you, too, you bastard.

The drive that had carried him this far, the passion for making this department incredible and that will to win whatever the cost was gone. Keith Dickhauser's complete and utter disregard for him, his ideas, his hard work and the disrespect and lack of support he had shown Vincent for nearly four years had finally vanquished his spirit. It was time to move on and he was not going to lift another finger to go outside of his basic job functions to help Keith be successful.

Mark was in Greenfield three days per week and Vincent now let him handle all office stand-up's. Vincent started arriving every morning at 8:30, canceled the morning manager meetings and stopped monitoring calls with managers unless they specifically requested it. Vincent stopped sending out reports, sent literally no e-mails except for the daily schedule (which no longer was accompanied by a litany on events and achievers from the day prior) and made it abundantly clear to everyone he was playing under protest and he was finished.

He still coached the people that wanted it, had passionate development meetings with those who were serious about being successful, but he was not going to kill himself another day for the undeserving and unappreciative bastard that was destroying what he had spent four years building.

Mid-week, Keith pulled Vincent into his office and it was one of the meetings where he told Vincent to close the door. Vincent sat.

"What the fuck is your problem?" he blasted, attacking right off the bat.

Vincent acted aloof. "What do you mean?"

"Are you going to pull your head out of your ass today and do your job?" the clearly frustrated Dickhauser boomed.

"Tell me one component of my job I have not done," Vincent responded calmly.

"Well, uh, you, uh, you're just not acting normal," Keith stammered.

"Acting? What part of my job is acting?" Vincent responded, definitely loaded for bear for this conversation.

"Well, you haven't been acting like yourself. You haven't been sending out e-mails…"

"That's not a mandatory part of my job."

"You haven't been getting here…uh…" Dickhauser trailed off and stopped himself.

"Oh, that's what this is about," Vincent laughed. "That I'm not getting here at 6 AM every morning and breaking my ass just so my opinions and advice can be ignored? You're right, I'm not."

Keith looked shocked and horrified all in one.

"I will do my job and I defy you to find something I'm not doing that is in my job description. But I am not going to kill myself for this place another day," Vincent said defiantly. "Period."

"Well, I also understand you have not been doing stand-ups in the morning. Mark is downtown tomorrow and I want you to have one to award the incentives," Dickhauser backpedaled.

"Done. Anything else?" Vincent asked, standing to leave.

"No," came the defeated reply.

Vincent was more proud of that Thursday stand-up than most all of his others of years past. He read the names of the contest winners and allowed the office to applaud, rather than bringing them down front and center, joking with them and praising them in front of the team as had become his trademark. Then, he folded the piece of paper, put it in his pocket and said merely, "Guys, like my T-ball coach once told me, play hard and have fun out there." And he walked off to stunned silence.

Jackson Taber, standing front and center and who had also been privy to a lot of Vincent's recent woes, said merely, "Brilliant."

Not long after, Keith came into Vincent's office and Vincent was sure it was to destroy him over the farce of a stand-up. He closed the door and sat down.

"Vincent, you can't go to the interview tomorrow," Keith said, fidgeting nervously.

"Excuse me?"

"Well, this investigation over those text messages to Abby is still ongoing. Lydia called me and said you can't go on the interview tomorrow."

That revelation struck Vincent like a ton of bricks. He was in utter disbelief.

"This is unacceptable. Let's get her on the phone," Vincent said.

"What?" Keith said, reacting with shock to Vincent's request. "No, I, uh, have a call in to her."

"Keith, what the hell is going on here?" Vincent asked. "I want to talk to Lydia immediately."

"No, I am handling this."

"This is my livelihood. What the hell are they going to do over a personal matter that has nothing to do with the company? This is ridiculous!"

"I will call Lydia back and see if we can meet on this to clear it up. Just call the guy and tell him you can interview next week."

"Next week, huh," Vincent said, his mind racing to try to figure out what was going on. "Please call Lydia. I want to talk to her today."

"I will do what I can," Keith said before departure. "Did you finish covering all of your appraisals?"

"I have a few left."

"I need them done today."

"How am I supposed to have positive meetings with these guys when you can't even tell me what the hell is going on here?" Vincent fired back, frustrated and angry.

"Let me try to call Lydia again. I will keep you posted," Keith responded.

Something was missing here. Why was Keith being so secretive? Vincent had not heard anything about those texts in three weeks — how could they resurface now?

After lunch, Vincent went to Keith's office, shut the door and sat down.

"Did you talk to Lydia?"

"I have a call in to her."

"Can we call her right now?"

"No, I am going to wait for her to call me back," Keith answered coldly.

"So you can't just try to call her while I'm in here?"

"No, I'm going to wait."

"Keith, this is my entire life. This is my career, and you can't even tell me what is going on. Forgive me for being a little untrusting, but how is this supposed to make any sense to me?"

"I don't know what to tell you."

"What to tell me?" Vincent shouted. "Tell me that you have my back. Why is it that in the last month, you had three different excuses as to why you weren't going to send me to Top Gun? Then somehow these text messages magically went to human resources. Now, you won't even pick up a phone for me, after everything I have done for you over the last four years?"

"How do you think I feel?" Dickhauser fired back. "Nobody had my back when I was under fire last year in that investigation."

"Whoa, whoa, why are you making this about you?" Vincent asked.

"I'm just saying," Keith said slowly, backing down.

"No, what I'm telling you is that this department would not be open if it wasn't for me. I have killed myself for you for four years, ruining two relationships because I was obsessed with this place, I work 10-11 hour days and am the face of this department and you can't pick up a phone for me?"

Keith stared blankly at Vincent.

"I will let you know as soon as I hear something," Keith said oddly. It was clear: Keith was not even willing to pick up the phone. He had lied to Vincent numerous times over the prior weeks. He had done everything he could to try to frame it that Vincent was not doing his job but had failed in that endeavor as well.

"Thanks," Vincent said, knowing what he had to do next.

Vincent left and headed back to his office. He closed his door and picked up the phone. He was under orders not to call Lydia but that did not stop him from calling Agnes Landry.

Vincent described the atmosphere of the last few weeks and that he knew Keith was up to something. Agnes revealed that Lydia did not forbid him from interviewing and stated she would talk to Lydia about his call. Ten minutes later, Keith came into his office.

"You can schedule the interview for Monday," Keith said. "And we have a meeting with Lydia downtown tomorrow morning at 11."

"I just have questions as to why she was not permitting me to interview. We don't need a meeting for that," Vincent answered.

310

"We are going to meet to clear up the text message business," Keith answered.

"Why would we meet in person? Do you want it to be downtown so you can just walk me out without a commotion?" Vincent asked.

"We're just going to meet to clear this up," Keith said again, warily.

"What should I bring?"

"I would recommend you bring anything that shows why you were in the state of mind you were in," Keith answered.

"Okay. Thanks for calling her," Vincent said, knowing full well Lydia had called him. This was extremely shady and Vincent had to get to the bottom of it.

Vincent came to play the following day, having stayed late the night before to print out hundreds of pages of supporting documentation, showing Abby harassing him on company time, letters to attorneys, court documents, the restraining order he had to file against her, a three page chronology of everything Abby had put him through, all the money she owed him and basically everything that would show why he blasted her antics the way he did. It was not difficult to show her as the villain.

He also went into it knowing he could expose Keith as the liar he was. Keith was nervous in the elevator before the meeting and tried to make smalltalk about work. They walked into the Human Resources conference room and took seats opposite Lydia; Vincent sat directly across from her and Keith sat a few chairs down.

"I assume you know why you're here," Lydia said.

"Absolutely – Keith said we were here to clear up this text message issue that I thought was already cleared up so that I can transfer out of the department," Vincent responded.

Lydia proceeded to delve into legal speak about the hazards of management treating non-management in this fashion, which was a complete 180 from her prior mantra of supporting him. Vincent spent an hour going over every document in his arsenal, his voice cracking twice as the memories and the horror of his relationship with Abby resurfaced.

"Okay, do you have anything else to add, Vincent?" Lydia asked.

This was clearly nothing more than a formality.

"Just that punishing me punishes my daughter and obviously also punishes Abby, so I have no idea what I'm doing here," Vincent answered.

"Well, I am going to meet with Dickie and decide where we go from here. We'll be back."

In the fifteen minutes from the time they exited until their re-entry, a million thoughts went through Vincent's mind. *Could this really be the end? How? How could something like this really spell the end for him?* Lydia had already told him she supported his stance. *Curse Abby – what the hell had she been thinking? Why would she put an end to her own child support? Why was Keith not pulling him out of the fire?*

It was all about to become crystal clear.

When Lydia and Keith came back in, this time Keith sat next to Lydia so they were both across the table from Vincent. Keith held a piece of paper in his hands, signifying to Vincent that this was the conclusion.

Keith barely read from it. It was a page four paragraphs long and Keith paraphrased two sentences. "Vincent, in light of recent events, the company has come to the conclusion that your unprofessional behavior can no longer be tolerated. Effective immediately, you are terminated from the business."

Vincent said nothing. He did not react. At Lydia's prodding he placed his identification badge and company-issued BlackBerry on the table. He got up, remained speechless, and walked towards the door making clear he was ready to depart. Lydia actually took a Kleenex and dabbed her eyes. Vincent was amazed this had actually gotten a reaction out of her.

Lydia walked with him and Keith stayed a little behind. They went down the escalators and Vincent took it all in: this company he had given his blood, sweat and tears to for 8 ½ years was kicking him out. It made no sense. But it started to very quickly.

Vincent's entire ABM career flashed before his eyes. That first interview with Belinda Appleton. Competing with Jake Stallings and Bambi Jennings and wreaking havoc on the sales charts and records as a rep. Murderer's Row, Shelly Cheekwood and Stacey Worth. Phoebe. Abby. The awards, cheering and accolades. Building a department from scratch and its rise and now certain fall. It was all over.

Keith caught up to them. "Vincent," he said rather quietly. Vincent stopped and said nothing, nor did he turn to face the man. "I'm sorry it came to this."

No, you're not sorry, Vincent thought. *You did this.*

"Vincent," Lydia said as he reached the turnstiles that, upon crossing, would make his exile complete. "Do you want to make arrangements with Keith to pick up your personal belongings?" Vincent looked at her, thinking for a moment. He had no desire to speak to that bastard again. "Mail them," Vincent said.

He turned and walked through the turnstiles, out the front door and, head held high, onto the streets of Minneapolis, unemployed for the first time in fifteen years.

"The Selling Game" by Vincent Scott
Chapter 13:
KEEPING THE FAITH, STAYING THE COURSE AND PICKING YOURSELF BACK UP TIME AND TIME AGAIN

Finding purpose and meaning behind the tasks we undertake is something many of us spend our entire existence trying to determine – sometimes to no avail. Fortunately, there is no mystery as to why we work: to provide, achieve, dodge boredom, answer a calling, keep from having the highlights of our day be *The Young and the Restless* or *The Price is Right* while we raid the fridge in our bathrobe, to overcome our fears and conquer the world.

Along with the agreement we entered into when we enlisted in our job comes the responsibility of not just a job done, but a job well done. We gave enough advanced billing to pack a movie theater so we can't be a low-budget stinker – we've got to be the high octane action thriller. We made a commitment to provide a service that is garnering a pretty penny and it all boils down to accountability.

To pay your debt to occupational society you have to hold yourselves and everyone you interact with accountable, be it subordinates, customers, or co-workers. Holding ourselves accountable means justification of how the day is spent and how our actions add up to fill it. We signed on the dotted line for a set amount of revenue to pay the piper and the piper is ready to collect. As Mark Twain said, "Virtue has never been as respectable as money." Money talks and those who make more are allowed to talk more.

To succeed in the selling game you have to be pretty darn autonomous. Everyone is an adult (though we like to deviate from that archetype from time to time – call it Peter Pan syndrome) and everyone needs to be able to do what it takes to deliver the expectation. Believe me, it is encouraged to go above and beyond! Delivery of less than potential is nothing but underachieving and a letdown; the results of which will be anything but positive. And whatever excuse you come up with to get the spotlight off of you is not accountability. It is less than what you committed to and will diminish your credibility.

If your results are not there, believe me – someone will analyze what you did with your time and they have every right to do so. If recommendations can be made to help you better allocate your resources and optimize your day, they will most certainly be made. Be open to feedback and learn from those who have found success in the very arena where you are seeking yours.

Be able to defend your decisions, actions and moves; without the ability of justification comes errors and failures. Sales is a thrill ride that would make

Walt Disney proud. It's about making lots and lots of quality pitches featuring loads of charm and witty banter with customers that don't know how to better themselves. You have to challenge them every step of the way, poking holes in what they do throughout the call and instilling self doubt in them so they will make the decision to heed your call. What you do with your day – be it in efficiency or effort or the words you choose to use – is up to you. These are variables you can personally manipulate. Take advantage of that power, because we are powerless in too many areas of life. Finding anything you have control over in the workforce is a rarity so you should seize that bull by the horns and hold on for dear life.

If you don't believe in your product, find another one to sell. If every pitch has you reeling on the defensive like you are in the middle of an interrogation on *Law & Order*, it's time to go.

Experts tell you it takes 21 days to form a habit and make something a way of life. One-hit wonders and flashes in the pan do not a successful career make; you are constantly going to be judged – both by what you have done lately and over the course of time. Consistency wins the race. Starting positive habits that will keep you in the upper echelon will not only satisfy you and your pocketbook, but it will pan out favorably in your career.

We talked about those who find early success and how it deludes them into thinking things will always be that easy. To stay the course you need to put several plans of action in place that keep you disciplined and on the road to achievement. Not many make it because not many have the restraint, courage and inner strength to not only take the hits but to trudge forward in the greatest way possible once they are delivered.

Keeping your wits about you and managing to repel negative energy is where it all begins. A heck of a lot of willpower must be involved in that process but it most certainly can be done. Many people hit daily, weekly or even monthly targets once or twice, which should be celebrated briefly, but can be a fluke. The mark of success is being able to achieve it over the long haul which takes tenacity and focus and turning positive behaviors into, say, a habit.

Function as if prior wins and losses did not happen. You cannot hang your hat on the time you won an award two years ago and you cannot hang your head and dwell on last week's bad call review. The sense of impending doom some carry with them is called "self-fulfilling prophecy"; they think so much about a negative outcome they practically will it into existence. We spend far too much of our lives worrying about unfortunate conclusions that never come to pass. When these pessimistic thoughts present themselves, dismiss them.

These principles apply to positive angles as well; you may achieve your annual objective in June but that by no means is a reason to ease up. You never know when you will encounter a lull in the action and you will wish you had seized more of the opportunities while you had them. Regrets are unprofessional and you have to protect yourself at all costs from having them. You will always be evaluated by the sum of your parts; if you have a good month and then string together some poor ones, your good one gets lost in the shuffle. It is never too late to redeem yourself with a sequence of stellar months but those in positions of power will always only care about who is in the current spotlight.

Think about names that ruled the movie, music and sports charts 10-to-20 years ago in contrast to 2 months ago or the ones there today. The names change and a frequent means to describe this phenomenon is "fifteen minutes of fame"; blink and you miss the careers of some of these people and acts. However, if you ask me, it is better to be considered one of those "has-beens" that made it big and achieved their dreams than to be a never-was who was afraid to go for it. Which are you?

Start your day off right every day. For many of you, that means coffee, breakfast or working out before you begin your sales day. Being sluggish means sacrificing potential opportunities and you never know when that big one will present itself or pass you by because you were not prepared. I know a lot of people who constantly put off bettering themselves; saying they will try harder tomorrow, next week or next month. Stop and reflect; life is far too short to allow ourselves to continue down a path that leads to nowhere. Seize the day and moment and don't let anything you do be less than superb.

Going into a day of selling, be it as a road warrior or a cold-caller, as a listless shell of yourself is not going to help anything or anyone. You have to be on your game all the time. Sales is about all the planets aligning at just the right times and places; that gatekeeper has to let you in, that decision-maker has got to be ready to hear your spiel and you have to deliver it with the right touch of finesse. Any false move and you are history. A poorly handled moment or miscue here or there and you are lost in space.

Recognize and acknowledge the monotony. Yes, it is a grind, a rollercoaster and it is going to eat you alive sometimes. Yet remember, you signed on for it and it is up to you to find ways to cope, persevere and break through. Your company and supervisors are not likely to provide you those coping mechanisms, so find something that pumps you up and gets your juices flowing. My personal favorite was blaring music on the way to work that made me feel like a million dollars. Whatever it is, find it and never miss a dose. "You're the Best" from the *Karate Kid* at a lofty decibel in my car every morning on the way to work always worked for me: that is enough to make anyone feel like a winner.

Get support groups going at work of people with whom you share opinions. Talking about excellence with people who exude it breeds and fosters and helps it spread.

Always keep your eye on the prize and stay focused on the big picture. While I am more than aware this is easier said than done, failure to do so will lead to derailment of the train with little likelihood at getting back on track. A few rough days can start a tailspin towards oblivion but you are always one sale away from the road back. That is exciting but frightening at the same time.

Do not lose sight of the light at the end of the tunnel, whether you are in an entry level position bitching about policy or you are the one making it. Before you embarked on this leg of the journey, surely there was some goal you had in your sights. Never let it leave and the loftier the better. Admit it, your aspirations are beyond knocking on doors and sitting on an automatic dialer so do not allow any outside force to keep you there and pin you to the mat. There are always bigger and better things you can accomplish by keeping yourself entertained with new challenges in the meantime.

Shamelessly steal tips, tricks and tactics that work wherever you may find them. Make them your own. You will always be a collection of your experiences; however, what you choose to do with these experiences and ideas is up to you. If you pick up a worthy tactic, be it from your peer, neighbor, a training session or, let's hope in this case, a book about sales, use it, put your own spin on it and make it better. Imitation is the greatest form of flattery and if you're lucky, someone will pick up from you, too.

Share your tips and tactics as well; this can be tough because people will always be out to assault you. Those attacks are greater the greater you are. The sum of our lives, however, is the contributions we make and I can tell you without hesitation that my greatest achievements (aside from my daughter, of course) are positive impacts I have had on others. That moment when you realize someone has bettered themselves because of something you did or said or aided in is a very rewarding one. Don't miss out on it because of your own selfishness.

Use visuals to jog your memory; no one, unless they are a cybernetic organism from the future, can scan information once and regurgitate it on command. Construction of a "perfect" sales call is a lot of repetition of words, phrases and attitude designed to win over the imagination of the recipient. A great line you used today may be tough to remember tomorrow. Write down what works and what doesn't because we never get anywhere if we fail to learn from the victories and defeats.

Write down your goals, sales or otherwise, and keep them prominently displayed, be it at your desk, by your bed or somewhere you will see them often. Keep track of how you are progressing, constantly reminding yourself where you have been and where you are going. People do not lose weight and keep it off because of diet and exercise; they lose it because they change their lifestyle. They lose it because they form – you guessed it – a habit of better living.

316

Never forget the importance the "numbers' game" plays in sales. Failure to remember its contribution to the lifeblood of sales is as detrimental as the trouble that befell those poor souls in *Gremlins* who fed the Mogwai fried chicken after midnight; it's a tragic oversight that causes all out disaster that could have been avoided. You may not be able to change the rules, but if you are not getting the results you want, do more. Nothing is stopping you in that facet of selling but you.

Your customers will constantly put you on the defensive. Design your strategy to turn it around on them; put the burden of proof on the customer and make them show you why your product or service is unnecessary or would be a detriment to them.

Finally, *have fun*. Stand up when you are in the middle of an engaging sales call. Enter into friendly competitions with peers. Get into passionate presentations. Keep the blood flowing in your veins.

Staying ahead of the curve in all areas will improve your luck. As Martin Scorsese says over the opening credits of *The Color of Money*, "For some players, luck itself is an art."

An inevitability of any job, sales or not, is failure. The difficult-to-swallow truth is that there are countless examples of scenarios where you will have no control on the outcome. There is something to be said for mastering the ones where you are in control however it is often how you react to those you do not that will determine your end result.

All things change. When talking about how life had taken its toll on him, Indiana Jones said, "It's not the years, honey, it's the mileage." In your mid-twenties you gradually start to feel differently about things. You start to see things in a brand new light due to a shift in responsibilities and physical changes you undergo. You can't do things the same way you once did them. Your priorities shift. You start to become the person you will forever be.

You have to rally behind small victories and keep your eyes focused on the trophy, which is the meaning of life, at all times. What is that meaning? As ironic as it is to hear someone as jaded and apathetic as me say this, it is love. I won't use clichés, but I will say that without love there is nothing to live for. The love and passion you have for your life's work, the love for friends and family and the love you discover when you become a parent. The trick is not letting those things become clouded because of the constant struggles, battles, or the cesspools that you will be thrown into on a sometimes daily basis.

People and situations and circumstances of life will always find a way to try to beat you down or let you down. Be selective in whom you put your trust, because most people will take your heart and break it, take your money and run, abuse you, use you, stick it to you, laugh behind your back, talk about you

…smile in your face while all the while they wanna take your place (the Backstabbers… *backstabbers*! Thank you to the O'Jay's.)

Heath Ledger's Joker had one of the greatest, hardest hitting and factual monologues in history a few years ago in *The Dark Knight*: "They need you right now, but when they don't, they'll cast you out. Like a leper. You see, their morals, their code, it's a bad joke. Dropped at the first sign of trouble. They're only as good as the world allows them to be. I'll show you. When the chips are down…these civilized people, they'll eat each other. See, I'm not a monster. I'm just ahead of the curve."

People can be evil,, rude, crude and despicable; it's a very imperfect world, and it pains one to think about it sometimes. But that, more than anything, is the reason to take what you want out of it and not let anything stop or deter you. Life isn't easy, but nothing worth anything is.

The point in all of this is that to become a true master of sales you have to care more about your charted course than damn near anything else.

The best advice I can give is that everything, be it joys and sorrows, bliss and suffering, good and bad, is just a blip on the radar.

Don't get obsessed. Obsession can drive you, but you have little left if you lose what you fought for and threw all your eggs in one basket.

You cannot force someone or yourself into this lifestyle. It has to be chosen and you have to re-commit to it every day or you might as well walk away. And don't get me wrong – it is not necessarily a bad thing to not be cut out for this way of life.

Life, no matter who it is living it or what trade you opt to pursue, presents the holder with a wide array of challenges and objectives. It's up to the person playing that game of Life to decide if they will take on the missions or not, and that will define their success based on the surroundings they select mixed with the ones handed to them. Whether malnourished in a third world country or a wealthy celebrity being stalked by a psychopath, something is going to ail you. It is your reactions and adaptation that will determine how time unfurls for you.

Don't worry about what other people think about you. Life, like a sales call, is about being able to look back and know you did everything you could, learning from it, and moving forward.

There is always something on the horizon, something you are chasing or that is chasing you, and the second you stop seeking out something better there is no purpose left. To lift a quote from (tragically, in my opinion, the worst James Bond movie if you do not count the unofficial ones) 1999's *The World is Not Enough*, "There is no point living if you can't feel alive."

Victories in anything can be few and far between. Seize them when they come. Hold on to their memory when they leave and give everything you've got to get that feeling again.

If you are the best at something you will always be under attack. You have to learn to let it roll off your back or it will eat you alive. Every one of us has something outside of work that beats us up; rise above everything holding you down. Bringing your terrible relationship or sick loved one or personal struggles into the workplace will only result in the quality of your business life sinking to one equal to your personal one.

You cannot allow yourself to give in to negative emotions. Consider the source and suppress your reaction, no matter what. If you fail to do so, the consequences could be disastrous.

There is no *happy ending*, there is merely reality. It is a reality that brings joys and a lot of sorrows. Sure, Hollywood may show you an ending that is nice and neat and leaves you feeling good, but if you skipped ahead minutes, days or weeks into the future of even those characters, that happiness would unravel as well. Their peaks and valleys of joys and misery last until the inevitable reunion show or sequel years later.

The connect-the-dots from one to the other is what will bring you joy. Enjoy every second of the things you cherish; the memories of those moments are the only things that will keep you afloat when the downpour of negativity tries to wash you away.

Life is interesting. It will beat the piss out of you and when you start to get up it beats you harder. You want to trust people but a lot of them burn you because they only care about themselves. The things coming out of their mouths sound great, but you should always judge people by their actions. Don't forget that.

However, in between each and every one of the trials and tribulations, there are unparalleled joys that make it all worthwhile. You will always sport the scars of life but the things that bring you joy will heal you, even if only for a moment. Life is a series of fairytales. There are damsels in distress, evil witches and warlocks, lots of frogs that think they are princes, an evil regime around constantly but fortunately for me, there was always my little princess. And that made me the dark knight that would be king.

No, it is not always fun or sexy or your first choice to get in tug-of-war matches with customers you know you can help but simply will not listen, but never forget it is the life we chose and you can master it if you try. Greatness is just a summary of the effort and struggles and achievements that led up to it.

Always set your goals higher than you could ever possibly reach. That way, when you barely fall short, you're still better than everyone else.

EPILOGUE

Vincent played no music on the drive home and placed no calls. The thoughts in his head were at fever pitch as he pieced together the chain of events that had led up to this conclusion. Danny Boyd had reported the text messages, yet had never taken action when Vincent reported Abby over actual harassment on company time and property a year and a half prior. She had sent instant messages on company computers and e-mailed during their court battle so much and so condescendingly he had no choice but to report it to her then-boss Danny, Mark and Keith. However, they had done nothing about it, much less fed it to human resources.

While Danny had actually engaged in an extramarital affair with a married subordinate and Keith separated the two by moving Danny to training, this time Keith intentionally offered to bring Abby back to the department. He knew the relationship was combustible and, given time, would be Vincent's undoing. What better way to get revenge against Vincent for his part in last year's investigation than hitting him in the relationship with his daughter and her mother. Dickhauser had shown his tell – the red face, quivering lip and stuttering – and deflected the question when Vincent asked how news of these texts got from Danny to Lydia. He had nonchalantly claimed he had no prior knowledge of them. Vincent knew this to be impossible – Danny had worked for Keith for ten years across three projects and would never have gone over Dickhauser's head to take out his number two without serious repercussions. Once, months prior, Keith merely *thought* Vincent was contemplating going over his head for something and it turned out he wasn't, but that misconception did not stop Keith from screaming and cursing at him before he found out the truth. He still could not put his finger on Abby's role in this, but that was irrelevant at this point. Keith had conspired with his boys' club to take him down, with Scott Kinsey's collaboration, and Keith had Danny report it so the blood would not be on his hands.

It was obvious his intention: take out the kingpin. Keith had never stopped talking about his own investigation, trying constantly to figure out who was behind it and he was vengefully bitter that no one had his back. No matter how his crimes were read to him, Vincent's involvement would have been abundantly obvious even if it was just the fact that every manager spoke out against Keith; Vincent was their leader and voice. Keith could not pinpoint one person who initiated the attack, but could certainly take out their leader and silence their voice. This would show the managers who was boss and made clear if they wanted to attempt a mutiny he would take out the head of the uprising. It was diabolical.

320

Vincent thought back to when he was in school and how Kay always told him that if he devoted the passion to his studies that he had for writing, basketball and just about anything but studying, he could have been tops in his class. If Keith had just fine-tuned his sinister mind and actually tried to help the department, which was his job, there would have been no telling the peaks they could have achieved. But instead, the man who constantly told people, "I don't hold grudges," proved once and for all that he was the most vengeful bastard of them all.

Keith Dickhauser decided that his reputation and quest for making someone pay for speaking out against him was more important than the department. A suspiciously timed blog post attack on Elizabeth and non-threatening, non-company related text messages during a week off from work to her mother spelled the end of Vincent Scott's tenure with ABM.

Keith wasted no time signaling that a new day had dawned and breaking the news of the fallen hero. He held a meeting back in Greenfield with the management team right after lunch to simply announce, "Vincent Scott is no longer with the business. I have nothing further to say about that." This sent the managers into panic and brought some to tears.

Dickhauser put in a requisition that afternoon to fill Vincent's job. He told the managers not to discuss it with reps; that he would handle it himself come Monday. Monday: the day Vincent was going to interview outside of the department so he could finally escape from Keith, Abby and Phoebe once and for all.

Vincent's phone erupted; he got calls and text messages of support from several of them right off the bat. Clyde assured him they would do whatever it took to sing the truth and bring him back. He urged Vincent to get the ball rolling with the ethics hotline to report Keith, Scott and Danny for this setup and conspiracy. Freddie told Vincent that he had gained a great deal of his respect and that meant he would do anything for him. Gina called distraught and in shock to make sure he was okay. Jimmy said Vincent was his family and that he would not take this lying down. Johnny told Vincent that this was worth any risk to his career to set the record straight; that Vincent had been there for him in the past and he would return the favor. Cal called him brother and said he would be there for him anywhere, anytime. Randall texted him and said they would talk very soon. Cathy was helpful with advice on attorneys and how to get the process in motion.

Several managers and reps mourned him across the street at Cullen's over drinks after work. They even called him and passed the phone around; Cal, Jimmy, Cathy and even a drunken Haley, surprisingly, put their two cents in. Reps and managers text messaged Vincent all night and weekend and he even heard from people that worked for him in Rockford. This was a shot heard 'round the ABM world.

Most startling of all, even Phoebe Wells sent Vincent an e-mail to his personal address saying she would do anything and everything she could to help if he wanted it. They had not spoken in over six months and yet she was apparently pledging support and was also spotted breaking down in tears upon learning the news of his demise.

Come Monday, Vincent sprung into action, calling the ethics hotline, visiting the Equal Employment Opportunity Commission (EEOC) office and applying for countless jobs. He was going to take Keith down and enact his vengeance if it was the last thing he did. For Vincent was now in a unique position: he had the time, money and resources to fight this until the end.

It was all so clear. The players in the conspiracy were obvious. There was the not-so-bright ex-fiancé who self-sabotaged her child support and bit down hard on the hand that fed her for three years. There was the opportunistic weasel of a clerical supervisor who saw the chance to again interview for the job he lost out on before in a courtesy interview. There was the condescending jackal of a commission manager who saw the chance to conceal his secrets. Finally, there was the head of operations, the hapless general manager who saw the chance to silent his biggest opponent and make clear to the world that no one messed with him without a price.

Keith Dickhauser also moved aggressively within the department, knowing full well that backlash against the wrongful termination of their savior would be imminent if he did not stop it. He quickly silenced the reps by threatening write-ups for anyone discussing it and for those who were sharing and spreading e-mails outlining exactly what happened to Vincent that implicated Keith as head of the conspiracy. He threatened the managers in closed-door meetings that if they so much as spoke to Vincent, their careers would be in jeopardy.

He also made several policy changes that Vincent had lobbied for over the last several months in an attempt to keep peace and minimize unrest. As for many of the procedures Vincent had in place that were synonymous with his name and success, Dickhauser did away with them despite the negative it had on the business. In short, Keith made Vincent's name a curse word in the house he built and tried to make it like he had never existed.

Most unsettling to Vincent over the first few weeks was the fact that several managers never called him. Also unsettling was that Abby did not either; not to check on him, not to see how he was doing or even to offer condolences. This only fueled his confusion over her involvement in his termination…until he learned just two weeks later that she had never reported him to begin with.

Abby had been upset after Vincent put her in her place and, deserved or not, sought advice from someone she hoped would talk to Vincent about not doing this again.

She first talked to one of her friends and co-workers from her clerical days, who was friends with Danny Boyd and turned her on to asking him for advice. Since Danny was one of the few people that knew both of them and their history, had his own long history of workplace romance gone bad and he had been Abby's former manager, she called him on their week off for his opinion. Abby was too naïve to be the wiser that Boyd would use the information for the forces of evil.

Danny told Abby he was going to "talk to someone for guidance," and called back shortly thereafter to inform her that he was going to report Vincent to Human Resources against her wishes, despite never having even seen the text messages. Who gave this "advice" to him? Keith Dickhauser.

Upon Abby's return to work after the holidays, Lydia Rawlings contacted her and forced her to cough up the text messages. Neither Danny nor Keith had ever seen them nor was anyone in the company ever supposed to. Keith thought they could carry out this plan, that no one would be the wiser and he could execute Vincent Scott.

Now Vincent had all the facts. All he had to do at this point was wait for justice.

*   *   *

The departmental conference room door was shut and was the only thing separating Vincent Scott from hundreds of reps and managers. He could hear their voices carrying on rabidly on the other side of the door, yet they had no idea what was in store for them.

Per prior instruction, Jimmy Sander sauntered to the front of the room and pressed a button on his laptop, starting up Mark Morrison's "Return of the Mack" and it boomed loudly throughout the room. Only a select few knew what it was to signify.

As the lyric, "I'm back to run the show" began to sound, Vincent pushed the door open with both hands and stood in the doorway, singing along to the tune. As people began to realize what was going on, there was an uproar of epic proportion and everyone got to their feet, cheering wildly.

Vincent only raised his hand, acknowledging the crowd, and he walked into the room and across to the front to address them all. People rushed to shake his hand, pat him on the back and embrace him. This is what he had waited all those hours, days and weeks for. This was his moment of vindication.

The cheering for him now was louder than at his best speech. Basking in the glow of the adoration, Vincent Scott had finally gotten the justice he deserved.

And then he awoke, on his couch in the dark, covered in a blanket.

The nice and neat Hollywood ending was not going to be his. This wasn't Hollywood.

The banishment and subsequent exile from ABM was quite a sobering experience for Vincent. Not only was it the first real vacation he had gotten in years but he learned just how quickly people abandon you after you lose your power. He learned that this big company had no interest in serving justice. He learned that fear and terror were how Keith Dickhauser was planning to move forward and, while it sacrificed everything the department had accomplished over its four years of existence, it was more important for him to keep intact his own job, enact his revenge and keep someone from infiltrating the network of lies he had tried so hard to foster and protect.

The agony for Vincent was the occasional self-doubt; was he really the pariah they made him out to be? Was he wrong? No, he decided. He would not change anything he did over 8 ½ years even if given the opportunity. Well, maybe he would have gotten involved with a female or two less, had a few less drinks with co-workers or pissed off a few less people. But, even still, he had been far too married to the job to ever find someone outside the company with which to forge a relationship. He had justified to himself that the alcohol was the only way he could cope with what the job and his life had imposed on him. And, at this point, after seeing the way his "friends" folded one by one and abandoned ship, a relationship or trusting much of anyone was out of the question. He had done things his way.

Vincent realized the tryst with Abby had wound up being his undoing. Had that never happened, had she not gotten pregnant and their relationship taken such a toll on his psyche, none of this would have happened. The blog post was an attack involving Elizabeth, which was the only reason it drew his anger. The text messages happened because of Abby's two-timing. However, in the end, rather than a job he hated or a relationship that drove him to medication, he emerged with nothing left but the thing that mattered most: his daughter.

It is utterly depressing waking up daily realizing the dream you just had of being at work was fake, having no place to go, realizing no one is thinking about you at that moment and the place you built and devoted your life to has moved on without you.

Vincent had accepted he would never have the "normal" family he used to want. He accepted that he will never be a run of the mill coward that goes along with unjust things the way they are. Most of all, he accepted his place in this world; he is an outspoken leader just trying to right wrongs in various shapes and sizes and risking everything just to feel something. He fights every battle, winning some, and spending the rest of his time doing penance for the ones he loses.

ABM's philosophy was to spend its money buying smaller companies and creating new technology and cutting costs by sending jobs abroad and price-gouging customers rather than investing in the people that slaved to make them successful. They employed lots of them but looked at them and treated them like numbers, and replaceable ones at that. They cared about bottom lines, not employees. They cared about dollar signs and reducing budgets, not customers, who were lost in the detrimental shuffle. That is why Vincent Scott did not fit into their picture.

Vincent would never forget that, for instance, once upon a time former adversary Dana Warsaw was a sales director who told her audience in a speech that she had never even been good at sales. She told the crowd that she had been very customer service-oriented, yet somehow she had politically risen through the ranks to a third-level position in sales. She hunted down and destroyed reps for breakfast because they had a bad call or a bad day. She had no way of relating to these workhorses because she had never been in their shoes. But this was the type of person who thrived in ABM's ludicrous hierarchy.

It was this type of small-mindedness and ignorance that was running ABM and companies like it that were satisfied with status quo instead of potential into the ground. The company had praised offices for cramming international calling plans on customer's bills that they had no need for, but when Vincent rallied his team around Internet sales, he was a villain. Rather than embrace him as a hero for the lives he touched and the tens of millions of dollars he brought to the company, ABM batted him down because he would not fall in line. Rather than acknowledge he had a gift no one else possessed, they would rather sacrifice an entire department just to prove a point and to protect the villain.

It was truly a case of David versus Goliath and the sad part in the immediate aftermath of the calamity is that not enough people were willing to take on the giant, be it out of cowardice or out of fear.

Truth is most people do not have the ability to lay it all on the line like Vincent had done. They have families, they live paycheck to paycheck and they have mortgage and car payments and are lucky to stay above sea level. This was quickly evidenced as the Monday following his dismissal, he was having a much-publicized "funeral" at Cullen's after the work day concluded and attendance was not what he expected.

The day had begun with Dickhauser confirming for the entire population of the department what a weekend of text messages and calls had already reported; that Vincent was no longer in their ranks. He announced it at the morning stand-up, taking less than ten seconds to eulogize him before walking away.

One of the many who showed support to Vincent was Union Steward Terry Fontana, with whom Vincent had shared a great working relationship over the years. Vincent had always been there when Terry needed him; when he was being harassed by any of the managers, when he was caught in political crossfire or just when he needed an ear. Terry sent an anonymously written eulogy to everyone on the floor's personal e-mail addresses that detailed exactly how Keith had set Vincent up and the department was enraged. When Keith caught wind of it he threatened to terminate anyone caught sending it around. While Keith had no right dictating what people did with their personal e-mail, he was quickly showing himself in his attempt to cover up his crime.

It also spread like wildfire that showing up to Vincent's funeral could be a magnet for the ire of Dickhauser. When all was said and done, he attracted Clyde, Frankie, Jimmy, Johnny and Cathy to lunch at the Chinese restaurant they frequented and ten reps, George Flaker, Randall Darwin and, surprisingly, Phoebe Wells to his funeral.

Vincent had no initial intention of reaching out to Phoebe, but after "the mastermind" Clyde Barton pushed him to do so because she could be helpful to the cause, he relented and responded to her peace offering. He was brief, made no mention of their past and merely thanked her and said he would take whatever aid she would give. At Cullen's, she was there for half an hour, said she would be there for Vincent every single step of the way until justice was served and told him that despite being somewhat serious with Denny, she still loved and would always love Vincent. She hinted there was hope for a future together, hugged him tightly three times before departure and pledged to go to HR Vice President Karl Farr with Vincent's story and ensure he heard the truth.

It seemed early on that Vincent would return swiftly.

However, Gerald Murphy, Keith's boss, came to town the following week to address the unrest. After getting Dickhauser's version of Vincent's sins, he sided with Keith when addressing the managers and spouted misinformation hinting that Vincent threatened Abby and got what was a long time coming. It was obvious Dickhauser was exploiting Murphy's complete lack of knowledge to intimidate the managers.

Then, Karl Farr told Phoebe to keep quiet with the truth and that being involved with Vincent in any capacity would only ruin her career.

Then, Agnes Landry and Lydia Rawlings started conducting their interviews of the managers after Vincent and a handful of them called in to report Keith's retaliation. However, they informed the managers that any information they provided would be sent to Gerald with their names attached, thus leaving them open to the same retaliation. They also lied to the managers and told them Vincent had named six of them on a list so they were only calling those six.

Finally, they ignored multiple requests from the managers to allow a fair investigation including anonymity. Needless to say, no one had the courage to talk. They alluded to knowing plenty about the situation that they would happily provide anonymously, but the ladies were not on a mission of truth. They were covering up for their political ally.

Considering one of the human resources directors in Minneapolis had once wound up the subject of a nationwide talk show due to his affair with a subordinate and he still had a job, clearly any powers that be could have taken Vincent's side in all of this. The truth was, they didn't. Keith had the right connections in the company through years of cover-ups, lies, golf and alcohol and now was when he pulled those strings to get his way.

And there it was; after just a few weeks of this, the tides were turning the opposite way and, one by one, people began to jump ship.

Cal Riley and Johnny Slade, his daily breakfast companions, whom he had hired, promoted, partied with, and who were even at Elizabeth's 2nd birthday party, left early on. Cal, after his initial pledge to be there for Vincent anywhere and anytime, stopped returning Vincent's calls or messages. He helped support his mother and sisters and was terrified, especially considering he had bedded many females of the office and was guilty of far more than Vincent, that he could be targeted if he failed to lay low. Slade, who said early on that he was going to do the right thing and stand by Vincent, folded when it started to look like he may not come back.

George Flaker, who was very vocal about the need for Dickhauser's removal, also chose to lay low. He had family in high places in the company and did not want to be socially linked to Vincent or have his name on anything controversial.

Frankie Rivera, who told Vincent that he respected him a great deal and that went a long way with him, disappeared after that conversation.

Randall Darwin and Maria Fernandez, both very fond of Vincent, kept tabs on him about once a month.

Dean Yamnitz, positioning himself to take Vincent's place, justified steering clear of contacting Vincent so he could stay politically clean. For all his positive attributes, Dean could never find the level of success he wanted because he did not have the audacity and rambunctiousness to complement his smarts and know-how. He was the opposite end of the spectrum from Vincent; where

Vincent's daring and boldness got him caught up in a political war with Keith Dickhauser, Yamnitz was a play-it-safe corporate type.

Gina Baker, despite being Dean's primary competition and eventual winner of Vincent's role, kept in regular contact with Vincent and the frequency never quelled. She was named Vincent's replacement a month after he was given the boot.

Oddly, Mark Rogers sent Vincent a text to see how he was that following Monday after the hammer fell. Mark was starting to see how corrupt, standoffish and impudent Keith was and Vincent had warned Mark about him the night before he was taken down. He told Vincent to call him when he was ready. Vincent responded that he felt like anyone who was betrayed, lied to and retaliated against would feel and that he was sure they would talk again.

Cathy Schumer was the most diligent in her devotion to her former leader. In addition to her initial legal advice, she checked on him, listened to him vent and kept him aware that despite the fact most everyone abandoned him, he was needed, missed and that the office very quickly collapsed in his absence.

Clyde Barton, while he originally saw Vincent as important to the cause of getting Dickhauser booted and knew a reversal of the decision to oust Vincent would accomplish just that, stayed in constant contact for the first several weeks. They speculated and discussed all potential outcomes while Clyde seemed fully in support of doing what it took to bring Vincent back. However, after the first month did nothing to resuscitate Vincent's career, Clyde started looking for a way to back out. When Agnes Landry's crooked "investigation" cited that Vincent named names of managers that could corroborate his story (which Clyde already knew was not true) he took it as his opportunity to very publicly abandon the operation as well.

Of all the fallout, the one that stung most was the disappearance of Jimmy Sander. The two had spent countless hours playing video games, grilling, Halloweens with the kids, birthday parties, etc., and had always been there for each other in times of need. However, as Jimmy's team's results were less than stellar and he was known publicly as Vincent's friend, he was already on Dickhauser's bad side. To protect his career, he backed completely away and never made the time for even a call, text or visit to see how his fallen friend was coping.

Eventually – practically every single one of them who had pledged allegiance, whom Vincent had lost his career for – vanished. There were no calls checking on how he was progressing. There were no invitations to do anything. There was silence.

Phoebe talked to him every day for a week and then stopped calling or replying to texts. Reaching out initially looked good on her part but she very quickly reverted to true colors. It was just as well; Vincent was starting to realize that everything was in the past for a reason. He needed to keep it there because that is where it belonged. People are exes for a reason, and in the case of these exes, it was more like fifty reasons apiece.

Clyde realized ABM was not going to do an about face anytime soon and he stopped contacting or advising Vincent. He even started lobbying support for his way of thinking amongst the other managers, prompting a complete collapse of whatever trust once existed in the team.

And while Vincent would have probably preferred being alone to the company of anyone but Elizabeth, the shows of support would have been comforting and nice during this painful and powerless time. In fifty years, people who had encountered Vincent would still remember him; he would never be one of those also-ran type managers or people that would dissolve in the annals of time. Vincent fought and never betrayed his principles despite the risks, and that is why he is a great man and leader. And despite what he lost, he would not change a single action from the last 9 years.

Had he made mistakes, been arrogant and abused alcohol frequently? Absolutely. But Keith Dickhauser was a lying, backstabbing bastard who had used Vincent until he became too much of a threat to his empire of lies and corruption. Abby Winters was a selfish gold-digging mooch, a liar and naive immature girl who passed her sexuality and what she deluded herself into thinking was her heart around like a used toy. Phoebe Wells was a manipulative phony, unreliable flake and a callous self-centered bitch that cared about herself and her image more than anything else.

And the support system – the multitude of reps and managers that built Vincent up, made him their king and pretended to worship him – came tumbling down like an avalanche when he was in need of them most. Just as Vincent's greatest strengths flourished in times of controversy, others were exhibiting their most glaring of weaknesses.

Vincent had become a byproduct of the world he had come to know. But to make a difference in the real world, to make a dent in the injustice and cruelty that is reality, he had to keep fighting by whatever means necessary. And he had a lot of fight left.

Abby may not have intentionally dimed Vincent out but she made clear she was still only interested in getting Vincent's money. She broke her silence after his termination weeks later only because she wanted a check from him and would call or come by but it was always in pursuit of funds. The credit cards Vincent had paid off years ago were once again in debt over new furniture, new clothes, a new computer, two new pets and a new car. Abby had moved two guys into her apartment since Vincent kicked her out and neither had jobs, meaning he was footing the bill. She was even moving out of the apartment she lived in that cost more than Vincent's to move into a condo that cost even more.

No more. He finally had the closure he needed to be done with her for good. She had ripped off his chance at a family and that was now something he would never forget or forgive. It was payback time.

Lastly, there was Keith Dickhauser. Vincent was relieved to no longer be in his world of oppression, of getting screamed at and never being good enough. It was ironic that the man who tried to claim to stand for truth and integrity turned out to be the biggest liar and cheat and Benedict Arnold of them all. Vincent had gotten too involved; he had given his all in the mutiny, gotten too close to unraveling the commission scam and the company allowed Keith to retaliate. For now, at least. Vincent vowed when it was all said and done he would do whatever required to bring down the dictator. Now, it was personal. Dickhauser could have let Vincent transfer out of the department but that would not have allowed him to achieve revenge. If he couldn't have him, no one could.

Vincent was fighting. He was drinking. He went days without shaving or showering or eating. He went back and forth between utter depression and hesitantly upbeat and applied for 50 jobs within his first week of unemployment.

He saw who had his back, who backstabbed him, who left him and who was part of the conspiracy. He saw the lengths ABM was going to in order to cover up what happened to him. He saw a lot of people for what they were: cowards. Vincent got e-mail happy with several senior executives in ABM, spelling out the entire conspiracy, but they would not even listen or care enough to make things right of their own accord. Bureaucratic bullshit had taken Vincent out and it seemed bent, at least for the moment, on keeping him there.

His thoughts were consumed with this obsession for vengeance; he could not sleep and when he did, his dreams were drenched with thoughts of being at work, in the midst of trouble and fighting for his job, or just trying to return. And these dreams would not stop or go away. And when he woke up, he had nowhere to be and practically no one who cared and his place of work – the place he painstakingly put together – was quickly collapsing without him.

He could not tell Kay or Vince, Jr. Not until he had a solution. Telling them would lead only to Kay's tears and weekly questions about what was going on, how the job search was faring and speculation on how Vincent needed to change his ways to better fit in with Corporate America. In his mind, the lesson had already been learned. Vincent had every intention of giving his parents full disclosure but only when it was over. When he would tell them tales of ABM's terrible business practices or Dickhauser's unethical treatment, they would merely offer up tales from their own work history to dilute his. At this point in his life, he did not want to provide them grief or burdens; now was time for them to enjoy their retirement and their granddaughter. He could only do it when he could come to them and tell them his new title and then fill in the blanks of the back story. The added pressure of their concern and upsetting them was not something he could emotionally contend with at this time.

The few remaining souls brave enough to keep in contact with Vincent would report the tragic news: the department was falling apart in his absence. Keith disbanded Vincent's schedule that had been unanimously voted to be kept in 2010 because he thought he knew better than Vincent and was quickly greeted with the worst months in department history. Keith eased the management workload and did what he could to calm the storm that was about to come as he knew Vincent's story could destroy him. Vincent had become too powerful and, in his panic, Keith thought the best choice was to eliminate him. However, the truth would eventually come out and even Dickhauser tried to ignore the eventual ramifications of that inevitability.

Also disconcerting was that everything Vincent had spent years accomplishing, such as improving efficiency by 50% his first year in power and the call grading process he created that worked wonders, were lost very quickly in the demise. The motivation, the driving force of the department was gone and, within just a few months the department, who had blown out expectations all four years Vincent was involved, was over $2.5 million in the hole in revenue for 2010. The year before at the same point they had enjoyed a $10 million surplus.

Unfortunately, however, Vincent realized that if he thought having all the facts and proof and witnesses in the world was enough to get swift justice, he was gravely mistaken. The legal process was slow and that was exactly what ABM was banking on: for Vincent to lose interest or move on. However, Keith Dickhauser had been shortsighted; his use of Vincent as a sacrificial lamb may have stayed his own execution but it did not cancel its certainty.

Vincent was left to wonder: what was ABM's purpose in his life? Elizabeth was the best thing that came out of his experience there by far. She made everything worthwhile and made his life worth living all by herself. He had a decorated résumé, but the crapshoot of applying for jobs and the fact around 1% of them actually resulted in a call made him weary. His superstardom may have stalled; his 100 mile-per-hour lifestyle may have come to a temporary halt, but he knew he was still going to take over the world. It was the waiting that drove him crazy.

He had built a department. He had changed lives. He had helped people, fought for people and made a difference. He had played hurt, heartbroken and sick. He had given ABM every ounce of himself and this is what he got in return from them. Thanks to all of that, whatever was next he could walk into it with no remorse over anything from the past. Not many people could say that.

It took quite some time for Scott Kinsey to sift through all of Vincent's e-mails and belongings, undoubtedly finding several amusing items among them, but Cathy Schumer volunteered to bring him the sum of his career: two boxes. Carrying in those boxes and welcoming them into his home was acknowledgment that it was over. A part of him never wanted to see them or take them back because that made it real. They sat there, unopened, as Vincent had no intention of opening them until this battle was completed.

Vincent was a rogue, rebel and renegade but he would not have had it any other way. He had an extremely strong case and was not going down without a fight, no matter how long it took. And his biggest battle, challenges and accomplishments were to come.

Though the job search took far longer than he ever would have imagined, bouts of depression wreaked havoc on his soul and hundreds left him for dead, something in the back of his mind kept him going. Someone like Vincent would surely bounce back and look back on this years from now as the best thing to happen to him. At least, he had to keep telling himself that so he did not give up.

He had become an adult during his time with ABM and whether they reluctantly brought him back or paid him a handsome sum to shut up and go away, he was determined to follow this through if for no other reason than to see Keith Dickhauser brought to justice. His wounded psyche would survive without the people who deserted him and despite the sting of their departure he would never take back everything he did for them. He would just know better going forward. Never get close to these people. Never again.

Vincent had learned the final lesson: do not hold on to anything too tight, no matter what it is. It makes it all the more painful when it is forcefully and unceremoniously ripped from you.

Vincent Thomas Scott III is a man, battered and bruised but standing. He is a crusader and one of the few people out there truly interested in the best interests of all. He is unquestionably flawed but does the best he can under the circumstances. He is a man who has made mistakes, but a great one nonetheless.

It is far too easy to judge others. The Bible itself says, "Judge not, lest ye be judged," so to tear Vincent down for all of his character flaws would be merely a potshot from a miscreant who could never walk a mile in his worn-out shoes. Those people would always be around but they could not keep him down. Vincent had been pushed or pulled into a lot of his problems, but the reactions he chose to have were his own doing and undoing.

Vincent is a tremendous Daddy, loyal friend and a true master of the selling game, motivation and communication. He enjoys it all and nothing – not Keith Dickhauser or any of his failed relationships – could take those things away from him.

332

It was pretty clear when he thought about it; God had pulled Vincent out of ABM and away from Keith, Phoebe and Abby because He knew Vincent would never do it on his own. He was finished with that job – mentally and physically drained to the point he could give no more – but he just could not let go of how it was all stripped from him unfairly, unjustly and unnaturally.

He missed some parts terribly and knew he would never have that again. Just the simple pleasures in controlling the schedule and the dialer and the reports and the meetings and his friends were so near and dear to his heart it was hard for him to let them go. Vincent knew it had to end at some point. He just never suspected it would end the way it did.

Getting used to the fact he was so good at what he did but was now on the sidelines with no immediate retribution was the painful part. And he had a constant reminder every time he woke up with nowhere to go. Time moves differently during unemployment; the days run into one another and it is one long stretch of nothing but limbo, yet you look up and realize you have lost days, weeks and months you can never get back and you have nothing to show for them.

And he was once again alone, with no one to pour out his soul to and no paychecks coming in, little remaining support and his typical life raft, Jack Johnson, was literally away at sea with the Navy. Regardless, no one could understand that as Vincent gained power, he also gained anonymous attacks and haters who strived only to tear him down. They knew his weak spots which is why they had temporarily succeeded in removing him from power. They could go too far because they did it under the guise of ambiguity. Vincent was the only one who suffered as a result of it because he had not until now learned to control his angry reactions.

Vincent had endured baptism by fire. Keith laughed first but Vincent would laugh last; unfortunately, at this point, there was nothing but guesswork as to when that laugh would come.

However, the extra time with Elizabeth gave him memories he would never regret or forget. The humbling experience he had been forced to endure ingrained in him who his friends were and weren't and what is really important in life.

On the nights Vincent did not have his princess, he sat alone in the dark contemplating his next move. He was unemployed, had been deserted by practically everyone he called friend months prior and felt like a completely different person.

He wished he had a dollar for every woman in his history that had told him they would always love him. He had a hell of a penchant for holding onto money but none of them were anywhere to be found.

In the blink of an eye, his career had been wrongfully ripped from him. Vincent had never failed to appreciate what he had. Others had failed to appreciate him.

He drew solace in the fact that in all of this, there was no former friend out there wondering why Vincent left them. No former employee was out there wondering why he let them down or stopped fighting for them. And no former lover was out there left in the dark on why it didn't work out or he stopped trying. When it came to his remaining obligations, he was unencumbered. His only duty was to raise Elizabeth to be the best lady he could. Being a single dad with no female aid was quite a challenge, but Vincent has not turned down a challenge yet.

Vincent wanted his defamed name restored, considerable pain and suffering acknowledged and his self made whole.

And, in the end, Vincent Scott lay in wait for the inevitable return of the salesman.

AUTHOR BIOGRAPHY

Carson V. Heady, 31, was born in Cape Girardeau, MO and first put in front of a typewriter at age 3. Back then, he typed mere sentences but as time went by it became much more.

At an early age, Carson was enraptured with writing short stories that incorporated his friends, family and himself into the plotlines. He entered and won numerous writing contests throughout the years and never gave up his dream of becoming a writer. In college, he took script writing classes and wrote a screenplay not long after graduation.

He entered the sales arena at age 22 and has found success at every level, from top-flight sales representative to a division leader over 200+ people. His devotion to the sales game occupied much of his time, but the desire to write never left his mind.

Once Carson realized his great aptitude in the game of sales, he decided to write his first novel – "Birth of a Salesman" – which told the story of a young man who came into prominence in the sales arena and doubled as a self-help sales advice manual to guide others to the level of success he achieved. He is a profound public speaker, superior corporate leader and, in addition to having letters featured in prominent magazines and local newspapers, he wrote his own bi-weekly column for his department.

Carson lives in St. Louis, MO, with his 2-year old daughter, Madison.

LaVergne, TN USA
13 October 2010
200618LV00003B/52/P

9 781935 444312